# The Truth of Broken Symbols

SUNY Series in Religious Studies
Harold Coward, editor

# The Truth
# of Broken Symbols

Robert Cummings Neville

STATE UNIVERSITY OF NEW YORK PRESS

Published by
State University of New York Press, Albany

©1996  State University of New York

For information, address State University of New York Press,
State University Plaza, Albany, N.Y., 12246

Production by Marilyn P. Semerad
Marketing by Fran Keneston

**Library of Congress Cataloging-in-Publication Data**

Neville, Robert C.
        The truth of broken symbols / by Robert Cummings Neville.
            p.    cm. — (SUNY series in religious studies)
        Includes bibliographical references (p.        ) and index.
        ISBN 0–7914–2741–2 (hbk.). — ISBN 0–7914–2742–0 (pbk.)
        1. Symbolism.   I. Title.   II. Series.
    BL600.N48   1996
        291.3'7—dc20                                                           95-2363
                                                                                         CIP

10  9  8  7  6  5  4  3  2  1

*For Ray L. Hart*

# CONTENTS

# PREFACE

I had first wanted to subtitle this book "Yes, There Are Cigars in Heaven." The idea came from C. S. Lewis who, in his *A Grief Observed*, remarked that there is some sense in which our plain tokens and hopes of happiness naively can be projected onto heaven. He, of course, longed for union with his late wife infinitely more than for a good cigar, and he took a dim view of those who do not expect heaven to be beyond earthly imagination. Nevertheless, in that symbolic context, a heaven without cigars would be oxymoronic for Lewis.[1] My wife, however, rejected the subtitle as vulgar for the subject of this book, remarking that cigars in our time are a symbol of death, not pleasure, and that they are a sexist token of pleasure at that. So there is no subtitle and I shall enjoy cigars with earthly finality.[2] But I shall also defend the view that there are contexts in which symbols that obviously are not literally true may nonetheless be taken to be true in broken innocence, including both hopes for heaven and addresses to personal gods.

---

1. See C. S. Lewis' *A Grief Observed*, the Bantam edition, pp. 28–29. His words are:

Talk to me about the truth of religion and I'll listen gladly. Talk to me about the duty of religion and I'll listen submissively. But don't come talking to me about the consolations of religion or I shall suspect that you don't understand.

Unless, of course, you can literally believe all that stuff about family reunions "on the further shore," pictured in entirely earthly terms. But that is all unscriptural, all out of bad hymns and lithographs. There's not a word of it in the Bible. And it rings false. We know it couldn't be like that. Reality never repeats. The exact same thing is never taken away and given back. How well the Spiritualists bait their hook! "Things on this side are not so different after all." There are cigars in Heaven. For that is what we should all like. The happy past restored.

And that, just that, is what I cry out for, with mad, midnight endearments and entreaties spoken into the empty air.

2. Infrequently, of course, and always out of doors, but with appreciation of Freud's thought that it is easier to understand what men really want, at least in some matters, than what women want.

The title itself has several levels of connotation. The phrase *broken symbol* was made famous by the theologian Paul Tillich.[3] He pointed out in many places, say in the first volume of his *Systematic Theology*, that religious symbols on the one hand engage us in what they symbolize and yet are different from that and hence no easy substitute.[4] In particular, religious symbols symbolize the infinite but themselves are finite.[5] The temptation to idolatry increases with the power of the symbol to engage the infinite in our experience. Religious symbols participate in what they symbolize, Tillich said, but also separate us from that. A broken symbol is one that effectively engages us but whose limitations are also known.[6] Heaven is not really a literal continuation of life after death with much

---

3. His actual phrase was "broken myths"; see his *Dynamics of Faith*, pp. 50–54. This was in his discussion of "demythologizing" but the points were made about all symbols, not only those of the form of mythic narratives.

4. After drawing a distinction between a sign which is wholly arbitrary and a symbol which is irreplaceable, Tillich wrote:

> Therefore, the religious symbol, the symbol which points to the divine, can be a true symbol only if it participates in the power of the divine to which it points.
>
> There can be no doubt that any concrete assertion about God must be symbolic, for a concrete assertion is one which uses a segment of finite experience in order to say something about him. It transcends the content of this segment, although it also includes it. The segment of finite reality which becomes the vehicle of a concrete assertion about God is affirmed and negated at the same time. It becomes a symbol, for a symbolic expression is one whose proper meaning is negated by that to which it points. And yet it also is affirmed by it, and this affirmation gives the symbolic expression an adequate basis for pointing beyond itself. *Systematic Theology* I, p. 239

See also the discussion in *Theology of Culture*, pp. 54.

5. See Tillich's *Systematic Theology I*, pp. 239–240: "The crucial question must now be faced. Can a segment of finite reality become the basis for an assertion about that which is infinite? . . . Religious symbols are double-edged. They are directed toward the infinite which they symbolize *and* [Tillich's italics] toward the finite through which they symbolize it." See also *Systematic Theology* III, pp. 109–110.

6. Tillich spoke of two kinds of corrupt symbols. On the one hand are dead symbols, which have simply lost their power. An authentic religious symbol for Tillich is one that actually establishes a person as subject of a revelation, which means being made into a New Being; thus a symbol functions authentically if it establishes such a change, or inauthentically if it does not.

A religious symbol *is* [Tillich's italics] true if it adequately expresses the correlation of some person with final revelation. A religious symbol can die only if the correlation of which it is an adequate expression dies. This occurs whenever

singing, visions of God, reunions with favorite people, smoking rooms for the gentlemen and separate drawing rooms for the ladies. Or golden streets, harp music, or lush gardens with sensual delights. Nor is God really a person like an old wise enthroned king, nor like a lusty mother, nor a disembodied personal spirit with a voice like the Cheshire cat's smile. These things all represent God as too finite, too much within the world, to be the world's creator or to be eternal and infinite in any other way.

---

the revelatory situation changes and former symbols become obsolete. The history of religion, right up to our own time, is full of dead symbols which have been killed not by a scientific criticism of assumed superstitons but by a religious criticism of religion. *Systematic Theology I*, p. 240.

The other corruption of religious symbols, according to Tillich, is idolatry, which is the identification of the finite symbol with the divine, neglecting the negative elements required by brokenness. See his *Theology of Culture*, pp. 53–67.

Tillich is famous for saying that the only literal, non-symbolic statement about God is that God is being-itself; see, for instance, *Systematic Theology I*, p. 238, or *Theology of Culture*, p. 61. Generally, however, he rejected all claims that representations of God are literal. But his position was subtle.

One should distinguish two stages of literalism, the natural and the reactive. The natural stage of literalism is that in which the mythical and the literal are indistinguishable. The primitive period of individuals and groups consists in the inability to separate the creations of symbolic imagination from the fact which can be verified through observation and experiment. This stage has a full right of its own and should not be disturbed, either in individuals or in groups, up to the moment when man's questioning mind breaks the natural acceptance of the mythological visions as literal. If, however, this moment has come, two ways are possible. The one is to replace the unbroken by the broken myth. It is the objectively demanded way, although it is impossible for many people who prefer the repression of their questions to the uncertainty which appears with the breaking of the myth. They are forced into the second stage of literalism, the conscious one, which is aware of the questions but represses them, half consciously, half unconsciously. The tool of repression is usually an acknowledged authority with sacred qualities like the Church or the Bible, to which one owes unconditional surrender. This stage is still justifiable, if the questioning power is very weak and can easily be answered. It is unjustifiable if a mature mind is broken in its personal center by political or psychological methods, split in his unity, and hurt in his integrity. The enemy of a critical theology is not natural literalism but conscious literalism with repression of and aggression toward autonomous thought. *Dynamics of Faith*, pp. 52–53.

All these issues will be discussed further in *The Truth of Broken Symbols*.

The question is, if we know that all the symbols are wrong, how can any be effective for us? In this secular age in which every transcendent reference is demythologized and everything else is deconstructed, how can people be gripped by the infinite toward which finite symbols so brokenly point? Secular or not, this is an age of religious fervor where rather simple symbols transform people's lives and orient them to things not of this world. Beyond the dubious appeals of fundamentalisms, beyond psychological needs resulting from disruptions of cultures, beyond energetic efforts to reconstruct traditional religions, across the globe our age is characterized by intense quests for and discoveries of the infinite, veiled in a motley of symbols.

This book is an effort to understand broken religious symbols, their powers and limitations. More, this is an effort to understand how religious symbols are true, when they are not true in any obvious or literal sense. The standard of truth was reflected in the title of one of my previous books, *Recovery of the Measure,* itself taken from a phrase of St. Thomas Aquinas at the beginning of *De Veritate.* Reality is the measure of our interpretations, and in religious matters therefore the infinite is the measure of our finite symbols. Because of this point, the topic of religious symbols is inevitably theological in the sense of conjuring about the infinite. The theory defended in *Recovery of the Measure* is that truth is the carryover of value from the object interpreted into the experience of the interpreter, in the respects interpreted, as qualified by the biological, cultural, semiotic, and purposive traits of the interpreter. This theory contrasts broadly with the Aristotelian one that speaks of the carryover of form, not value. Forms are the bearers of value, but when one checks on the validity of the carryover one looks for the commonality of value, appropriately qualified, not commonality of form. The relation of form and value is explored at length in my *Reconstruction of Thinking.*

An important new purpose for studying religious symbols has emerged in the last several decades, namely, as a way to get at the content of theological claims. The old purposes were of two respectable sorts. Anthropologists and other social scientists, including philosophers of culture such as Ernst Cassirer, study religious symbols as important parts of cultural systems. This is an objective analytic purpose and, despite recent postmodernist criticisms of objectivity, it remains an important and legitimate purpose. The other sort of old purpose is practical, that is, the purpose that religious practitioners have of mastering their own symbol systems, of obtaining competence in reading their lives through the symbols of their religious tradition, and of attaining the soteriological benefits of their symbols. This practical purpose also remains important and legitimate.

The new purpose for studying religious symbols is as a hermeneutic entry for theology, that is, for attaining religious truth in critical, correctable ways. The elementary content of theology takes its rise from religious symbols as found in liturgies, hymns, scriptures, practices, and other places of symbols in religious life. However theology transforms the symbols for the sake of coherence and precision, theology still needs critical access to the symbols in their concrete use, and this requires studying the symbols as symbols. The novelty of this purpose comes from recent changes in the conceptions both of the roles of religious symbols and of theology.

At the beginning of the twentieth century most scholars construed religious symbols, even whole systems of symbols, as instruments for symbolizing some intention or feeling other than the symbol itself. Thus anthropologists could ask whether the symbol systems of neolithic tribes are as good as modern science for symbolizing nature, and whether the symbols of animism, or polytheism, or monotheism, or trinitarianism, or pantheism, are adequate for symbolizing the religious object. Now, by contrast, most scholars have come to reject the instrumentalist approach in favor of a pragmatic construal of religious symbols.[7] The pragmatic construal takes religious symbols to be what Charles Peirce called "leading principles" which guide behavior, particularly habitual behavior.[8] When behavior becomes consciously problematic the leading principles can be objectified and represented abstractly so that they can be criticized, alternatives contemplated, and the problems of behavior addressed. As leading principles, religious symbols actually shape reli-

---

7. I recognize that this contrasting of instrumentalism and pragmatism must seem strange to students of John Dewey who popularized both and identified one with the other. See, for instance, his *Essays in Experimental Logic*, in the introduction to which he explains instrumentalism and throughout which he illustrates it; see chapter 12, "What Pragmatism Means by the Practical" in which he discusses Peirce and James. Nevertheless, there is a clear distinction between instrumentalism in the sense of using symbols as instruments and the pragmatic understanding of symbols explained above.

8. Sometimes called "guiding principles" and closely associated with his theory of hypothesis, "leading principles" occupied Peirce's attention from his early essay, "Some Consequences of Four Incapacities," (1868; CP 5.264–317) through his famous essay, "The Fixation of Belief," (1877; CP 5.358–387) to his late "Issues of Pragmaticism," (1905; CP 5.438–463). Citations are to the *Collected Papers,* the citational form of which is expressed in the bibliography.

gious life. Seventy-five years after Peirce, Wittgenstein developed the notions of language games and forms of life that were taken to express much the same conception of symbols in religion, although Wittgenstein's model suggested symbols as a closed or rounded system of signifiers.[9] For Peirce, systems of symbols guide behavior for engaging the world, and hence his symbols are always referential in ways to be explained below. Both traditions agreed that religious symbols are to be understood primarily as shapers of religious life either, as in Peirce's case, in reference to the divine or, as in Wittgenstein and Derrida's cases, in compliance with religious forms of life.

While the scholarly understanding of religious symbols was shifting from instrumentalism to pragmatism, its understanding of theology was shifting from a paradigmatic identification with Western metaphysical theology and its counterparts in other traditions, such as Nagarjuna's theology, to an existential understanding of theology that is cross cultural. By existential I mean that theology is not only a representation of the divine but a representation shaped by the life situations of the theologians or the religious community within which theology might work. By cross cultural I mean that theology aims to be true in representing the divine, and therefore needs to be true in all cultures, however diversely they might symbolize the points at issue. Whereas particular religious groups might practice theology with a concentration on their own traditions' symbols, if they claim their theology is true they imply that their assertions can be made persuasive to anyone from any tradition willing to take

---

9. See Wittgenstein's *Philosophical Investigations*. Wittgenstein's ideas have been influential in a conservative direction as providing a conceptuality according to which Christianity, being a life-world of its own, cannot be criticized from the outside. Questions of truth or orthodoxy become translated into questions of orthopraxy, playing the Christian language-game right. George Lindbeck's *The Nature of Doctrine* has some affinities with this line of thought, although it is far more sophisticated than the simple move I have just indicated. On the leftish or radical side Wittgenstein's ideas have supported the ideas of Derrida and the deconstructionists who say that religious symbol systems are closed wholes without external reference and are therefore untenable because logocentric. Whereas for the conservatives languages games are places within which to hide confessional theology from criticism, for the radical deconstructionists they are proof that the symbol systems cannot be taken seriously at face value ever. For the latter, see Mark C. Taylor's *Erring*, his helpful anthology, *Deconstruction in Context*, and *Deconstruction and Theology* by Thomas J. J. Altizer and others including Taylor. For an interesting theology that combines both of these approaches, see Don Cupitt's *Life Lines* and *The Long-Legged Fly*. Cupitt is explicit about taking the main point from Peirce, as in the latter book, p. 16.

the trouble to investigate the matter thoroughly. Theologians at the present time are far from effective actual practice of crosscultural theology because the scholarly world lacks good comparative categories. Nevertheless, the critical understanding of the breadth of cultural sensitivity needed for sound theological argument is in place. This point will be discussed at greater length at several places in this book, particularly in chapters 4 and 7.

The topic here is heir to a powerful discussion of religious symbolism in the twentieth century. Ernst Cassirer's monumental *Philosophy of Symbolic Forms,* Susanne K. Langer's more efficient (more insight without the necessity of monumental machinery) *Philosophy in a New Key,* and more recently Janet Martin Soskice's *Metaphor and Religious Language,* among many others, provide a rich philosophical tradition. The empirical work of anthropologists and phenomenologists of religion such as Edward Tylor, Gerardus van der Leeuw, and Mircea Eliade to mention only a few, as well as the vast outpourings of studies in history of religions, have provided sophisticated analyses of many important religious symbols.

The late twentieth century is a problematic time for studying the truth of broken symbols because of the juxtaposition of the points made in the previous paragraphs. The last paragraph quickly listed contributions to the understanding of symbols from the social sciences and humanities. These all deal with the nature of symbolism within the world, as it were, where the referents of symbols as well as their interpretations are worldly. But the previous paragraphs claimed that the referents of religious symbols are not finite things within the world but the infinite, lying beyond the world in some sense. This claim of course needs much qualification and justification (see chapter 2). Surely not all religious symbols are about Brahman, God, or even non-theistic parallels. Furthermore, most that are refer not to Brahman or God as infinite, wholly and simply, but to Brahman or God as connected with the finite world, for instance as creator, judge, or redeemer. Even more, examples of symbols taken from theistic traditions are likely to hide biases and limitations that might affect the distinction drawn between the finite and infinite. All these qualifications aside, however, religious symbolism refers to what most humanistic and social scientific positions say cannot be symbolized. This is even more obviously true in the cases of Buddhism symbolizing Emptiness, or Confucianism the Principle of Heaven, or Advaita Vedanta symbolizing Brahman without qualities. The problem is not just the standard issue of metaphor—using a sign to signify something other than what the sign usually signifies. It is that the infinite part of the referents of religious symbols is precisely what finite things in the world cannot stand for. As was remarked in the old debate about the analogy of being, there is an infinite distance between the finite and infinite.[10] It would seem that no finite set of interpretive transformations could turn a finite thing into a symbol of the infinite.[11]

Yet, as remarked above, religious thinkers for thousands of years have known that the gods they symbolize are not finite as symbolized, really and truly. With the positive, kataphatic, claims in the symbols there also have been negative, apophatic, claims. This means that there is no innocence in the remark that the study of religious symbolism is theological as well as semiotical. In addition to the standard and now threadbare secular skepticism of our age, theology must cope with making sense of the divine as sufficiently connected with the world as to be symbolizable with finite images and yet sufficiently non-reduced to the world as to be the referent of religious symbols. There is no difficulty deconstructing the referents of religious symbols so that they seem to be topics of moral, political, or psychological discourse. But if that were done, of course, we might as well have suggested without argument that there are no genuinely religious symbols, symbols that refer to God. The topic needs a non-reductive account.

In light of this, perhaps the recent studies of religious imagination are even more important than the social science and philosophical studies of symbols and symbolism mentioned above. Almost universally acclaimed as the pioneering work is Ray L. Hart's *Unfinished Man and the Imagination: Toward an Ontology and a Rhetoric of Revelation.*[12] In its train have followed distinguished books by Amos Wilder, John Bouker, David Tracy, Gordon

---

10. For the classical doctrine of the analogy of proper proportionality, see Thomas Aquinas's *De Veritate*, Q. 2, a. 11. For a modern exposition and defense see James F. Ross's *Philosophical Theology*. For the critical point made in the text, see Austin Farrer's *Finite and Infinite*, p. 53; for my own discussion, see *God the Creator*, pp. 16–22. For a view of the analogy between God and the world that does away with all infinite distance, see Charles Hartshorne's essay on analogy in *The Logic of Perfection*.

11. For a sophisticated development of the claim that finite characterizations of things in the world can be transformed through a series of intellectually examined steps into characterizations of God as infinite, contrary to what seems to be the case, see Paul Weiss's *Modes of Being*, chapter 4.

12. Elizabeth A. Johnson (1993, p. 283) writes: "The importance of image and the imagination has been an issue in religious studies for at least two decades, triggered into prominence by Ray Hart's insightful *Unfinished Man and the Imagination.* . . ." See also Fritz Buri's review article, "American Philosophy of Religion from a European Perspective."

*humans must have a way to discover the positive or negative lived implications of a presumption of value*

Kaufman, Avery Dulles, Margaret Miles, Garrett Green, John B. Cobb, Jr., and Schubert Ogden.[13] The discussion carried on in these works and others lies behind this study, especially a reading of an early draft of Wesley Wildman's forthcoming *The Quest for a Classical Christology*.

Not only has religious imagination been studied theoretically, as in the books just mentioned, we are in the midst of a massive criticism of traditional religious imagery by a worldwide feminist movement. Nearly all religious traditions have been strikingly patriarchal in their religious symbolism, and the practical implication of this (see 4.3 and 6.1 below) has been the subordination of women in religion (and elsewhere). The number of important feminist criticisms of religious symbols is far too great to list, but at least the following is a good sample: Katie Cannon, Anne Carr, Rebecca Chopp, Mary Daly, bell hooks, Elizabeth A. Johnson, Catherine Keller, Sachako Murata, Rosemary Radford Ruether, Valerie Saiving, Marjorie Suchocki, Susan Thistlethwaite.[14] The forceful challenge to patriarchal symbolism requires serious reflection on the various things symbolism is good for, both its representative powers and its practical transformative powers. Understanding how symbols can do the bad things feminists point out and also what is involved in changing, supplementing, criticizing, and replacing them are major concerns underlying this study.

In the long run the theological truth might be that there is no infinite, no God or divine matters, indeed no specifically theological truth. Religious symbols, then, would be thoroughly spurious insofar as they refer to the infinite or divine. But let that be a conclusion, not a premise. A study of religious symbolism should begin from phenomenologically open premises. In these prefatory pages it can be noted that I have previously defended at length a theory of God as the infinite creator of everything determinate, for instance in *God the Creator* and *Eternity and Time's Flow*. If these defenses were taken to be valid at face value, however, they would prove far too much for a general theory of religious symbols. They would prove one particular theory of the divine as transcendent, a theory not universally accepted even in one religion, let alone all the religions that have religious symbols. What is needed for a theory of religious symbols is a prima facie acceptance of the fact that

---

13. See the references to them in the bibliography. My own book *Reconstruction of Thinking* focuses on the constitutive power of imagination and its role in religion.

14. See the entries for these scholars in the bibliography.

they can engage their objects in some significant ways and mean what they say about those objects in some significant ways. Chapters 2 and 3 will explore these points.

Put in a preliminary and anticipatory form, the thesis of this study is that religious symbols are to be understood through three related and overlapping but quite different kinds of analysis. The first is the study of what religious symbols refer to and how they refer. Only by distinguishing a class of religious referents is it possible to say in any more than a conventional form what makes a symbol religious. The argument will be that religious symbols refer to something that constitutes a boundary condition of the world, or of a conception of the world. As a boundary condition it is both finite in the sense of being part of the founded world and infinite in the sense of adumbrating what would (not) be there if the world were not there as founded in the boundary condition. Chapter 2 will analyze reference.

The second kind of analysis places symbols within semiotic systems and traces out their coded connections. This is to analyze their meanings in a strict sense as the meanings of signs. Within a semiotic system, a symbol has a coded extension of objects to which its meanings might refer; these are a symbol's extensional referents, contained within the semiotic system and not necessarily the same as the intentional referents, which are the things to which the symbol is intentionally referred in an actual interpretation. The meaning-analysis of religious symbols involves showing how symbols are embedded within symbol systems, and how symbol systems relate to one another, interdefining and overlapping. The analysis also spells out the distinction between network meaning, which has to do with semiotic codes, and content meaning which has to do with persons internalizing and becoming competent in the symbols' meanings. Chapter 3 contains the main expression of this kind of symbolic analysis.

The third mode of analysis focuses on the contexts in which religious symbols appear in actual interpretations. Both the content of meaning and the nature of truth vary from context to context. Although the contexts for religious symbols are as varied as religions, three roughly distinguished contexts are to be discussed in chapters 4 and 5. The first is the theological context in which symbols are used to come to understanding and truth. Theology is used in a broad sense that encompasses the normative reflections of non-monotheistic religions as well as monotheisms, and also reflection on theological topics by those who might not be religious. Theological contexts are those in which religious symbols function most directly as representations. The second context, or family of contexts, is the involvement of religious symbols in shaping life in its practical dimensions. Obviously this involves explicit religious communities but also religious dimensions of secular areas of life. In this context the truth of religious symbols is less a matter of adequate representation than effectiveness in conforming life's shape to the implications for life of the religious realities to which the symbols refer. The third context, closely related to the second, is the involvement of religious symbols in personal devotional life, in transforming the soul or leading on to enlightenment or perfection. In this context religious symbols are often exaggerated and fantastic, at a far remove from theological symbols aiming at accurate representation. Devotees talk with their gods and imagine all sorts of things that are not "true" in a representational sense but that address the spiritual condition of the person. The truth of symbols in a devotional context has to do with effectiveness in spiritual progress; chapter 5 is concerned to study both the deviance of symbols in devotional contexts from mere representative functions and also the checks on their truth.

Religious symbols can be perversely demonic as well as positive, as they are intended. They are demonic if they turn against their religious functions. They can also be demonic in offending against morality, justice, psychological health, the ways cultures perceive things, and a variety of other normative dimensions of life; this is discussed in chapter 6. Therefore, in their practical implications religious symbols always need a check on their normativeness; effectiveness in practice is not enough.

Reference, meaning, and interpretation in context are the three main elements in a theory of signs that has learned from the semiotics of Charles Peirce. The theory of signs is of course more general than a study of religious symbols, a particular kind of sign. But the general theory provides the context for the distinction of the modes of analysis of religious symbols, coupled with the observation that such symbols have social, moral, psychological, and other consequences extending beyond their symbolic significance.[15]

---

15. The theory of signs here follows Charles Peirce in noting that every interpretation involves a triadic relation. Of his many discussions, one of the best is in CP 2.227–382. There is a sign which relates an object to an interpretant in some respect. The interpretation is an act that engages an object to which it refers by means of a sign which it takes to stand for the referent in a certain respect, and the interpretant is a sign that completes and represents the interpretation. Put yet another way, an interpretation intends an object by referring a sign to it in some respect. Object, sign, and interpretant or interpretation are three things, each of which may be something in itself but which has these characters men-

tioned by virtue of its roles involved in the triadic relation as referent, sign, and interpretant. The word *interpretant* is used when the act of interpreting is meant to be objectified as an object by another interpretation; an interpretant is an elicited meaning of a sign which is itself a sign. The word *interpretation* is used when the act of taking a sign to stand for an object in a certain respect is meant.

Although connected, each of the three roles in the triadic interpretation relation needs study. Clearly central is the role of being a sign. Signs have determinate characters as set within the coded structure of a semiotic system of signs. Within a semiotic system, signs are involved in complex networks that express for each sign connections with two other sets of signs. One set is the signs of objects to which a given sign's structured meaning might refer; these are the extensional referents of the sign, and are networked parts of the sign system. The other set is the collection of signs that constitute the meanings the sign might have for various of its extensional referents; this set constitutes the sign's extensional interpretants which are also networked parts of the sign system. The sign, its extensional referents, and its extensional interpretants are all integrated parts of the semiotic code. The code itself can be studied as a complex object, as it is by linguists, philologists, and historians. Signs with their extensional referents and interpretants are grouped within systems, and systems of systems. A given code has an historical development, with shifting network connections between signs and their extensional referents and interpretants, perhaps becoming more or less determinate as connections are made or unmade. The relations within a living code among signs, their extensional referents and interpretants, constitutes that code's logical space.

The study of semiotic codes in this sense, which is the principal preoccupation of European semiotics, abstracts from the actual or dynamic use of signs to interpret. In a dynamic act of interpretation a sign is intentionally referred to an object in a certain respect. Internal to the act of interpretation, the object engaged is an *intentional referent*. In many circumstances, the *intentional referent* is something signified by one of the sign's *extensional referents*. But in metaphor, for instance, the intentional referent is something different from what the sign's network code of extensional referents would include. The study of how signs refer to intentional referents within an actual or dynamic interpretation is different from a study of the sign's code of extensional referents and moves beyond the code to the use of the code to engage the object intended in an interpretation.

The obvious importance of the study of intentional referents for those signs that are religious symbols is that it is the locus of questions about the reality of those referents and about how referents which are not finite natural objects, or not only finite natural objects, can be intended. A study limited to the meanings of signs within a semiotic code need not raise the question of the reality of referents or of how complicated kinds of referents such as emptiness or God might be intended.

Although interpretation is a triadic affair of sign, object (referent) and interpretant, there is a fourth element, the respect in which the sign stands for its object as taken by the interpretant. An act of interpretation takes a sign with its coded structure to stand for an intentional referent in a certain respect. On the one hand, this involves selecting for use a configuration of the sign with certain of its specific extensional referents and meanings. So, for instance, the noun sign *coat* has among its extensional referents signs of a kind of outer *garment* and signs of an applied *layer* of a substance, such as paint; among its extensional meanings are signs distinguishing coat garments from hats and shoes and also signs distinguishing colors, textures, ages, and adherance of applied layers of a substance.

Running throughout the discussion is the problem of the nature of truth regarding religious symbols, especially as it varies with context. The general hypothesis about truth in all its senses is that it consists in the carryover of value from the object interpreted into the interpreting person or community, in the respects in which the sign interprets the object, as qualified by the biological, cultural, semiotic, and purposive nature of the interpreters.[16] Carryover means different things in representational theological contexts, organizational practical contexts, and devotional contexts where the value is a transformation of the soul. Chapter 7 summarizes and systematizes some of the various elements of truth in religious symbolism.

A special word needs to be said about the use of the word *symbol* in this study of religious symbols. Following Cassirer and others, I take *sym-*

---

An act of interpretation is required to engage an intentional object, say a house, and interpret it with *coat* referring (intentionally) to its paint and taking the paint to be of a good color; the act selects certain extensional referents and meanings to go together, and to be usable as a complex sign for engaging the house in respect of whether it should be repainted. On the other hand, an act of interpretation engages its intended object, to which it refers its sign, in a certain respect. The intentionality in interpretation involves selecting both the object and the respect of interpretation. The sign employed legitimates the connection of the object and the respect of interpretation by means of its network structure; metaphoric interpretation makes a connection between object and respect of interpretation not strictly legitimated by the sign's extensional semiotic structure. Of course, metaphors can become extensionally coded into semiotic systems over time. Perhaps someone once said that paint covers a house like a good coat on a person; or perhaps someone said this garment covers a person like a coat of paint. Or perhaps the meanings were always distinct, like a bank for money and a bank of a river, although susceptible to subsequent analogizing. The intentional meaning that an interpretation draws from a sign referred to an intentional referent is a function in part of the *context* of interpretation. That context involves the interests and purposes affecting the object chosen for reference and the respects selected for interpretation. Sometimes the contexts involve fairly straightforward and direct attempts to figure out and represent objects. But most contexts involve the construing of objects as incidental or supporting elements in the process of larger ongoing activities. Most interpretations are not conscious inquiries but the habitual responses to things that take them as background and foreground elements for ongoing action and enjoyments. Sometimes interpretations are intimately involved with changing or affecting things. The context needs to be understood in order to analyze the connections among intended referents, respects of interpretation, and signs in semiotic constellations of extensional referents and meanings.

16. The hypothesis regarding truth is elaborated in detail, in connection with the theory of interpretation and a cosmology to show how truth can be carryover (a causal notion) of value (not form, which is a function of value), in my *Recovery of the Measure*.

*bol* to be the generic word for all kinds of religious signs of the divine (or however we might define what religious signs signify). As generic, religious symbols include myths and religious narratives, theological ideas, particular notions such as karma or sin which are defined in one or more symbol systems, the symbol systems as such, religious acts such as liturgies or private meditations that move through and overlay various symbol systems, as well as architectural and artistic symbols with religious content, books, songs, devotional objects, and the like—anything that can be referred to a religious object and can bear a religious meaning. In chapter 3, I will introduce some distinctions to sort these things into kinds, for instance, schemata, schema-images, replicas, and symbol-fragments. But we should note here that a very wide range of things can be religious symbols in the generic sense.

Within Peirce's (and others') semiotic system, however, symbol has a much more restricted meaning, namely as a sign with a conventional reference, in comparison with signs that have iconic or indexical references.[17] Peirce's narrow meaning is not used in this study. Rather, the broader meaning of symbol is retained. As is fairly obvious, most if not all religious symbols have conventional content, most are also indexical in referring to something beyond what they completely express, and most are iconic in the sense of referring to reality as like this story, this myth, this theory, this system of interdefined symbols, or referring to Jesus' cross as like the cross on the altar. This point is important not only to avoid terminological confusion but because some scholars reject the view that religious symbols refer to reality at all in the intentional sense, being confined to coded extensional references. They cite the inner intentionality of myths and narratives, claiming that there is no intention of saying reality is like what the myth says; but this is to forget that the iconic is a kind of reference. More of this in chapter 2.

Having begun so bravely, it is important here near the beginning to call attention to some of the limitations of this study. One is that I shall assume that the reader is familiar with religion and religious symbols. Only a few will be analyzed in detail, and then not so much to understand the symbol as to understand what goes into its analysis. To assume otherwise would require a volume longer than Eliade's and would be beyond my capabilities. Another limitation, consequent on the first, is that the symbols to be discussed will be those with which it is reasonable

---

17. CP 2.292–308.

to assume most English readers have familiarity. Thus most of the symbols common to the denominations of Christianity and Judaism can be treated with great familiarity, including gestures, architecture, and music as well as nodal texts. Symbols peculiar to one branch or denomination will not be so commonly familiar. Symbols of Islam, of Asian religions, and of primal religions will be limited to those of familiar texts, architecture, and art, not gesture, ritual, or music. English readers are likely to know about davening and kneeling to pray, but they would not likely know about the direction in which to process around a Hindu stupa; they might know from art or yoga classes about sitting in the lotus position, but not about its signficance for "wall meditation."[18]

A third limitation is that, even if the readers were genuinely cosmopolitan, as many are, and if I were sufficiently erudite to discuss all or most of the world's religious traditions in sophisticated detail, which I am not, there still is not the knowledge to be had for a comprehensive discussion. The reason has already been mentioned, namely, that proper comparative categories for relating religions and their symbols do not yet exist. Most of the comparative categories that we have were put forward by the great nineteenth-century translators of the texts of world religions into European languages; categories are required for translation. Great as that work was, and deeply indebted to those translators as we still are, the translation equivalents have not been subjected to critical scrutiny for their capacities to register subtle differences. Where they have, most have been found wanting. We are still awaiting what Francis X. Clooney calls "comparative theology" in which the texts of each religion are read in, or inscribed in, the others, allowing a faithful conversation, each with the others.[19]

Therefore, the discussion will focus mainly on Western, theistic, indeed Christian symbols, with frequent references outside those traditional lines for comparative support. In regard to this focus it should be

---

18. "Wall meditation" is a form of Zen practice, popular in Korean Son Buddhism, in which meditators face a wall, not in order to turn away from one another nor to limit vision but rather to be *like* a wall—just there, with no distinctions of subject and object, meditator and topic, self or others. The wall meditation is paired by Bodhidharma as entering into enlightenment "by practice" along with the approach through faith, "entering into communion with primordial reality." See the profound analysis of this in Park Sung-bae's *Buddhist Faith and Sudden Enlightenment,* chapter 8, "Bodhidharma's Wall Meditation," which includes a translation of Bodhidharma's text from his *Treatise on the Fourfold Practice through the Twofold Entrance.*

19. See Clooney's *Theology after Vedanta.* See also my *Behind the Masks of God.*

noted that I myself am a Christian and thus have a special interest in understanding symbolism in that tradition; let the reader beware of this bias. What may be concluded about religious symbols from such a study, if the analyses are good ones, may have reference to only a small domain of religion. On the other hand, perhaps the findings and arguments have greater generalizability than can be claimed now. Although the examples of symbols I shall analyze in detail come from the traditions I know best, I attempt to cite symbols to illustrate points from a variety of traditions, often counterbalancing theisms with religions sometimes characterized as non-theistic, or anti-theistic.

This book has grown out of four lectures delivered at Seattle University in January, 1994, where I had the very great privilege to be the Toulouse Lecturer. The Toulouse lectures consist of the public Toulouse Lecture and separate presentations to the Thomas More Society, the Philosophy Department of Seattle University, and the Northwest Society for Phenomenology and Existential Philosophy. I thank both old and new friends in Seattle for the invitation and for stimulating critical discussions. I especially thank Patrick Burke who made the invitation and coordinated the lectures. If this book has grown a long way from those talks, it is because of the helpful discussions they received in Seattle.

I thank Boston University, especially its President, John Silber, and its Provost, Jon Westling, for granting a sabbatical leave for the spring semester of 1994 during which most of this was written. They both have gentle regard for deans who believe their scholarship should have support. In addition I thank Donald Treese, former Associate General Secretary of the Board of Higher Education and Ministry of the United Methodist Church, and John Harnish, the current Associate General Secretary, for permission to spend much of the spring semester in the flat of the Association of United Methodist Theological Schools in Cambridge, England. That place is in the midst of a great university and yet is sufficiently distant that few people felt it worthwhile to interrupt my studies. I am deeply indebted to Kenneth Cracknell, head tutor of Wesley House, and to Arnold Browne, Dean of the Chapel at Trinity College, in Cambridge for their extraordinarily gracious hospitality during my stay there.

Religious symbolism has held an important interest for me since the age of twelve when I realized there are problems here. I cannot begin to list those friends and mentors who have stimulated and influenced my thought; surely all those mentioned in prefaces of previous books have been important for this topic too. But I would like to single out Helen

I. Baldwin and Raymond T. Shepherd as my principal conversation partners on religion from the time I was twelve until I left home for college, probably the most formative period. Over the years I have had instructive sustained discussions with William Desmond, Joseph Grange, Jay Schulkin, Marjorie Suchocki, William Sullivan, and Carl Vaught. Among recent colleagues I should single out those with whom the topic of religious symbolism has been explicitly comparative, especially Judith Berling, John Berthrong, Sharon Peebles Burch, Francis X. Clooney, David Eckel, Paula Fredriksen, Livia Kohn, Anthony Saldarini, Merlin Swartz, and Wesley Wildman. An early draft of this manuscript received helpful criticism from the anonymous reviewers of the State University Press, and from John Griswold, William Eastman, and Robert J. Sadowski, C.S.P.; extensive page by page comments from the last two guided a very considerable revision. Bud Heckman provided commentary on and proofreading for a late draft, for which I thank him.

The most important learning experience for me regarding religious symbols has been preaching, an activity often required by my position as Dean of the Boston University School of Theology. Many people have encouraged my preaching, for which I am grateful but who thereby cast doubt on their own judgment. Of those who have taken special pains to correct my preaching, I thank Horace T. Allen, Anthony C. Campbell, J. Harley Chapman, Elizabeth E. Neville, Imani-Sheila Newsome, Sean Recroft, J. Paul Sampley, John Silber, William Sullivan, Jon Westling, and Wesley Wildman. The most astute critic of sermons (not only mine) is Ray L. Hart who has expended great and caring effort to develop my ear for symbolism, and is the author of the most important book on religious imagination in our time. I am pleased to honor his friendship by dedicating this book to him.

All quotations from the Bible are from the New Revised Standard Version Bible, copyrighted 1989 by the Division of Christian Education of the National Council of the Churches of Christ in the United States of America.

# CHAPTER I

# What Religious Symbols Do

What do religious symbols do? Obviously, many things in many contexts. In religious contexts, religious symbols are supposed to help save people, shape communities, and tell the truth about what they represent. Each of these points is important for the study, or at least this study, of religious symbols. The first section of this chapter will discuss issues concerning the relation of religious symbols to religion, asking what makes religious symbols religious. The second will consider the approach to religious symbols as instruments of salvation, and will conclude that, even if their primary value is soteriological instrumentality, they still are representations and should be examined regarding their truth. The third will look at approaches to religious symbols that construe them primarily as shapers of communities, and will also conclude that, however much they have a shaping function, they still need to be understood as representations. The fourth section will then consider summary issues concerning what it means to be a religious representation.

## I.I. SYMBOLS IN RELIGION

A study of religious symbols needs to acknowledge two traits of the subject matter. One is that the use of religious symbols is an activity of interpretation, a semiotic practice. Religious symbols are supposed to symbolize something. What do they symbolize? How do they refer in symbolizing? What kinds of meanings are involved? How can they be interpreted and under what conditions? Under what conditions are they true or false? These and like questions concerning the nature of religious symbols as signs are to be expected in a study of any kinds of symbols.

The other trait is that religious symbols are supposed to be instruments of transformation, of shaping religious, familial, and other communities,

1

of leading the soul to greater perfection, or the person to enlightenment, or to attunement. These transformations go beyond the mere interpretation of what the religious symbols mean. Encountering the symbols is supposed to lead to a transformation of personal, social, or cultural character. Sometimes this might mean only that, when the symbol is properly interpreted, people will behave, think, and feel differently, as when learning the morally relevant facts leads to improved moral behavior, or when learning what a work of art means leads to greater appreciation. But at other times, transformations of behavior, thinking, and feeling occur, or are supposed to occur, when the symbols are brutely encountered with no interpretation, or a wrong interpretation.

Transformation of people happens with many kinds of symbols, of course, but to a very high degree with religious symbols. Religious symbols are supposed to be instruments of salvation, or enlightenment, or basic attunement. Some people, indeed some significant branches of religions, believe that these soteriological purposes are much more important than inquiry into the truth, at least for the business of religion; for them, religious symbols are to be judged almost exclusively on the basis of their soteriological instrumentality, regardless of whether they are true. The Buddhist doctrine of *upaya* is an extreme example of this last view: symbols are merely expedient means to enlightenment.[1] Perhaps also Tertullian's vexing remark that he believed in Christianity *because* it is absurd is an affirmation of the exclusive priority of soteriological

---

1. On Buddhist practice aimed at enlightenment or samadhi, see *Traditions of Meditation in Chinese Buddhism,* edited by Peter N. Gregory. Of course, Chinese Buddhism is not the same as Indian or Tibetan Buddhism, but it is the source of the most common Western apprehensions of Buddhist meditation and practice. On *upaya,* see all the articles in that volume. For further technical studies see *Buddhist and Taoist Studies I,* edited by Michael Saso and David W. Chappell, and *Buddhist and Taoist Practice in Medieval Chinese Society: Buddhist and Taoist Studies II,* edited by David W. Chappell. For more popular approaches see the Zen Buddhism of the San Francisco Zen Center in Sunryu Suzuki's *Zen Mind, Beginner's Mind* or the Tibetan Buddhism of Naropa and the Karma Dzong in Boulder, Colorado, in Chogyam Trungpa's *Cutting through Spiritual Materialism*; taking symbols as representations rather than skillful means (*upaya*) is often a form of "spiritual materialism." Perhaps the best single exposition of Buddhist thought, especially Zen thought, on all these topics is Park Sung-bae's *Buddhist Faith and Sudden Enlightenment*; Park treats *upaya* with the doctrine of the Two Truths as the culmination of the Buddhist understanding of faith, a topic neglected in most Western expositions. He then integrates faith with practice and enlightenment, all as dialectically, not sequentially, interconnected.

instrumentality in doctrinal symbols rather than a peculiar logic of doctrine.[2] Anyway, in religious practice creeds are recited often without understanding, hymns are sung with attention to harmonic feeling but not words, symbolic postures are sat in, gestures made, processions followed, sunrises and night skies grooved on—all for effect and often regardless of interpretation. Like reciting "nonsense" mantras, engaging at least some religious symbols is to be understood causally, not only, or even at all, hermeneutically.

That religious symbols are supposed to have causal effects as well as interpretations does not mean they always in fact have the effects they are supposed to. Feminists have argued that symbolic language, and even some elaborate theological doctrines, have consequences quite the opposite from what would be supposed to be their meaning or intended causal consequences. Chapter 6 studies a case of this in detail. Therefore, a study of religious symbols must examine how they function in context, with causal consequences of various sorts and interpretations dependent on the context.

How do we hold together the hermeneutical and the instrumental traits of religious symbols? By examining them in the context of religious practice attempting to engage its object, not merely as a species of signs in semiotics. There is good precedent for this. The influence of anthropology on the study of religious symbols has emphasized their embeddedness in religious practice, and in religious dimensions of society beyond religious cults.[3] We should also be wise to the causal consequences of religious symbols that run counter to their explicit meanings and counter even to their religious functions as a sociologist or anthropologist might recognize them. Historians and cultural critics or moralists can discern non-systematic consequences of religious symbols. To make much progress with this, we need to inquire more deeply into the nature of religion itself as the context or partial context for religious sym-

---

2. See Paul Tillich's discussion in *Systematic Theology I*, pp. 150–151, and *II*, p. 91. In the later place he says the phrase *credo quia absurdum* is wrongly attributed to Tertullian; I cannot find the direct quotation in Tertullian. Kierkegaard, of course, was the one who developed the connection between faith and absurdity *ad absurdam*; see, for instance, his *Concluding Unscientific Postscript*, the chapter on "Truth as Subjectivity," say, at pp. 191–195. In *Philosophical Fragments*, p. 43, Kierkegaard attributes the phrase to Tertullian.

3. Consider, for instance, the importance of Emile Durkheim's *The Elementary Forms of the Religious Life*.

bolism. What difference does religion make to the functioning of symbols?

Of course there is an even more pressing reason to look at definitions of religion, namely, to say what makes some symbols religious. What is our subject matter here? Or if that is too blunt a question, What are the issues in defining our subject matter? The scope of religious symbols is almost impossible to indicate because religion itself is not easily defined.

One could take a denotative approach and say that religious symbols are those playing major roles in the world's religions, including Buddhism, Christianity, Confucianism, Hinduism, Islam, Jainism, Judaism, Shintoism, Daoism, primal religions such as the traditional ones of Africa and Oceania, shamanisms of Asia and America, and post-Axial Age variants and blends such as Mormonism, Sikhism, and Ba'hai. This list could be extended and subdivided indefinitely, but sooner or later most important religious symbols would have been encompassed.[4] Such an approach

---

4. This approach is, perhaps by necessity, that followed by anthologists, authors of introductory textbooks on religion, and generalizing comparativists. An influential introductory text such as John B. Noss's *Man's Religions* just starts off with "Primitive and Bygone Religions" that are treated anthropologically, with some discussion of anthropological definitions, and then deals with thirteen religions or religious movements. James W. Dye and William H. Forthman's anthology-with-commentary *Religions of the World* solves the problem of definition by recognizing "major" religions. Arvind Sharma's collection of "state of the religion" essays by contemporary representative religious thinkers, *Our Religions*, treats the Big Seven and defines its topic with this first sentence: "The world of religion is composed of the religions of the world, seven of which—Hinduism, Buddhism, Confucianism, Taoism, Judaism, Christianity, and Islam—are presented in the covers of this book. Geoffrey Parrinder's *World Religions From Ancient History to the Present*, a collection of articles by scholars of twenty one religions or religious movements, begins with the Oxford English Dictionary definition of religion as "the recognition of superhuman controlling power, and especially of a personal god, entitled to obedience," accepts it [!] and then proceeds to add other things one might want to say about religion, in no apparent order and with no coherence. In his *The World's Religions*, Ninian Smart, a sophisticated philosopher of religion, raises the question of the definition of religion, notes some difficulties with particular examples of attempts to define the essence of religion, concludes that we cannot define the essence of religion, and then lists seven dimensions that together are to be found in religions: the practical and ritual, the experiential and emotional, the narrative or mythic, the doctrinal and philosophical, the ethical and legal, the social and institutional, and the material dimensions. The problem is that these dimensions apply to most social institutions: the government, the economy, the judiciary, the educational system, and so forth. However important it is to look at these dimensions, they do not have anything specific to do with religion, and Smart really answers the question of the definition of religion by listing them; as an historian his list is fullsome and subtle.

would not say what makes a symbol religious, however. It would miss religious symbols that are not taken up into organized religions. Its sole advantage as an approach for defining religion is that it indicates where to look for counterexamples that would not fit some normative definition of religious symbols. Running through a list of religions at the beginning of a study of religious symbols is an important reminder of how catholic our conceptions need to be.

Another approach is to attempt a normative definition of religion. Such a definition would be presupposed at any rate in any attempt to give an account of religious symbols. Nevertheless, two common lines of definition should be marked for avoidance at the outset. One, associated with anthropology and sociology, defines religion in terms of cultural and social functions.[5] Of course religions have such functions and many of them are unique to religion. But religion also deals crucially with individuals in some ways that transcend social and cultural origins. The other, associated with philosophers such as William James and Alfred North Whitehead, picks up precisely the individual focus of religion and defines it as what people do with their solitariness.[6] Important as this is, it misses the social and cultural parts.

---

5. Durkheim has already been mentioned. In sociology Max Weber is likely the most important figure; see Part III *From Max Weber*, edited by Gerth and Mills. Sociologists of knowledge dealing with religion, such as Peter Berger, will be discussed later.

6. William James was deeply aware of the elements of religion neglected by his famous definition, and pointed them out, claiming that his definition pertained only to the studies contained in *The Varieties of Religious Experience*, in which he wrote in chapter 2, "Religion, therefore, as I now ask you arbitrarily to take it, shall mean for us *the feelings, acts, and experiences of individual men in their solitude, so far as they apprehend themselves to stand in relation to whatever they may consider the divine.*" Note the reference to the divine, to which my text shall return.

Whitehead, too, was more circumspect than his famous definition : "Religion is what the individual does with his own solitariness," in *Religion in the Making*, p. 16. The profundity and fruitfulness of his ideas require that his definition be put in context, reading from pages 16 to 18.

> No one is invariably "justified" by his faith in the multiplication table. But in some sense or other, justification is the basis of all religion. Your character is developed according to your faith. This is the primary religious truth from which no one can escape. Religion is force of belief cleansing the inward parts. For this reason the primary religious virtue is sincerity, a penetrating sincerity.
>
> A religion, on its doctrinal side, can thus be defined as a system of general truths which have the effect of transforming character when they are sincerely held and vividly apprehended.

Perhaps the whole enterprise of attempting to define religions is misguided. Under criticisms deriving from deconstruction and postmodernism, we have become wary of "essences." Perhaps there is no "essence" of religion of which the religions are species. Of course the language of "essences" reflects a formalist Aristotelian metaphysics that few people follow these days[7]. But the empirical question is a good one. Are there traits common to the religions, and perhaps found sporadically outside

---

In the long run your character and your conduct of life depend upon your intimate convictions. Life is an internal fact for its own sake, before it is an external fact relating itself to others. The conduct of external life is conditioned by environment, but it receives its final quality, on which its worth depends, from the internal life which is the self-realization of existence. Religion is the art and the theory of the internal life of man, so far as it depends on the man himself and on what is permanent in the nature of things.

This doctrine is the direct negation of the theory that religion is primarily a social fact. Social facts are of great importance to religion, because there is no such thing as absolutely independent existence. You cannot abstract society from man; most psychology is herd-psychology. But all collective emotions leave untouched the awful ultimate fact, which is the human being, consciously alone with itself, for its own sake.

Religion is what the individual does with his own solitariness. It runs through three stages, if it evolves to its final satisfaction. It is the transition from God the void to God the enemy, and from God the enemy to God the companion.

Thus religion is solitariness; and if you are never solitary, you are never religious. Collective enthusiasms, revivals, institutions, churches, rituals, bibles, codes of behavior, are the trappings of religions, its passing forms. They may be useful, or harmful; they may be authoritatively ordained, or merely temporary expedients. But the end of religion is beyond all this.

Accordingly, what should emerge from religion is individual worth of character. But worth is positive or negative, good or bad. Religion is by no means necessarily good. It may be very evil. The fact of evil, interwoven with the texture of the world, shows that in the nature of things there remains effectiveness for degradation. In your religious experience the God with whom you have made terms may be the God of destruction, the God who leaves in his wake the loss of the greater reality.

In considering religion, we should not be obsessed by the idea of its necessary goodness. This is a dangerous delusion. The point to notice is its transcendent importance; and the fact of this importance is abundantly made evident by the appeal to history.

7. On these issues see John D. Caputo's *Radical Hermeneutics*, David L. Hall's *Richard Rorty: Prophet and Poet of the New Pragmatism*, and Frank Lentricchia's *After the New Criticism*.

organized religions, that make them religious, in contrast to other traits common to religions having nothing to do with religion, such as being human activities, involving people of different ages using symbols, taking place on the Earth, and so forth?[8] We should look for attempts to distinguish religious from non-religious elements.

A third approach, then, expressed best in recent years by Paul Tillich, takes religion to be that dimension of life, including both individual manifestations and those appearing in cultures and societies, that constitutes a response to the divine, the absolute, the infinite, or the unconditioned.[9] An old-fashioned Western way of saying this is that religion has to do with the bearing of God on human life. An obvious difficulty with this approach is that to this date it is not clear whether non-theistic religions such as Daoism and some forms of Hinduism and Buddhism have analogues to the Western notion of the divine. In their popular forms they have altogether too many gods and in their philosophical expressions seem to unify these by transcending divinity to something beyond theism. Related to this difficulty is the fact that the very idea of *religion* arose out of the self-reflection of the Western theistic religions, and some scholars claim that it simply does not apply to some of the phenomena that Western thinkers have catalogued in the above list as religions. The problem here is an empirical one for scholarship. We need comparative categories with academic legitimacy, that do not now exist, to facilitate the examination of "religions" regarding whether some analogue of divinity is a common trait.

The preliminary evidence, however, is positive more or less. Anthropologists and phenomenologists of religions such as Tylor, Frazer, Otto, van der Leeuw, and Eliade have amassed extraordinary amounts of data that illustrate the commonality of at least the sacred or holy, if not something transcendently sacred or holy.[10] Of course their works are mutually inconsistent in their interpretations of these data and we now

---

8. The dimensions of religion listed by Ninian Smart at the beginning of his *The World's Religions* are like the latter.

9. See, for instance, chapter 1, "Religion as a Dimension in Man's Spiritual Life," and chapter 4, "Aspects of a Religious Analysis of Culture," in Tillich's *Theology of Culture*; or the pervasive discussion of Spirit in his *Systematic Theology III*. Tillich's technical definition of religion is "the self-transcendence of life under the dimension of spirit"; see, for instance, *Systematic Theology III*, p. 96. That definition is too technical to connect much with my own argument at this stage, although later it will be apparent how it connects with my discussions of self-transcendence, dimensionality, and spirit.

10. For their compendious works, see the bibliography.

appreciate the degree to which any data-gathering is already theory-laden.[11] But precisely because of the great variations in their theories, their inconsistencies and diverse classifications, the commonalities that do show through likely have some point. Probably the case is that *religion* roughly describes the collective human responses, individually and socially, to the divine as sacred or holy.

Whether the distinction between the sacred and profane parallels those often drawn in Western theisms between the infinite and finite, God and the world, the transcendent and the natural, can be left to later reflection. Suffice it to note for now that even in Western symbolism the symbols vary systematically by context. The God of storms, trials, mercy, persecutions, and death (see the Tindley hymn, "Stand by Me," quoted in chapter 5) is existentially vivid in personalistic images. Yet Jews, Christians, and Muslims also say that God creates all these things and hence transcends them; in each of those traditions theological moments occur when personalistic images are explicitly denied, when it is affirmed that God is, for instance, simple, something no personal or even individualized being could be. Therefore even within monotheistic religions there is a spectrum of contextual construals of symbols for God, from representations of God as a concrete personal individual to representations of God as *esse*, Being-itself, a mystical Godhead, or the God beyond Gods. We can call this a "personalizing/form-transcending spectrum." The same spectrum of contexts is found in Mahayana Buddhism when worshippers pray for help from Guanyin on the one hand and affirm that even Emptiness is empty on the other. The spectrum or something

---

11. See my *Normative Cultures*, chapter 2, for a detailed discussion of value-ladenness, based on a reconstruction of Peirce's theory of theories.

12. Western scholars have often given very great contrast to the religious Daoism that dances with gods versus the philosophical Daoism of Laozi and Zhuangzi. Recent scholars have argued that this is exaggerated; see Livia Kohn's discussions in the first chapters respectively of her *Taoist Mystical Philosophy* and *Early Chinese Mysticism*. The exaggeration has occurred, perhaps, because Confucians from Xunzi onward liked and learned from the Daoist philosophical texts and rejected their rites and pantheon, whereas religious Daoists were often from the lower classes and did not have access to the highly refined, discussion oriented, religious practice of Confucians, even though there are striking parallels between medieval and later Daoist projects of self-cultivation and those of the Song and Ming Dynasty Neo-Confucians. But the point about the spectrum holds whether or not the philosophical Daoists of the Dao that cannot be named are the same people as the religious Daoists of temple ceremonies and exotic mystical practices.

much like it occurs in Daoism when priests entrance themselves to inquire of gods about divinitory questions on the one hand and on the other say that the Dao that can be named is not the true Dao.[12] Vedantists worship Isvara as the creator of the world but say that Brahman truly is without qualities. The personalizing/form-transcending spectra in these religions, from concrete, devotional, and personalistic images to abstract, theological, and ultimate ideas, are at least similar to the monotheistic cases. The difference is that for the non-monotheistic cases, there is no one symbol, like *God*, which moves through all the positions on the spectra. Yet what does remain constant in all the religions, characteristic of all the positions on the spectra, is the sense that the religious "object" symbolized is holy or sacred.[13]

The elementary limitation with saying that religion is the human response, individually and collectively, to the divine and its analogues is that nothing at all is said in that about the human response. Of course, religions differ in their responses, including in what they take the divine to be, as has been noted. Some scholars, often associated with history of religions or with deconstruction or both, go so far as to argue that the category of *religion* is not only parochial but useless: what we should study are religions, not religion. Surely we need to be wary of any attempt to define a single essence of religion. Nevertheless, every reflective thinker about the religions, from social scientists to mystics to ecclesiastical bureaucrats, agrees on three main classes of religious responses: rituals, spiritual practices aimed at perfection or approximation to the holy, and intellectual representations of what the religion is about. These can be spelled out briefly here and illustrated copiously later.

Rituals can be collective or personal, elaborately cultic or more diffuse as in philosophical Daoism. There is much scholarly debate about just what rituals are about.[14] At least one of the most important features

---

13. *The Sacred* has become a binary notion in contrast with the *Profane* because of its technical employment in the classificatory systems of Durkheim, Eliade, and others. *Holiness* is a vaguer and hence more useful notion here, insofar as it can mean *sacred* in the dichotomous sense but also indicate a dimension of everything. See Tillich's *Systematic Theology III*, pp. 98–110.

14. Indeed, ritual has become a popular topic lately. A classic anthropological work is Victor Turner's *The Ritual Process*. Jonathan Z. Smith's *To Take Place* is a history of religions theory about ritual. Francis X. Clooney's *Thinking Ritually* is a groundbreaking study of Purva Mimamsa, the Hindu school focusing on ritual. Tom F. Driver's *The Magic of Ritual* is a theological analysis of ritual as it functions, or ought to function, in Western societies. The ancient philosopher who best understood ritual was Xunzi.

code, creed, cult → Yerkes characterization

is that they epitomize symbolically and rehearse the "work" to be done in order to relate rightly to life relative to the sacred. In paleolithic times the problem was food, and rituals had to do with the hunt and fertility. At the dawn of civilization the problem was ordering larger-than-clan societies, and rituals had to do with order and lordship. Part of ritual's intent is defined by the pervasive felt problematic situation of the people and part by the role of the sacred in this.[15]

The second class of religious responses is the efforts and practices separate from ritual that aim for greater holiness or perfection on the part of individuals particularly and also of groups. These include prayer and meditation, fasting, religious quests, and a host of more exotic practices. But they also include the vast tissue of practices involved in communal religious life. From monasteries to very loose consciousness of the religious dimensions of ordinary life, including societies' reactions to specific historical phenomena—floods, barbarians, exemplars of virtue and vice—religious responses include the organization of life to "relate appropriately" to the sacred.

The third class of religious responses is the development (and sometimes criticism) of representations of the sacred and of strategies or postures to relate to it. These intellectual responses might be mythic or take some other form such as theology or commentary on sacred texts and objects. They express how religious people try to think about the sacred and its bearing on life. Here is the direct source of religious symbols per se. But religious thinking is expressed throughout rituals and spiritual practices as well as throughout other kinds of religious responses that might not be as common as these three. Religious symbols for thinking about the divine shape many relatively unthinking religious activities.

A provisional understanding of religion (not a formal definition), then, is that it is the responses in rituals, spiritual practices, and representations to the holy or sacred and its bearing on life. Religion might include other

---

15. I have discussed ritual, cosmologies, and spiritual practices as defining characteristics of religion in *Soldier, Sage, Saint*, chapter 1, and *Behind the Masks of God*, chapter 10. The Greek root of the word *liturgy* meant *public service*, including but not limited to *public service to the Gods*. For this reason I play upon ritual as the "work" of setting things right for the people in the cosmos. The Chinese word for what we would translate as *ritual* (*li*), means not only ceremony but also gift or present, connoting the establishment of a relationship through an action directed at the acknowledgment of someone else. The ancient Confucians argued that the rituals by which people give proper acknowledgment to one another, to nature, and to the divinities themselves constitute civilization with its social habits. I have discussed this sense of ritual at length in *Normative Cultures*, chapter 7.

important features, and religions surely have many important features that are not common to them all. This understanding, however, gives a preliminary context in which to ask about religious symbols. Reference to the sacred in religious symbols will be advanced beyond the stage of preliminary discussion in the analysis below where it will be argued that religious symbols refer directly or indirectly to borderline or worldmaking things, to things having to do with the very worldliness of the world, thus referring always jointly to the finite border and to the infinite within which the border is constituted. This is related to the personalizing/form-transcending spectra where the former contexts for symbols emphasize the location within the world of the person or group at which the borderline situation is encountered and where the latter contexts on the spectra relate to the borders themselves and what lies beyond them. If this argument has plausibility, then the onus of justifying transcendent references to divinity will be greatly lessened. In fact, the difficulty will be to show that merely sacred things such as rocks and trees can be religious symbols in the sense of having the infinite side of the contrast. They can, if they help define worldliness for a person or people.

The cultural contexts for religious symbols, namely rituals, spiritual practices, and representations, will also be discussed at much greater length below. Ritual, however, usually will be treated within a more generic head, that of the roles of religious symbols to organize life. Ritual practice is the paradigmatic sense of life organized around religious symbols and yet both the whole of the life of a religious community and the wider non-religious community are affected and shaped by religious symbols. In the course of this book, therefore, some of these preliminary orienting assumptions will be given greater justification and plausibility.

From what has been said so far, it is apparent that the study of religious symbols, or at least this study, is normative as well as descriptive. Actually, there is no such thing as a purely descriptive study. Even empirical word-pictures of things, or simple classificatory schemes, bear the values involved in taking the descriptive terms and classifications to be the important things to know about what is described.[16] Describers should be prepared to give reasons why their descriptive selections are the important ones, which reveals the normativeness of their descriptions. Analytical studies of symbols too have their weighted terms for

---

16. That description is value-laden need not be construed as a fault. In *Normative Cultures*, chapters 1 and 2, I analyze this problem in detail.

analysis, for functional divisions, and for the timing of when to analyze what in what order.

That all studies are normative has a deeper reason as well, namely, one based on the nature of definition. The fashionable critique of essences does not prove that things lack identifiable form but that what forms are selected to define and describe them reflects judgments about what forms *in them* are important or valuable to describe. The importances come not alone from the interest of the describer or definer but lie within the character of the thing if the definition and description are to be true to the thing. How the importances function in the thing is very important to know about it. Therefore, we should be wary of attempting to define or identify things such as religious symbols in a Platonic way by reference to some ideal form, for instance, "a religious symbol is a symbol that genuinely communicates God or divine things to the interpreter." If this line is taken, then many things that anthropologists, sociologists, psychologists, and ordinary people take to be religious symbols will not be such if they are old-fashioned, misunderstood, dead, demonic, idolatrous, or plain ignored. Also, while saying that most symbols used in religion are not really religious symbols (because today is not a religious time), this Platonic line, which was followed by Tillich in a surprising gaff, will lead to proclaiming just about anything and everything to be a religious symbol if someone somewhere is spurred to see the "depth dimension" in it.[17] Far better it is to say that religious symbols are the symbols found in the rituals, spiritual practices, and reflections of religions that have the sacred or divine as their direct or indirect object. Where they fail to communicate because they are ignored, dead, misunderstood, or untimely, and where they miscommunicate because they are demonic or idolatrous, those very adjectives can be appended to them as religious symbols, various ways of being bad religious symbols. Meanwhile, we recognize that part of the analysis of religious symbols is to say when and how they symbolize well, and in what senses.

## I.2. SYMBOLS AND SALVATION

The understanding of religious symbols to be advocated here is presented in part as a corrective to other approaches, particularly to one. That is the family of positions saying that religious symbols are all fictions as far as their symbolic function goes, and that their function in religions is as

---

17. See his *Systematic Theology III*, pp. 111 ff.

instruments of salvation (or as instruments of something wholly unreligious, thus reducing the religious to something else). This is a powerful position because there is a profound truth in both of its clauses, at least for many symbols. First, many religious symbols are indeed fictions, often fantastic works of poetic imagination. Second, many if not all religious symbols are used at one time or another for soteriological purposes.

Consider the point that at least some if not all religious symbols are fictions of poetic imagination (perhaps all those that are not are dull and unpoetic!). Indeed, poetry is too tame among modes of creative imagination. Many religious symbols are, or were in their original models, clearly works of deranged, intoxicated imaginations. Whether the intoxication is by inspiration of divine or demonic spirits, or by some vegetable product drunk, eaten, or smoked, or by deprivation or pain, is not to the point of the symbols' fictitious character. One thinks of fantastic visual images, from the man-beast paintings in the caves at Lascaux to Tibetan mandalas to African masks to William Blake's etchings to the religious murals and paintings of Marc Chagall.

Even so-called illustrative art, such as paintings and sculptures of Brahma, Buddha, Jesus, Krishna, Mary, Siva, or any pantheon, is fictional in the sense that no one knew what the original subject actually looked like, if there were originals. Music is obviously fictional. Architectural religious symbols might have some iconic elements, such as high vaulted ceilings pointing to heaven or stupas recalling worshippers to the organs of origin, but still there is much fiction in architecture. As to texts, although some might appear to be "literally" about their subjects, no one doubts the poetic side in the mythopoeic imagination. Not only myths but religious histories such as the books of history in the Jewish Canon are also fictional, though perhaps in widely different genres of fiction. Many religious symbols are ancient time out of mind and, because we cannot imagine individual authors of them, or even authorship as such, it sounds strange to call them fictions: nobody "made them." Still, they are products of human imagination and do not represent anything in a literal way.

As to religious symbols being instruments of salvation, or at least being used for that purpose whether they work or not, the difficulty is to find any exceptions. Perhaps some very dry and abstruse ideas in theology are relevant only to some narrow intellectual truth about a divine matter, the understanding of which makes no palpable difference to religious living. Other than that, religious symbols, however they symbolize and have perhaps an intellectual meaning, are taken up as shapers of religious living. The interesting questions are not about whether they have instrumental use but about how they are used, the conditions for their effectiveness, the practical interactions of symbols with one another and with other parts of life. I will have more to say about this in chapters 4 through 6. Even in the case of very abstract theological and philosophical conceptual symbols, I am convinced that some thinkers do use them as instruments for engaging the divine in transformative enlightenment.

The position I oppose here conjoins those points to say that the symbolic or representational function of religious symbols is unimportant and that they are misleading if interpreted symbolically. Rather they are to be understood in terms of their functional use within religions for religions' own ends, collectively, and perhaps honorifically, called "salvation" "enlightenment," or "attunement." There are several variants of this position.

One variant believes that there are no religious objects, that religion is false regarding its cognitive assumptions, and that therefore religious symbols cannot symbolize anything truly. What they mean to symbolize is simply not there. But their meanings can be foisted upon people who are then used for exploitative purposes.[18] The people themselves are deluded. Perhaps the delusion is self-delusion, which is how many secular people view religious people today; perhaps the delusion is perpetuated by a manipulative class. In either case, the use of religious symbols should be looked on with some cynicism, according to this position. Even if religious practice has some good side benefits, such as supporting family life, national pride, or a work-ethic, people are deluded to believe that there is any such thing as divinity, salvation, enlightenment, or spiritual uplifting about which religious symbols purport to inform practitioners in their symbolic function.

Another variant of this position, at the opposite extreme, holds that there really and truly is such a thing as salvation but that it is merely a peculiar state of affairs or kind of awareness, without reference to anything holy or transcendent. All religious symbols, and practices such as chanting mantras, have value only insofar as they serve the culture leading to the soteriological end. This variant is a borderline case, barely representing a religion at all, though it is affirmed by some Zen Buddhists preaching to Americans (possibly because they think Americans are supposed to be pragmatic!).[19]

---

18. Long before Marx, Glaucon and Adeimantos argued this case to Socrates in Book II of Plato's *Republic*.

19. See Suzuki's *Zen Mind, Beginner's Mind*.

This position is more intelligible in its near neighbor which says that, although there are many transcendent and sacred things to be symbolized, including miracles, transfigurations, and objects with sacred powers, attention to symbolizing these things often gets in the way of true religious ends. Enlightenment or salvation requires becoming free from the compulsion to symbolize, as well as from other compulsions. This is the position of more orthodox Zen Buddhists in Japan, Korea, and China.[20] Their legends are fantastic, their art imaginative, and their theology highly intellectual, often dependent on the metaphysics of Hua-yen Buddhism. Religious symbolism is just fine and may in fact at times be soteriologically instrumental; but often enough it stands in the way of enlightenment to the suchness and emptiness of the world. Perhaps the way to describe this position is that, although some symbols function religiously as means to salvation, other symbols, or the same symbols for other people or in other circumstances, cease to be religious even though they are "about" religious subjects. At any rate, the Zen Buddhist concern is only for the soteriologically instrumental use of things, and of symbols only if the symbols do not get in the way but function as skillful means.

In between these extremes are many variants. Most derive from the historical and social sciences that are interested principally in the ways symbols function within religion regardless of direct representational value. Intellectual historians, for instance, can say what people took the symbols to mean and discuss how those meanings functioned in religious history without inquiring into whether the meanings were valid, or in what sense they might be valid. They might be concerned, for instance, with how certain symbols strengthened or weakened a religion's connections with civil authority. They might also be concerned with the moral or aesthetic functions of symbols, whether they helped or hindered care for the poor or the stimulation of innovative artistic activity. In these instances some historians are quite willing to make normative moral and aesthetic judgments, but not theological judgments about the validity of religious symbols regarding what they purport to symbolize.[21]

---

20. On the distinction between immediate enlightenment or samadhi and that mediated by upaya, see Daniel Stevenson's "Samadhi in Early T'ien-t'ai Buddhism"; for the issue in Zen, see Carl Bielefeldt's "Ch'ang-lu Tsung-tse's *Tso-ch'an* and the 'Secret' of Zen Meditation."

21. Interesting recent examples of historical studies are Judith Herrin's *The Formation of Christendom* (1987), Thomas F. Mathews' *The Clash of Gods: A Reinterpretation of Early Christian Art* (1993), and Samuel Hugh Moffett's *A History of Christianity in Asia* (1992). These are all important books honored with lavish scholarly praise. Herrin's and

Moffett's are definitive comprehensive surveys of their fields for our generation. Mathews' overturns the previously definitive view of early Christian art that it sought to emulate imperial rule in its representations of the authority and work of Christ; Mathews shows, to the contrary, that Christian art turned away from imperial analogies at each strategic opportunity to make the connection.

Herrin says at the outset that she is not a believer (in Christianity or anything else religious, presumably). Her statement of her historical approach is worth quoting.

> Belief is often taken for granted as a given fact, whose characteristics can be assumed at all levels of society, the most sophisticated and the least educated. Rather than make that assumption, I prefer to try and examine the meanings of belief for early medieval believers. This is a delicate business not only because of the inherent difficulty of grasping the significance of faith for people so distant from us, but also because medieval religion is sometimes conceived, and criticised, as the chief support of an unchanging and fixed social order. While beliefs certainly did unite and restrict medieval Christendom, they seem to me infinitely more complex than they are often thought. There are a great many subversive aspects to belief, and medieval culture was more varied than ecclesiastical leaders cared to admit. *So I make no apology for studying religion from the viewpoint of a non-believer; the history of faith is far too important to be left to adherents alone.* (pp. 7–8, my italics)

Much of what she means by "belief" is the taking of Christian symbols to be true; her text analyzes creedal controversies in detail for their political significance but little for their theological significance. Note her strong approval of diversity. This is not merely a matter of setting the record straight in the face of later medieval attempts to read greater unity into early Christianity than existed; if that were her point she simply would have objected to the later medievals as being factually mistaken, perhaps because of their own biased beliefs. No, her objection is to the possibility of "adherents" being able to grasp what is "far too important" in the history of faith to be readily available to the believers' own eye, presumably cultural richness and diversity. Of course she does not suggest that believers could not obtain the objectivity to be good historians; only that if they do it is because they rise above the historical vision of believers alone. Her moral and cultural points are subtly made with massive and persuasive erudition.

Mathews has no similar forthright statement of faith or non-faith. One suspects, however, great sympathy with the early (and late) Christian movement. His negative argument against the received imperial interpretation is framed as a devastating review of the evidence and non-evidence. The positive argument for his own interpretation of early Christian art is consciously guided by the theological principle that power-orders are to be reversed, the high brought low, the lowly elevated to spiritual power. That point is unusually consonant with contemporary liberal Christianity. In matters where contemporary religious consciousness would be offended, for instance in the symbols of Jesus as a magician, Mathews is scrupulously non-committal about their symbolic validity, dealing only with their symbolic meaning for potential Christians.

Moffett is a Christian seminary professor and was a missionary teacher in Korea; there is little doubt that he holds at least some of the major Christian symbols to be valid under some interpretation or other. His handling of evidence is no less objective than

Historical studies powerfully shape the way reading people think about symbols, even those who are professionally religious such as seminarians and clergy, and the view that religious symbols play important historical roles but have no important symbolic meaning as regards their validity is widespread.

Social scientists employing synchronic models might on average, in comparison with historians, be more convinced that the full treatment of religious symbols lies in their functioning within religion and the larger society and more hostile to the suggestion that questions of validity are important. Much of this stems from the fact that synchronic social science models are supposed to be reductive, that is, to explain only what can be explained by their constants and variables; this is their virtue. If some other considerations can be left out without altering the roles displayed by religious symbols within the model, so much the better for the model. Many social scientists construe a high degree of cultural (and thus religious) alienation to be a required if not inevitable affect of scientific practice. Social scientists who do affirm the importance of questions of the validity of religious symbols often do so by extending their discipline to include theology.[22] Social scientific approaches to religious symbols are also widespread in their influence.

What are we to make of these different expressions of the position that religious symbols are instruments of salvation but not (in any interesting way) more than fictions regarding what they are supposed to sym-

---

Herrin's or Mathews's (though the evidence is often different in kind). Like them he does not discuss the validity of the symbols, for instance whether Nestorianism might be true, but only their historical roles. His discussion of the fifteenth- and sixteenth-century decline of Christianity in Asian in the last chapter is dispassionate, unromantic, and almost ruthless in its dissection of contributory causes. Yet the penultimate paragraph of the book is the following:

> There are times when history can only be described, not explained, and perhaps the history of Christianity in Asia is best left as one of the mysteries of the providence of God, whose ways, as seen from a Christian perspective, are not our ways; nor are his purposes ever entirely made known. But from that same Christian perspective, history does not end with despair but with hope.

22. Peter Berger is the outstanding example in our time. His work in sociology of knowledge applied to religion has defined the field of sociology of religion. Yet he has also written influential theology books informed by his sociology. In religion he is a Lutheran Christian with a very strong devotion to high liturgy; in theology he is close to the twentieth-century liberal Protestant emphasis on experiential foundations for religious belief.

bolize? The first and most obvious thing to say is that we should learn as much as possible from the various functions they reveal religious symbols to have in religion and society, both toward salvation and toward other ends. No point at all is to be gained by rejecting their positive contributions just because they neglect the important question of the validity of symbols.

The second and more important thing to say is that a distinction needs to be made, with differential responses, between simple neglect to raise the question of validity and neglect in principle stemming from systematic reductionism. With regard to the former, it might be the case that the discipline approaching religious symbols is simply not much good at dealing with questions of validity which it should therefore set aside. In regard to the latter, however, there is no reason in principle why historians, or even sociologists for that matter, could not expand their discipline to enter into careful theological evaluations of religious symbols just as they move into normative morals, politics, and aesthetics. Peter Berger and Robert Bellah, both sociologists of religion, have done just that.[23] Some might believe that normative ethics, politics, and aesthetics are easier than theology because they do not deal with the transcendent or because there is a consensus around the former but not the latter; those are doubtful beliefs, however, as scholars of ethics, political theory, and art would be the first to say.

Reductive rejections of issues about the validity of religious symbols need to be recognized for what they are. How and why the questions of validity are not raised need to be determined in each case. It needs also to be asked whether the principles of reduction make their positive conclusions deceptive when they are reintegrated with less reductive studies that do include questions of validity. Finally, questions need to be raised about how to combine reductive studies with one another, each reducing in different ways, and with studies that approach the questions of validity. Although the present essay will not undertake that higher level issue, it should be borne in mind.

In discussing the "fictions only" views of religious symbols the question of the symbols' validity has emerged as extremely important. Certainly for religious people the question of validity is uppermost, especially in this time of religious change and alienation. But for inquirers

---

23. Although their approaches are very different, both are concerned with the roles of alienation in modernity that inhibit religious commitment and conviction. See their works listed in the bibliography.

after the truth, which surely we are if we are studying symbols, the question of the truth of the symbols simply cannot be ignored. As remarked earlier, the study of religious symbols includes normative dimensions. Also emergent from the discussion of the variants on the "fictions only" position is a sensed need for some distinctions that can guide subsequent discussion through the pitfalls of questions of validity. Six topics can be singled out for mention here, each to be expanded upon below.

First is the topic of a religious symbol's *meanings*. Religious symbolic meaning is accessible in at least one sense to any discipline equipped to study what a symbol intends to assert of its object. The analytical and phenomenological study of meanings can go on without raising the question of whether there is an object or situation to which the symbol refers. Actually, the question of meaning is more complex than this, as will become apparent below. The above point holds for what will be called "network meaning," that meaning which consists in the network of assumptions and inferences around the symbol. As children learn languages, so can scholars learn network meaning. Network meaning is coded and involves the issues mentioned earlier of extensional reference and interpretants, in contrast to intentional reference and interpretants. "Content meaning" is more difficult to access because it involves experiencing the content of the symbol's meaning, not just moving through its semantic, syntactic, and pragmatic networks. More on this in chapter 3.

The second topic, obviously, is the *reference* of religious symbols. To what do such symbols refer and how? Do their objects of reference exist? The preliminary definition of religious symbols in the previous section employed the notion of reference to the sacred or divine.

Religious symbols do not refer at all, of course, unless someone uses them to interpret reality. The third topic is *interpretation*. Interpretation is what puts symbols into play. This is the domain of intentional reference and interpretation. Sometimes we elide reference and interpretation into coded meaning, assuming that meanings mean to assert something of their objects and that the interpretations of the objects through the symbols is implicit in their meanings. But as we have seen, meanings can be analyzed without raising the questions of reference, even under the assumption that religious symbols do not refer to anything. It is also apparent that the interpretations of religious symbols are dependent on contexts in ways meanings are not; in fact, if meanings were not common to different contexts we would not recognize that they are different interpretations of the same symbol. Chapter 4 will discuss this in more detail.

Meaning, reference, and interpretation together lead to the fourth topic, *engagement*. Religious symbols, under a given interpretation, either do or do not engage the interpreters with that to which they refer.[24] If they do, the symbol is a living one. If they do not, the symbol is dead. A religious symbol might have the capacity to refer to a real object; but if it is not properly interpreted, the symbol will be dead. It might be interpreted so as to have great power and influence within the interpreters' lives and yet not refer to anything real; it will still be dead or demonic as a religious symbol however powerful it is psychologically, politically, or in some other way. Symbols are alive if they engage their interpreters with their objects. The symbolic function of religious symbols is to engage people with the sacred or the divine.

But engagements also should be true, and *truth* is the fifth topic. Stated in a preliminary way, religious symbols are true when their meanings accurately describe or evaluate what they refer to and communicate this into the experience of the interpreters. Truth thus is the accurate carryover of the nature of the religious object, in the respect interpreted, into the interpreters by the vehicle of the meanings in the interpreters' symbols; chapter 7 will explore this in more detail. Religious symbols can be false by being idolatrous, that is, identifying their referent with the meaning of some finite, non-divine, or profane thing and not indicating how that meaning does not apply quite adequately. The historical dialectic concerning idolatry is what, in the history of religions, has moved religious symbolism from simple reference to spooky things as sacred to the characterization of the sacred in terms of some special bearing of that which is not just another object within the world. Critique of idolatry is what spreads the personalizing/form-transcending spectra from the former to the latter end. More of this below. Religious symbols also can be false by being demonic, that is, engaging the religious object with the interpreter so that the object's nature becomes falsely ingredient in the interpreter. Instead of the interpreter having the divine carried over, according to the respects in which interpretation is made, the interpreter receives a biased element of the divine that perverts the divine nature. History is full of divinely charismatic villains and religions sometimes have difficulty identifying their own demonic abberations.

---

24. Engagement is the point that focused Tillich's interpretation of the truth of religious symbols: they must participate in what they symbolize, and correlate the interpreters' subjective responses with the revelatory material. See *Systematic Theology I*, pp. 239–240.

The sixth and final topic that has emerged from the discussion so far is that religious symbols have *consequences* beyond their interpretations. Often these are the implications traced by historians or laid out by synchronic theories of social causation. Extra-interpretive consequences are especially important in studying religious symbols because many people have pointed out that they sometimes are disastrously at odds with their interpretive intentions. Feminists have rightly accused many religions of having symbols that reinforce patriarchy, even though none of the symbols in a given religion intends that.[25] Religious symbols can have political consequences, as historians like to note. They can also have artistic consequences, and many other kinds. Extra-interpretive consequences are sometimes as important to study as meaning, reference, interpretation, engagement, and truth. This review of the issues to which we are pushed by consideration of the position that religious symbols are only fictions with no representational function amounts to a justification for the topical outline for this book as already sketched in the Preface.

## I.3. SYMBOLS AND COMMUNITY

Whereas the last section discussed the family of approaches to religious symbols that regard them as fictions that might have soteriological instrumentality, this section will focus on the approaches that treat religious symbols as shapers of communities in religious respects. Like the previous, this too is an approach to understanding religious symbolism with great plausibility but to which my approach here is a corrective. We have already observed one very important sense of life-shaping, that is, the instrumental capacity of symbols to lead to fundamental attunement, enlightenment, or salvation. The theme of shaping needs generalization at this point. I shall consider two main forms of this approach here. The first is the cultural-linguistic approach to religious communities and the second deals with religions' contributions to the larger cultures within which they live.

The cultural-linguistic approach to religions has the splendid merit of being able to display how religious communities are constituted with both diachronic and synchronic dimensions. Religious symbols are what tie a community together with its past and they also, by virtue of their networked meanings, tie disparate parts and functions of the community into systematic interconnection. These, of course, are normative or ide-

25. See for instance, the discussion in Elizabeth's Johnson's *She Who Is*.

alistic statements: when religious symbols are live and sufficient, they make these tyings-together. Most of the time the symbols are fragmented in various ways and so are the religious communities, often precisely because of the symbolic deficiencies. *Tying-together (again)* is the very meaning of the Latin roots of the word *religion, re-ligere.*

The cultural-linguistic approach, as used for instance by George Lindbeck, arises from the anthropological method developed by Clifford Geertz and others to provide *thick descriptions.*[26] A thick description is a phenomenological account of how the meanings of a symbol are united in the symbol itself but have connections with other symbols across a culture.[27] Each symbol in the network shapes and gives meaning to some part of cultural behavior, and the elements of behavior are coordinated through the network of symbolic meanings. This entails that mere physical or functional descriptions of behavior, for instance producing and exchanging goods, dancing and singing according to certain patterns, building houses and traveling about, are insufficient for analysis. We had long known that such physicalist and functionalist accounts leave out the intentionality of the people engaged in such behavior: that is not how they see, feel, understand, or orient what they are doing. But construing those behaviors as shaped by symbols introduces intentionality into the account. People engage in meaningful behaviors, because of the meanings and the motives carried by the meanings in the symbols shaping the behaviors, and these behaviors are meaningful in terms of one another because of the network character of symbolic meaning. Whereas a *thin* description might try to describe the behavior shaped by a single symbol or a functional system, a *thick* description fleshes out the interconnections of the many symbols, shaping all sorts of different kinds of behavior, networked together. A thin description in fact is merely an abbreviated one: no symbol has meaning only in itself, rather in the vast networks within which it is nested, and therefore can be described fully, with its shaped behavior, only as part of the larger nest. Even *thick* is a relative modifier of descriptions because no live cultural system can be fully described, only epitomized in its main networks of symbols.

---

26. George Lindbeck in *The Nature of Doctrine* focuses principally on doctrinal symbols, but most of his points hold for all religious symbols. Geertz illustrated the power and complexity of his method in a classical description of the symbolic function of cockfighting in Bali, in his essay "Deep Play." See also Geertz' *The Interpretation of Culture.*

27. "Phenomenological account" is no innocent phrase. The essays collected in Sullivan and Rabinow's *Interpreting Social Science* spell out some of the complexities.

To acknowledge that societies are cultural-linguistic systems is not to imply that they are completely systematized symbolic wholes with every symbol networked with every other. Most societies in fact are congeries of different cultural-linguistic systems expressed in different ethnic groups. Moreover, cultural-linguistic systems of symbols can be more or less tight. Some can approach the extreme of total institutions in which every bit of every behavior is regulated by its symbolic roles relative to other behaviors and to the whole.[28] Some can approach the opposite extreme with such vagueness in the networking—the symbols can lead to any number of mutually exclusive other symbols without determinate preference—that the society's lack of social cohesion borders on fragmentation and anomie.[29]

The same is true of religious communities. Some are organized so tightly by religious symbols—every symbolic behavior has one and only one determinate implication for every other potentially symbolic behavior and all behaviors are shaped by the symbols of the religious system—that all of life is regulated by the complicated but univocal meanings of the religious symbols. Others are organized with only some behaviors shaped by religious symbols and with much vagueness in the network connections of those symbols to other symbolically shaped behaviors. In between are religious communities in which, say, behaviors in common worship are shaped by religious symbols of timing, liturgical order, what is sung, recitation of certain prayers, topics of preachments, collections of money and what the money can be spent on, which persons perform which roles, and the like. These communities might have religious symbolic networks that are vague with respect to what worshippers should wear, how they should breathe, what they should think about while in service, what architectural spaces are required, and the like. Other communities can shape those other behaviors with religious symbols networked together. Religious communities do not exist only in worship. They do others things such as teach, bring comfort and aid, and pursue political and moral goals in the larger community. These other behaviors can also be shaped more or less tightly by networks of religious symbols. And then of course the members of a religious community have other aspects of their lives that might be shaped very little by the network

---

28. On total institutions, see Erving Goffman's *Asylums*.

29. This is the point, for instance, of Peter Berger, Brigitte Berger, and Hansfried Kellner in their *The Homeless Mind*.

implications of their religion's symbols, such as family life at home, athletic activities, pursuits of artistic interests, economic, political, and convivial activity. Some religions have attempted to develop religious symbolic networks that would shape absolutely every aspect of life. But there is too much plenitude, variability, and density of life for this to be much more than a dream; even a brilliant rabbinate cannot provide interpretations fast enough. Often, as in the stereotype of the puritan culture, the attempt of religions to regulate everything, including one's gestures, dress, thoughts, and feelings, is taken to be odious.

Part of the pluralism of religious life today is that in most countries a given cultural-linguistic religious system shapes only a small sphere of behavior with much determinateness, leaving vague symbolic implications for the rest of life. Those other spheres of life are shared with people of different religious symbolic systems. The consequent interactions of religious systems provide opportunities for extraordinary enrichments— not just an innovative modification to a symbol within one's own cultural-linguistic religious network but sudden access to much or the whole of an entirely different religious system. Such enrichments, however, threaten the integrity of any religious system involved, for better or worse. Not every Jewish family wants a Muslim son-in-law. Perhaps in our pluralistic time one important criterion for the health of a religious symbolic system is the degree to which it is flexible in accomodating itself to other religious (and anti-religious secular) systems without losing its integrity.

Having emphasized the synchronic elements of religious symbols in their networked capacity to coordinate and give meaning to disparate behaviors, it is appropriate to add the historical dimensions of religious symbols. All symbols, of course, have a history. Even verbal symbols for newly discovered entities or traits in physics, such as *quarks* and *spin*, are plays on antecedent meanings. The same is true for the new jargon of computer use that is quickly becoming generalized in the languages of the world. Given the rapidity of technological and other kinds of change, hardly any symbol has a plain default meaning.

Religious symbols are among the most ancient kind, and often illustrate great jolts of meaningful change. Consider, for instance, the symbol of the messiah, which enters the Hebrew Bible meaning merely a person annointed for a special honor, for instance athletic or military victory, surviving another year of life, being head of the family, or whatever, including being marked as king. In 1 Samuel the prophet Samuel annointed first Saul and then David as kings over Israel. The striking shift in meaning here is that before Saul, Israel had no king. Or, put more accurately, Yahweh, the great warrior who brought Israel out of Egypt, was himself king and acted through his prophets. See 1 Samuel 8 where Yahweh listens to the pleas of Israel for a real flesh and blood king who can lead them to war against the Philistines, and then warns them of the cultural down-side of flesh and blood kings, all before acceding to Samuel to anoint Saul. Suddenly *messiah* has accrued the meaning of a king who is a god-surrogate. Furthermore, the kingly ideal includes the powerful norms of protecting the weak, looking out for widows and orphans, and executing God's justice, as well as the conventional kingly norm of dealing with external enemies of Israel, who were, of course, also enemies of Yahweh, Israel's God. After Saul and David the next person to be called messiah in the Bible was Cyrus king of Persia, no king of Israel save as its conqueror but in fact a surrogate of Yahweh, now become the God of all nations, again protecting Israel by sending the exiles back to Jerusalem (Isaiah 45:1). *Messiah* hence meant someone executing the will of the God of all creation. With reference to Jesus, all those connotations were enfolded in a transformation of the means of rule, from military authority to faith in God that celebrated lowliness and meekness; Jesus also changed the image of the Head of heaven, which was still described as a kingdom, from warrior-king to loving, provident parent. Some shallow Christians today might think of God only as parent and of Jesus only as meek, long-suffering persuader; but they miss the depths of the symbols, those earlier layers of meaning. Meek Jesus is still Fell King; and God the Father is, underneath, the Holy One of Israel.

Sometimes, of course, changes in religious symbols are not mere accruals but downright reversals, denials of previous meanings or at least of aspects of previous meanings. Feminists in all religions, for instance, hope that the patriarchal symbols or dimensions of symbols can be rejected, perhaps while sustaining other dimensions of the symbols. But even reversals bear the historical marks of the reversing.

By attending to religious symbols in their depths, religious communities can be in continuity with their past development, often with their founding. It is commonly said that only the theistic religions have a strong sense of historical consciousness in the Western sense. Nevertheless, part of the richness of religious symbols consists in the fact that they have a history. Many symbols begin as classical motifs, such as the creation story in Genesis 1, the Buddha's first sermon, or the Analects of Confucius, which then are embellished in diverse, often mutually contradictory ways, by subsequent developments of the religion. Songs, vestments, and architecture can have motif-deep symbolic histories: the Christian house-churches of the second century became the basilicas of the third and then the cathedrals of the thirteenth. The historical careers of symbols, their impacted laying-down of many levels of development, provide a far thicker sense of community continuity than retrospective affirmations of personal allegiances across generations and centuries, and across divergent cultures.

When the question is asked what makes symbols religious in this cultural-linguistic sense, the first answer is that they are co-implicated developments of the motifs that have defined the religious community. The growing, shifting, but ever reintegrating symbolic behaviors of the community provide the scope of definition. But then we must ask what made the motifs religious in the first place, and how we can tell when the religious community has subtly been transformed into something else, for instance, a political entity cloaked in religious symbols. The answer to both of those questions is that the symbols in their networks need to have some reference to the sacred or divine. To this question we shall return.[30]

Allusion has been made already to the fact that sometimes the network connections of a system of religious symbols extend beyond the religious community itself into the larger community. There is a special sense in which every culture has a religious dimension constituted by certain religious symbols affecting the whole society, namely, the symbols having to do with obligatoriness. To be human is to be under obligation and one of religion's general cultural functions is to provide cultural symbols for this, in two senses. First, religions symbolize the fact that the human condition is to be obligated in the first place. They might do this in the way of the Hebrew Bible, representing human beings as in a covenant with their creator which has laws for people and obligations of other sorts for God.[31] Or they might do it by representations of people and nature as being either within or without attunement or harmony. There are a host of motifs in the world's diverse religions. Those motifs

---

30. On the point that the cultural-linguistic approach needs also to raise questions of reference, see Maurice Wile's succinct discussion in *Christian Theology and Inter-religious Dialogue*, 1992, 36–39.

31. The idea of covenant in the Hebrew Bible was actually a version of a much more widespread notion of covenant; see Robert Murray's *The Cosmic Covenant.* The Biblical covenants include those with Adam and Eve concerning the garden, with Noah, Abraham, Moses, and David, all of which affected the New Testament (Covenant) claim that Jesus instituted a new covenant. The idea of the covenant has been discussed by

in their original form might be lost in modern secular culture. Few Americans, for instance, trace their sense of obligation to Yahweh covenanting with Adam, Noah, Abraham, or Moses; yet the social contract theory, which undergirds modern Western consciousness, is a thickened, accrued meaning of the covenant motif. When the religious symbols of obligatedness die away completely, or become so faint as to be ineffective, the peculiar kind of relativism falls upon the land which believes that everything is permitted because nothing is obligated. The second religious contribution to the cultural sense of obligation is to provide measures for how well a culture is living up to its obligations. The specific contents of obligations are of course dependent on the specific religions involved, the larger culture which has many determinants of morality, and the exigencies of the situation. But religions have the symbolic task of recalling societies to face up to their obligations whatever they are. Standing under "prophetic judgments," as the theistic symbols have it, is as much part of the human condition as being obligated in the first place. This is why religions have so often been strong moral forces in their societies. They are distinctive not so much for the content of morality, although there are specific traditions there, as for symbols for judging whether people are living in such a way as to address their obligations. The Confucian symbols of the great as opposed to small person, the individuated rather than the alienated person, deal with this.[32] All the traditions have such symbols. Where they are lacking in a society, relativism in yet another sense takes hold: nobody is to be called to account.

The two ways in which religions contribute to obligatedness and judgment in society can be called civil religion.[33] The symbols that inform civil religion do not need to be different from those that shape practicing religious communities. Indeed, they at least must derive from common religious symbolic motifs if not from direct applications of contemporary religious symbols. Practicing religious people sometimes do not like the category of civil religion. They believe the society ought to be plainly religious or acknowledge its separate secularity. This is to mis-

---

nearly every Biblical theologian but was especially important in Puritan theology. It was a primary metaphor for society for Robert Bellah in his *The Broken Covenant*. See also my *Theology Primer* which uses the idea of covenant as a metaphor for an ontological definition of the human condition, as hinted at in the remarks in the text here about obligation.

32. See my discussion of Confucianism in *The Puritan Smile*, chapter 2.

33. See Bellah's *The Broken Covenant* for a discussion of civil religion.

understand the public function religion has irrespective of the vitality of the *community* of believers.

We have seen that religious symbols do indeed shape life, both the life of a religious community and the life of the larger civil society which might be quite separate from the believers' community. Much is to be learned about religious symbols by treating them as shapers of life, and this will be pursued again in connection with discussions of religious symbolic meaning, interpretive contexts, and extra-interpretive consequences. But regarding the question of whether religious symbols symbolize truly, that issue cannot be ignored if we are going to be able to tell what makes the symbols religious in the first place. If the symbols are not religious as they purport, how then do they have the authority to define human life as obligated? This brings the discussion around to the point of symbolic representations.

## 1.4. SYMBOLS AND REPRESENTATION

At last we come to the approach to religious symbols that underlies all the others to be employed here, the semiotic approach. Semiotics takes the symbols to be signs of objects for interpreters. Relevant questions then have to do with the truth of interpretations, which includes asking whether there really are religious objects whose nature is what the symbols mean to say they are to interpreters who engage those religious objects by means of interpreting the symbols. (That complicated circumlocution is required by the theory of signs and theory of truth sketched in the Preface and elaborated in chapter 7.) Semiotics treats symbols as representations that might or might not be true.

Theology, of course, is the approach to religious symbols that emphasizes the questions of symbols as true representations. I have argued in the cases of the other approaches that the theological mode of inquiry should not be ignored. But the theological approach by itself is as one-sided as the others. While not necessarily claiming that religious symbols need to be interpreted in literal terms, theology wants the interpretations to be precise and the conditions for truth all spelled out. When theology encounters symbols whose primary context is soteriological instrumentality or the shaping of community life, theology is likely to neglect those dimensions. The symbols typical there are likely to seem fantastic and exaggerated to the theological eye, or pragmatic and not really religious. The tolerance of general ambiguity and the insistence on particularistic contextual interpretations typical of soteriological or communal shaping contexts make theology nervous. That religious symbols represent the sacred to interpreters might not be the most important thing they do, given the context in which they occur; therefore theology's questions might be out of place.

The study of religious symbols in their saving and shaping functions represents a kind of rebellion against the older theological approach. Indeed, to study religious symbols as such, rather than the divine as symbolized, marks an important intellectual revolution in Western thinking. When the symbols of a given religious tradition are fresh and living, people see through them to the divine. They do not notice the symbols as such any more than they notice the glass in a window or think about columns of mercury when hearing the temperature from the TV weather announcer.[34] When another religion with different symbols is encountered, however, attention is suddenly called to the symbols as such, as if the window were dirty, or shown to be a photograph, or the weather announcer cited a description of temperature that made no reference to degrees. When symbols are suddenly made manifest as symbols, they are liable to be broken.

This study of religious symbols, then, reflects the state of being beyond the dominance of the theological approach. One way of reading my argument is as a plea to remember the enduring contribution of theology to the study of religious symbols, namely with respect to their validity as representations. It is still possible, of course, to do theology by concentrating on the divine and referring to the nature of religious symbols only where they are problematic. But in the present theological situation, affected by the secular skepticism of modernity and by the present vivid encounter of different religious traditions with one another, the religious symbols are always problematic. Paul Tillich and George Lindbeck meet in addressing this situation in Christian theology. Tillich's *Systematic Theology* continues the traditional topics of theology, but at every point along the way treats what other theologians have called doctrines or dogmas as *symbols*. His very late book, *Christianity and the Encounter of the World Religions*, deals with the plurality of symbol systems. Lindbeck has moved to the social sciences and their functional approaches in order to gain legitimation

---

34. On the very important distinction between symbols used to "see through" and symbols which themselves "appear," see Patrick A. Heelan's *Space-Perception and the Philosophy of Science.* His topic is the perception of scientific entities, such as "temperature as degrees of mercury." But his examples include visual perceptions and illusions, especially in art.

for some of the basic theological ideas. By emphasizing semiotics, my approach here joins with Tillich and Lindbeck in setting theology in a larger context. The semiotic approach can sustain both the theological focus on truth and the social science study of truth's vehicles.

The approach to be taken here follows Peirce in the triadic theory of semiotics, in emphasizing interactive engagement and learning, and in focusing on transformations of symbols rather than static coded syntactic, semantic, and pragmatic relations. But there is a special problem in dealing with religious symbols, for their objects are not the ordinary kind with which one can interact to clarify and improve one's signs and interpretive habits. Even worse, the logical objects referred to by religious symbols are both finite in the ordinary sense but also explicitly not that. Religious symbolic reference includes the implicit if not explicit caveats that the finite part of the logical object is not really what the reference is getting at, or at least not the whole of it. Therefore engagement, in which the objects have a corrective force, is problematic in the religious case. Problematic, though not impossible. Indeed, in religious traditions emphasizing revelation the understanding of religious learning is that the initiative comes from the object of symbolic reference rather than from interpretive moves. Of course, there is always an interplay between the interpreter's handling of the signs with which the religious referent is approached and the religious object to which reference is made.

Seeking representational truth in the case of religious symbols is less well described in the metaphors of science making controlled experiments than in the metaphors of piety. *Piety* here means a disciplined practice of comporting oneself before the object so that its nature comes through with minimal distortion. Piety before nature is a learned appreciative way of letting natural things be and living so as to register them but not interfere. Piety before the religious object is also to let it be without forced redescription, to register it within one's own (or one's community's) life, but to acknowledge the initiatives of the religious object. Non-interference with the divine is living in accordance with it, where the divine is relevant to one's life.

Setting aside the possibility that there is some kind of immediate, intuitive, non-symbolic registration of the religious object, all other registrations of the divine are symbolic. Piety before the sacred then means the disciplined development of symbols and their interpretation that register the divine within the interpreters without distorting the sacred in the respects interpreted, and then living in light of these registering interpretations without running counter to the divine, participating where relevant in the initiatives that flow from the interpreted divine nature.

There is a continuum of piety in religious interpretation running from passive deference on the one hand to active incorporation on the other. The extreme of deference would be mystical usages of empty or near-empty symbols, symbols whose meaning comes from the process of definitizing other symbols. The extreme of incorporation is where the religious object is so taken in to the interpreter's life that the (important) forms of that life are replaced by the divine. Like the coincidence of opposites, the second extreme also is a mystical mode, though more active than the first, indeed an intensification of personal acts to become the divine act rather than passive registration of letting the religious object be.

From deference to incorporation, this kind of piety involves symbolic interpretation. Symbols always mediate the religious object and the interpreter. Only through symbols can a religious object be referred to. Only through symbols can there be a content (even emptiness) ascribed to the objects. Only through symbols can the object be interpreted so as to relate to the life of the interpreter and interpreting community. The question of the truth of symbols has to do with whether they foster proper piety before the religious referents rather than subjecting those referents to distorting interpretive purposes. This is not to say that pious religious interpretations should not be guided by human purposes, conscious and unconscious. Most religious symbols interpret the sacred in respects that do bear upon human purpose, and the divine nature can be represented truly or falsely in those respects. The ideal piety rather is to say that the symbols guided by interpretive purposes should not distort the religious reality in the respects interpreted.

Underlying the rhetoric of piety regarding symbolic representation is the more general theory of truth sketched in the Preface and that will be spelled out in detail in chapter 7. It can be restated here as the carry-over into the interpreter of the object of interpretation in its value-nature, its importance, by means of the symbol, in the respect in which the symbol stands for the object, as qualified by the biology, culture, semiotic systems, and purposes of the interpreter. By "value" is meant what the object has achieved in its own nature; by "importance" is meant how that value or nature bears upon the interpreter as mediated by the respect in which the symbol purports to interpret.[35] The "value"

---

35. On the difference between value and importance in knowledge, see my *Normative Cultures*, part 4.

of religious objects is complicated because, in an obvious sense, only the finite side is the achievement of anything valuable; if there is an non-obvious sense in which the non-finite side of the religious object is valuable, that will have to be made out. The next chapter shall address this issue, characterizing religious objects as involving an integrated contrast between finite and non-finite elements.

By the qualifications of "biology, culture, semiotic systems, and purposes" is meant that the religious object needs to be transformed to the stuff of the interpreter's experience and life. Thus the carryover must respect the fact that religious symbols and their interpretation are activities of people with meat-brains, not computers nor angels. It must address the cultural conditions that frame what is important to interpret and that affect the respects in which interpretations are made. The carryover also must involve the interpreter's symbol systems, although of course those are evolving in the process of interpretation; symbol systems are social as well as personal. The carryover must also be qualified by whatever is relevant in the object's importance for the interpreter's purposes.

Because of the qualifications or transformations involved in the carryover, truth is a correspondence of interpreted value in the interpreter with the value defining the object's nature, subject to the respects in which the object is interpreted. This contrasts with the Aristotelian view that the carryover is one of form. Obviously the form is changed in the transformations of objects to the forms of human experience. The correspondence question is whether whatever important is achieved, realized, or accomplished in the object is registered without distortion in the interpretation, however selective that registration as determined by the respect in which the object is interpreted.

I mentioned earlier that interpretations are encoded within semiotic systems. That is, within a semiotic system of religious symbols, some symbols refer to other symbols and are interpreted as having both representational and practical meanings, all expressed within the system. Scholars can learn to decode the possible interpretations as carried within the system. From this, some thinkers conclude that all interpretation takes place within the system of symbols, with no external reference. But on the contrary, the pragmatic theory of interpretation notes that actual interpreters use the symbols, and indeed the entire symbol system—whole theologies, myths, symbolic patterns—to engage sacred realities. The relations among the symbols within the system are extensional. But the use of the symbols with their systemic network connections to interpret reality is intentionality. Thus, the advocates of thick description have gone only part of the way toward integrating intentionality into descriptions of religious behavior. Beyond a thick description of symbolic life we must note that religious people intend to say that reality itself is like what the symbols say. Religious people by and large do not believe they are meaning to behave competently according to their symbols; they believe instead that reality is such that this is the way they ought to behave. The distinction between extensional interpretation within symbolic worlds and intentional interpretation of the world by means of the symbols is at the heart of this approach to understanding religious symbols, as will be elaborated in the following chapters.

The questions of truth can be framed many ways. Following Aristotle we can ask whether the objects referred to are as the interpretation says. Or we can ask whether the symbols employed are the right or best ones to interpret the object in the respect in which interpretation is sought. Or we can ask whether the interpretation has been framed in ways within the interpreter that keep it correspondent with the object. Falsehood in interpretation can consist in the referents being other than what is symbolized (which would include being non-existent if the symbols assert existence), or in the symbols being clumsy, biased, distortive, or plainly wrong in representing the object in the respect in which they are supposed to, or in the interpretations being distorted by how they are received in the ongoing process of the interpreters.

This characterization of truth is no more partial to religious matters than to scientific, critical, political, artistic, or philosophical ones. Modern scientists hope to interpret the values of things insofar as they can be registered in symbols of measurement, especially mathematical measures; these values have to do with structure and causation. Critics aim directly to register the values in their objects and compare them with other values and ideals. Political thinkers aim to understand how the structures and processes of society reflect matters of justice and other kinds of value. And so on. The interesting problems of truth in religious symbols have to do with the peculiar, not-wholly-finite character of their referents.

An implication of this argument about truth is that in all spheres, not only religion, truth is a matter of piety. The truth of any representation is measured by the nature of what it represents.

Throughout this chapter the word *significance* has been used to refer to objects interpreted by symbols. Significance has two related meanings. One is shadowed in its etymology, namely that symbols' significance has to do with their being signs. The recent discussion has spelled out a bit of what the sign-character of symbols is. Chapter 2 will explicate the relation of religious symbols to their objects or referents. Chapter 3 will explicate the meaning of symbols themselves. Chapter 4 will deal with the interpretation of symbols. Signification, significance in this sense, has to do with this triad of interacting functions. The other meaning of significance is importance. An object interpreted by a sign has importance or value in the interpreter. If the interpretation is true, that importance or value should correspond to value in the object, in the respect in which the interpretation is made and as subject to the qualifications mentioned. Significance thus means that what is important in the object is registered as important in the interpreter, in the appropriate ways.

These remarks indicate that the idea of value or importance is the one to watch in subsequent discussions. They also indicate the self-reflexivity in the claim at the end of the first section of this chapter that all description of religions and religious symbolism is normative.

# CHAPTER 2

# Symbols Break on the Infinite

Religious symbols need to be understood in terms of their referring, their meanings, and their interpretations in various contexts. The first of these, reference, is the topic of this chapter. I suggested in the previous that religion in part is to be defined as an orientation to the sacred or divine, taking due note of the fact that these terms themselves need definition and that their generalizability among religious traditions is problematic. To start with a theological or philosophical definition of the sacred or divine, even if that defintion were not in itself controversial, and then to classify as religious those symbols that refer to the sacred or divine so defined, would be arbitrary. It would short-circuit empirical studies of religious symbols. In the context of a study of religious symbols, the approach to the sacred or divine must be made through an analysis of religious symbolic reference. Then, should we come to a philosophical or theological argument for the reality of sacred referents, it would be understood that such an argument is itself symbolic, with its own kinds of critical reference. Therefore a beginning needs to be made through a discussion of semiotics or the study of signs, focusing on reference.[1]

## 2.1. REFERENCE, MEANING, AND INTERPRETATION

The interpretation of things involves an irreducibly triadic relation among signs, their objects, and the interpretants that interpret the signs as standing for the objects in a certain respect. Perhaps we should even

---

1. There will still be arbitrary elements, of course, for instance the choice of the theory of signs employed; see the Preface. But the arbitrariness will be located within the topic under discussion and thus will have a better chance of being exposed and corrected by the matters at hand.

go so far as to say that a tetradic relation lies within interpretation because the *respect* in which signs interpret objects is not reducible to signs, objects, or interpretants, although it is contained in the intentional process of interpretation.[2] At any rate, signs, objects, interpretive respects, and interpretants can hardly be discussed separately. This holds for interpretations with religious symbols as for any other kind. Therefore the focus on the reference of religious symbols in this chapter needs to be kept in the context of the larger view of interpretation.

The meanings of signs can be analyzed as such, prescinding from whether the signs are actually used in interpretation or are referred to objects. So prescinded, the meanings of signs are functions of networks of interrelated meanings organized syntactically, semantically, and pragmatically. These networks include synchronic symbol systems and also connections and overlays of the historical evolution of the various parts of the sign-code. The meanings of signs are accessible to anyone with the means to decipher their synchronic codes and historical evolution. The study of the meanings of signs in this abstract sense prescinds from whether there are any objects to which the signs might be applied interpretively and also from the conditions under which the interpretations of objects by means of the signs can take place. Chapter 3 will focus on the meanings of signs by that kind of prescinding.

In one sense, reference itself is a function of the meaning of signs—they mean what they refer to; some philosophers, for instance idealists and postmodern decontructionists, construe reference to be no more than what signs mean.[3] Surely the meanings of signs include pointers to their referents, as well as characterizations of those referents. Reference itself is a relation between a sign and its object or referent, constituted by the interpretation that refers the sign to the object. Similarly, the interpretations of signs can be construed as functions of the signs' meanings because the meanings legitimate some interpretive inferences and not others. But interpretations are also determined in part by the interpretive context in which the signs represent their referents or objects. Interpretation is a relation between a sign and its meaning or interpretant that

---

2. See Neville, 1989, chapter 15, for an analysis of intentionality in interpretation. See my article, "Intuition," for a criticism of Peirce concerning the "respect" of interpretation and concerning his claim that all relations can be reduced to triadic, dyadic, or monadic ones. I suggest there that his system might be improved by adding *fourthness* to his categores of *firstness, secondness,* and *thirdness.*

3. See David Weissman's discussion of idealism and realism in reference, in his *Truth's Debt to Value,* 1993, chapters 2, 4, and 5, also pp. 53–64.

obtains when the sign is referred to its object in a certain respect. Interpretation, it must always be remembered, is a triadic process in which signs are taken as representing the objects to which they are referred by the interpretation or interpreter, resulting in new signs, interpretants, that constitute the meanings. Therefore it is possible to look not merely at meaning but at the referring relations between the sign and its object and at the interpeting relation between the sign and its interpretant. Reference itself is neither the sign nor the object but a special relation into which those are put by the interpretation; the interpreter refers the sign to the object, or refers to the object by means of the sign. The senses in which reference and interpretation are functions of meanings are all contained within the extensionality of a semiotic code; they are extensional references and interpretations. But the senses in which reference and interpretation refer beyond the signs to real objects and are interpreted in actual practical life are the intentionality of interpretation; these senses are intentional reference and interpretation.

According to Peirce, there are three principal ways by which signs relate to objects: as icons that mimic the objects, as indices that are causally connected with objects and point in that way, and as symbols that are conventional. Because I use the word *symbol* in this study as the generic term for sign, we may represent Peirce's categories as iconic, indexical, and conventional references. Nearly all religious symbols are sufficiently complex that they have conventional, iconic, and indexical reference at once. We shall look at these in turn.

A symbol has conventional reference when its references is determined in part by a semiotic code. Any symbol that is part of a tradition is conventional, because traditions are coded. We might imagine two partial exceptions to the generalization that all religious symbols are conventional, at least in part. One would be the first encounter with something that bears a numinous quality. If Kant is right about infinite sublimity being conveyed by the depths of the night sky, then the first persons on their first clear night might have had a non-conventional sign of the infinite. But if they told someone about the experience, or looked again the second night for the sublime sight, the experience had been made a convention. Moreover, that first night the sight of the night sky would be a diaphanous reference with no hint of a distinction between the sky seen and the infinity to which it refers: infinity would be seen in the sky. For reference to be dynamic and not merely diaphanous, the sight of the sky would have to be in a conventional symbol system with other references to infinity that could be coordinated with the sky. Most religious symbols are in systems of multiple reference so that the reference is not experienced as merely immediate. When the astronauts photographed the Earth for the first time from lunar orbit, that was a "first sight." But the photograph was already a conventional symbol because of its place in a symbolic system that gives meaning to perspective on the human place. The other possibility of a non-conventional symbol is a metaphorical first reference in which the conventional reference is displaced and the symbol is referred to something different. In a technical sense, the metaphoric reference is non-conventional, but it depends for its meaning precisely on negating or transposing its conventional reference; furthermore, once the metaphor is made and understood it becomes part of the semiotic system, and hence conventional again. The structuring of symbols by semiotic systems will be considered at greater length in the discussion of meaning in the next chapter.

That a symbol is referred iconically means that its object is referred to as being *like* the symbol. Symbols with iconic reference thus have a complex internal structure that their referent is interpreted to be *like*. There are many kinds of likeness, of course. Perhaps the least plausible is the positivists' conception of an isomorphic mapping of reality by scientific propositions. This is the view Richard Rorty attacked as the "mirror of nature."[4] The only hope for its plausibility lies in the chance that reality itself is composed of discrete little bits of positive substances with positive attributes, each element of which could be mirrored in a scientific proposition. Descartes, with his view of simples, and the early Wittgenstein, with his "metaphysics" of logical atomism, attempted to make good that hope.[5] Scientific theories, like any complex symbols, interpret their object in certain respects and not others; other symbols are required to pick up what those objects are in other respects.

---

4. See his *Philosophy and the Mirror of Nature.*

5. Descartes argued in the *Meditations,* the *Rules for the Direction of the Mind,* and the *Discourse on Method,* as well as nearly everything else he wrote, that proper study consists in breaking the subject matter down into parts simple enough to be understood completely on their own; then, by reconstructing the whole out of the assembling of parts, one also understands the connections one has made in the reconstructing, thereby understanding everything—the basic constituents and their connections. Wittgenstein believed that the logical way to represent this was according to the logical atomism he developed in the *Tractatus Logico-Philosophicus.* For a criticism of that kind of Cartesian metaphysics, including its functionalist expression in the work of Jerry Fodor, see my *Recovery of the Measure* (1989), chapter 2.

Religious myths and narratives are also icons. They refer to their objects as being like their internal structures in certain respects. This point has fooled some recent thinkers into believing that myths and narratives are not referential at all.[6] The confusion comes from the fact that symbols within the myth or story refer to other symbols within the myth or story, and when people are "thinking mythically" they are interpreting things, perhaps even the meanings of their own lives, within the coded contours of the narrative; they take themselves to inhabit the myth with nowhere else to stand. They do not think of the religious object except in terms that are part of or compatible with the myth, or cluster of myths and narratives. But it does not follow from this that the myth as a whole, or in parts relevant to attention at the moment, is not taken in interpretation to refer to reality. For a mythopoeic person, what the myth says is what reality is like in the respects the myth is intended to interpret. Asked if the myth could be just a made-up story, the mythopoeic person would say No, it's the story of reality. A post-mythopoeic person would say that the myth is a made-up story with its own integrity, a system of symbols shaped as a narrative, and so forth, but could equally well say that the myth truly says what reality is like in certain respects. A post-mythopoeic person might also say that reality is more like some myths than others, or that several myths need to be networked or overlaid to express reality. For both mythopoeic and post-mythopoeic people to think mythically, their myths refer to reality as like how it is.

---

6. I am referring, of course, to Derrida and the deconstructionists who expand the notion of *text* to the point that any apparent reference is *intratextual*; in the mythic world, there is no reality outside the myth. Part of the deconstructionist argument is to interpret interpretation as a dyadic relation between signifier and signified, not a triadic relation with a dynamic engagement of reality by means of symbols. At a far more subtle level, Francis Clooney comes close to the denial of reference for complex iconic symbols, those of the Advaita Vedanta philosophy in his case. He begins by citing Michael Riffaterre's theory of fictional truth according to which a fiction, such as a novel, has verisimilitude to real life without referring to actual events; within the novel there are relations of truth among levels of thematic discourse such that they express an iconic truth about life even though the events described have no reference. So, Hamlet's indecision says something about anyone's indecision even though no one else has Hamlet's problems about what to do about his father's murder. Clooney then moves to say, "By analogy—and it can only be such, for though textual Advaita's truth cannot be adequately described as a fictional truth—we can understand how truth can be said to reside in the upanisads and in the Advaita Text, and how that truth is real, demanding and efficacious—without having also to maintain that there is an extratextual reference for this truth." See his *Theology after Vedanta*, p. 80, and Michael Riffaterre's *Fictional Truth*. The Hamlet example is mine.

In the most basic sense, iconic reference is disclosive.[7] That is, the lineaments of the myth or story, their internal structures, are taken to disclose or reveal something. Reality is then experienced in part as it is disclosed to be. In a disclosive iconic reference there need not be a separate naming of the object that is disclosed in the myth. That would be to say that mythic thinking always recognizes that it is a symbol for something else. Nevertheless, if the myth or story is disclosive it is intended referentially: if someone suggests to the believer or the moved hearer of the story that reality is not like what the myth or story says, the response would be to say "O Yes it is!" For the believer, it is the reality, the object, that is disclosed in certain respects, not the myth or story that is internally interesting without further implication. Of course, the respects in which myths and stories interpret their objects are complicated to figure out. They do not do so in allegedly isomorphic mirrorings of structure. In what respect does Conrad's *Heart of Darkness* refer to reality? In the respect that the character Kurtz confronted the Horror? No, that reference is internal to the story, an extensional reference within the story's little symbol system. In the respect that the horror of the heart of darkness characterizes all human experience? Unlikely. In the respect that it is a possibility for everyone that most of us are weak enough to forfend? Perhaps. In the respect that reality for humans is in some deep sense dark, and that to take that dark reality to heart is to confront the horror? More likely. The story as a whole refers to some aspect of reality, such that it discloses that reality to readers in some respect. But the respect of disclosure for most readers is far tamer than the respect depicted in Kurtz's experience within the story. The lineaments of the story polish up some part of the grain of reality.

Religious symbols, including myths, stories, parables, and the like have as their general real referent the divine. But in what respects do they iconically disclose that referent (or those referents)? Precisely because myths are disclosive, the answer to that question always has to begin from within the myth, however far it might move beyond it, and hence there is no general answer any more than there is a general myth.

For post-mythopoeic people, and for literary critics reading stories who ask what they might mean, their own symbolic systems are coded so that the myths and stories as a whole are referred to an extensionally defined referent within the system. That is, within our sophisticated semiotics we express the idea of reality, or the divine, or human life relative

---

7. See Brockelman, 1992, chapter 2.4.

to the divine, as the object of the myth or story, and can formulate the ideas of disclosure, and of better and worse disclosures, and of disclosures of the object in different respects. The argument of the last few paragraphs has attempted to express a symbol system about reference in semiotics itself that, I would like to persuade the reader, discloses something about religious reference. If the reader takes it seriously as a good or bad disclosure of something about symbolic reference, then the reader is taking my argument as an iconic reference (good or bad) to the realities of symbolic reference.

The distinction is important to recall between the extension of symbols within a coded semiotic symbol system, with extensional referents and extensional interpretants, and the intention of symbols in a real act of interpretation. A myth can be analyzed as a complex symbol system, where elements refer to other elements with various meanings. This is an extensional analysis and has nothing to do necessarily with mythic thinking. Mythic thinking, however, is using the mythic system itself, or a relevant part, to interpret reality. In mythic thinking, the myth itself refers or is referred iconically to reality as engaged. If there is any truth to the myth, it is disclosive.

Indexical reference is a symbol's pointing to or indicating its object, whatever else it says iconically or conventionally about the object. Indexicality has many forms. Peirce thought the paradigm is direct causation: the effect is an index of the cause. But there are other forms of referring by indicating. To the extent that religious symbols refer to that which is not wholly finite, to that which transcends determinate identity, to what I shall shortly analyze as finite/infinite contrasts, to that extent religious symbols refer indexically. For religious symbols to be at all apophatic, to take back what they seem to assert, to suggest that the divine is more than is said, or not quite what is said, is for them to be indexical.

At least some religious symbols are powerfully indexical in a revelatory way, that is, as something like what Peirce thought about causal indices.[8] Something in or about the divine shocks us and calls us to attention, although what we find when our attention is commanded is a matter of iconic and perhaps conventional reference. The initiative comes from the symbol-object to become an index pointing to something else. When, in the *Bhagavad-gita*, Krishna manifests himself to Arjuna as Vishnu, "brighter than a thousand suns," that was an index for something Arjuna had not seen before.[9] When Moses comes upon the burning bush and

8. See Peirce's CP 2.283–291.
9. Bhagavad-gita, chapter 11.

discovers it to be not merely a strange natural phenomenon, it is an index for an aspect of divinity he had not previously encountered.[10] Both Arjuna and Moses came to those indexical epiphanies with complex symbol systems that allowed them to supplement the indexical element in their symbols' reference with thick interpretations referring iconically and conventionally. But the indexical quality of the references was new and revelatory. That an indexical reference is revelatory does not mean that the divine causes it in any strict sense, although that is sometimes the interpretation, as is the case with the Krishna and burning bush examples. It does mean, however, that something turns a thing into an indexically referring sign, revealing an object we had not otherwise understood to be there. Such revelatory symbols are usually also disclosive in their reference. The brightness of Vishnu iconically discloses the heat (*tapas*) of creation. Although fire often symbolizes divine creativity also in Hebrew symbology, in the case of the burning bush it is not the fire but the speech that iconically discloses the divine will for Moses' mission.

Although it is possible to introduce the distinctions between the conventional, iconic, and indexical elements of reference, the discussion is radically incomplete without treating also the various elements of meaning. Before that, however, certain other introductory remarks need to be made about the "respect" in which symbols refer to or interpret their objects.

An interpretation of a religious object takes a religious symbol to represent the object in a certain respect. It might have taken a different religious symbol to represent the object in that respect. The symbols differ in their meanings and therefore give rise to different interpretations of the object, forming the interpreter's experience differently. The subtle point to notice is the *respect of interpretation*, subtle because it is usually expressed silently by the kind of symbol involved. For instance, "red" and "new" are symbols that can be used to interpret a house; the former represents the house in respect of color and the latter in respect of age. There is no ambiguity because the respects are understood in the kinds of things redness and newness are. But to interpret a person with the symbol "lovely" is ambiguous; is it in respect of how the person looks, as an ideal bride on her wedding day, or is it in respect of character that might be lovely despite homely appearance? The symbol allows of both interpretations, and the context of interpretation determines which respect is in play.

---

10. Exodus 3–4.

The problem of understanding respects of interpretation is especially complicated in religious interpretations. Which respect is in play when a Christian interprets God with the symbol of "rock" of salvation? Surely not a geological respect. How does that respect relate to interpreting God with the symbol of "spirit"—"God is spirit"? Are spirits softer than rocks? Or is relative permeability irrelevant to the different respects in which both symbols are used to interpret God? Certain symbols in the Christian tradition interpret God as personal while others interpret God as the creator of everything personal. Are these contradictory symbols interpreting God in the same respect? Many theological debates suppose so. Or do they interpret God in different respects as rock and spirit do? A truly irenic theology would find some integral respect in which every favored symbol can interpret God without contradiction. Some scholars, such as John Hick, believe that all the world's religions can be made compatible this way, with one religious object symbolized by all and with many different respects of interpretation derived from different cultural histories.[11] But the empirical situation is more complicated, I believe. At least the situation is empirical. We first have to analyze the various symbols and clarify the respects in which they can be used to interpret the religious object to see how the respects, and thence the symbols, relate.

That signs are interpreted as referring to their objects in only certain respects can be understood with the help of some ideas from Justus Buchler's metaphysics of natural complexes.[12] Every thing, suggests Buchler, can be understood in terms of its complex of traits each of which lies within some order. So, the house has traits, among others, that lie in the orders of color (red) and age (new). Each order has several positions within it (such as red, yellow, blue, etc.; new, recent, lived-in, venerable, antique, old, etc.). Therefore the thing is determinate with respect to the positions of its traits in each order. It is also determinate with respect to the diverse orders in which its traits are located.

With regard to interpretation, to use Buchler's ideas, we can say the orders are respects of interpretation and the symbolic meanings are locations within those orders that are taken to characterize the object. The process of interpretation selects the orders within which the object's

---

11. See, for instance, Hick's *Problems of Religious Pluralism*.

12. See Justus Buchler's *Metaphysics of Natural Complexes*, 1966; for Buchler's own theory of interpretation see his *Toward a General Theory of Human Judgment*, 1951, and *Nature and Judgment*, 1955. The discussion here focuses on his metaphysical categories because of the uses to be made of them.

traits can be located. Or, the object (as in perception) presents traits that can be grasped by interpretation as being positions within certain orders. An interpretation is *irrelevant* if its respect of interpretation is no order within which the object has traits; it is *mistaken* if its interpreting sign mislocates the trait within the order (as blue rather than red). Variations and qualifications of this scheme can be elaborated at will.

Metaphoric symbols occur when the order customarily associated with the symbol is not the respect involved in the interpretation. Consider Homer's "rosy fingered dawn." "Rosy fingered" falls into the order of colored hands; dawns do not have hands. The real order of interpretation is something like the appearance of light and clouds in the sky and the metaphor says that the position in that order has the light of a rose color and its disposition arranged in cloud streaks with the shape of fingers. A successful metaphor presents not only the trait but the unexpected order in which it is to be located by the interpretation.

"God is the rock of my salvation" is a powerful and non-problematic metaphor. But it is among the few such, regarding lack of ambiguity, in religion. To say that "God is my Lord" is more difficult. A subtle theologian will point out that God is being interpreted in the order of determiners of my main life-agenda and is being located as first relative to the positions, say, of my President, my wife, and my own desires. A less subtle reflection on the claim, however, might construe the respect of interpretation to be the order of political office held by God, in which God has the position of being my liege-lord, and from which it would follow that God is the kind of being who can hold political office, thus requiring an iconic sense of a heavenly court. Insofar as the whole mythic system of a heavenly court is referred as iconic of divine things, it is in respect of something like making sense of the cosmic powers involved in human obligatedness. What is the order (or orders) involved when symbols of God as personal are used, say, in prayer? Are they orders that take their personal elements from the relation to human persons praying? Or are they orders that can place God as personal independent of the human relation? Many theists say the latter, speaking to God as a person in prayer, recognizing that whatever God is, God must be at least personal in some higher sense, and therefore be an individual being (which all persons are). Many Buddhists, while not recognizing God on the metaphysical or theological level, on the other hand, pray to "God" as personal, asking for help and giving thanks just the way theists do, but visualizing "God" in the image of Avaloketishvara or Guanyin and knowing both that this is only a visualization and that the reality of Buddha-mind is more like a compassionate principle than a person; the Buddha-mind is certainly not individual.[13] Is the quality of person in God merely in the order of visualizations, or has it a more objective reference?[14] When Advaitins and other Hindus refer to Brahman as *sat, cit,* and *ananda,* there is yet a different array of respects in which Brahman is being interpreted or pointed at.

These questions are matters for specific analyses of the symbols, referents, interpretations, and respects of interpretation involved. Much philosophical theology is an attempt to specify the respects in which religious symbols refer to their objects. This can be reconstrued as an analysis of the orders within which religious symbols fall insofar as they can be referred to their objects, the real orders, not the apparent ones. Buchler emphasized a special trait of his analysis, namely, that all traits and all orders of traits are on the same ontological level. None is more real than any other. This is Buchler's principle of *ontological parity.* He claimed it was a common failing among philosophers that they would privilege one order as more real than another, for instance substances as more real than attributes or relations, or principles as more real than their manifestations, or the other way around. As an analysis of orders within interpretation, where they are the respects in which interpretations are made, this point is valid: any order of traits is as much an order of traits as any other order of traits. But the orders of traits also are in various higher-order orders of dependence, causal, ontological, and otherwise. When other philosophers commited Buchler's sin of ontological priority, the contradictory of ontological parity, dependencies of various sorts are what they had in mind.[15] So too when philosophical theologians inquire about what orders of interpretation apply to God irrespective of our visualizations and which are orders that can be denied when we subtract our visual and other metaphoric projections, they have in mind some scheme of orders of dependency. Whereas it is just as true that God is

---

13. For a clear example of just how abstract and non-personal Buddhist metaphysics really is, including its claim that Buddhism has no metaphysics, see Raimundo Panikkar's *The Silence of God: The Answer of the Buddha;* for the reasons behind my snide reference to no metaphysics, see my review of that book, "On Buddha's Answer to the Silence of God." For a fascinating and multifaceted discussion of personalizing the Buddha, responding to relics, making pilgrimages, and the like, see Malcolm David Eckel's *To See the Buddha.*

14. For a sophisticated discussion of this from the standpoint of a Christian theologian who wants to say that God is a personal being, see Pannenberg, 1988, chapter 6.2,4,7.

15. See Buchler's "On a Strain of Arbitrariness in Whitehead's Philosophy."

the rock of my salvation as that God is my Lord or that God is the inde-terminate Creator of the entire universe of rocks, Lords, saving events, and determiners of my life's agenda—those traits have parity as traits. But that God is the Creator is the condition on which all those other traits depend in various ways. Philosophical theologians delve deeply into those metaphysical issues which can, relative to religious symbols, be rephrased as the issues concerning the orders or respects in which God or the sacred can truthfully be symbolized.

Let us not lose sight of Buchler's point about parity, however. The orders or respects within which religious symbols interpret God are often complexly involved with the contexts of the interpreters. Even pure the-ology is carried out by theologians in an academic or religious context. Perhaps it is true to symbolize God, in the context of visualizations for meditation, as large, red, hairy, female, and girdled with skulls; perhaps in the context of prayer, the respect in which God is interpreted involves a personal mirroring and personal symbols are true. None of this is to say yet that these symbols are true overall but to point out that their truth is relative to the respects in which they are referred to their objects, respects that are functions in part of the interpretive context. Buchler's point is that, taking into account the respect of interpretation, that God looks like Kali or is to be addressed and listened to like a person, is just as true of God as that ultimate reality is empty or that God is the mystical abyss whence arises all determinate things.

Therefore a major clue for our inquiry into how to understand and assess religious symbols is that their reference is always in some respect. Identification of the interpretive respect is necessary for understanding how the symbols, with their constellations of meaning in fact refer to their objects. Symbolic meaning abstracted from the respect of reference is misleading. That would be like thinking that the Rock of my Salvation is geological. If the interpretive respect of reference is understood as an intrinsic qualification of the reference, then all true interpretations can be taken at face value: these might be equally weighty truths, that God is a Rock of Salvation, that God is the Lord of Agendas, that God is to be visualized as large, red, hairy, female, and girdled in skulls, that God is the Creator of all determinateness, and that God has perhaps furnished heaven with cigars!

Many more considerations of reference need to be woven into this account, however. Most especially, it is necessary to identify the referents of religious symbols by some characteristics that make it defensible to use language such as "God," "the Sacred," "Buddha-mind," "Emptiness," "the Absolute," "the Unconditioned," and so forth. The thesis to be argued is that all religious symbols have a primary reference directly or indirectly (as determined in the respect of interpretation) to boundary conditions contrasting the finite and infinite. The additional thesis will be argued, mainly in chapter 5, that religious symbols have a secondary reference to the state or stage of the interpreters' characters, both individually and communally. Thus the shape or structure of symbols for referring to the primary divine referent is affected by how that reference can be made for the specific interpreting character at hand. The secondary reference is not to be confused with special kinds of interpretants of meaning. It is rather that God can be symbolized as a rock *for people in need of support,* as a warrior king *for people in political danger,* and as spirit *for seekers after enlightenment.* But God cannot be symbolized as a Father *for people whose father abused them.* Chapter 5 will discuss in greater detail the variations of the interpreters' characters that affect secondary reference. For most of the remainder of this chapter, primary reference is the topic.

The key to this argument about reference is an understanding of the general operation of the imagination within which religious symbols are to be found. Its steps are the following: first to establish the religious character of imagination; second, to indicate how imagination functions in reference so as to engage experience with its objects; and third, to define the reference of religious symbols as finite/infinite contrasts.

## 2.2. IMAGINATION AS RELIGIOUS

To begin with imagination, the first and most important thesis to assert is that imagination, in the sense of the most primary or primitive organization of human experience, is religious, regardless of whether it contains any specifically religious symbols of God or related matters. By *imagination* is meant, not the functions of fantasy, as when we would say a person has a lively or creative imagination, but rather the elementary capacity to experience things with images.[16] In order to make out what may at first appear as an extraordinary connection between imagination

---

16. The importance of imagination in the inventive or creative sense is itself very great for an understanding of religious symbols. Many important symbols are themselves truly fantastic. This different but related sense of imagination will be discussed in chapter 5. For theological purposes these two senses of imagination need to be combined. See, for instance, Ray L. Hart's *Unfinished Man and the Imagination,* 1968; also Fritz Buri's "American Philosophy of Religion from a European Perspective: The Problem of Meaning and Being in the Theologies of Imagination and Process."

and religion, I shall spend some time analyzing imagination. Four points will be made about how imagination is to be understood.[17] Because imagination is so important for understanding religious symbols, the technical philosophical points here are worth the effort. After these four points about imagination, two further points will be made about religion in imagination so as to make out the claim that the primitive organization of human experience is religious, whether explicitly so in terms of organized religion or not.

The first point, argued exhaustively in his way by the philosopher Immanuel Kant, is that imagination is what makes the difference between experiencing something and merely responding as a reaction in vectors of forces.[18] In contrast to Kant's transcendental account, which treats understanding the imagination as a condition for explaining nature and natural causation, my account here treats imagination as a part of nature continuous with semiotic behavior. Imagination is the peculiar kind of causal synthesis, found in human beings and higher mammals in various degrees, that integrates impinging conditions which might not have experiential form in such a way that they take on experiential form and so become parts of experience and subject to reference in interpretive experience. Imagination is the mental synthesis that integrates various impinging stimuli according to the forms of experience, which are images in the most generic sense. Among the most elementary kinds of images are those that allow stimuli to be integrated in spatial and temporal fields, and in fields of relative value or importance. Whereas ordinary, non-experiential, causal reactions respond to a stimulus, now as modified only by the other stimuli, now demanding response, experiential reactions through imaginative synthesis take stimuli to be in a temporal continuum in which other things are earlier and later. Whereas ordinary, non-experiential, causal reactions respond to a stimulus only in terms of the locations of the vectors of forces impinging on the stimulus, experi-

---

17. Underlying those points is an elaborate theory I developed in *Reconstruction of Thinking*, chapters 5–8. Whereas that particular theory of imagination is not asserted as established here, it does prove that the points that are asserted here can be cashed out in detail; other theories of imagination might do just as well regarding these points. I have learned much from Ray L. Hart in these matters.

18. Kant's most useful discussions of imagination in this sense of the primal base of experience are in the *Critique of Pure Reason*, the "A Deduction," rather than the "B Deduction," and in the chapter on "Schematism." Kant's *Critique of Judgment* discusses imagination in the creative and fanciful sense, which is also important for understanding religious symbols.

ential responses through imaginative synthesis react to stimuli as being in a field. Whereas ordinary, non-experiential, causal reactions take things to be only as important as their force eliciting the reaction, experiential responses value things in patterns relative to other values.

In short, in experience things are integrated *so as to have the form of a world*, with temporal, spatial, and valuational dimensions. Also, there are many other dimensions that go into making up an experiential world, as phenomenologists have outlined for us; some of these will be discussed shortly.[19] The dimensions of experiential worldliness have to do also with the positions of humankind in the world, or the position of the tribe, or the individual. All of these are constructed from and by imaginative forms or images according to which the stuff for experience is integrated into experience itself. Imagination is what integrates things into the experiential form of being in the world.

Imagination is thus the elementary kind of causal process in human beings that gives rise to experience integrated with the forms of experiential worldliness. This is by no means to say that imagination creates real objects, or that the objects of the world do not exist on their own irrespective of the activity of imagination. David Weissman has shown with great wit the folly of inferring that, because experience has integrative forms of its own, arising from imaginative synthesis, there is no real world to which experiential images refer or can be referred.[20] Indeed, the pragmatic restraints on elementary imagination are such that our

---

19. The phenomenological idea of the "life-world" was elaborated by Husserl; see, for instance, his *Ideas*. Husserl himself did precious little description of the phenomenological life-world. For that, on the topic at hand, see Edward S. Casey's wonderful books, *Imagining, Remembering*, and *Getting Back into Place*. The phrase *worldmaking* was popularized by Nelson Goodman in his *Ways of Worldmaking*; Goodman's topic is imagination in the artistic as well as Kantian experience-formation sense, and his approach is that of analytic philosophy committed to a kind of pragmatism. That neo-pragmatism in the hands of philosophers such as Richard Rorty has evoked the profound critical response of David Weissman in his *Truth's Debt to Value*, in which he warns that emphasis on the worldmaking character of imagination might lead to the thesis that interpretation has no reference to the real world: if we can just make up a world, why is there the obligation to get the truth about something? How is there even the possibility of that? My thesis is that the human imposition of imaginative forms of order on natural stimuli is part of a natural process that does indeed allow for intentional reference to reality as engaged through imagination. For the sake of strategy, I place the first discussion of religious imagination in this chapter on reference which is in thorough agreement with Weissman against the anti-reference people.

20. See Weissman's *Truth's Debt to Value*.

images need to represent the world very well indeed. In a certain way, at least some of our basic images are like maps, and they are good to the extent the terrain is the way they represent it. Maps are iconic in a plain sense. Furthermore, in actual experience, human beings are like other natural organisms interacting with their environment, as Dewey liked to say. We do not ordinarily scan our experiential images like an inner map and then make inferences to realities outside. Rather, we engage those realities in the real world as guided by our shaped imagination (more on engagement in the next section). Iconic interpretation in imagination discloses reality in certain respects. The question of whether the world is really like the images in our experiential world is a question of interpretation, not of imagination as such. Interpretations always carry ontological commitments, imagination on the face of it does not.

Another sign of the naturalness of imaginative synthesis, albeit found highly developed only in human beings, is that it is itself a synthesis of syntheses of syntheses, most of which are to be understood in terms of non-experiential modes of causation. Perceptive elements in imagination are syntheses of syntheses of physical events and light coming through chains of syntheses of bodily reactions in eyes, ears, skin and nerves. There are also layers of syntheses of the imaginative body itself, chemical metabolic syntheses, the interdependent maintenance of the skeletal, muscle, and organ systems, diurnal and seasonal rhythms, patterns of excitation and rest, a kind of inner bio-psychic dance reflective also of the environment. There is no hard and fast line distinguishing imaginative forms of synthesis from others that usually have been approached with physical classifications. That internal physical activities can be brought into explicit religious imagery has long been known by ascetics and tantric practitioners.[21] Imagination is as natural as digestion, with imagistic forms of synthesis rather than chemical ones. Imagination connects experience with the rest of the world by virtue of the nesting of its syntheses in other natural syntheses. Scrooge was right to wonder whether Marley's ghost was an undigested bit of beef rather than a divine messenger.

Within experience all other forms of thinking, willing, and enjoying take their rise from imagination. They all have imaginative forms, that is,

---

21. Livia Kohn (in *Early Chinese Mysticism*, chapter 1) has used Julian Davidson's distinction between ergotropic and trophotropic activation to build an elaborate theory accounting for various forms of Daoist mysticism. Ergotropic activation turns the sensory and motor systems on high, as in rage, or as cultivated by dancing dervishes; trophotropic activation turns them down very low, as in yogic prana meditation.

are based on images, however else they might also be formed. Interpretation has logical forms in addition to imaginative ones, for instance, and presses issues of truth in ways imaginative forms do not.

The second point about imagination is to single out what might be called *perceptive forms*. Prescinding from the question of the truth or veridicality of perception, as a matter of imagination alone perception has a form, or a variety of forms. Perception has the imaginative structure of distinguishing focal things in the midst of a background. The foreground-focus-background relations are extremely complex and various, as has been shown by many phenomenological analyses and Gestalt psychology. They are constitutive of the experiential trait of distinguishing "things" and discriminating areas and levels of importance. Of course even the basic imaginative elements of spatio-temporal field connections suppose that there are things articulating places or times.[22] Distinctions of importance also involve distinguishing things from their background and from one another. The imagistic forms for the distinction of perceptible things from their background are more basic than those distinguishing one perceptible thing from another. The overall imaginative form of the experiential world has the complex character of many things, each distinguishable from its background and also distinguishable from one another, but so entertained that experiential focus can be on one thing or another, or on several, or on comparisons, but never on all things discriminated at once with no background left over. In respect of the variable quality of focal attention, the experiential world is a (possible) representation of the real world, and different from it in certain aspects of imaginative structure.

The third point, perhaps implicit in what has already been said, is that perceptible things with their background have the additional imaginative form of *appearance*. They present themselves as the way real things appear to us. They do not seem like fantasies or fictions but the way real things are relative to us experiencers. Although interpretation can treat (special arrangements of) images as representations, the images themselves, in their perceptive thing-in-background imaginative structures, have the intentional vector quality of real things appearing. Only modern European philosophers would ever think they are trapped within the mind, as if the mind contemplates only its own mental stuff. Rather, it is the nature of mental stuff—imagination—to make the world appear.

---

22. It can be argued, in fact, that space and time in their real and objective sense are constituted by the characters of spatio-temporal things rather than as containers in themselves. Whitehead held this view. I defend it in *Recovery of the Measure,* chapter 8.

The discussion so far has spoken as if visual perception were the paradigm for experience, and perhaps in the Western tradition of philosophy this has been so. But clearly this is an abstraction. Even when phenomena of all the other senses are added in, experience is much richer than sensation. Things that appear in experience include one's emotions and those of one's neighbors; institutions and their effects, for instance political, educational, and familial; ideas, traditions, cultural projects; obligations in morals, politics, arts, descriptions, theories—anything at all that can be experienced as real can appear in experience, shaped by the imaginative forms of appearance. Many if not most of the things that appear are shaped themselves by human signs, including images as well as interpretations and theories. For theories that sharply distinguish mind and body this mixture of human imaginative and interpretive conventions with the natural would be problematic. The present theory is naturalistic, however, and therefore counts the mental and other artifacts of human beings as part of nature, capable of appearing in experience.

The fourth point about imagination is that appearances have relations of importance amongst one another.[23] The experiental field where things appear in connections with one another out of their backgrounds is organized as much by the relative importances appearances have to one another as by spatio-temporal or other field structures. Experience takes things as having values, relative to one another, against their backgrounds, and in relation to the perspective of the experiencer.

Importance thus suggests a three-fold orientation of value. (This analysis abstracts out what are densely mixed in appearances.) On the one hand, things that appear are achievements on their own, relative to their backgrounds. Their imaginative form as appearances focused against the background indicates how they integrate elements of value in the background that would not be integrated without the appearing thing. In more objectivist language, this would be called *intrinsic value*; the interpretive question of truth asks whether the intrinsic value that appears to be achieved is really what it seems. On the other hand the importance of appearances has to do with how they condition one another's value. Hot sun is intrinsically an achievement of energy concentration but it is also good for the growth of corn. Much of the imaginative structure of experience has to do with shaping the bearings of things on one another regarding what is good or bad for them. Usually this is translated into a

---

23. This discussion of importance summarizes a more nearly complete discussion in my *Normative Cultures*.

physical dimensions of space and time, and as the revelations of beauty and inventions of new wickedness jolt our images of the value dimensions.[27] Relative to all these considerations, the fundamental images of the place of humanity, its true ground, heart, and destiny, also changes. That we no longer take world-tree mythology seriously does not mean we cannot understand the religious symbol systems in which the ancient Norse did.

Now imagination in this basic function of worldmaking, including the place of the human, is always religious, because it is world construct-ing. This very important thesis, if true as I have argued, justifies the attention scholars of religion have paid to imagination as such. Imagina-tion cannot frame its experiential elements in a human way without the orienting importance of certain pervasively or seasonally appearing images that function as boundary conditions for worldliness. Religion is the name of the cultural enterprise that shepherds the symbols of the boundary conditions. This does not define religion, but it points to one of its most important cultural locations. Peter Berger calls the religious mythologies and theologies that represent these conditions the "sacred canopy." Rituals and spiritual practices celebrate these conditions and aim to bring people into better attunement with them.

Organized religion is not always or even often the source of the sym-bols of the boundary conditions. They might come from science, from the arts, and from moral discoveries and practices. But their function is religious if they serve to frame the dimensions or boundaries of experi-ential worldliness. That science concocts them is for the sake of scientific truth, not religious mythopoeic world construction, yet they can function as world-constructing images. That artists create them is for beauty or some other aesthetic purpose, but they can function for world construc-tion. Moralists and jurists are concerned for the good and right, but their images can shape a culture's very sense of world. One of the cultural responsibilities of religions is to attend to good, beautiful, and true images for the purpose of world construction. In our time, religions thus need to be intimately involved with science, the arts, and normative practice. But though those images or symbols can be constructed intentionally for a variety of other purposes, the purpose of defining the boundary con-

---

27. It can be argued that the world-constructive elements for us are not trees or pri-meval times or divine fiats but rather the conditions of determinateness. Determinateness, epistemologically represented as the property of being distinguishable and measurable, is how modernity defines what makes the world worldly. This is my argument in *A Theol-ogy Primer,* chapter 3.

ditions of experiential worldliness can hardly ever be served directly. Though new symbols can be developed by individuals and groups, that they, and not the host of other invented symbols, turn out to be symbols of world-constructing boundary conditions is a function of other factors. Theistic religions often think their symbols are revealed; even Confucius, eschewing interests in gods, thought he was merely passing on the golden heritage.[28] Whether any symbols articulate the true boundary conditions of the real world is an interpretive question of truth, a very complicated matter because of the indirectness in religious symbols and issues of their secondary referents, of which more later.

The sixth point is that, where the experiential organization of the appearances of the world clusters symbols around those boundary conditions, the very form of imagination lends itself to expressions of contingency. That is, the world itself is experienced as dependent on those boundary conditions. When the World Tree is felled, the world begins to collapse. When the ancient primeval time is let slip past, through the forgetting of ritual, it no longer powerfully sustains the world which sinks into profane decay. In the present time the once authoritative symbols for the source of value and importance have lost their grip for many in secular cultures, and people despair that pure relativism might be true. Or people fall into a kind of cultural narcissism in which they oscillate between grandiosity born of the belief that they create all value themselves and flattened affect in which everything seems worth nothing.[29]

This sense of contingency can be given precise philosophical definition.[30] Suppose that, for late modern cultures, the boundary conditions include those having to do with determinateness and what makes such an abstract element as determinateness especially significant for the orienting of human life (there may be many other boundary conditions too). This sensibility developed from the early modern conviction that what is real can be measured in some sense—the senses of "measurement" are now quite diverse. Determinateness can be analyzed as the transcendental condition that all determinate things are harmonies of

---

28. *Analects* 7.1

29. See the analysis of cultural narcissism in Lawrence E. Cahoone's *The Dilemma of Modernity*. He traces the causes to philosophical problems, but his interpretation gives them religious force.

30. See my *God the Creator*, chapter 8. Of course, contingency does not have to be given the technical metaphysical analysis that appears here in the text in order for the general point to be appreciated. In fact, if readers don't have an experiential sense of contingency, the metaphysics is likely to be whistling in the wind.

essential and conditional features. The essential features are unique to each thing in some sense and the conditional ones are how the things condition one another; so every determinate thing is conditioned by at least some other determinate things, and each is also a harmony of its essential and conditional features. If any of these traits is missing, the thing is not determinate, lacking either a reality of its own, relations with things with respect to which it is determinate, or the harmony of these features.

Relative to essential features, ways of signalling the uniqueness of things can become symbolic of the things' contingency. Much of the religious symbolism of romanticism has to do with the contingent but transcendent and world-constructing importance of something's (or everything's) uniqueness and its struggle to sustain that in an engulfing world. Relative to conditional features, ways of signalling the connections of things, the mutual hang-togetherness of the world, the overarching unities of diversities, can become symbols of contingency. Without conditional features, reality would be chaos, and the symbolic figures of gods bringing order to chaos are ancient; they form deepseated motifs in nearly every religion. Relative to the harmonies of essential and conditional features, the ways of signalling the integrities of things can become symbols of contingency. These are the symbols of balance, and of achieved actuality, of definiteness, of making a place for oneself: non-romantic celebrations of human integrity, the durability of mountains, the first ten seconds of the Big Bang. These symbols point to the contingency of sustaining a thing's nature and place amidst defining conditions with unique integrity. With all of these, the very structure of the experiential world can be experienced as contingent, which of course means that the world appears contingent (whether it is in fact again, is a question of truth involving interpretation, not sheer imagination). The most developed symbologies for total contingency have been developed in Indian religions from Vedic times forward, including the Buddhist distinction between form and emptiness and its doctrine of *pratitya-samutpada*. Western theisms also early moved from the idea of God as orderer to God as creator of the stuff to be ordered as well.[31] Even earlier than symbols of cosmic creation were symbols of the life of the human soul and its mortality, which also are fundamental pointers to contingency, at least to the contingency of whatever makes human life meaningful as such.

---

31. This was present in Justin Martyr and Tatian, and became very explicit in Irenaeus. See J. N. D. Kelly's account in his *Early Christian Doctrines*, chapter 4.

The logic of the borderline contingency conditions, registered in at least many of the symbols of them, is that they mark the boundary between the finite and the infinite. That is, by focusing on some finite thing as a boundary condition orienting the experiential world (the world as it appears, the experienced world), they suppose a contrast with what would be the case without the boundary condition. No world tree, no centered sphere of human existence; no primal time, no meaning to consequent time; no determinateness, no thing at all, nothingness, emptiness. The finite condition is disclosively referred to as actual; its infinite contrast is transcendent. The infinite can be merely the absence or nonexistence or ineffectiveness of the finite boundary condition. It can be construed causally, as Brahman manifested as Isvara the creator, or the infinite Christian creator. Or the contrast can be expressed as a mythic action, Marduk slaying Tiamat, or any number of other ways. Precisely in being symbolized as contingent, as the focal points of contingency, as those things on which all other worldly orientation hangs, the boundary conditions are imaged as finite/infinite contrasts. They also, in that, are symbolized with an underlying contingently actual/subjunctively potential contrast.

I propose to use *finite/infinite contrast* as a technical term for the primary direct or indirect referent of religious symbols. Finite/infinite contrasts are what I mean by the *divine*. They deserve that meaning, as I shall argue through the rest of this book, because they mark what is experienced as a special condition defining worldliness or world construction. Finite/infinite contrasts have been approached in this section through an analysis of imagination and interpretation in experience. But if their interpretations are true, they are realities, or structures of reality. Even as imaged in experience, finite/infinite contrasts have the form of being disclosures of reality, not of being mere images themselves.

In this usage, the *infinite* is not universally honorific. That honor comes only in those symbol systems affirming that the infinite itself gives rise to the finite. Many theisms assert that God is not the infinite in this literal sense of non-finite but is a being who creates and thereby overcomes the infinite nothingness of the abyss. The point of the argument here is to call attention to that particular structure of imagination, in its elementary function of synthesizing things into an experiential world, that focuses on the world's contingency as resting on certain absolutely crucial finite/infinite boundary conditions. Those conditions are represented as a contrast of finite and infinite.

2.3. IMAGINATION AS ENGAGEMENT

The second main thesis about imagination is that, although in itself it is neither true nor false, imagination is the way by which we engage the world.[32] This is but an anthropomorphic way of putting the earlier point that imagination is the special synthesis that turns causal stimuli into the stuff of experience. Although human beings do bounce about as lumps of matter, they also respond to the world experientially. The images that shape their imagination determine what things they respond to and how those things are interpreted. Different religious images determine different global engagements of the world. In ancient times people engaged the distant stars as if they were gods determining human destiny; now we engage them as enticing frontiers. Sometimes we engage the world with courage and vigor; other times we are alienated and self-deceived. Imagination by itself is the means for the particular engagements underlying our culture.

One can approach the point from an evolutionary perspective. Great adaptive power lies in being able to synthesize causal impingements into experiential forms that allow for relating to things distant in time and space. A homely example serves to make the point. The reptile and amphibian brain and ocular nervous system allows for synthesizing perceptual experience in a visual field with three dimensions. Mammalian brains, however, can do that and also imagine rotating objects in the visual field so as to experience them as having backsides. Frogs sit on lilly pads and flick sticky tongues at flying food; cats can creep around birds from behind. If frogs had evolved the experiential ability mentally to rotate an image of their prey, they likely would also have evolved more sneaky locomotion than hops. Human beings, of course, have much more involved synthesizing senses for experience, and they have evolved both physical attributes and cultural ones to fill the niches opened by their elementary forms of experience. Those niches in turn breed more subtle experiential images. The elementary human image of distances out of sight allows for images of "everywhere" or at least "beyond the

---

32. My use of the metaphor of *engagement* is intended to stand in contrast to metaphors such as *decoding* common in some Continental philosophy and *mirroring* in much analytic philosophy, especially philosophy of science. The roots of the metaphor are found in pragmatism and existentialism. From pragmatism comes the primary referent of engaging with nature, where biological analogies come to mind. *Engagement* is my variant on Dewey's *interaction* or *transaction*, with more of a connotation of intentional behavior. From existentialism comes the problematic of engagement versus disengagement, inauthentic engagement, engagement in bad faith, idolatrous or demonic engagement. For a proper discussion of norms of engagement, see my *Normative Cultures*, chapter 5.

mountains there and the sea here." Because organisms need to engage their environment in order to sustain themselves, keep safe, grow, and reproduce, the ways they synthesize their responses to things so that their activity is organized are engaging elements. For human beings imaginative synthesis is the outstanding distinctive mode of engagement.

We can always ask whether our engagements are true to reality, or at least as true as our culture allows. *Interpretation* is the name for the family of cognitive activities within experience that treats images as true or false. An image by itself is not an assertion; an image interpreted in experience is taken as representing its object. So, within interpretation, although not in imagination alone, the questions of truth are raised. Stated more aggressively, interpretation asks how things are truly to be imaged. To ask that question is already to be engaging the things. Imagination forms the stuff of interpretation: all interpretive ideas are images of one kind or another. Yet beyond imaginative form, interpretation has the additional forms of logic or truth-seeking. Religions do not treat their symbols as images alone but as disclosive interpretations.

Beyond both imagination and interpretation we can ask whether our engagements are comprehensive or fragmentary. If they are comprehensive, it is because our interpretations are formally organized into theories. Theory is a third family of cognitive activities. Theorizing also takes place by means of images, and theories are to be treated as interpretations that are true or false. But in addition, theorizing has to do with gaining a synoptic vision of a field, with gathering many objects under a complex head. Some kinds of theorizing are like modeling, where the structure of the model is sought to be a mirror image of the objects modelled; other kinds of theorizing are more complex. Among these are the systems of religious symbols, their networks of interrelated meanings. The forms of theorizing are different from and additive to those of imagination and logical interpretation.

In addition to imagination, interpretation, and theorizing, there is a family of practical cognitive activities associated with the pursuit of responsibility.[33] We can ask whether our engagements are responsive to

---

33. As has been noted earlier, imagination, interpretation, theorizing, and the pursuit of responsibility are the four families of thinking based on valuation in the several respective senses examined in my trilogy, *Axiology of Thinking*. Volume 1, *Reconstruction of Thinking*, deals with imagination; volume 2, *Recovery of the Measure*, deals with interpretation; volume 3, *Normative Cultures*, deals with theorizing and the pursuit of responsibility. All are involved with engaging reality, but all depend on imagination as the elementary form of the possibility of engagement.

the various norms framing our responsibilities. Both organizing life in light of religious symbols and cultivating the leading of our souls are practical activities responsive to norms. So, in fact, is the practice of theology.

All these considerations affect whether we engage the world well or ill. Imagination alone puts us in experiential touch with things. With interpretation our touch can be accurate and true. With theory our touch can be comprehensively oriented. With the pursuit of responsibility our touch can be practical and efficacious in how we live. Engagement, rather than mere causal bouncing, is the human mode of being in the world, and it is made possible through imagination, interpretation, theorizing in the broad sense, and practical activity.

I would not want sight to be lost of the crucial function of engagement performed by imagination just because interpretation, theory, and the pursuit of responsibility seem so much more important. Focus is difficult to keep on engagement because there are few images that enter into discourse that are not also involved in interpretation, reflective of theoretical orientations, and relevant to action. But engagement is not reducible to interpretation and the rest that builds on interpretation. If there are no images, nothing can be used representatively as a sign to interpret reality. If there are no images in which certain real things appear, they simply do not appear and no interpretation can be made of them; without images of how a large ball could seem flat on the surface, no one could experience or contemplate experiencing the world as round; without higher mathematical images quarks and spin could not appear; without images of God, God could not be engaged.

Nevertheless, we can have images that, through their imaginative structures as appearances, refer to real things but do not effectively engage them. The non-engagement problem is not that they are false, although that too may be so. The problem is that their imagistic structure stands in the way of making interactive contact with things. Philosophy professors often try to give their students images (language and concepts) with which to engage philosophic issues, but the images sometimes do not work to engage the students. If our image of natural objects is that they stand ready at hand to be used instrumentally for technological purposes, as Heidegger says, we cannot engage nature in its beauty and other intrinsic and conditional worths.[34]

Religious symbols are intended to engage people with the real boundary conditions or finite/infinite constrasts to which they are interpreted

---

34. See Heidegger's *The Question Concerning Technology*.

to refer. They can fail to do so for at least two reasons, that they are dead or that they are idolatrous. No religious lament is more common than that the current society, or at least our children, do not engage the ultimate conditions that are the religious referents. The symbols that worked in former times no longer engage. They fail to refer indexically and iconically, and their conventional structure can be limited to semiotic codes in extensional reference alone. Is the fault in the new generation? Are the old symbols mistaken? Are they true in the contexts where they do engage? Can we have new symbols for realities anciently referenced? These questions indicate the complexity of the connection between engagement and interpretation of the truth of the symbols.[35] I lament the decline of engaging religious symbols; so did my parents; so did my grandparents. It is hard for us all to recognize the rise of new symbols for religious engagement.

Symbols can also refer idolatrously. That is, although they seem to refer to the finite/infinite contrast they refer to something else instead. The problem is not with their meanings or interpretants, as if they mistakenly ascribe false attributes to the divine. The problem rather is with their reference, ascribing attributes possibly appropriate to the divine to something else instead. The deep dialectical polemic in the Hebrew Bible against idolatry is aimed at the finite side in various finite/infinite contrasts that gets disconnected from the infinite side in the contrast. The Hebrews were particularly exercised about divine symbols such as statues and pictures that they thought were easily shorn of the transcendent element. Verbal and architectural symbols, and natural symbols such as light and thunderstorms, and occupational symbols such as the king, warrior, shepherd, or parent, did not bother them so much. This point is complicated by the Hebrew effort to distinguish the cult of Yahweh from surrounding cults that employed many graven images; the Hebrews were probably too hard on the cults of their neighbors which indeed did find the transcendent in their graven images. The Hindu cults focusing on Siva, Krishna, and the great multitude of other gods did not have the Hebrews' problem. They, on the contrary, could see the infinite in a great many finite things, perhaps in anything. When pressed about the infinite side, the Hindus could unify their gods under higher gods, always ultimately one highest God, usually depicted as creator like

---

35. Tillich was particularly sensitive to the effects of dead symbols. See his discussions, for instance, in *Theology of Culture*, p. 53, and *Systematic Theology I*, pp. 106–118. Whether symbols are living or dead is closely related to Tillich's theory of the *kairos*, things happening at the right time; see his essay, "Kairos," in *The Protestant Era*.

Isvara-Brahman. The Hindu sense of infinite and universal oneness was so powerful, however, that the danger in their eyes was forgetting the finite side in the finite/infinite contrasts. Hence the resolute polytheism that finds the infinite in this finite thing, and that, and that other.[36] Polytheism might be a misleading Western descriptive category for Indian religious history, because that history arranges its references to the divine around resolutely single and deep sources such as Brahman or the empty Buddha-mind, as monotheist in its own way as the West Asian religions in theirs. Polytheism does not mean the simple assertion of many gods all on a level, or a primitive kind of pantheon, because many Indian religions such as the varieties of Buddhism with polytheistic symbols at the devotional level also deny most forms of theism at sophisticated levels; it means a response to a form of idolatry. Idolatry of the easy swoop to infinity is just as bad a way of corrupting finite/infinite contrasts as losing the infinite in the finite. Too quick a reference to the infinite loses the particularity of the world and the infinite is emptied of significance.

Western monotheisms arising from the Hebrew dialectic as well as Indian polytheisms have both soteriological devotional paths and theological paths leading to purified experiences of finite/infinite contrasts. Both engage the transcendent. But their dominant concerns with idolatry are opposite. Thomas J. J. Altizer has shown that the concern for idolatry of the finite led the West to be able to conceive the finite world in wholly secular terms; his own Christian theological project to re-engage the divine thus has to take the form of the "death of God," referring to the transcendent infinite separated from the potentially idolatrous finite, and the assertion of a kenosis or emptying of the infinite into the finite, with no remainder.[37] The obverse concern about Hindu polytheism is that, because just about any finite thing can be the bearer of the infinite, finite things commonly can be neglected in their plain finite character, with a resultant lack of attention to ethics and matters of mate-

---

36. See Diana Eck's marvelous *Encountering God*, in which she recounts her experience as a transcendently oriented Methodist Protestant going to Banaras to study Hinduism and finding Gods on every corner and worship of them as devoted as anything Christian. Her study illustrates the distinction between the two kinds of anti-idolatry: the West Asian fear of losing the infinite in the finite and the South Asian fear of losing the finite in the infinite.

37. In his recent work, Altizer sets the background for his interpretation by a study of epic literature of the West in *History as Apocalypse*. Then see *Genesis and Apocalypse*, chapter 6, "Emptiness and Self-Emptiness," and *The Genesis of God*, chapter 5, "Genesis and God."

rial existence. The point of both concerns about idolatry is to maintain
the finite/infinite contrast. Symbols are idolatrous when they refer to
either side without the other.

The division of idolatries occasions reflection on the notion of *contrast* in the term finite/infinite contrasts. *Contrast* is a technical term in
Whitehead's philosophy to mean the unity of two or more things, not
under a higher inclusive thing, but just because they fit together.[38]
Moreover, it means that the things contrasted cannot be themselves, or
understood themselves, save as being in the contrast. True, Whitehead
himself intended contrasts to unite two or more finite things, not finite
and infinite. Christian medieval philosophy was deeply concerned about
the "relation" between the finite and infinite. Thomas Aquinas and
Duns Scotus had quite different ways of articulating the contrast, using
the terms *finite* and *infinite* themselves. Hegel showed that the infinite
cannot be a mere negation of the finite, which leads to what he called a
"bad infinite" of one negation after another. We do not have to solve
this problem here in order to use the notion of a finite/infinite contrast
to articulate the direct or indirect referent of religious symbols. In fact,
the very generality of our account of religious symbols needs to be
friendly to the whole array of ways of contrasting them, however much
some are better than others on philosophical grounds. The Indian religions of Hinduism and Buddhism have philosophical discussions of the
infinite and finite that are analogous to the history of Western thought
on the matter, though often with somewhat different models.[39]

Regarding religious symbols, my overall argument is now becoming
more complex. Because they image the very foundations and limits of
the world or what can be imagined, the truth of religious symbols must
be extremely complex, that is, organized comprehensively with some
sense of theory, at least in networks of symbols. Furthermore, their truth
can be grasped only when they successfully engage interpreters with
their objects of reference. Because religious symbols deal with such basic
matters as how we ought to live, a successful engagement means making

---

38. See his *Process and Reality*, p. 22 and *passim*, where he defines contrasts as the
eighth category of existence: "Modes of Synthesis of Entities in one Prehension, *or* Pat-
terned Entities." For a more elaborate discussion of contrasts in their depth and aesthetic
intensity, see Part 2, chapter 4, of *Process and Reality*, "Organisms and Environment."
With due deference to Whitehead, I am extending his notion to the composition of finite
and infinite things.

39. See Clooney's discussion in *Theology after Vedanta*, chapter 5, of "naming the
infinite" in Amalananda in comparison with Thomas Aquinas.

how we ought to live an effective practical part of life. Put in religious terms, the more divine matters are accurately grasped, the more people are transformed, enlightened, or saved, at least within certain limits. Engagement is crucial for interpretation, theory, and responsibility.

But surely religious symbols are different from most other kinds of symbols because they refer in part to what is not of this world. With these remarks about imagination and engagement, we are on the track of religious symbolic reference.

## 2.4. RELIGIOUS SYMBOLIC REFERENCE

Hypothesis: Religious symbols are those whose primary reference, direct or indirect, is to a finite/infinite contrast, that is, at least partly to the divine or the infinite.

How can this be made plausible when our ordinary suppositions are that reference is only to objects within the world? The answer is that religious symbols are those religiously functioning images that so shape the worldliness of the world that they also indexically point beyond it. As shaping the basic dimensions of the world—its temporal and spatial structures, its values and importances, and the place of the human in all this—religiously functioning images refer to what makes the difference between cosmos and the transcendent.

Some would say, as noted above, that beyond the cosmic dimensions of worldliness lies chaos. Others would say the creator, or creators. Yet others would say sheer nothingness. Whatever one's theology in this regard, or what parallels theology in non-theistic religions, the other side of worldliness is not finite. It is indeterminate, infinite. Therefore at least some of the religiously functioning images refer not only to finite structures shaping worldliness but also to what stands between the finiteness of the structured world and the infinite. They express what makes the difference so that there is not sheer chaos, not only the yawning abyss beneath creation, or blank nothingness. Of course the characterizations of what lies beyond the imaged boundaries of worldliness are always at least partially through negation. We have no positive conception of chaos, nor of a creator without creating, nor of sheer nothingness. The negation comes from the sense that the shaping dimensionalities of worldliness are finite structures like those contained within the world, and yet are what make worldliness possible. They are finite structures, referred to by images that also have in-the-world meaning such as trees, mountains, creative potmaking (Genesis 2:4b–7), and Big Bangs. But their religious imaginative function is to allow for the synthesizing of reality as experienced-world-as-such. Thus, as Tillich said, they participate not only in mundane imaginative uses but also in the world-founding powers of what lies beyond them, or of what would be if there were no worldliness.[40]

Better to understand these matters, three questions must be addressed. First, what does reference mean here? Second, what is the difference between direct and indirect reference? Third, what is the dialectic of affirmation and negation in religious symbolic reference?

Reference itself, I have argued, is a function of at least two things, the extension structured into the meaning of the symbol and the interpreter's act, objectified in the interpretation, of referring to the religious object by means of the symbol. The symbols themselves are "appearances," in the sense discussed earlier. They are imaginative organizations of effects from the world so as to make something in that world appear in experience as world-forming. Thus the religious symbols have their own internal extensive referring conditions that specify to what sorts of things they might be referred. Indeed, as mentioned, some philosophers think reference is nothing more than these internal referring conditions. Among the conditions, as part of the imaginative structure of appearance, is the indexical reference that there is a real referent, a real object, that is symbolized by what the symbol means. That is, the symbol is not self-contained in a flat sense but contains an internal indicator of its object that is supposed to be as the symbol says. The question of truth, of course, asks whether there is such an object, which leads to the issue of interpretation.

The second element in reference is the role the symbol plays in an interpretation that takes it to represent the religious object in some respect as being what the symbol means. Here the interpreter actually engages the symbol's object by means of the symbol. The interpreter refers to the object by means of the symbol and its internal referring conditions. Whereas the symbol's internal referring conditions are extensional, stating to what kinds of objects it can be applied by imaging those objects it makes appear, the interpretation refers intentionally to the real object as indicated by the symbol and by the act of taking the symbol to stand for the object in a certain respect. The act of interpretation is how the interpreter intends the object.

The possibility of error is of crucial importance here. What if ultimate reality is indifferent rather than compassionate? What if nothing is lovely, only useful or harmful? What if the symbol says that God is wise, and the

---

40. See *Systematic Theology I,* pp. 177, 239ff; *Theology of Culture,* pp. 54 ff.

interpreter takes God to be wise, but there is no God, or God is foolish, or there is no respect in which God legitimately can be interpreted with cognitive symbols? We must say that the object, identified in the interpreter's intention by means of the symbol's meaning and the matters pertaining to the purposes and respect of interpretation, is not in fact as the symbol interprets it. Not Marley's ghost but an undigested bit of beef. Not the Lord of the Universe but a memory of Daddy projected by hope or desperation onto the cosmos. There are no interpretations without objects, and all interpretations coordinate the object interpreted with the extensional references in the symbols used. But the objects might be very different indeed from what they are interpreted to be by the symbols, in fact with differences that make all the difference, such as not really God but physiological disturbances or psychological projections. That Achilles killed Hector might not really be true in history; the real symbol is a song long sung that (falsely) sounds like the real thing and is true only as an icon of martial struggle, the real object, not of Troy's history.

The matter here is related closely to issues of the respect in which the object is interpreted and the fact that so many symbols, especially religious ones, are indirect. The interpretation that Achilles historically killed Hector (assuming that both are fictional characters) interprets Achilles and Hector in the respect of being historical figures. That respect is inappropriate for the Homeric epic, supposing in fact that there is no historical truth to the tale. What Homer's tale disclosed about reality is not in respect of an historical report but in respect to something about martial heroism. Error can arise as much from interpreting the referent in an inappropriate respect as from interpreting it in an appropriate respect with the wrong symbol.

What is the relation between the extensional reference internal to the meaning of the symbol and the intentional reference of the overall act of interpretation? The interpretation picks up the meaning with its extensional reference, and also the respect of interpretation, when it engages the object in an interpretive act. Suppose the extensional meaning of the symbol does not point to referents of the sort engaged by the interpretation. Then the interpretation will have to be metaphorical. Whether the metaphor works, of course, needs to be decided by a subsequent interpretation analyzing the meaning of the former interpretation. Insofar as religious symbols refer extensionally only to finite things in the world, all religious interpretations will have to be metaphorical, at least in part, if the interpretation refers to the infinite and well as finite side in the finite/ infinite contrast. Insofar, however, as religious symbols have a depth that internally includes reference to the contrast, including the negations involved in the non-identification of the infinite with the finite, the symbols themselves are metaphorical; this is different from an interpretation making metaphorical use of a symbol that is not itself a metaphor.

The references both to error and to metaphor require that I no longer postpone a discussion of the indirectness of religious symbolization. The difficulty, of course, is that the interpretation of religious symbols is indirect in so very many senses. Many of these have been discussed above. First of all, religious symbols have many layers of meaning, as I will explore in the next chapter. The layer of meaning focused by the symbolic object or name or gesture may not itself have religious reference, but gains it through connection with another layer of meaning in its constellation of symbolic continuities; so, a cross on a Christian altar refers to God not directly but indirectly through its connection with the symbolism of Jesus' crucifixion. The symbol at its focus level refers indirectly by means of the extension of reference of a symbol at some other level. Some layers of meaning are expressive of synchronic networks of symbolic implications. Indirection might come from the religious reference lying in the extension of some symbol with which the original symbol is systematically connected, as the Christian eucharistic elements are connected symbolically to the death and resurrection of Jesus which themselves have religious reference to the contrast between finite and infinite. Other layers of meaning are connected as historical overlays and make religious reference through a layer whose historical significance is different from the focal layer. For instance, (as will be explored in chapter 6) the religious references of animal sacrifice, once living for the ancient Hebrews and Christians, are not living today and therefore can refer religiously only when constellated to some contemporary symbols system with analogous religious reference. Perhaps the most important thing to say about indirection in religious reference regarding meaning is that religious symbols refer indirectly on many levels all at once and in many different senses that might not be expressible in common terms.

Regarding the kinds of indirection that come not so much from the meanings of religious symbols as from the interpretations of them, we have already noted certain important features of the interpretive contexts. For instance, in the theological context symbols are interpreted in terms that express the cognitive interests of establishing the limits of the usefulness of symbols, the integrative interests of combining symbols, the hierarchical interests of comparing levels of abstraction, the practical interests of finding guidance from symbols, and the rest. Perhaps all of these theological approaches can be summarized as making sense of life through the symbols. The religious references of the symbols can thus become indirect in the sense of being incidental to the making-sense project, as well as in all the ways mentioned above concerning indirectness in meaning. The direct religious reference of primary symbols can be transformed to assumptions or presumptions, suppositions or presuppositions, by the practical project of making sense.

Then of course there is a multitude of ways in which religious interpretations are part and parcel of the complex task of organizing life, both within religious commnities and in the larger public. The earlier discussion in 1.3 of the cultural-linguistic approach of symbols should be recalled. Sometimes, as in teaching and some parts of worship, religious symbols are used directly to refer to their religious objects. But most often, and in many, many layers of practice upon practice, the religious symbols are assumed, presumed, supposed and presupposed, in their direct reference and are interpreted indirectly for practical purposes. Often the direct interpretive uses of religious symbols can be analyzed without discernable remainder into the practical interpretations that would be picked up in a cultural-linguistic thick description. Only a phenomenological or theological or philosophic approach would say that the symbols so practically contextualized also have reference to the sacred or God. The very material texture of religious symbols is most often the stuff of practical life—song, dance, ritual, eating, and so forth. Chapter 4 will argue that religious symbols in a practical context have doubled interpretants, giving both representational and practical meanings.

Another source of indirection is that religious symbols refer to God or the sacred (or the Unconditioned, Absolute, and so forth) as present in some worldly thing. Often for Western theistic religions the worldly things are historical events, or mythic events in some "other" sacral time. But there are also sacred objects, for instance, mountains or trees, sacred revelatory words recorded in holy scriptures, sacred postures, gestures, places, people, and so forth. That these worldly things are sacred, according to my argument, means that they are sites of the finite/infinite contrast. They are finite things that themselves are boundary markers of the finite and the infinite, where the elementary forms of the world have taken shape that give orienting meaning to human life, or to the life of a person or group, that signify cosmic differences. Whereas the religious symbols as imaginative elements construct the formal contours of the experiential world, as interpreted they represent the real world as having those contours too. It is not just the imaginative conception of Yahweh binding himself to Israel in the Exodus and wilderness wandering, it is the Exodus and journey itself that is symbolized to bear the presence of Yahweh establishing the covenant. Here the indirection comes from the fact that all the elements that refer to the infinite side are borne by references to the finite side. Yahweh is not represented as only infinite but as Hebrew-speaking (and writing), fiery by night, cloudy by day, purposeful, vengeful, extraordinarily impatient, and tending to break apart mountains and destroy people when he gets too close, but also as "merciful and gracious, slow to anger, and abounding in steadfast love and faithfulness" (Exodus 34:6). Yet the symbolic account in Exodus is also filled with edges to the symbols that indicate that this is no ordinary speaker and lithographer, no merely large bonfire. The symbols intensify the finite to show that more is meant. Yahweh's "persuasions" of the Egyptians start with magicians' tricks but quickly move to threaten Egyptian identity by killing *all* their firstborn sons. The fire and cloud are more effective as weapons than any imaginable army. The Holy One of Israel has not negotiated an alliance with Israel but *created* a new nation that can destroy itself utterly by faithlessness. Yahweh's holiness modifies, qualifies, transforms the finite things in which it dwells, and the dwelling is always temporary, and apparently wearing on the abode.[41]

Thus religious symbols refer indirectly because of the polysemous layered and networked characters of their meanings, the diverse practical intentional contexts within which they are used (rarely for the purpose of getting a direct interpretation of the divine or sacred) and the fact that all reference is through finite worldly elements. These points will be explored in later chapters at greater length. A word here needs to be said about the dialectic of affirmation and negation in religious symbols, although that topic too will be developed at greater length in what follows.

The interpretation of religious objects that has been offered here is that they are finite things that have some world-constructing importance, either in a cosmological sense or a sense having to do with the ground, meaning, and goal of human life. Because of this importance, the real object is not the finite thing as such but the finite thing in contrast with the infinite, with its supra-finite context, with the situation that would obtain if the finite thing did not exist or have its world-constructing importance. In short, the contrast has to do with the importance of the finite thing for the contingent existence of the world, in some respect, or the world of human meaningfulness.

---

41. See the development of Yahweh's holiness as a finite/infinite contrast in sermonic terms in the homily in chapter 5.3 below.

How can we test this hypothesis about religious objects? Part of the test is the fact that it makes sense of what the sociologists have discussed as "world-construction" without requiring an implausible lack of realism about the difference between the real world and our representations of it.[42] The main part of the test, however, is to review religious symbols of all sorts to see whether it is plausible to describe their objects as finite/infinite contrasts. That review, of course, is impossible. But some initial remarks can be made in a survey defense of the hypothesis.

First, notice that all objects taken to be sacred or holy are to some extent "uncanny."[43] There is a quality about them that is extraordinary. This would not be significant if the objects were not otherwise ordinary. One's clan totem is an animal or bird like any other, except for the fact it connects the clan to the gods. The burning bush was easily recognized as a burning bush, except that it also spoke and was not consumed. The sacred *kami* stone is like any other deposited by a glacier or by a sacred stone store delivery person, except that it contains a spirit around whom one should orient oneself. The leper is cured, like any other happy patient, but by no visible medicines. Lazarus speaks; but he had earlier been dead. The holy or sacred is an uncanny transformation of what otherwise would be only ordinary, and it is a religious symbol or the object of religious symbolic interpretation precisely because it is not only ordinary. All religious symbols are surrounded by other symbols interpreting what the holiness is supposed to mean.

The Axial Age religions formed religious symbols that were explicit about referring to what is on the other side of the finite, symbols of gods who create the cosmos, or who establish laws and ways of life, gods who intervene on behalf of people in salvific ways, principles such as Heaven and Earth that compose the cosmos, the Dao that can and cannot be named, the Brahman that is the real identity of each human soul, and so forth.

Buddhism is frequently cited as an exception to the very kind of point being made here. But attend to the following myth from the text of the fourteenth-century Tibetan Rnying-ma-pa Buddhist, Klong-chen Rab-'byams-pa:

> Prior to everything, samsara and nirvana being not divided, nor dividing, nor to be divided, Samantabhadra, the teacher whose dominion is perfect, arose from the primordial ground—the expanse that is self-

---

42. For instance, Berger and Luckmann.

43. See Rudolph Otto's *The Idea of the Holy*, chapters 1–6; Van der Leeuw's *Religion in Essence and Manifestation*, Part 1, especially chapter 4.

emergent pristine cognition, the nucleus of the Sugata—as the manifestation of the ground. In the instant that he emerged from the ground, because he recognized this to be self-manifest, then owing to the three self-emergent principles he seized his imperial realm in the spontaneously present precious enclosure, the great primordial purity that is the original site of exhaustion, the field of the vase-body of youth. The enlightened attributes of renunciation and realization being perfected, he achieved buddhahood in the manner of the dharmakaya, and abides thus inwardly clarified. . . . Subsequently, from the expressive play that arises from the original ground as the manifestation of the ground, mundane creatures appeared as if bewildered without cause for bewilderment, as in a dream. Seeing them thus disturbed, his compassionate excellence was aroused.[44]

Cultures differ, of course, regarding the nature of the world and what transcends it, regarding the boundaries defined by contrasts. The

---

44. Translated by Matthew Kapstein in Kapstein, 1992, 63–64. Kapstein argues that this is not a creation myth, and the reason is that there is no creator god or demiurge (75–76). Although it appears that the ground speaks in the voice of the original Buddha, Kapstein argues that the tradition has always regarded this to be a metaphorical representation. Why does a creation myth have to have a separate creator or demiurge, however? The mystical tradition of Eckhart, for instance, would argue that God is the great abyss of nothingness from which the world emerges as a creation; for many other Western theologians, deeply wedded to the language of creation, especially creation *ex nihilo*, God becomes a determinate being only in reference to determinate creation. The point of the present theory is that the transcendent ground (in the Buddhist case) is not finite. As to the mythical terms being metaphorical, of course; if the Buddhists recognized metaphor as metaphor from the beginning, that is remarkable but does not obviate the point. The ontological issue is what the metaphor refers to. Kapstein's own theory (62) is that the myth is an attempt to resolve a three-way tension within Buddhism: that the world is thoroughly law-like, that the world contains beings whose ignorance brings them trouble, and that it is possible for these beings to overcome their ignorance and hence their troubles. With Kapstein's subtle interpretation, the myth can be shown to exercise this intellectual function. But that it has a functional role does not mean that it has no intentional reference, which he assumes it lacks. The denial of reference flies in the face of the phenomenological meaning of the myth, and could be legitimated only by the double claim that there could be no transcendent references and yet the myth must be true in some other (perhaps functional) sense. The importance of the vast ontological tradition in Buddhism is precisely to legitimate the peculiar kind of transcendence to which Buddhism appeals, contrasting the formed and empty, the illusion and the reality. The theory developed in the present text explains how the Buddhism myth can have a transcendent reference, marking an original creative "eternal" moment in which pure consciousness or clarity (Samantabhadra) arises from a ground with no division and hence no consciousness.

Mahayana Buddhist form/emptiness version of the finite/infinite contrast is strikingly different from the Jewish world/God version. Cultures
also differ both in the systems of symbols and in their histories of systems
of symbols with which they develop new symbols of the transcendent.
But there seems to be a peculiar dialectic that they all share.

On the one hand, all the symbols of the transcendent are identified
in terms of their connections with the world. On the other hand those
identifying connections all are also represented as not being the transcendent "in itself," or as it is by its own nature. The Dao that can be named
is not the true Dao. There is Brahman "with qualities" but then there is
Brahman "without qualities." Even Neo-Confucian Heaven and Earth,
when considered out of their conjunction that constitutes the world, are
not determinate. In the West this point about God was given sophisticated expression in the apophatic theology of Pseudo-Dionysius; but it
was also the answer Job got out of the whirlwind.

An elementary part of religious reflection is that the worldmaking
images, including those having to do with the human condition, are
interpreted precisely as worldmaking. Eliade called this the recognition
of the sacred.[45] The point of the reflective interpretation is that the world
is taken to be the way the dimension-shaping images represent it to be.
Of course, civilized post-mythopoeic peoples know those images are
only metaphorical, but we have no better images than our best ones.
When religions, or cultures, interpret their worldmaking images as
worldmaking, they are acknowledging that those images participate in
what lies beyond the world as well as what is in the world they define.

This is not the place to attempt a categorization of religious symbols.
It should be noted, however, that because religious symbols are definitive of cultures, and local to them, those of other cultures often seem
bizarre. Immanuel Kant, the great German philosopher, probably picked
out the two fundamental families of theistic religious symbols when he
marvelled at the sublimity of the starry sky above and the moral law
within.[46] For theistic religions, at least those deriving from West Asia,
worldliness is most often imaged as the boundaries of the physical cosmos
and the interior of the human soul as hedged by obligation. For both

---

45. In *The Sacred and the Profane* and elsewhere.

46. See his *Critique of Practical Reason*, where he begins the Conclusion, p. 166:
"Two things fill the mind with ever new and increasing admiration and awe, the oftener
and more steadily we reflect on them: the starry heavens above me and the moral law
within me."

Daoism and Confucianism, the human soul is important, not so much for its moral obligations, but for its aesthetic obligations of harmonization, some of which have moral implications; they find little of world-making religious interest in the edges of the physical cosmos but are deeply moved by a kind of interior intensity of spontaneity and perceptivity of worth. For many kinds of Mahayana Buddhism this world is an insignificant one of a number of worlds and the soul evaporates into the Buddha-mind when one turns inward, but worldliness is marked by how one relates to the arising and ceasing of experiential contents. Therefore quite different things become religiously symbolic in different religions, not just cosmos, history, and human destiny, as in the West.

The language of world-making is perhaps misleading in its cosmological connotations because most religious symbols have to do with the human sphere and how it relates to divinity. Symbols of evil and judgment, divine love and redemptive events, liturgies rehearsing salvific histories and sanctifying practices all are shaped by religious symbols. What makes these symbols religious, however, and not mere functions of traditions shaping meaning, is that the meaning involved is the relation of people to their very status relative to worldliness as such and what lies beyond that. Common elements such as bread and wine can become sacred. What makes symbols religious, whether cosmological or domestic, abstract or concrete, is that part of their reference is to the borderlines of worldliness and to what lies on the infinite side of the world's finitude.

Another way of looking at all this is by means of the distinction introduced earlier between the primary and secondary referents of religious symbols. The primary reference is to the finite/infinite contrast. But the secondary reference is to the symbolic structure of the interpreters' experience such that the world and its boundaries are conceived the way they are. For *West Asian* experience, the boundaries are at the edges of the physical cosmos. For *South Asian* experience the boundaries seem to have more to do with the sources of identity and value. For *East Asian* experience the boundaries have to do with discord and attunement. (These, of course, are crude generalizations.) But then the secondary referents are far more specific than these general structures of experience. The religious symbols refer to what would be finite/infinite contrasts for the young rather than the old, for the religiously immature rather than the mature, for women rather than men, for a person with just this spiritual situation and history rather than some other. The secondary referents are to be understood in large part in terms of the meaning-world of the individuals and groups at hand. Hence the discussion of meaning in the next chapter is an important next step. But the secondary referents become truly important in understanding religious reference mainly in the case of devotional symbols in which the state and stage of the spiritual life of the devotee determine what meanings can refer to the finite/infinite contrast, the topic of chapter 5.

# CHAPTER 3

# Finite Meaning Infinite

## 3.1. A COMPLEX MEANING: THE EUCHARIST

Precisely because religious reference is so dialectical, treating images as the border-limits of the finite and infinite, of the human and divine, religious meanings are extraordinarily complex. Whereas we might take specific things to be religious symbols, for instance the primeval tree or mountain, or an historical event creating a people such as the Exodus, or a person such as Jesus or Laozi, in fact those objects or persons function religiously only as imbedded in a rich imagistic texture of meanings. The Buddhist creation myth quoted at the end of the previous chapter is a case in point. Religious symbols are always in networks of symbol-systems. Because it is so easy to identify specific things as religious symbols without realizing how essential their networks and layers of meaning are, it will be worthwhile to give a phenomenological analysis of a symbol in some detail, one less complex than a complete mythic view of the world or a complete theology. Like a complete mythic world or a complete theology, however, this symbol with its associated symbol systems is an icon of religious reality.

For purposes of analysis the discussion will focus on the symbolic meaning of the Christian eucharist. By no means shall I give anything like a complete account of the meaning of the eucharist. Indeed, I shall attempt to prescind from those layers of meaning that have been contentious in Christian history and to discriminate only the blandly general elements of meaning on which nearly all Christians in nearly all ages and places would agree.[1] Scholars of Christianity will be embarrassed by the brevity

---

1. What a foolish generalization to attempt! Nevertheless, readers will be prompted by it to think of one exception after another, all even better illustrating the levels of complexity I mean to point out.

and swiftness with which whole symbol systems of meaning are sketched; entire volumes have been written, often in contention with alternatives, about the meanings summarized here in a paragraph or two. My point is to illustrate some of the complexities of symbolic meaning, however, not to develop a finally acceptable interpretation of the eucharist.[2]

It might seem as if the Christian eucharist is already too complicated a symbol. Things would not really be simplified, however, if we were to discuss the theological symbol of the Trinity, or the prayerful symbolic gesture of kneeling. Besides, the belief that analysis should begin with simple examples is a false Enlightenment belief, false because nothing is simple and the appearance of simplicity is attained by a complicated act of abstraction whose assumptions are hidden behind the thing abstracted. Furthermore, no theory is good if it handles only the obvious; a theory needs to handle hard cases. Even so generally approached, the meaning of the eucharist as religious symbol falls into at least nine layers.

The first layer of meaning is that the eucharist involves food, the bread and wine. The bread and wine have a double meaning that is emblematic of the central double figure of the crucifixion and resurrection. On the one hand they are emblems of the broken body and spilled blood of Jesus in the crucifixion. They symbolize his pain and suffering, not only in the crucifixion itself but all the vicissitudes of his life. They also indicate that much of his suffering—all so far as we know from the Christian gospels— came from the misunderstanding, ill-will, or contrary preoccupations of others. Both his religious establishment and the judicial establishment turned against him despite his innocence. Consuming the eucharistic elements thus means in part that the worshipper accepts the life in which one bears a cross, the life in which there is suffering and pain, perhaps premature death, surely much incomprehension, failure, fragmentation, and all the other kinds of disabilities characterizing Jesus' life.

On the other hand the elements of bread and wine are emblems of nourishment, of new life in resurrection, new growth, new joy. Psalm 104:15 lists wine and bread, along with oil for the face, to be special

---

2. Readers might want to consult Laurence Hull Stookey's *Eucharist: Christ's Feast with the Church* for a fulsome though still schematic development of the elements of the eucharist. He does detail some of the major controversies of interpretation, such as over the transubstantiation doctrine, and he gives a far more complete discussion of the history of the eucharist than my text does. Moreover, he describes several actual eucharistic services so that those who have not attended might know what goes on. On one useful level, his is a liturgist's how-to-do-it book.

divine graces for gladdening and strengthening the human heart. (The early Christian symbologists did not neglect the reference to oil, either, in their recounting of the annointing of Jesus with nard just before Passover, Mark 14:3–9.) The eucharistic meal is the nourishment of the baptized, those awaiting the triumphant meal with Jesus in heaven; Matthew 26:20, Luke 22:28–30.

The double figure of crucifixion and resurrection in Christianity means that the Christian rises to new life through faithfulness to God while embracing life that is a series of crosses. Therefore, consuming the eucharistic elements means taking in nourishment for a new life that rises out of the brokenness and suffering of ordinary life in which Christians find God. The double meaning of bread and wine as food, both suffering and nourishment, has synchronic network connections with the symbols of crucifixion and resurrection and all they mean in turn. Hardly any symbol within the Christian life is out of touch with the network meanings of the eucharistic elements.

The second layer of meaning employs the broken-body, spilt-blood imagery of the crucifixion to associate Jesus with the sacrificial lamb whose death atones for human sin. This symbol system is controversial today and will be examined in much greater detail in chapter 6 where the entire symbolic strategy of the atonement as an explication of the mechanism of salvation is criticized. The root of the sacrificial imagery is the tradition of temple sacrifice described in the Torah. The underlying logic is that human beings have broken the Mosaic covenant with Yahweh by sin or ritual impurity and need some way to repair it. Nothing human beings can do on their own can repair things from Yahweh's end. So Yahweh devises the sacrificial procedures as something people can do to reestablish the covenant relation. The important point is that the rubrics of the sacrifice rituals are a gift from Yahweh, offering a way back into the covenant. That people have to give up something, some grain, a pigeon, a goat, lamb, or ox, does not mean they buy their way back in, only that they recognize something of the value of their deviance; all grains and animals are Yahweh's anyway, and Yahweh has no need of them. Christian atonement imagery embellishes this, representing Jesus Christ as the sacrificial lamb (in the Torah the animal was a goat). Some versions of the atonement sacrifice say that only a creature as great as God's own Son could be a sacrifice deep enough to redeem human sin. Because so many of the sacrificial rituals of the Torah had to do with cleansing after ritual impurity, "washing in the blood of the lamb" became a Christian symbol for purification. The strength of the

sacrificial imagery is that it resists the reduction of sin to mere moral cul-
pability; as Ricoeur has shown, stain and impurity signify an even deeper
sense of sin than immorality.[3] This level of meaning connects the sacrificial symbol system with all the other symbolic meanings of the blood
of Christ. Yet another symbol system associated with the atonement sacrifice is to liken Jesus to the sacrificial lamb (or goat) that was ritually
slaughtered on the eve of the Exodus from Egypt and whose blood on
the door warned the angel of death away from killing first-born Hebrew
boys; in this symbol system, Jesus the sacrificial lamb takes the place of
the first-born who is marked for death.

The third layer of meaning in the eucharist consists in the fact that
it is a common meal. Typically it is celebrated by members of a congregation in attendance at the liturgy. But part of the meaning of its commonality is that this congregation joins with all the other congregations
across the world. Indeed, the meal is really a continuance of the meals
the congregation had in the past and that Christians through the ages
have eaten. Whereas baptism is the universal symbolic entry into the
Christian community, the eucharist is the symbolic exercise of membership. Of course much else is involved in membership in the Christian
movement than the eucharistic liturgy, and this has varied widely over
time and place. But the eucharist, despite its various forms of celebration,
symbolizes the continuities and solidarities of the Church. To twist the
symbolic imagery only slightly, the eucharistic meal is the way the Body
of Christ takes nourishment.

In addition to the solidarity of the community thus signified, there
is a fourth layer of meaning in that the common meal is a reenactment
of Jesus' table fellowship. The common supper was one of the principal
contexts in which Jesus taught his disciples. More than that, it was where
they became friends, took on interrelating roles, learned to care for one
another, and became a community. Most of all, it was where, with food
and wine, they came to enjoy one another's company, particularly the
company of Jesus. That kind of friendship and colleagiality is paradigmatic
for human relations within Christian communities, a foretaste of heaven
which is also sometimes symbolized as a feast. Christians should be able
to know one another, share stories, celebrate good things and bear one
another up under bad things, joke together, work out angers, tease, and
take pleasure in one another as people do who have ideal table fellowship.

---

3. See Paul Ricoeur's *The Symbolism of Evil*, 1967.

The liturgy of the eucharist itself is not table fellowship but an emblem of that. In his instructions for the eucharist Paul told the Corinthians (1 Corinthians 11:17–34) to have dinner at home first precisely because the Corinthian congregation could not manage a living table fellowship. But a truly important layer of meaning in the eucharist is its reference to that early paradigm of community instituted by Jesus himself.

A fifth layer of meaning is that the eucharist is a commemoration of Jesus as an historical figure. It is a reenactment of the Last Supper just before the crucifixion and resurrection. Those events were not accidental but came out of what Jesus had been and done, his ministry, his ill-fit with the political and religious establishment, his teachings and the preparation of disciples, and all the other things that made up the historical particularity of his life. By remembering Jesus, especially through the focal drama of Passion Week, participants in the eucharist locate themselves in their own particularity as disciples of Jesus. There is a particular historical chain of events from the life of Jesus down to his remote followers that gives those followers identity, perhaps the main part of their identity. Christians are defined particularly by a lineage, and the commemoration of Jesus is an abbreviated rehearsal of that lineage.

A sixth layer is the symbolic network that consists in the meaning of the words of institution. Within Christian symbolism, Jesus himself is the incarnation of the Word of God through which the very creation was accomplished. The prologue to John's gospel says this in so many words:

> In the beginning was the Word, and the Word was with God, and the Word was God. All things came into being through him, and without him not one thing came into being. . . . And the Word became flesh and lived among us, and we have seen his glory, the glory as of a father's only son, full of grace and truth. (John 1:1–3, 14)

The baptism scenes in the synoptic gospels say it indirectly. Mark, for instance, says

> In those days Jesus came from Nazareth of Galilee and was baptized by John in the Jordan. And just as he was coming up out of the water, he saw the heavens torn apart and the Spirit descending like a dove on him. And a voice came from heaven, "You are my Son, the Beloved; with you I am well pleased." (Mark 1:9–11)

The symbolic elements are those of Genesis 1: primeval water, divine wind or spirit, and the Voice that makes something out of these. The symbolic resonances of the divine Word in Jesus are triggered when the words of institution say "this is my body" and "this cup is the new covenant in my blood." The Word that creates the world is the Word that creates a new reality in the Christian community centered around the eucharist. For Christians, this is not just a religious rite among others, but a rite that accomplishes a new reality.[4] Perhaps in all religions the important rites are of this sort. Of course, the network connections of the eucharist with Christology are vast and the eucharist does not signify the whole Christological story. But its connections with Christology are a significant layer of meaning.

The layers of meaning discussed so far all refer to the synchronic networks of symbolic references we can presume to be intended self-consciously from the first centuries of the Christian era. These, however, grew upon more ancient historical symbolic resonances that might not have been recognized as such in Christian times.

The seventh layer of meaning comes from the fact that Christianity arose during a period of severe cultural dislocation. From the sixth century B.C.E. to perhaps the rise of Islam in the seventh century C.E. multicultural empires held sway. These created the conditions of the Axial Age, as Jaspers has called it, which forced individuals to define their personal identity and their moral responsibilities in ways that transcend traditional cultural definition.[5] Because of the unification of China on the one hand, and India on the other, as well as the succession of Near Eastern empires— Babylonian, Assyrian, Neo-Babylonian, Persian, Hellenic, and Roman— people were forced into a broader ecumene than was defined by their local tradition. Often people had to speak a putatively universal language such as Koine Greek as well as, or in preference to, their native tongue. Often they were moved from their home village with its graveyard to foreign parts, usually to anonymous cities. When individuals could no longer define themselves in terms of clan, village, and graveyard, they had to seek definition as individuals per se. The great religions of the Axial Age—Daoism, Buddhism, Confucianism, Hinduism, Zoroastrianism, Judaism, Christianity, and finally Islam—offered ways of relating first to the Ultimate and then to folk of choice, not kin, and to places of unpre-

---

4. I suspect there are very few rites in any religion of which it could be said it "is just a religious rite among others." All rites are intended to accomplish some work, if the theory presented in 1.1 above about ritual as the work of orienting the people to the ultimate is plausible.

5. See Jaspers *The Way to Wisdom*, chapter 9. Jaspers figures the Axial Age to have been from 800–200 B.C.E.

dictable destiny. Christianity is clearly a religion of this type. It celebrates a direct relation to God and a religious community of those who choose it rather than are born in it. The eucharist celebrates this in the fact that those who come to partake of the common meal themselves choose to come. The table fellowship accepts those of no kinship relation, those of backgrounds as diverse as Jew and gentile, community outcasts such as prostitutes and embezzlers, and those whose language and customs are different save for the sharing of the Spirit. In the background of the eucharist is the recognition that others who are partaking are vastly different from oneself, and the community is not what a traditional society might expect. In our own time, this pluralism and search for individual identity in a world bereft of traditional determination is extremely important. The eucharist has come to seem more important than before in this layer for people acutely aware of the pluralism of our age.

The eighth layer of meaning refers back behind the Axial Age to the advent of civilization in which the most important problem was the establishment of law and order. Or at least order. Civilization arose when agricultural methods and circumstances allowed for the feeding of a larger population than was required for agricultural work alone. Surpluses required a protective army of soldiers who were non-producers and they also allowed for a burgeoning of population with producers of commodities and scholars whose profession was to contemplate holy things and predict when to repair the dikes. The simple rules of clan governance were inadequate for this situation. Orders of justice, which treated people as citizens rather than as sisters or uncles, had to be imposed, and the imposition fell to strong people, usually men, who developed the office of warrior king. Axial Age civilizations in China, India, and West Asia grew up on earlier civilizations in which kingship or leadership had been established as a paradigmatic office. Yahweh was surely modeled on the warrior king who led Israel out of Egypt and established the kingdoms around Zion. The idea of the Messiah was a particular adaptation of this, emphasizing the righteousness of the king who not only protects people from external enemies but regulates internal justice protecting widows, orphans, and the poor who were victimized by the prevailing social order. When Jesus is addressed as Lord, which is the presupposition in the eucharist, and when he himself used the image of the Kingdom of God, the pre-Axial Age concern for the imposition of just order is involved. Feminists have pointed out the overwhelmingly male orientation of the concern for lordship, the imposition of just order to establish the reign of God. However biased, it is part of the meaning of the liturgy acknowledging the Lordship of Christ over Christians' table fellowship, community, and work.[6]

The ninth layer of meaning is rarely acknowledged because its archaeologically deep heritage is so remote and threatening. It is the nevertheless obvious point of cannibalism, eating the flesh and blood of Jesus Christ, however metaphorically that is taken.[7] Cannibalism itself is a reli-

---

6. I have tried to state this thumbnail sketch of the rise of civilization and the role of imposed order in it as vaguely as possible to make it seem innocuously true. See the works of world history such as William McNeill's *The Rise of the West* that compare the rise of civilizations in Egypt, Mesopotamia, India, and China. Concerning the feminist point, Tikva Frymer-Kensky's *In the Wake of the Goddesses* which details how the fairly even distribution of goddesses and gods, in their authority over matters of civilized life, in the early Sumerian empire became biased in favor of the gods. That is, activities such as writing and singing state laments, which were originally women's work under the supervision of goddesses, were taken over by gods and men. By the time of the Biblical Yahweh, he had both the maternal and paternal roles. Does this suggest that ever increasing numbers of people and complexity in civilization required ever more coercive means to impose order, with coercion being a male prerogative, or at least something easier with greater upper body strength? Even when Yahweh like a mother nourished the children of Israel with manna from heaven while they fled from Egypt, the primary image of Yahweh was that of the warrior leader.

7. The traditional words of institution are similar in Matthew 26:26–29, Mark 14:22–25, and Luke 22:14–22; also 1 Corinthians 11:23–26. Matthew's version is:

> While they were eating, Jesus took a loaf of bread, and after blessing it he broke it, gave it to the disciples, and said, "Take, eat; this is my body." Then he took a cup, and after giving thanks he gave it to them, saying, "Drink from it, all of you; for this is my blood of the covenant, which is poured out for many for the forgiveness of sins. I tell you, I will never again drink of this fruit of the vine until that day when I drink it new with you in my Father's kingdom."

The Gospel of John associates a foot-washing ritual with the last supper instead of the eucharistic blessing, and cites Jesus' eucharistic words instead as part of his answer to the angry response of people to his feeding five thousand people with five barley loaves and two fish, John 6:5–14. Jesus claimed himself to be the bread of life, John 6:35, 51, and then said, John 6:53–58:

> "Very truly, I tell you, unless you eat the flesh of the Son of Man and drink his blood, you have no life in you. Those who eat my flesh and drink my blood have eternal life, and I will raise them up on the last day; for my flesh is true food and my blood is true drink. Those who eat my flesh and drink my blood abide in me, and I in them. Just as the living Father sent me, and I live because of the Father, so whoever eats me will live because of me. This is the bread which came down from heaven, not like that which your ancestors ate, and they died. But the one who eats this bread will live forever."

gious symbol of the paleolithic age of hunters and gatherers. The great hunter who feeds the people is in close attunement with the forces of nature in the beasts of prey and the timeliness of their accessibility. To eat the flesh, especially the brain, of the hunter is to partake of something of his virility, of his spiritual power. Cannibals who hunt their neighbors for food are seeking the powers and virtues of those whom they consume. Just as God told Ezekiel to eat the scrolls with the divine words so as to be able to preach them (Ezekiel 3:1–3), so our primitive forebears across much of the world thought they could assume the powers of accomplished people by eating them. Why else would Christians eat Jesus, or emblems of his flesh and blood? Civilized people, of course, are not cannibals because that requires murder, which is against just order and is forbidden by the king. But civilized people perform cannibalism in symbolic form for the same reason paleolithic people ate one another's flesh: the hope of assuming their power, especially sacred power. What Christian does not want to incorporate Christ? The food of the eucharist is the body and blood of Jesus, however symbolically that is interpreted. The eucharist is only symbolically cannibalistic because that layer of primitive meaning was overlaid by an archaeologically subsequent layer insisting on the order of justice and condemning murder.[8]

These nine layers of meaning, as well as a host of others not mentioned, enter into the symbolic meaning of the eucharist. Even these are very generally stated. They do not get to the issues that separate Roman Catholics from Orthodox and Protestants, let alone those that separate Lutherans from Calvinists. These layers of meaning have been so vaguely stated here as to make little or no reference to the liturgical and material forms in which the eucharist is celebrated. But even at this very general level it is apparent how complex its symbolic meaning is and a discussion of the complexities of this brief discrimination of symbolic layers has general significance. The rest of this chapter will develop some of this general significance, illustrated by the analysis of the eucharist, in three parts. Section

---

8. The eucharist is explicit in symbolizing that the cannibalism is only symbolic. Part of the background of the controversies over transubstantiation has to do with keeping the distance from the real body and blood of Jesus while also asserting a real connection or presence. But bread and wine are obviously symbols of human flesh and blood. If the early church had given that symbolic significance to rare roast lamb *au jus*, which Jesus and the disciples probably also ate at the Last Supper, the archaic psychodynamics of cannibalism might have been too close to the surface, not sufficiently distanced as symbolically symbolic.

3.2 will develop some formal structural distinctions regarding symbols. Section 3.3 will analyze the notion of network meaning already used informally, and relate network meaning to what I call "content meaning." Section 3.4 then returns to the analysis of the eucharist and show various senses in which its symbols refer to the infinite in finite/infinite contrasts.

3.2. THE STRUCTURE OF SYMBOLS

Some further distinctions need to be made before proceeding with an analysis of kinds of meaning in which religious symbol systems are involved. Three distinctions will be made: between symbolic schemata and symbolic schema-images, between symbols and symbolic replicas, and between symbolic complexes and symbolic fragments.

Kant distinguished between imaginative schemata and schema-images.[9] The schema for a circle, for instance, is a line the points on which are all equidistant from a point outside the line. The schema is the inner logic of the symbol. A schema-image of the schema of a circle, however, is a round plate or a hubcap.[10] A schema-image is something in experience or imagination that embodies the logic of the schema but need not be interpreted in terms of the schema. So plates might be interpreted in respect of food rather than circularity and hubcaps in respect of shininess. Schemata themselves are imaginative symbolic forms that

---

9. In his *Critique of Pure Reason*, the chapter on "The Schematism of the Pure Concepts of Understanding," B176–187.

10. See Kant, *op. cit.*, B181.

> This much only we can assert: the *image* is a product of the empirical faculty of reproductive imagination; the *schema* of sensible concepts, such as of figures in space, is a product and, as it were, a monogram, of pure *apriori* imagination, through which, and in accordance with which, images themselves first become possible. These images can be connected with the concept only by means of the schema to which they belong. In themselves they are never completely congruent with the concept.

Kant's theory of imagination, especially as expressed in the A edition of the Transcendental Deduction in the *Critique of Pure Reason*, is very important for the theory of imagination I have defended in the previous chapter and in *Reconstruction of Thinking*. I do not, however, accept Kant's strong claims for a pure and transcendental *apriori*. My account, like that in the A edition Deduction rather than the B edition, is more genetic; at best, schemata are *apriori* for schema-images only in a sense like C. I. Lewis's "pragmatic *apriori*."

translate realities (Kant said "Pure Concepts," but that was a limit of his idealism) into the imaginative stuff of experience. The realities cannot be expressed or experienced except as schematized. This is another way of saying that imagination is what makes experiential engagement possible.

Analogously we need to distinguish religious symbolic schemata from religious symbolic schema-images. Two of Kant's own examples illustrate the point. I mentioned earlier that he thought two things especially sublime, where the finite and infinite meet: the starry sky above and the moral law within. Obviously people had been looking reverently at the night sky ever since Homo sapiens looked up. Although in each case it was a particular sky, with particular arrangements of stars that on no two nights could be exactly alike, all had the qualities of immensity and people could get the general idea or image of the night sky. These various sky-views are schema images of Kant's infinite sublimity. Many people, of course, looked at the sky without thinking of sublimity or infinity, just as people can look at plates with respect to food and not see circularity. If other people, however, thought the night sky signals infinity or unmeasurable vastness or something else defining religious depth, they were taking the sky to be more than the vision recorded on their retina. They took the schema-image to bear the religious symbolic schema of the cosmic edge itself. Otherwise Kant's point would not be comprehensible. His point holds for people in the Southern Hemisphere whose sky he never saw, it holds for astronauts on the moon, and it most likely would hold for people or percipient sentient beings on planets in other galaxies with a night sky.

An analogous point could be made about the schema and schema-image of the moral law. Every inner sense of morality is culturally conditioned: Kant's Prussian sensibility regarding duty lies in humorous contrast with a Sicilian sensibility; but Prussians and Sicilians can agree on Kant's point that duty is a religious symbolic schema for the ontological foundation of conscience while having quite different schema-images of what duties are. The religious symbolic schema of the great World Tree or the cosmic mountain doubtless arose because people saw some particular big trees and mountains which became for them schema-images. Persons such as Moses, Jesus, Confucius, Krishna, or Buddha can become symbols of religious depth, each in different senses in these examples, because the particular images of them get to be interpreted in light of more basic religious symbolic schemata. When this happens, the ordinary images of the person, the mountain, the tree, the moral sense, or the night sky are transformed into schema-images of religious symbolic schemata. Some hasty phenomenologists of religion might be tempted to derive a large-scale classification of possible religious symbolic schemata that can be approached through various, perhaps inconsistent, religious schema-images. Whether a univocal and universal set of religious symbolic schemata exists, however, is an empirical matter to be studied after proper comparative categories are developed.

It would seem that the schema-image precedes its schema. We first directly encounter plates, Buddha, Confucius, Krishna, the night sky, and moral duties, and then we come to see them as images of more basic schemata. But in fact things are taken to be schema-images only insofar as the relation to the schema is also affirmed. People can relate to all these things which might also be schema-images without interpreting them as schema-images at all; prophets have no honor in their own country.

Whereas the meanings of religious symbols lock their schema-images into the logic of their schemata, it is through the logic of the schemata, not the schema-images alone, that reference is made to the finite/infinite contrast. The wine and bread of the eucharist, on the first layer of meaning, are schema-images of the schemata of Jesus' suffering and death on the one hand and his resurrection on the other. The death and resurrection make direct reference to the finite/infinite contrast that Christians take to define what is important in human life. The cross and empty tomb are also schema-images of those schemata respectively. Wine, bread, cross, and sepulcher are religious symbols because they are schema-images of schemata that refer to some finite/infinite contrast. The finite/infinite contrast cannot be experienced or imagined except through some schemata. What we call a religious symbol can be either a schema of some finite/infinite contrast or a schema-image of that. Most people identify the symbol in terms of the schema image, and may not be conscious of the fact that the interpretations they make of it are really functions of the logic of the schema through which reference is made to the finite/infinite contrast. Both schemata and schema-images can be interpreted and exegeted by other symbols. This illustrates another dimension of the complexity of indirect reference discussed in 2.4

A second distinction needs to be set alongside that of schemata and schema-images. Charles Peirce distinguished between a sign, which is always general in some sense, and a replica of the sign, which is always particular.[11] Both religious symbolic schemata and schema-images are

---

11. See Peirce, CP 2.315.

signs, whereas instances of them are replicas. Any wine or bread will do for the eucharist because any can be schema-images of death and resurrection, suffering and nourishment. But the symbolic act of the eucharist involves some particular bread and wine. Storekeepers will not think of their particular loaves and bottles as replicas of religious symbols unless they closely associate themselves also with the eucharist. But communicants will see the particular loaf and cup as replicas of the religious symbols, both schema-images and the schemata. The cross is a schema-image within Christianity of a religiously important part of Jesus' life; the crosses on altars, walls, and around necks are replicas or tokens. The biblical text is a vast set of schema-images of religious symbolic schemata; the Gideon Bibles in hotel drawers individually are replicas. Most if not all religious symbols have actuality only by means of existentially particular replicas. The eucharistic elements in a given liturgy are particular bread and wine actually blessed and consumed.

Yet a third distinction needs to be observed, namely between symbolic complexes and symbolic fragments. Any religious symbol of importance or history has a multitude of layers of meaning. The symbolic meaning of the Christian eucharist, for instance, has meaning as symbolic food, as a common meal, as a commemoration of Jesus, as an artifact of the creative Word, as a form of religious practice in a world of alienated traditions, as an expression of the political metaphor of the reign of Christ as Lord in the Kingdom of God, and as a cannibal ritual. Each of these layers has network meanings connecting it with other religiously symbolic matters, and non-religious matters. Much of the time when we talk about religious symbols we mean the whole complex. Some of the time we mean only one or several of the parts of the symbol, being concerned, say, with the quality of a particular way of celebrating the eucharist as a common meal. What makes the fragment religious are its roles in the larger symbol complex even though it can be interpreted on its own and perhaps with explicit exclusion of or inattention to other fragments in the complex.

Much attention has been called in recent years by Hans Frei and others to narrative structure in religious disclosure and by phenomenologists of religion such as van der Leeuw and Eliade to mythic complexes, narrative and otherwise.[12] I argued in 2.1 that myths and narratives have both an internal semiotic structure within which symbols are extensionally inter-

---

12. See Frei's *The Eclipse of Biblical Narrative* and *Types of Christian Theology;* Van der Leeuw's *Religion in Essence and Manifestation* and Eliade's *History of Religious Ideas.*

preted in terms of one another and also an external semiotic function in which they serve as signs intentionally referred to reality and disclosive in their whole texture. As reconstructed by the distinction between symbol complexes and symbol fragments, the interpretations of things within the narrative and mythic structures are matters of symbolic fragments. The interpretation of life in terms of the myth or narrative itself is a use of them as symbol complexes. It makes no difference whether the story as a whole is called a "single complex symbol" or a "symbol complex." Most particular interpretations use symbol fragments identified as schema-images, and refer and interpret these fragments according to the logic of the schema of that fragment which fits into the logic of the schema of the entire myth or narrative, the schema of the symbol complex. This is another example of the complexities of indirect reference.

An actual symbol complex requires either replicas or the habit of replicating it. Thus the eucharist as a symbol complex is not only the idea of the eucharist, the directions for speaking and acting, and the schematic and schema-imagistic meanings involved. It also requires the actual celebration, with particular bread, wine, people, a particular recitation of the words of institution in a particular quality of voice, and so on. Even when we are talking about those religious symbols that are theological ideas, their actuality must include also their being thought by someone, or the readiness of someone to think them. In our discussions of religious symbols, even when seeming to make reference to the whole complex, we usually ignore their actuality and assume that nothing important is involved in their replication.

The point of the distinction between symbol complexes and fragments is to raise to consciousness the fact that sometimes fragments on their own do not refer to finite/infinite contrasts. Only when interpreted as parts of a larger complex do they do so. The symbolic complex of which fragments are parts is itself an icon for religious reality. Yet it is perfectly legitimate to call a fragment a "religious symbol," bearing in mind its place in the larger context. For instance, some Christian communities associate different colors with different liturgical seasons and deck the eucharistic table and priestly garments accordingly. Discussions by liturgists of the colors as religious symbols can be quite detailed and elaborate, but what makes them religious is their connections with the larger complexes in which distinctions of liturgical seasons are schema-images for the Christian schemata of divine redemption.

The importance of the distinctions drawn in this section can be illustrated further with reference to several examples, beginning with the eucharistic ones. The schema of the meal itself is the very general idea of drawing divinity into oneself, or changing oneself into the divine. The Christian twists on the schema have to do with the attitude toward suffering and the relation of life to death. The schema images are those of the meal, the ingestion of bread and wine. The acts of eating at repeated eucharistic liturgies are replicas of the schematized images. The bread and wine themselves are fragments of the larger story of Jesus' life that can serve to image joining with divinity only in connection with interpretations of who Jesus was supposed to be, the events of the last supper, the larger symbolic resonances of bread and wine, and so forth.

The schema in the level of meaning having to do with solidarity with other participants in the eucharistic liturgy is the idea that humankind as a whole has a religious problem, not just certain people, and that the response to the problem expressed in the liturgy is a matter of human solidarity. Anyone who is human might be a eucharistic participant. The schema-image is the concrete act that anyone can replicate, namely, the participation in the meal in any number of forms. That schema-image is a fragment of a larger system and articulates who should come to the meal and why; similarly, the schema itself is a fragment of a larger scheme relating individuals to humankind.

The level of meaning associated with table fellowship itself has as its schema the proper relations between persons, expressed generally as love but particularly as the friendship, communication, instruction, and learning about one another's identity that can be schematized in concrete imagery as the kind of meal Jesus had with his disciples. The schema-image for relations between persons is the meal, the schema is the ideal for those relations. Replication here means not only the many instances of the eucharist but also the fact that eating together frequently is necessary for table fellowship to be what it needs to be in order to be a schema image of true friendship. The table fellowship is but a fragment of the larger practices of Jesus teaching, healing, and leading his disciples about the countryside and cities.

The level of eucharistic meaning commemorating Jesus' historical life has as its schema the continuity of transpersonal individual identity, that is, that Christians are part of something larger than themselves that has personal characteristics. The schema-image is the church in its historical continuities as the body of Christ, activated in the celebration of the eucharist. In this sense, each individual Christian is not a replication of a general Christian norm but rather a unique if minor extension of the particularity of the historical existence of Jesus-plus-church. The complex schema-image of which this commemorative element is a fragment is the whole of symbolic ecclesiology or the understanding and organization of the church, including the division into different churches.

The schema of the level of meaning associated with the I Am elements in the words of institution has already been mentioned as the creation of things. The schema-image is the voice that calls things into being, perhaps the voice of the king but construed as much more fundamental. In the eucharistic there is a nesting of symbolic schema-images from the specific words of Jesus to the explicit use of I Am language in John's gospel as noted above to the I Am language of the Hebrew Bible to the mystery of creative evocative voice that Biblical religion shares with Hindu devotion to Vac. The other side of this level of eucharistic meaning is that the participants become new beings. The schematic idea here is that of human renovation, and the schema-image is that people become like Jesus and parts of his extended ministry. That this is replicated in each eucharistic service acknowledges the point that becoming a New Being is a slow process.

The schema in the Axial Age level of meaning is the relation of the individual to God, which is required to be a matter of freedom. The schema-image is the voluntariness in the joining of the fellowship. Furthermore, the capacity for free response to the divine is a universal characteristic of being human, in this schema, and is more important than other characteristics that might divide people. Therefore, the eucharistic schema-image admits people of all types to the table fellowship, based on their free confession of loyalty to Jesus as Lord, about which more shortly. The Christian schema-image is only one of several, others being found in other Axial Age religions, each of which schematizes the point about free human response and responsibility to God. The eucharist is obviously a fragment of the much larger symbolic complex that includes table fellowship as mentioned above, stressing the difficulties of making friends with very different people.

The level of meaning associated in the eucharist with Lordship has the schema of divine initiative and human response. The order in the world that is most real is that imposed by God and to which human beings need to be obedient or deferential. This is schematized in the images of the kingdom of God and deference to Jesus as annointed Lord. These of course are fragments of larger symbolic complexes of human beings lying under obligation. There is another schema of Lordship, less evident in the eucharist, namely that of the human quest to find something or someone to whom to be devoted. Christians have found their

Lord in Jesus and their devotion can rest there. Both schemata of Lordship have to do with devotion to a sacred person and the tasks set by that person. Most religions have some schema-image or other for Lordship in the senses of both schemata.

The cannibalistic level of meaning has a similar schema to the first level having to do with food, namely, becoming or joining with the divine by eating it. At the cannibalistic level the special twists are taking on the virtues of the ancestor or hero. The same schema is to be found in the Confucian rituals of filial piety in which the children are to take on the virtues of the ancestors. Whereas the Confucians develop schema-images of acts of deference, the cannibals and Christians develop schema-images of eating, incorporating. Because in the eucharist it is symbols of the flesh and blood of Jesus that are consumed, the cannibalism is set in a wider complex that negotiates the substitutes of bread and wine, replicated by the specific loaves and chalices full in the particular celebration.

These remarks about the eucharist illustrate certain aspects of the distinctions between schemata and schema-images, between symbols and replicas, and between symbolic complexes and symbolic fragments. Consider also the following symbols, the first of which has already been mentioned, heaven, and the subsequent four of which will be treated in 5.3–4, fire, water, the abyss, and light. Each of these is a symbol that can occur in many contexts.

Heaven is a schema-image consisting of an icon derived from a customary or idealized representation of earthly life that schematizes the idea of a person relating closely to the divine without complete identity. Heaven schematizes the human-divine relation by spatializing it: there is distance between the person and God, yet the space is filled with connecting places. Heavenly space differs from ordinary space because the divine can occupy a position there, though not, at least not easily, in ordinary space. Heaven is related to, and involved in, the schema-image of the spiritual journey in which one approaches (or fails to find) the divine; the journey involves an essential reference to time, as heaven does not. The geography of heaven is variously appointed, like a garden, a house with many rooms, a banquet hall, a place of reunion with dead friends, and so forth, all imaging people's spatial proximity to the divine. When the divine is imaged as in heaven, it is as a being who occupies a place; much of the plausibility of the personalistic symbols of God comes from the fact that in heaven God must be in a place, only a being can be in a place, and if God is a being then the being is at least as complex and excellent as a person. Schemata of the divine-human relation that do not have to maintain connection without complete identity, such as utter alienation or complete identity in beatific or mystical vision, do not require the spatialization characteristic of schema-images of heaven.

The next four symbols—fire, water, the abyss, and light—are far more abstract than most discussed so far; yet each is a schema-image of one (or several) fundamental religious schemata of finite/infinite contrasts. Fire is the schema-image of spontaneous holiness, and that in several dimensions. It images creativity, as in the Vedic Agni-fire ritual, or in the mystical philosophy of Boehme. It images the implied judgment in holiness, as in the refiner's fire or the coal that purified Isaiah's lips (Isaiah 6), or in an eschatalogical conflagration. It images the tempering of the worshipper to prepare for meeting the holy, the refinement of dross. The interesting thing about the schema behind fire is that it is a kind of spontaneous activity in which the divine constitutes itself as holy. Fire seems to come from nothing and exists only in its activities. Fire is a schema-image of divine spontaneous self-constitution of holiness while doing something such as create a world, motivate Moses, purify Isaiah, or, as in the Agni-fire, to recreate the heaven of the Gods. To meet God going through fire is to encounter the holy in the activity of being itself. When Yahweh descended to Mt. Sinai to talk with Moses, he nearly burned the whole mountain (Exodus 19:16–25).

Water, by contrast, is the schema-image of that which is deep, permanent, difficult, unstable, and yet the medium of religious achievement. Crossing the river to the other side is a symbol of salvation in Buddhism, Judaism, and Christianity. Currents are swift, waters are stormy, they teem with sea monsters; and yet with the presence of the divine they are buoyant. Water is a symbol of the infinite density of life. Its practical implications have to do with faith and skill in navigating the depths. Behind all this, water is a symbol of the infinite density of chaos before creation of form, a chaos through which we can live if we are connected to the divine that manages chaos. To accept life is to launch out through the water, with faith, courage, and hope that the God who brings order out of wind and wave will carry one over in the power of the Buddha, the Dharma, and the Sangha.

The abyss is the schema-image of the infinite as not needing the finite, as prior to or unconditioned by the finite. The abyss is approached by stepping over the verge of the finite; it is a place (or non-place) we get to by going to the edge, or by imagining the world explicitly emptied of all the things that give it definition. By contrast to the unconditioned abyss, we are conditioned by dependency on the fruitfulness of the abyss.

Spiritually to step off into the abyss is to commit oneself to the indefinite, abandoning all means of self-definition. The abyss can be fearsome beyond measure, or true home.

Divine light, by contrast, schematizes the perfect presence of the divine in all the finite things, making them be what they are and illuminating that without distortion. Wholly and infinitely positive, as light contains all colors, light is the schema-image of a doubled schema, namely the creative power perfectly and immediately present and suffusing all created things and at the same time being more real and important—glorious—than any or all the things. On the first side, divine light is complete illumination; on the second, blinding. Both are schema-images of pure divine presence.

These five symbols—heaven, fire, water, the abyss, and light—are schema-images of five central aspects of finite/infinite contrasts, at least as symbolized in some traditions: relation, spontaneity, infinite density, unconditionedness, and presence. Different traditions pack these symbols in systems differently, with different specific images, and often with twists and shifts of meaning in the elementary schemata. I am not suggesting, as a Kantian might, that the schemata are apriori religious universals. The generality of their occurance is an empirical matter. Nevertheless, I am suggesting that the way the schema-images work is a function of the logic of the schemata they schematize. In this quick sketch of the symbols in terms of their schemata and schema-images, it has been easier to begin with the latter and infer back to the former—and my method has been more intuitive than analytical here. One could also attempt to move the other way—from schemata to a variety of schema-images that would schematize them. Either way, when reflecting on religious symbols, it is important to see what schemata lie within as the inner logic of images, how images are either general as symbols or particular as replicas, and how symbols in all these respects are often fragments of larger networks of symbolic systems. Once we are aware of these distinctions, the sense in which something is called a "religious symbol" in any particular discussion is easily made out and confusion avoided. With these distinctions in mind, we can turn to the discussion of relations among symbols, of their connections in networks or systems.

### 3.3. NETWORK MEANING AND CONTENT MEANING

The discussion several times has made reference to symbol systems as networks of meaning where on a given level several other meaning systems are engaged. Much of the richness of religious symbols comes from the complexity of network meaning. Because of this, no religious symbol has only one meaning, or even one cluster of interdefined meanings. Networks lead inference from one cluster of meanings, one set of inter-defined symbols, to another. This needs further analysis with some technical distinctions.

*Network* is general, in the technical way I define the term here, with respect to two senses, system and overlay.[13] Systems are synchronic networks and overlays are discursive networks. The first is most obvious. With regard to signs, their systems include their syntactical structures, their semantic meaning relations, and their pragmatic roles in interpretation. We may set aside the last of those three as a major topic in chapter 4. Syntactic and semantic systematic connections are the topics of the study of the meanings of signs as such. Perhaps the distinction between syntactics and semantics has been overdrawn. At any rate, given the metaphoric character of religious symbology, the syntactic grammar of the symbols varies with their semantic meanings.

A symbol has a system of meanings in a sense explicated by Kant's thesis that concepts are rules for unifying manifolds.[14] The manifold can be conceived as the content of the concept in the sense the manifold things are the other representations that the rule in the concept legitimates as interpretations. The meaning of a symbol is expressed in other symbols in terms of which it can be interpreted, which are thus called its "interpretants." The systematic network meaning of a symbol is more encompassing than merely the other symbols that interpret it, however, for it also has to do with the systematic connections of the symbol with the various contexts in which it can be interpreted in different respects. Bread and wine can be interpreted as the body and blood of Christ in the context of a eucharistic service but not in the context of a meal at Musial and Biggie's Restaurant in St. Louis. Within a eucharistic service they can be interpreted as signs of the solidarity of the Christian move-

---

13. I first drew a distinction between network and content meaning in *The Tao and the Daimon*, chapter 11. The discussion here is an extension of that early presentation but adds many nuances and also some shifts in emphasis. The distinction between system and overlay networks is an example.

14. *Critique of Pure Reason* A 106. "But a concept is always, as regards its form, something universal which serves as a rule. The concept of body, for instance, as the unity of the manifold which is thought through it, serves as a rule in our knowledge of outer appearances."

ment across space and time with respect to their being schema-images replicated in diverse Christian communities. But with respect to their actual replicas in diverse communities, they are signs of disunity and schism, of exclusionary practices and mutually contradictory theologies.[15] A symbol's network system is all the other symbols its meaning legitimates as its interpretation, as coordinated by contexts and respects of interpretation. Put in other terms, a symbol's network system meaning is the structure of its extensive referents and extensive interpretants in the semiotic system within which it is coded.

The other symbols which are a symbol's meaning themselves often have systems of meaning of their own. Thus the meaning of one symbol leads from symbol system to symbol system. The first layer of the eucharist's meaning connects the bread and wine to the system of meanings associated with suffering and nourishment, in turn connecting to the crucifixion and resurrection of Christ, in turn connecting to the identity of Christ in Christological doctrine, in turn connecting with symbol systems of God as creator and as Spirit, and so on. Sometimes these connections can be highly mediated by intervening symbol systems and have only vague connections with one another. The immediate symbol system of eucharistic bread and wine is only very indirectly connected with most aspects of the immediate symbol system of the Holy Spirit; nevertheless, at one time the Orthodox Church objected to the Roman Catholic use of unleavened bread because that was taken to deny the Holy Spirit which is symbolized by the gaseous leavening. In Trinitarian symbologies, so important for the Orthodox Church, the symbol systems of each person of the Trinity are so coordinated that "the act of any one person is the act of the others also." Therefore, the Orthodox insisted on interpreting what kind of bread to use in respect of its Trinitarian symbolic connections, whereas the Roman Catholics interpreted what kind of bread to use in respect of its historical continuity with Jesus' Passover Meal, the Jewish feast of the unleavened bread.

Inter-systematic connections also exist, or can be established, between what can be discriminated as layers of network meaning. So it is possible to connect the suffering and nourishment meanings of the

---

15. Not only have Christian communities fought with one another over the interpretation of the eucharistic elements, the very name for getting booted out of a Christian community is *excommunication*, meaning exclusion from participation in the eucharistic communion.

eucharist with the solidarity meanings and with the table-fellowship meanings. But this reflects an abstract theological interest in transforming layered meanings into systematically connected and interpretable ones. Systematic connections of systems of symbols give the whole of the religion's symbolism a synchronic and intelligibly mediable form. Layered meanings have a different form, that of a discursive sequence that is "activated" all at once.

Layered meanings are such that the symbolic act, whether merely intellectually interpreting something with the symbol or the more complicated act of the liturgy, immediately exercises all the layers of meaning at once. Participating in the eucharist, in one and the same act, is an affair of suffering and nourishment, of sacrifice and redemption, of the solidarity of all Christians, of affirming an historical identity relative to Jesus, of grounding the community in the creative words of institution, of being religious in the Axial Age form of personal and voluntary communal responsibility, of affirming the importance of Jesus as Lord, and of consuming the divine being's flesh. Of course, the participants do not think consciously of all these levels. In fact, some may think consciously of nothing but the roast in the oven at home. But the meaning of the liturgical act, the meaning embodied in participation in it, includes all those levels at once.

The networks of overlayment among religious symbols can have varying degrees of internal resonance. Minimal resonance would be where the same symbolic act simply has two different meanings, both present and perhaps true, but unrelated. If participation in the eucharist is delaying the cook's attention to the burning roast or to the sneaking fear that the oven was not turned on, that level of meaning has little resonance from the other levels of eucharistic meaning mentioned.[16] On the other hand the resonances can be so thick as to qualify each layer by the others. So, the cannibalistic layer provides the very form of the eucharist—eating symbols of human flesh and blood—despite the fact that the roots of this symbolism might be denied on other layers; the political layer of lordship gives identity to the body eaten—not neighboring warrior nor tribal father but king; the level of personal responsibility qualifies both the relation to the lord and the conditions of cannibalism—voluntary; the words of institution mean that the participants'

---

16. Obviously *my own* system of eucharistic meanings includes my mother's fretting about the roast while the communion service seemed interminable.

king whom they each acknowledge is divine; the person of Jesus, however historical, is not only historical but also all of the above; the table fellowship commemorated is not really like eating at home but has the uncanny dimension of being in the presence of God, king, the one chosen to be eaten; the solidarity is not community for its own sake but the community of those peculiarly related to uncanny Jesus; Jesus as atoning sacrifice is not merely like the Torah's scapegoat but is the sacrifice of the one who was host at dinner, albeit an uncanny host; the tokens of suffering and nourishment are qualified in their references to crucifixion and resurrection by all the other layers' meanings. To the extent there is resonance among the overlayed systems of meaning, the symbol has depth. To the extent the symbols on any layer are systematically connected to other symbol systems, the symbols have extent and reach. The power in symbolic meaning comes not only from the importance of the things that are brought within their systematic reach but also from the massing of overlays that resonate in depth.

The modern problem with the overlayment networks of religious symbols is that frequently some of the layers are objectionable, taken on their own. Cannibalism is gross; kingship is undemocratic; some Christians do not want to be in solidarity with others who also celebrate the eucharist but wrongly, and so forth. The symbolic systems reflecting first-century Hellenistic culture, compared with modern science, have a primitive and false geography for heaven and hell; Jesus cannot return on clouds of glory without a space ship with a heat-resistant nose-cone, a silly image. Yet these meanings are objectively layered and cannot be removed or decoupled simply by choice. A communicant cannot *choose* to regard eating the blest elements as non-cannibalistic. The attempts in some modern religions to purge their symbol systems of mythic and morally objectionable elements results only in transforming the symbols into instruments of deliberate intention, acts of human will, rather than symbols of ultimate realities. To construct a new imaginative symbol genuinely engaging the divine while avoiding objectionable figures is very difficult. Purified symbols are also boring.

Two kinds of responses are to be made to this problem. One is to recognize that the more complex religious symbols partially dislocate us from our own culture and its various intellectual and moral perspectives. The eucharist, like important ceremonies in all religions, is decentering, dislocating; it pushes participants to the limits of their centered world, and over. It helps to know that, in the deep identity that religion supplies by relating persons to the infinite as well as the finite, people are paleolithic cannibals and servants of a civilizing strong-man as well as friends of Jesus faithful to God through suffering. Though moderns might not believe in life after death it helps to know that, in the identity to which they are stretched through eucharistic symbols, resurrection is their heart's true home. How they might cope with devotionally powerful symbols whose suppositions are an incredible cosmology is a major topic in chapter 5.

The other response is that where the resonances of one or several layers need to be limited, circumscribed, reinterpreted, or plain rejected, as in the case of the patriarchal implications of lordship taken by itself, dampers and counter-symbols need to be built in to the layers where the offensive resonance is to be denied. Thus, the symbolic layer of the just king limits the cannibalistic layer so that we should not murder. The patriarchal implications of the lordship symbol system can be supplemented by other systems that give leading places to women; to the extent the lordship system not only ignores but positively suppresses women, as for instance it positively suppresses political democracy, explicit criticisms can be put into other layers so that lordship never impacts the eucharistic symbols without the countering criticisms also impacting in effective forms. The Axial Age layer of personal responsibility and voluntary association contains the roots of criticism of lordship and the fostering of democracy, and these roots have branched widely in the culture modern Western Christians bring to the eucharist. Those same Axial Age themes of personal responsibility underlie the feminist critique of patriarchy, but in this respect they have branched much less fulsomely, hardly at all until our time, and without much impact on eucharistic liturgies. I shall return to the issues of moral judgment of symbols in chapter 6, and to how this bears on the truth communicated through deeply resonant overlays of symbols in chapter 7.

The discussion of this section so far has dealt with meaning as defined by the relations among symbols within a semiotic code. I have characterized it as a network with two related kinds of symbol groupings, systems of symbols and overlayments of systems of symbols. I have also called attention to the resonant interactions of networked symbols.

Coded extensional meaning is not the only kind of meaning a given religious symbol has; it also has existential meaning in actual intentional interpretation, which I call *content meaning*. Whereas network meaning has to do with semiotically coded patterns of signification, reference, and inference, and with patterns and resonances of overlay, content meaning has to do with what is involved in *experiencing with a symbol*. Whereas one can symbolize something or enact a religious symbol such as the eucharist while thinking of something else entirely, one cannot have content meaning except by experiencing the world through that meaning. The content meaning is the network meaning as an actual experiential symbol, actually disclosive. Religious symbols are not merely network meanings that could be programmed into computers so as to connect with other meanings. They have a content such that to live with those symbols experientially is also to experience their content. When symbols function in an intentional context, when they are used, it is their content meaning that functions, regardless of what the network meaning might suggest. Whereas network meaning by itself is extensional meaning, related to extensional referents and interpretants, content meaning is intentional meaning, related to intentional referents and interpretations. Many Christians participate in the eucharist with conscious and subconscious reflection on the network meanings in the nine layers just discussed and more. What is the content meaning they experience?

The content meaning of religious symbols is two-fold, the internalizing of network meaning and experiencing the layered meanings through one another, through their resonances. On the one hand, the content meaning of a religious symbol might include some or all of the network connections. Thus, internal to its lived experience, the eucharist as the consumption of food might include the express feeling of the sufferings of life as on a cross as well as the feeling of nourishment for new life and its oncoming problems. Often enough the Christian in communion might think or feel nothing of this but is distracted by other concerns. The adept, however, has made these and perhaps other elements of network meaning parts of the internal conscious and unconscious experience of the eucharist.

On the other hand, content meaning includes internalizing the layerings of meaning that are not systematized together in consistent ways. The whole symbolic exercise of the eucharist involves not only the food with the crucifixion/resurrection figure but the connotations of the table fellowship across the ages, the commemoration of Jesus' historical definition of himself and later Christians, the shock of meeting the Creator in the words of institution, the assignment of responsibility to individuals and voluntary communities in an alien world, the acknowledgment of the political realities of justice and the kingdom of the Lord, and the eating of Jesus the hero who gives Christians power to be human in the face of the divine mystery. For this stack of overlays to become content meaning the persons would have to interpret their referent or referents not only through the symbolic layers separately but together through their multiple resonances.

People can learn the network meaning of symbols and play them as games. Children and converts learn religious symbols through their network meanings. But religions also urge persons and communities to take on the content meanings, to be able to feel together the network implications and the many layers of inconsistent meanings. Theological wisdom and spiritual depth consist in making the encounter with the infinite through religious symbols dense and intense with content meaning. Who can say how the eucharist is an encounter with God? No one layer of meaning without the others can stand easily by itself. No one part of the network on any level can stand by itself without bias, distortion, and, from the outsiders' perspective, silliness. Together the networks and layers of the eucharistic symbol engage Christians with some of the important limiting structures of worldmaking for their world. Because of the vastness of network meaning, hardly any one attempt to express the meaning of a religious symbol can be more than part of the story. Because of the multitude of layers of incommensurable network meanings, no symbol can be exhaustively or truly expressed by even a complex statement. Religious symbols require polysemic interpretations. But when the network meaning is internalized and experienced as content meaning, all the systems and layers are felt together.

Perhaps this is best understood by considering a negative example of how content meaning can break down or be partial. Suppose a person were enculturated in a very narrow community with no experience of cultures different from his or her own, and with only the vaguest sense of history, "the old days." Now that person might have a strong experience of the content meaning of the eucharistic elements as symbols of suffering and nourishment, because those things are fully expressed in his or her culture. But regarding the solidarity with Christian communities around the world and through the ages, the person would have only abstract network meaning. And the person would probably be horrified to think of cannibalism in association with the familiar words, "Take, eat, this is my body." Because both the cannibalism and the solidarity-in-diversity layers enter this person's experience only as networks of (minimally) interpretable symbolic systems, those absent layers not only are missing from the content experience of the eucharist as a whole but also from the resonances they ought to provide for experiencing suffering and nurishment. Suffering would be selfishly interpreted in terms of the conditions of the person's narrow culture and it would not be appre-

ciated in its extent; nourishment would be appreciated only in its triumphant goody-goody sense, not as something resulting from the innocent
death of another human being.

Much religious growth and development consists in turning the network meanings of important symbols into content meanings. This hold
for both communities and individuals. The importance of content meaning
is also reflected in the concerns discussed above about problematic elements
in various symbolic layers. On the positive side, a destructive symbolic
element that remains only a network meaning is less powerful than if it
is taken to the content of the heart, though it is still possible because its
implications can direct behavior. On the negative side, the correctives
against destructive symbolic elements need to be embraced as serious content of the heart if they are going to be effective. Feminists point out the
need for compensatory liturgies, prayers, and songs that are not merely
symbolically corrective in a network sense but that also can be taken to heart.

A final comment about content meaning is that it is yet another dimension of engagement. The dimension discussed earlier is that imagination
forms the possibility of engaging the world through symbolic forms. The
dimension associated with content meaning is that engagement means we
have to take the symbolic forms and what they symbolize to heart. Engagement is not only the semantically and syntactically ordered response to
finite/infinite stimuli. It is also people constituting their hearts and characters by the symbols of the divine. Whereas interpretation on the one
hand refers to the divine interpreted, it also refers to the reality of the
interpretation in the interpreter. Interpretations according to network
meaning make interpreters competent at following the networks' rules.
Interpretations that involve content meaning make the souls and practical
lives of the interpreters bear the objects symbolized in the respects interpreted. Competence at network meaning is what is so nicely rendered
by Lindbeck's cultural-linguistic approach. Internalization of the divine
through content meaning is the main focus of those to whom Lindbeck
ascribes the experiential-expressive approach to doctrine.[17]

The discussion of content meaning has called attention to the concrete act of interpreting symbols and the intentional contexts within
which this is done. But before turning to a more complete reflection on
that, it is important to ask in summary fashion how finite symbols can
mean finite/infinite contrasts.

---

17. See 1.3 above.

3.4. MEANING THE INFINITE

Now we are in a position to support the claim in chapters 1 and 2 that what makes religious symbols religious is that they refer to some finite/infinite contrast, by means of the illustrative analysis of the meaning of religious symbols in the present chapter, with some obvious qualifications to the argument that need to be acknowledged or repeated here. One is that religious symbols are immensely more complicated than can be rendered fully in any philosophic hypothesis. Therefore the distinctions that have been offered here concerning systems and layers of meaning and modes of indirect reference only begin to scratch the surface. Another is that the fairly simple philosophic ideas about symbols as signs and about finitude and infinity at the boundaries of world-constitution have no hope of enlightening the complications of religious symbolism unless they are unpacked and elaborated through the analysis of cases. Therefore this chapter has approached the problem of religious meaning by the interpretive unfolding of some elements of a particular religious symbol, the Christian eucharist, that is likely to be somewhat familiar to readers who can remember and reflect on its words, symbolic actions, visual elements, smells, and music. Chapter 5 will undertake the analysis of another polysemic example, a sermon set in a worship service with an anthem, hymn, and scripture lessons. A third qualification is that this approach to religious symbols does not assume that there is an essence of them. The attempt to distinguish religious symbols from others by means of the discussions of religion in chapter 1 and reference to finite/infinite contrasts in chapter 2 aims to lay out important features of religious symbols, not to assert that the distinctions involved carve up the world neatly. There may be symbols everyone would agree are religious that do not fit this understanding at all; perhaps those associated with Theravada Buddhism are a case in point. There may be symbols that are borderline cases respecting religion on the one hand, and morality, politics, psychology, aesthetics, or some other domain on the other: these "domains" are not defined by essences either, although some of the crucial connections will be discussed in chapter 6.

These qualifications having been noted, it must be admitted that the thesis at hand, that religious symbols mean to refer to the divine as located in finite/infinite contrasts, is a strong claim. It entails that there is the divine as so located and that, whatever functions religious symbols play as spelled out in cultural-linguistic thick descriptions, they (or at least those to which this analysis is relevant) also refer to the divine.

Chapter 4 will argue that their practical functional roles need to be understood at least in part by their transcendent reference.

The remainder of this chapter will discuss various senses in which the levels of meaning distinguished in the Christian eucharist involve reference to some finite/infinite contrast. The crucial distinction to bear in mind is between intentional and extensional reference. The former obtains when an interpreter refers to a religious object by means of some religious symbol in an interpretation that includes the object as well as the symbol and its interpretation as standing for the object in some respect. This is not the topic of the current discussion except when religious symbols are treated as parts of interpretive symbolic activities (which the eucharistic liturgy is). Extensional reference, by contrast, is how the meanings of symbols define the referents in the semiotic code to which they can be referred. Included within the meanings may be clues and assumptions about the respects in which the symbols might be intentionally referred. But because so many religious symbols (if not all) are metaphorical, and metaphor involves the interpretation of an object with a symbol in a respect for which the common extensional meaning of the symbols would not seem to be pertinent, the assumptions within the symbols' meanings about the potential respects of interpretation should not be assumed as defining their actual intentional referring in interpretations.

Consider the first level of the eucharistic analysis on which the bread and wine symbolize the crucifixion and resurrection of Christ with implications for the themes of suffering and nourishment. The principal religious reference here is the obvious one to death and life. Although particular persons' life and death are involved, Jesus' and also the participants' in the eucharist presumably, life and death are symbolized as fundamental themes of human existence. Part of the meaning of the identity of Jesus is that his death (and the suffering that led to it) symbolizes the death of every human being, and that his resurrection symbolizes the return to life or the triumph over death available to every human being. Theological systems differ in how they explain the ways in which Jesus' death and resurrection symbolize universal human implications; some of these are expressed in the second level of interpretation, concerning sacrifice. However the symbolic role of Jesus as stand-in for every person is explicated, that role is involved in the eucharistic elements. The meaning of life and death as human existential conditions is a central borderline finite/infinite contrast addressed in the symbologies of nearly every religion, not always with the same outcome. In reincarnation religions, *life* is the problem and death is the nirvanic solution (in the senses of life and death that would be understood by Westerners), opposite to the Western construction of life as the fulfillment of the soul. The short span of human years, the finite element in the reference, is contrasted with the infinity of a person's non-life. This infinity is at minimum the nothingness out of which people come, and the void into which they return. The point of the crucifixion/resurrection reference is that the infinity side of the contrast is the fulfillment, not the mere void, of life. The ending of life lived Jesus' way is not mere emptiness (as Westerners would understand that) but fulfilled life. The symbols of the post-resurrection appearances of Jesus all make that fulfilled life slightly unfinite; resurrection is not more life of the finite kind; Lazarus had more of the finite kind and there was no religious significance to that at all (only to Jesus' power to bring it about). The resurrected life encompassed by God is not subject to the conditions of finitude. That Jesus was supposed to "ascend" upward was only a metaphor meaning that he no longer appeared to his friends but still was fulfilled in God. This crucifixion/resurrection reference to finite life-death and its infinite background asserts that the infinite fulfills the finite. The entire symbology here is set within a system that also asserts that the infinite background is the source of the finite, a very fruitful and fulsome void indeed. There are many subsidiary or indirect references to the contrast of the finite conditions of life, including death, and the infinite fulfillment of resurrection, in the eucharist. What is affirmed of Jesus is affirmed also of the communicants, as noted. The sufferings of life are not only emblematic of the human condition for everyone but Jesus' attitude toward suffering, accepting it as part of faithfulness to God, is normative for how to live life Jesus' way, and hence to get one's own life into the position of being in the finite/infinite contrast whose infinite side is fulfillment or resurrection. The nourishment in the elements is not only for getting through finite life in faithful fashion but also symbolizes the meal to be enjoyed on the infinite side in resurrected life, the heavenly banquet.

The finite/infinite contrast in the second level of eucharistic meaning, that concerning sacrifice, is as obvious as finite life with death versus infinite fulfillment in its contrast. The background to the sacrifice idea in ancient Israel was that the sacrifices were aimed at restoring the covenant. The covenant itself was what gave meaning to the people of Israel, their true identity, and it came from the creator of the universe. The finite/infinite contrast is that identity-giving by God. As the Christians took this up in various ways they took the scale of sin to be universal to all humans. Although not anyone save in Israel had been part of the original covenant with Moses (and before him Abraham), the sacrifice of Jesus made possible the cleansing of everyone's sins and the establishment of a new universal covenant. Part of the legitimation of this change lay in the universal covenants with Adam and Eve and with Noah. Covenantal identity, and the vicissitudes of following it, are finite/infinite contrasts contributing to the construction of the world in which the human condition is meaningful. The divine infinite transcending the world is its creator in establishing the covenant and sending aid for its repair. In the systems of symbols variously interpreting Jesus as the sacrifice for the sins of the world, Jesus is identified both from the finite human side and from the divine side. The symbolism does not work if Jesus is treated merely as a good human being.

The third level of eucharistic meaning, that of the solidarity of the Christian movement in the common meal, is less obviously a reference to a finite/infinite contrast than the first two levels. It might seem to be merely a political or social assertion of solidarity, like the ethnic claims for solidarity so widespread throughout history. But to the contrary, precisely what is common to all the celebrations of the eucharist across space and time is the symbolic reference to Jesus in the first and usually the second symbolic systems discussed already. The community is not merely a social whole, not merely the continuity of a movement, but a community unified in its reference to death, life, and redemption through Jesus. By virtue of these references, the community itself is understood to be constituted by an ultimate finite/infinite contrast as itself a special holy community. The most direct and common symbols of this have to do with the Christian church as the Body of Christ animated by the Holy Spirit. High church theologies make the Christian community itself a finite/infinite contrast in which the infinite Spirit dwells to animate finite activity. Other symbols for the church make the same point but often with a bit more mediation through traditions, scriptures, and leaders. In any number of variant symbol systems, Christians view the church, either in itself or as normed by a finite/infinite contrast with the Holy Spirit, as the creative or constituting infinite side.

The fourth level of meaning, the eucharist as Jesus' table fellowship, can indeed be interpreted as having no transcendent reference. Some people today who demythologize all religion out of Christianity and make it an ethical or social enterprise still take the table fellowship to be both a communal ideal and an instrument of ethical culture. But for most Christians, the table fellowship recalled in the eucharist cannot be understood apart from the specific teachings of Jesus at the table, mainly concerning the reversal of the priority of the rich and powerful on the one hand and the poor and humble on the other. The table fellowship was supposed by Jesus and the disciples (according to the symbolism in the eucharist) to be an image of heavenly fellowship. The central finite/infinite contrast in Jesus' table-teaching was that worldly rankings do not count for God; in fact, they can be reversed. Therefore the friendship and camaraderie of the disciples is not only that, but also the beginnings of a redefinition of human relationships. Then in addition to this central finite/infinite contrast in the table fellowship are all the resonances of the other layers of meaning that define Jesus as himself a finite/infinite contrast, his death and resurrection as an alteration of the human condition, and so forth.

The fifth level of eucharistic meaning has to do with establishing or enacting, or reiterating, actual connections between the historical Jesus and the communicants in congregations, identified in the ways mentioned above and in other ways symbolized throughout Christology. There are indirect references to all the finite/infinite contrasts mentioned so far regarding Jesus' identity, deeds, and the church. The central direct finite/infinite reference is the quasi-personal relation to Jesus symbolized in the commemoration. Although Jesus is not an ordinary contemporary of later celebrations of the eucharist, he is related to them in direct historical time, and therefore the communicants can define themselves in terms of that relation. In that relation, Jesus is the savior to the communicating persons, the one in whom they relate to God. Jesus historically commemorated thus in part defines each person's confrontation with God. In Christian communities that are very hesitant about elaborate Christologies and substantialist definitions of the church as the Body of Christ, the commemorative personal relation to the historical Jesus is very important.

The sixth level of meaning in the eucharist as analyzed above has to do with the words of institution. They repeat those spoken by Jesus who is himself interpreted to be the creative word of God, as in Genesis 1 or John 1. However different Christians interpret what happens to the bread and wine in consecration, an elementary meaning of the words of institution is that they have been made the locus of God just as Jesus was made the locus of God. Perhaps not *just like* Jesus, but in symbolic analogy. The consecrated bread and wine symbolize the presence of the infinite in the finite, as in the symbol of the incarnation.

The seventh level of meaning was described as the Axial Age traits of the eucharist, symbolizing the general relation of human beings to God as having individual personal responsibility. This is symbolized in the constitution of the eucharistic community as voluntary (not hereditary), as diversely comprising peoples from different cultures who accept one another not first because of their own bonds but because of each individual's bonds to God, as itself called by Jesus' appeal to voluntary responsible discipleship, as defined by Jesus' personal faithfulness through crucifixion to resurrection, and by a host of other systematically related symbols. The central finite/infinite reference here is the same throughout all the Axial Age religions, namely a redefinition of the individual rather than the land-and-kin defined clan as that which bears responsible relation to the ultimate, to emptiness, the Dao, Brahman, or God.

The eighth level of meaning in the eucharist expresses the lordship theme as the problematic of enforcing justice in a community too large for kinship norms. From Egypt and Mesopotamia to the capitals of China, kings were regarded as divine or divinely supported. Kingship is the imposition of order in situations where it does not flow out of naturalized social habits such as a clan. Whereas the imposition of order may not be a full symbolizing of what is involved in heaven's creation of the earth, for cultures at the rise of civilization (city-building) the imposition of order was the most important part. When the legendary sage kings Yao, Shun, and Yu tamed the rivers, domesticated plants and animals, and taught their people signs, rituals, and other vehicles of culture, they were acting under the Mandate of Heaven. When Yahweh, whose word created the world out of the chaos of water and wind as in Genesis 1, anointed David to impose just order on Israel and its environment, the messiah-king role was set for Jesus, who was taken by the early Christians as Lord in the sense of that developing ontological condition. The finite/infinite contrast is the very direct one of finite order issuing from the infinite God where otherwise there would be chaos.

The ninth level of meaning, that the eucharist is a cannibalistic eating of Jesus, of course has all the indirect references to the finite/infinite contrasts defining Jesus. But in addition, simply as cannibalism it has a finite/infinite reference, even if a strange one. So far as we know there is no proper conception of the infinite as such among primitive practitioners of actual cannibalism, no negative dialectic of denial of mere finitude. On the other hand eating human flesh was not regarded as merely one among many sources of protein. Cannibalism is the *uncanny* appropriation of another's identity. It is a marking of the transference from one person to another of a personal identity, perhaps with special powers. The finite/infinite contrast referred to here has to do with the acquisition of normative identity: it comes not through natural means of heredity and learning only, but through incorporation of someone else who has it. Without the incorporation of the other, one's identity is not complete. An analogous idea lies behind filial piety in Chinese society: filial piety is not just taking care of the elderly but working through learning to incorporate their virtues, honoring them by taking on their strengths. Cannibalism is a less figurative means of incorporation. In the case of Jesus, the incorporation is the taking on of the life and death and resurrection of one who is human enough to be eaten but divine enough to save. Jesus, of course, is not the only god-man whose body is supposed to be eaten. The finite/infinite contrast in cannibalism is the sense that human life or character is not wholly natural but of uncanny origin. Life does not come only from life, as from mothers and fathers, *but from death*. The setting of the cannibal theme in all the other Christian symbols greatly domesticates it, and revises definitions of God and personhood, and supplements the reference with symbols of divine incarnations. But the raw cannibal reference to eating the broken body of Jesus in order to attain to his triumphant life remains a resonance throughout the other levels of eucharistic meaning. Without the cannibal theme, the eucharist does not properly incorporate death into life.

In this analysis *symbolism* has been spoken of in a general sense because the focus has been on how symbolic meanings contain extensional references to finite/infinite contrasts. There has been symbolism in several senses, however, as distinguished in the second section of this chapter. For instance, the symbolic schema of God the infinite acting to transform the finite human condition salvifically has lain behind the schema-images of raising Jesus, sending Christ as sacrifice, being present in the community as spirit, and in the words of institution. The schema of God the infinite creating the finite has been imaged in the lordship theme, in the words of institution, and in the gratitude that is part of the table fellowship. All the discussion of the actual celebration of the eucharistic liturgy, the blessing of the elements, the speaking of the words of institution and so forth, have called attention to the fact that specific things and acts have to be replicas of the symbols (schemata and schema-images) if any actual symbolizing is to be done. There have also been many examples of relations among symbolic fragments and symbolic complexes. The bread and wine, for instance, are fragments that have religious reference only in connection with the body and blood of Jesus which themselves are schema-images of the redemptive transformation of the human condition. The words of institution are like fragments. A full account would have to make many finer distinctions.

The case has now been made that religious symbols, at least to the extent they are like the Christian eucharist, have complex networks of systematic and overlayment meanings that refer extensionally to finite/ infinite contrasts. The finite/infinite contrasts of course are defined in terms of the symbols and no attempt has been made to suggest that they are real except as possible extensional referents. Nor has the attempt been made to justify them even as symbolized as being symbolized correctly. The very notions of finite and infinite are foreign to all the particular symbols mentioned here and appeal must be made to the reader's senses of metaphor and analogy to accept the references discussed as instances of that set of notions. The topic will still be approached from several other angles, however.

# Taking Symbols in Context

## 4.1. INTERPRETATION AND INTENTIONAL CONTEXTS

Now that we have rehearsed some sense of their polysemic scale we can focus on the interpretation of religious symbols, although interpretation has been under discussion all along. A sign or symbol is interpreted to stand for or represent its object in a certain respect. Whereas chapter 2 focused on the relation of referring between the sign and its object, and chapter 3 on the meanings of signs themselves, this chapter focuses on the relation between the sign and the interpretant. Of course these distinctions are artificial within the activity of interpretation itself. Interpretation integrates signs with their objects so that the objects become embedded in the interpreter as mediated by the sign's meaning. Nevertheless, certain features of interpretation have prominence in each of the relations studied, that of a sign to its object, to itself, and to its interpretation.

To focus on the relation of religious symbols to their interpretation requires making some careful distinctions between some notions we have not had to distinguish carefully heretofore: interpretants of the extensional and intentional species, and interpretations as intentional acts. An *interpretant* is the meaning of a sign that is assigned to a referent in an act of interpretation. The various elements of the levels of meanings of the eucharistic symbols discussed in the previous chapters are all examples of interpretants. In a semiotic code, a range of interpretants is networked with signs, which in turn are networked with a range of extensional referents. The interpretants so coded are the *extensional interpretants* of the signs, and can be understood by studying the code, as we did by example in the previous chapter. The extensional interpretants are the meanings of the signs.

A semiotic code is made determinate by systems upon systems of symbols related by defined sets of symbols that articulate coded ranges of extensional referents and extensional interpretants for each symbol. The extensional referents and extensional interpretants are themselves all symbols. The triadic interpretation holding among them, relating them as symbol, referent, and interpretant, does not make any of the elements in the semiotic code other than symbolic.[1] The coded systems of symbols with their extensional referents and extensional interpretants is what much of the analysis of religious systems consists in for many students of the subject, such as Eliade; religious meaning is a matter of symbol systems, although usually some attention is paid to the practical religious contexts where the meanings are appropriate.

The temptation is great to assume that extensional interpretants have something like a propositional form: $f(x)$, or "God is great."[2] The propositional form, however, is closely related to the subject-predicate structure of Indo-European languages, and Chad Hansen and others have argued with considerable cogency that this is not characteristic of Chinese.[3] In Chinese, for instance, there are no terms that might not function as predicates in some expression or other, whereas in most Western languages there are terms that can function only as subjects, a point Aristotle used to argue for his theory of substances. (A substance is that the name for which cannot function as a predicate of something else.)[4] The temptation of the propositional form beloved of Peirce and Whitehead is that it would tie semiotic codes to formal logic.[5] But given the openended

1. Peirce argued that *sign* is the generic term of which *symbol* is a species; accordingly we should say that every element in a semiotic code is a sign, not a symbol. But because we are studying religious symbols, which are symbolic in a proper sense, that difference does not mark an important difference here. This was noted earlier.

2. As a logical matter, there is some controversy regarding whether "God" is a proper name; if so, then it is more complicated to symbolize "God is great" by the simple propositional function $f(x)$. The controversy is not important for the illustration at hand.

3. See Hansen's *Language and Logic in Ancient China* and *A Daoist Theory of Chinese Thought*. See also Lenk and Paul's *Epistemological Issues in Classical Chinese Philosophy*.

4. See Hansen's "Term-Belief in Action: Sentences and Terms in Early Chinese Philosophy," in Lenk and Paul.

5. Peirce was one of the inventors of the symbolic logic of relations and Whitehead was coauthor with Bertrand Russell of *Principia Mathematica*, the founding document of symbolic logic studies in the twentieth century. In Whitehead's metaphysics, "proposition" is a technical term for a possibility that offers a way of reconciling the conflicting demands of diverse entities for integration in a new singular entity; it has a logical subject derivative from the diverse entities prehended and a logical predicate or conceptual form

variety of symbol systems, particularly those used to refer to such peculiar objects as finite/infinite contrasts, the best we can say of the form of an interpretation is something like the following: "Symbol $x$ referred to extensional referent $m$ in respect $g$ means $p$ in symbol system $x$, and it means $q$ in symbol system $y$; symbol $x$ referred to extensional referent $n$ in respect $g$ means nothing in symbol system $x$, $r$ in symbol system $y$, and $s$ in symbol system $z$." And so on. The possible interpretations of that sort within a semiotic system can be called *extensional interpretations*.

The primary meaning of interpretation, however, is as an *intentional* act of actually interpreting something for which the semiotic code contains possible forms. An *intentional* interpretation is an act within a real context of using symbols to interpret a real object. Thus, at a eucharistic service, one person can be interpreting the elements as connecting the congregation with the great fellowship of Christians united by the eucharistic meal, another can interpret them as food for renewal, while a third might be distracted to think rather about the roast at home in the oven, not interpreting the symbols by any of the symbols' own systematic extensional interpretations but in terms of other associations—food, roast, did I remember to turn on the oven? As we shall see in the next chapter, a person might make a complex series of interpretations that add up to positioning them all in a transformative world of symbols.

An extensional interpretation is a coded possibility for an intentional act of interpretation. An *intentional interpretation* has existential location; it is an act, or part of a more complex act of interpretation and action. An intentional interpretation uses signs to engage intentional referents. These signs might be entire extensional interpretations, as in the case of a myth used iconically to interpret reality. But we have seen that sometimes, in the case of metaphor for instance, the intentional interpretation might engage its intentional referent with a symbol whose extensional referents in the code do not include that engaged referent. In these cases, the intentional interpretation is *dynamic*, meaning that it makes a change from the extensional interpretations possible. That *dynamic intentional*

---

derivative from the forms of prehended things. Although the metaphysical position is complicated, I believe there is nothing in principle that would prevent the expression of a proposition in terms of the propositional logic of *Principia Mathematica*. Whitehead's use of *proposition* in the metaphysical sense departs from the Aristotelian tradition of saying that subjects (substances) are never predicates because Whitehead claims that previously actualized entities (substances or actual entities) enter into the composition of emergent entities, and thus are multiply located, both in their own space-time position and in that of the emergent entities.

*interpretation* might subsequently become encoded as another extensional interpretation. Perhaps all extensional interpretations of religious symbols began as dynamic intentional interpretations, stretching a previous code in new ways to interpret the peculiar intentional object. But until that happens for a particular intentional interpretation, it remains dynamic, poetic, making a new connection. Many complex intentional interpretations, such as sermons preached once, always maintain a poetic, dynamic quality, acting out of but transgressing the structures of the codes at hand by combining extensional interpretations in new ways. The next chapter will analyze a sermon that does this.

Intentional interpretations always take place in some kind of intentional context which is their existential location. There is always intention or purpose behind interpretation, and this is over and above both the meanings of the signs and their extensional relations to objects.[6] The contextual intentions do have to do with the intentional interpretations of symbols referred to objects, for they determine why this sign is taken to represent this object. The intentions also have to do with the respects in which signs are taken to represent their objects, a point to which I shall return. The intentional contexts in which interpretations are made, in conjunction with the meanings of the signs as discussed in chapter 3, determine the meaning-contexts of the signs. In the matter of religious symbols, the meaning-contexts of the signs are extremely important because almost always idiosyncratic relative to commonsense meaning-contexts.

The meaning-context of a religious symbol is that part of the intentional context of interpretation within which the symbol legitimately can interpret its object. As I mentioned before, the context in which the Western God can be called a "rock" is circumscribed and quite clear. The meaning-context in which God can be called "lord" is broader and yet not so clear. The meaning-contexts (there are probably several) for treating God with personalizing symbols are extremely controversial. Unlike West Asian religions, which tend to call the religious object "God" in all or many meaning-contexts, South Asian religions tend to shift the label from one god to another or from gods to non-theistic referents as meaning-contexts change. A meaning-context is the scope within which meanings of a certain sort can be ascribed to their objects, outside of which those meanings have no legitimate application to those objects.

---

6. This general point is the central doctrine of American pragmatism. See John E. Smith's *Purpose and Thought: The Meaning of Pragmatism.*

One determinant of a meaning-context is obviously the symbol's meanings themselves with their extensional references. Insofar as a meaning-context is determined by the structure of a semiotic code, it is the aggregate of the extensional interpretations within which a given symbol has extensional referents and extensional interpretants. The definitions of the symbolic systems in the semiotic code cannot be the only determinant of a meaning-context, however, because most if not all religious symbols are metaphoric and regularly are applied outside their extensional references. Another determinant is the intentional context of interpretation because the purposes and other elements in the intentional structure determine the respects in which it is relevant to interpret the object. In a theological classroom it is highly relevant to inquire into internal division within God as pure unity or Trinity, and to deny in that context that God in essence, accidents, or existence is anything like a rock. In a foxhole, however, that God is the rock of salvation is far more relevant than the trinitarian controversies which are unreal in that meaning-context. The differences here have nothing to do with degrees of literalness or metaphoricity but with relevance to the purposes at hand.

The *respects of interpretation* are very difficult to understand. They are themselves the fourth term in what Peirce otherwise rightly characterized as the triadic interpretive relation of object, sign, and interpretant.[7] They are the form of the act of interpretation itself that embraces the object and interpretant as mediated by the sign or symbol. As red interprets a barn in respect of color and not in respect of height or use for horses or cows, the respect of color is what determines the relevance and irrelevance of redness, numbers of stories, and what kinds of animals are cared for within. To interpret with respect to color is obviously a function of purpose in the intentional context of interpretation. But it is also a function of the object: barns are the kinds of things that have color. Yet again it is a function of people having repertoires of possible symbols that can interpret in that respect; before modern science no one could interpret physical matter in terms of molecular structures, although that would have been relevant to many purposes, and matter itself was always capable of being interpreted in that respect.

Understanding the respect of interpretation is the key to understanding the powers and limits, that is, the meaning-contexts, of religious

---

7. Peirce was mistaken, or at least misleading, to call interpretation only triadic, if the analysis here is correct, although he did note the role of the respect in which signs interpret objects. See my article, "Intuition."

symbols. Within the respect of interpretation, a given symbol is either right or wrong. The respect selects the real referent which might not be the same as, although obviously related to, the extensional referents. The respect also reflects the legitimacy or illegitimacy of interpreting the object with these symbols for the purposes in the intentional context. Part of the difficuly of formulating the right question when asking whether a given symbol is true is identifying the respect in which it alleges to interpret its referent in the meaning-context at hand. The crudity of most European Enlightenment criticisms of religious symbols is that they ignored the respects in which the symbols interpret their objects, and the limitations of meaning-contexts, and supposed that the symbols employ the meaning-contexts of Enlightenment science to interpret God and the world in the same respect scientific ideas do.[8]

Furthermore, identifying and understanding the respect of interpretation is crucial for correctly understanding and critically assessing the truth of symbols that are historically deep and different, or that are fragments of more complex symbols. For instance, in our own time we do not ordinarily interpret eschatological matters in respect of geography because our geographic symbols exclude eschatological significance. But if we were in a culture where geographic symbols be indeed eschatological, say that of the Hellenistic first century, we can see that, in interpreting the crucified Jesus with respect to eschatology, it would be appropriate to say he went *down* to hell, because death means location in hell which is down, and then *up* to heaven at the Ascension, because unsullied camaraderie with God takes place above the stars. Or if we live in a time that rejects metaphysics or at least the metaphysics of substances and hypostases, we can think there is no respect in which God can be interpreted in those terms and that the controversies of the third through fifth centuries about just how to do so are meaningless. But if we bracket that supposition of our own time and ask what we would say if we were to interpret God in those respects that so dominated the age of the great councils of the Christian movement, then we can tell the better from the worse answers.[9] Christians for whom the creedal controversies are part of the resonant heritage of their theological symbols can affirm (or deny)

---

8. Satire, as used by Swift or Voltaire, for instance, consists in interpreting symbols according to meaning contexts and respects of interpretation that are deliberately different from the original intention, for the purpose of ridicule.

9. For a standard magisterial study of how early Christian theologians used Greek philosophy, see Kelly's *Early Christian Doctrines*.

a given line of creedal development by supposing that the ancient respects of interpretation can be given limited, reconstructed, or corrected places within a contemporary theology.[10] These extremely complicated matters remain to be sorted out here with more extended analysis and examples.

The concrete intentional interpretation of religious symbols in experience is the concern here. An interpretation consists in the impact of the symbol's referent, usually some one or several finite/infinite contrasts, on the experience of the interpreter or interpreting community, as mediated by the symbol; this impact is the symbol's content meaning integrated into practice. The interpretation is not the repetition of the symbol. Nor is it the naked presence of the divine, as if that were possible in finite experience. Rather, the interpretation is the difference made in experience by the referent, God or related divine matters, as the symbol makes the referent effective. Because interpretations always take place in intentional contexts, the effective difference of a given symbol takes different forms; the content meaning is also supplemented by practical consequences. In theological contexts, the interpretation takes the form of cognitive representations of the religious referents. In the intentional contexts of practically ordering life according to religious symbols, the effectiveness of the divine symbols, if truly interpreted into the assumptions and habits of social life, consists in forming the social practices to acknowledge the divine matters and their practical implications. In the intentional contexts of spiritual formation, which shall be analyzed in chapter 5, the interpretation of divine symbols takes the form of leading the soul to greater recognition of the symbolic referents and to disposition of habits to acknowledge and identify with them. In short, the interpretation of religious symbols in practical intentional contexts is to make the divine effective in shaping life in those contexts. If the symbols are to be interpreted, and the symbols are true, they make their referents effective in life.

The effective and accurate presence of the divine is much of what is meant by salvation, in theistic religions, and by enlightenment in several

---

10. One might say that Christians ought not affirm a line of creedal development until they actually reconstruct it in some contemporarily defensible meaning-context. But that is to place theological responsibility on all Christians; a practical division of labor allows for community solidarity where specialized theology works for all. In a strict sense, of course, to the extent a person's salvation depends on theological orientation, the responsibility for that orientation cannot easily be passed to another, once the individual has reached the age of reason.

other religions, although this point must be qualified. The nature of salvation, enlightenment, or the soteriological transformation is an extremely complicated topic about which religions say different things and about which almost nothing has been said here. So we must rest tentatively with religions' supposition that the accurate and effective presence of the divine is salvific, enlightening, or positively transformative in some general sense.

There are other qualifications. Having noted that symbols occur in complex systems that constitute their network meanings, I have not sufficiently stressed how loose, flexible, and incomplete those systems are. Religious quarrels nearly always have to do with differences over networking. Religious symbols are nearly always problematic for some people because of contradictions or lacunae in networking. At best we can say that religious symbols are vaguely true, acknowledging much that is controversial or undecided in their networks. As to content meaning, symbols are similarly vague, sometimes filled with over-determined images, sometimes lacking crucial images.

Further qualifications of the identification of symbolic truth with salvific effectiveness come from reflecting on what might go wrong. Religious symbols might be engaging for some people but dead for others; the networks of a given symbol might contain both live and dead symbolic connections. Engaging religious symbols might be true or false; surely their networks contain mixtures of both. The practical interpretation of false symbols is idolatry or even demonry if the referent genuinely engages the divine. Furthermore, even the true and effective interpretation of religious symbols in the practical intentional contexts of life might have consequences stemming from other social conditions that negate their clear practical intent, as for instance in the development of patriarchy. So, clear pure cases of true and soteriologically effective religious symbols are rare today and probably in every age. Nevertheless, the function of symbols is to engage us with the realities to which they refer so that in the processes of engagement we can learn from error and modify the symbols so as more accurately to orient our experience to the realities. This is true of the symbols of common sense, of science, and of poetry. It is also true for religious symbols whose referents are made known only at the borders of the world itself.

The topic of kinds of intentions within which religious symbols are used supposes an understanding of the occurrence of religious symbols in life that may not be obvious until pointed out. Only very rarely, save in theological contexts, do people in religious life actively try to symbolize something, say, only in trying to develop a new liturgy to celebrate a special event or in creating new visual, musical, or architectural symbols. The direct intention of symbolizing is a matter of art whose practice pervades religion but is not the whole of it. Rather, religious symbols are most usually employed in contexts dominated by other intentions. The intentions of theology are to understand divine matters which are themselves the objects of religious symbols; but theology is often concerned about the limits and contexts of religious symbols. The intentions of organizing religious life through worship, community interactions, prayer, and social expressions are shaped by religious symbols in many ways, and sometimes the symbols are instrumentally employed as well as presupposed as shaping. The intentions of leading one's soul, or the souls of others, likewise are shaped by religious symbols and very often use symbols as instruments of discipline and the further shaping of imagination and heart.

These rather theoretical and general points about interpretation need now to be fleshed out by discussing several important intentional contexts for religious symbols. With regard to each context I shall ask how religious symbols have reference, meaning, and interpretation and how the context affects reference, meaning, and interpretation. The next section will begin a discussion of theology as a context for representing the divine cognitively, a discussion that will be resumed in chapter 7 on the topic of truth. Section 3 will discuss the practice of religion in cultic life as a context for religious symbols, focusing on the ways those symbols shape cultic practice. Section 4 will discuss three intentional contexts outside of cultic life in which religious symbols have important shaping functions: public or political life, "ordinary life" in the sense Charles Taylor has defined that term, and extra-ordinary life as defined by some context-stretching project other than religious or spiritual perfection itself. Then chapter 5 will deal with the context of devotional life or spiritual discipline, the context within which many religious symbols themselves are shaped.

4.2. THEOLOGY

By *theology* here is meant the fairly restricted intellectual task of thinking about divine matters, including both divinity and things within the world such as human beings, culture, and history in the respects in which they relate to divinity. *Divinity* is a comfortable word in theistic religions, as is *theology*. Some people associate theology exclusively with Christianity, and take theology to be the historical and normative study of Christian doctrine.[11] In this narrow usage, theology as Christian is contrasted with commentarial reflections as in rabbinic Judaism and with reflections on law as in Islam, as well as with the combination of aphoristic sutras and oral commentarial traditions in theistic Hinduism. Usually the not-so-hidden motive in this narrow usage is the desire to protect Christian theology from having to relate to critical opinions outside its own confessional community; or else it is the motive of non-Christians to bottle up Christian theology so as not to have to take it seriously.

But the narrow usage is not justified either historically or normatively. The word theology comes from Plato, perhaps even from Xenophon, not from a Christian source, and originally meant the study of the gods and divine matters, as defined here. Furthermore, the early Christian theological apologists such as Justin Martyr took theology to be discussions about divine things *with people who were not Christians*. It was the inclusive intellectual medium in which Christians attempted to explain and justify themselves over against other theological views.[12] Moreover, even the very earliest Christian theological writings, the letters of Paul addressed to Christian congregations, assumed a context in which Christian theological points had to be expressed, explained, and justified in a culture broader than and different from the culture of the original events. The Galilean Jesus and his company needed to be explained to the sophisticated Hellenistic Jews in diaspora, such as Paul's own family, and then to the larger non-Jewish Hellenistic world. If there is truth to the early traditions about Philip and Thomas taking Christianity to Africa and India, then the cultural translations of the first generation of Chris-

---

11. Avery Dulles comes close to this position in his *The Craft of Theology*, chapter 1, "Towards a Postcritical Theology." His argument is that, in rejecting the "critical" skepticism of Enlightenment thought, we now should view theology as operating within the believing context of the faithful. He almost suggests that making theology responsible to a larger public would be a return to skepticism. In fact, skepticism needs to be treated as one would any other position: sympathetically and critically.

12. Wolfhart Pannenberg, in his *Systematic Theology I*, pp. 1–8, acknowledges the pre-Christian Greek origin of the word *theology* and notes that it was explicitly used by Christian authors, for instance Clement of Alexandria, by the second century. In their use, the early Christian writers would count all the Biblical (Hebrew Bible) writers as theologians as well as pagans talking about God. Pannenberg does not himself expand the use of the term to include thinkers about divine things from traditions that were not part of that early discussion. He writes as if Christian theology were a topic and a discipline of its own without essential connections with non-Christian theologies.

tian thinkers extended even beyond Hellenism. Theology never was just what Christians had to say but the topic area about which they had something to say. The form of Christian theological expression is particular, but no more theological than other particular ways—Pagan, Jewish, Muslim, Upanisadic, or whatever—of thinking about the topics of divinity.

Not all religions are theistic, of course, and secularism is explicit in its denial of theism. Nevertheless, if some religions have non-theistic views, that constitutes a response to the topic areas about which other religions take theistic views. Secular culture and non-theistic religions have well-formed and well-argued views about why theism is inappropriate.[13] These too can be called "theological" because of the commonality of the topic, recognizing a certain anomaly in naming the topic after only one kind of many possible positions concerning it. Although, in practice, people who call themselves professional theologians are likely to be positive about divinity (even if their opponents believe they betray positive assertions), the word *theology* literally means *study of gods or divinity* and that study might conclude that there are no gods and that divinity is a psychological projection. The anomaly is justified by its historical roots, moreover. Reflection about the general topic began in cultures that were "in the middle of" cults of the gods, as it were. This is obviously true for early Semitic religions, for European Paganism, and for Vedic religions. Julia Ching and Norman Girardot have argued for mythopoeic theism in the roots of Confucian and Daoist Chinese cultures.[14] That some of the world's civilizations have developed non-theistic approaches to the topics does not take away from the topics themselves which, in light of the history and for need of an inclusive name, can be called "theology."

This use of the term *theology* is still restricted to the intellectual task of thinking about divine matters and as such contrasts with broader uses that include everything in theological education or even any kind of thinking done by religious people.[15] The restricted sense of theology as

---

13. Perhaps the most sophisticated recent expression is Panikkar's *The Silence of God, The Answer of the Buddha*. See also Michael Martin's *Atheism* and *The Case against Christianity*.

14. See Ching's *Confucianism and Christianity* and Girardot's *Myth and Meaning in Early Taoism*.

15. These are uses of *theology* common in Christian seminaries, for obvious and legitimate reasons.

intellectual involves the aim of thinking well about divine matters, which means with some discipline and right-positioning. There are degrees of discipline distinguishing the amateurs from the professional academic theologians, with professional religious leaders usually being somewhere in the middle.

My discussion of theology here has aimed to be descriptive, that is to describe the phenomenon of disciplined and critical thinking about divine matters that takes place in all religions and in anti-religious cultures. All that can be called theology because its various versions constitute the intentional context of wanting to represent putatively divine things rightly. "Mere description" is impossible, however, and normative issues have hovered around the edges of defining theology as a "disciplined and critical" approach to the topic of the gods. The meanings of discipline and criticism have taken widely different forms through the ages and across the religious and anti-religious cultures of the world. For descriptive purposes, they all count. But we may also ask what constitutes truly disciplined and critical thinking, that is, the best thinking our own culture can envision. The terms of the present academic discussion have been set by David Tracy's distinction among subdivisions of theology as fundamental, systematic, and practical.[16] For Tracy, fundamental theology is the discourse about God open to everyone, concerned primarily with the truth of theological theories, and preoccupied with competing concerns about the nature of truth and method in theology; this is often called "philosophical theology." Systematic theology might also employ some philosophy but is the "reinterpretation of the tradition for the present situation."[17] Systematic theology speaks from within a religious tradition to members of that tradition or to outsiders concerned with the tradition, and aims to be faithful to the tradition's symbols, interpreting and reconstructing them; both confessional theology of Barth's sort and apologetic theology of Tillich's sort are Protestant versions of what would fall within systematic theology. Practical theology is what is engaged by a movement or group convinced that some kind of social change is the theological imperative; it is characterized by an insistence on the commitment of the theologian to the relevant associations and experience of the topic practiced upon, although the topics of various practical or *praxial* theologies are diverse and sometimes in conflict.

---

16. See his *The Analogical Imagination*, chapter two, especially pages 56–79. Avery Dulles draws a similar distinction in his *The Craft of Theology*.

17. *Op. cit.*, p. 64.

Tracy intends these categories to be both descriptive and normative; that is, they describe most of what theologians claim is good theology today, and they together are mutually reinforcing and require one another. For theology to be public, and to relate to the publics of society, the academy, and religious communities, all three need to be practiced; they are subdivisions of the one discipline of theology, for Tracy, even though most theologians specialize in one kind or another.

These categories indeed are very helpful, both for recognizing different genres of theology and for sorting some unhelpful turf disputes. But there are some other considerations to be taken into account as well. The first is that the line between fundamental and systematic theology gets fuzzier the more it is examined. What systematic theologian working within a church or religious community would not need to address philosophical questions about the nature of truth being asserted and how that tradition's claims for truth can be related to apparently counter claims within the tradition or arising from another source? Are Barth, Tillich, Rahner, and Pannenberg, who write systematic theologies, not also fundamental theologians as part and parcel of their reinterpretation of their traditions? Have they not often been called fundamental or philosophical theologians, sometimes in criticism, despite the fact each is explicitly a traditional Christian church theologian? On the other side, how far can fundamental theology go without internalizing disciplined interpretations and appropriations of the symbolic material of religious traditions? Only the most abstract of European Enlightenment theologians can talk about religion in general for very long without presupposing the symbolic structures of some particular religions, for instance theisms. I suspect that the better distinction is not with regard to audience or with regard to antecedent community commitment but rather with regard to approach. There is the approach of philosophical theology that can bear upon any theological topic. And there is also the approach of critical hermeneutics, intepreting the traditions and analyzing their bearing upon present circumstances. Furthermore, there is a third approach that is not registered as important in Tracy's scheme, namely comparative theology. Comparative theology is not the mere hermeneutical mastery of several traditions because that by itself would not say how they are related. Nor is comparative theology philosophical reflection about commonalities and differences, because philosophy by itself does not have the terms of comparison. Rather, comparative theology is the mutual dialogue of religious traditions that gives rise to a new vocabulary for comparison bringing the traditions into real theological relation. In the interests of truth, hermeneutical tradition or church theology needs to be complemented by comparative theology in order to see itself from the outside. In the interest of generality of content, philosophical theology needs comparative theology so as not to be blind-sided by parochial assumptions. So the three, philosophical theology, tradition or church hermeneutics, and comparative theology need each other, even though individuals might practice one to the relative neglect of the other. Chapter 7 will return to the question of the community of theological discourse that needs these and other disciplined approaches.

Having defined the intentional context of theology as the intellectual concern to understand divine matters, a word should be said about the common assumption among Christians who are theologians that this intellectual context is itself *normatively* located within a tradition of religious practice. Two dimensions of this issue need comment here. One is the claim that theology is always thinking in and for a religious community or tradition.[18] I have argued here that sometimes it is and sometimes it is not. The best way to conceptualize this is to say that there are two, perhaps nested, intentional contexts, the more purely intellectual concern and the concern to provide the intellectual work for the practice of a faith. The latter intentional context is part of the practical organization of cultic life, which will be discussed shortly. The need to distinguish the contexts comes not only from the fact that some people think interestingly about divine matters who are not themselves practicing members of a cultic tradition but also from the fact that even the cultic practice of theology wants to be true and therefore ready to learn whatever might be known by those outside the cult.

The second dimension of the assumption is that competence in theology cannot be had except through *faith seeking understanding*. This is a

---

18. James Evans writes in *We Have Been Believers*, pp. 1–2:

> Genuine theological judgment requires a praxiological commitment to the community of faith. Theologians as theologians cannot tell other Christians what they should believe; rather their task is to help the community understand more clearly what they do believe and to assess those beliefs in light of the major sources of Christian revelation.

Avery Dulles would agree with this; see his *The Craft of Theology*, chapter 1.

It is not clear how far this extreme statement of in-group theology stems from the fact his focus, although not in this statement, is on African-American theology. If I am right that this is not theology but ethics, the quoted remark is an ethical exhortation, not a setting of the conditions for theological discourse.

more complex matter in several senses. First, there are deep problems of comparative categories that make communication difficult among different theological traditions, a topic already mentioned and to be explored further in chapter 7. Second, theological thinking is complicated because the symbols are so complicated and easy to misinterpret. The criticism lodged above against European Enlightenment approaches to religious symbols, namely, that they usually failed to be sensitive to issues of meaning-context and the subtle respects in which symbols interpret the divine, illustrate the problem. Third, because religious symbols in theology, as in other intentional contexts, mean to engage the divine, theologians too must engage the divine, at least in a theological way, and perhaps faith or devoted cultic participation is required to make the engagement. There is no general answer to this issue because religions differ greatly on the nature of faith and appeals to revelation, both of which are important theological topics themselves.[19] The difficulties in gaining access to competence in theology do not, however, obviate the need to distinguish theology's own intellectual intentional context from other practical contexts in which it might also need to be imbedded.

Theology's context can be analyzed in terms of its bearing on religious symbols, on their theological reference, and on their interpretation.

As to symbols, most of the religious symbols involved in theology are verbal, with exceptions. Among the exceptions are theological meditations on the cross, on music, on the activity of prayer, and so forth, to use symbols from Christianity. Kukei's theology was mainly reflection on ritual.[20] So was Xunzi's.[21] So was Jaimini's *Purva Mimamsa*.[22] So was at least some of Bavaviveka's thinking.[23] These ritual examples are schema-images of symbols, as are theological reflections on relics, works of art, and holy places. The typical symbols in theology, however, are the big ideas named in scriptures, creeds, confessions, and seminal theological works, the schemata themselves however approached through schema-images. Because of the vast amount of work done in the past century on the nature of language, including religious language, many

---

19. I have dealt with other dimensions of the relation between participation and critical theological thinking in *The Tao and the Daimon*, chapters 10, 11, and the Postscript.

20. See Thomas Kasulis's "Philosophy as Metapraxis."

21. See Edward Machle's *Nature and Heaven in the Xunzi.*

22. See Francis Clooney's *Thinking Ritually.*

23. See David Eckel's *To See the Buddha.*

are tempted to use linguistic symbols as the paradigm case of symbolism. Even Suzanne Langer, whose brilliant and influential *Philosophy in a New Key* contains an extensive discussion of musical symbolism, focused primarily on linguistic symbols. To the extent linguistic concerns are paramount in understanding religious symbolism, attention needs to be paid to extensive and detailed treatments of religious language such as in Janet Martin Soskice's fine book, *Metaphor and Religious Language.*

The theological deployment of religious symbols comes close to making verbal symbolism paradigmatic. Nevertheless, as New Testament scholars have shown, theology arose out of liturgy and song, and out of practical needs to figure out how to live religiously in a world whose glorification was not immediate. However one ultimately judges George Lindbeck's cultural-linguistic theory in *The Nature of Doctrine*, he is surely right as far as he goes about the cultural context for the origin of much theological symbolism, cultural in the worshipping, praying, and singing sense, not in the purely linguistic sense.[24] For present purposes, theology's verbal religious symbols are one part (or several parts) of a continuum of symbol-deploying behaviors that shape religious life.[25] Perhaps all theological ideas are religious symbols, classifiable according to distinctions of the sort made earlier. Paul Tillich's *Systematic Theology* is a masterpiece of displaying the symbolic character of the great Christian doctrines.

Moving from symbols themselves to reference, the ancient question for the theological context is whether all theological ideas refer symbolically rather than literally. The reason for believing so is that, in one way or another, theological ideas directly or indirectly refer to the infinite by means of finite symbols. Even the symbol of the Infinite itself has as one of its two main schema-images something like the mathematical notion of always being able to add another unit—always another year, always another place across space. The other main schema-image is also finite and negative—the infinite is what you get when you take away all finite determinations.[26] It would seem then that every idea attempting to convey something about the divine should be recognized as a broken symbol, and if it is not broken it is idolatrous.

---

24. A basic critical question from the philosophic standpoint of the present study is that Lindbeck's approach seems to cut theology off from the questions of truth. Avery Dulles agrees with the importance of symbols in theology—the subtitle of *The Craft of Theology* is *From Symbol to System*, and he would argue strongly for referential truth.

25. See chapter 3.2 above for further analysis.

26. See Pannenberg's discussion of infinity, in his *Systematic Theology I*, chapter 6.2.

On the other hand, how would one know to deny part of a symbolic reference, or to claim that it is limited, if one did not have at least one purely positive and non-symbolic claim? Duns Scotus was one of the first systematic theologians to make this point and Tillich himself claimed that the thesis that God is Being-itself is literal and non-symbolic.[27] By virtue of a dialectical understanding of Being-itself, Tillich thought we could discern what to deny in limiting all symbolic claims about divinity. The problem is, the so-called dialectical understanding of Being-itself is a matter of symbolic knowledge. All that is required regarding the positive ground for making a negation is a relative grounding. That is, the limitations of one symbol can be asserted from the standpoint of another symbol that is not limited in the respects in question. That other more inclusive symbol might be limited in its own way—indeed it would have to be; but that limitation need not be distortive in expressing the limitation of the first symbol.

These points reflect a confusion of distinctions. One is that between apophatic and kataphatic symbols or symbol-assertions; it is here that Scotus' point holds, that something positive is required to assert a negative, and here the above remark also holds, that only something relatively positive is needed. Another apparently similar distinction is that between the symbolic and the literal, and the question is what is meant by *literal* in the case of religious symbols. If literal means that an extensional interpretation is applied without further metaphorical alteration to an intentional object, then a great many highly metaphorical symbols can be applied literally to the divine, as so many theologies insist. But if literal means that any symbol, being finite, must have a finite extensional referent, with a denial of the legitimacy of coding religious metaphors in semiotic systems, that amounts to a denial of the possibility of referring to finite/infinite contrasts. Even if one rejects my analysis of religious objects as finite/infinite contrasts, nearly every theology has said *something* like that. In this sense of literal, all religious symbolization of the divine is *symbolic*. Tillich's "Being-itself" is symbolic, not literal, in this sense, as he would be the first to say, given his dialectical analysis of Being-itself. In the general semiotic theory employed here, *symbol* means any kind of sign, some of which can be literal in the sense of non-metaphorical and others of which (all primary religious ones) are non-literal.

Regarding reference, then, the theological context employs religious symbols that have the structure of referring to finite/infinite contrasts,

---

27. See Tillich's *Systematic Theology I*, pp. 238 ff.

which means they are broken symbols. If those symbols are adequately encoded in a religious system, they can be intentionally referred literally to the divine in the sense that they need no further metaphorizing. The extensional referents are here assumed to be adequate to the intentional referents. On the other hand, theology often deals with symbols that are inadequate, and are revealed to be so by various forms of theological dialectic and criticism. In these cases, theology stretches the extensional referents in intentional reference, and perhaps then changes the coded extensional referents. In any case, in its attempt to be true to the peculiarities of finite/infinite contrasts, theology cultivates dialectical awareness of the difference between extensional and intentional reference.

Regarding the bearing of the theological context on interpretation, several points need to be made.

First, insofar as the theological intention is fairly pure, that is, to seek to understand divine matters truly, interpretations of religious symbols are treated as *hypotheses* about the divine. Hypotheses are not necessarily tentative. According to Charles Peirce, all of our intellectual habits, including those we cannot conceivably find ways to question or doubt, have the form of hypotheses more or less confirmed. But where theology is concerned about the truth of its symbols and the assertions made with them, it treats the symbols as hypotheses in many ways. Theology can attempt to construct symbols to express things other symbols cannot; this construction is like guessing and it lies behind all efforts at system-building. Theology can attempt to explicate symbols into other symbols better understood; it can attempt to draw out the implications of symbols for cognitive and practical experience; it can survey other things known about religion that bear upon the confirmation, deconfirmation or modification of symbols; it can relate symbols according to consistency, coherence, applicability and adequacy to the questions raised.[28] The aim of systematic theology is to present a coherent set of symbols, coherent in some defensible sense, that expresses the truth about divine matters.[29]

Second, theology is concerned not only with what symbols assert about the divine when they are involved in interpretation but also with

---

28. I discuss Peirce's theory of hypothesis in *The Highroad around Modernism*, chapter 1; my own theory of theories as hypotheses is in *Normative Cultures*, chapters 1–4.

29. Theology's intention is hardly ever pursued purely, of course. Very often the practice of theology is folded back into the intentional context of organizing religious life and leading souls. In these instances theology often becomes more particularlized and less systematic.

the meaning-contexts in which particular symbols engage us with the divine reality properly. Symbols, like any hypotheses, are context-dependent. Valid within the context, they do not properly engage their object outside that context but become silly, distortive, or idolatrous. The Psalmist can say, as we have seen, that God is the rock of salvation without many people extending his symbol to a geological context. That Yahweh is symbolized as a warrior-king for Israel finds proper engagement in the context of Israel's struggle for national identity; but it is a distortive symbol when extended to the context of spiritual life, as Jesus implied when he said the Lord of the Kingdom of God is a father, not just a warrior. There may be many contexts in which God is adequately symbolized as a person, but the context of theodicy is not one of them, as Job learned. In the theodicy context, God cannot be symbolized as a person within the world interacting with people on moral terms. Our current science understands the universe as a process of expanding gasses clustered in galaxies, stars, and planets. The reasons earthquakes kill people have to do with plate techtonics, not divine personal intentions. People get sick because of germs, not divine punishment. Nations overwhelm other nations because they themselves are under migratory pressures, or because they have an expanding economy or population, or because individuals are greedy and the cumulative force of that is colonialism, or because superior technology shifts the balance of power, not because they are executing divine foreign policy.

Theistic religions are in danger of idolatry, theologies note, because to give up personalistic notions of God is often too difficult even when the context is obviously supra-personal. As a result, mysticism is usually anomalous within theistic religions because it relativizes personal symbols of God very quickly. Theisms also are an easy prey to an obviously untenable spirit-body dualism, depreciating the body, because God is symbolized as the paradigmatic person and God has no body.[30] Christian theology has many alternatives to personal symbols of God, including that of the Trinity which is not the symbol of a person in any ordinary sense. Much of theology's interpretive business with religious symbols is sorting the contexts of their appropriate use. The peculiar character of the meaning-contexts of religious symbols is made more apparent when religions are compared in which similar symbols have different meaning-

---

30. That God is conceived as a spirit with no body is true on many theistic theologies. There are interesting exceptions, however, where the world is conceived as God's body, as in the theologies of Ramanuja and Charles Hartshorne.

contexts. Buddhism, for instance, is not a non-theistic religion as so many people say: it recognizes thousands and thousands of gods. Buddhism, however, does not put divinity into the meaning-context of ultimacy on the spectrum of religious objects, as do monotheisms, and hence it has a very different theology. The topic of theology includes all positions about ultimacy (the finite/infinite contrasts) as well as gods at the less than ultimate level of daimons.

Third, theology deals with many different symbol systems that are not systematically networked together but rather overlain. God is rock and warrior and king and father and Spirit and lover and being and creator; and the deep water, the abyss, the mother, and a host of other things, each with its appropriate context.[31] The contexts often overlap or confuse with one another. When interpreted together systematically the symbols seem contradictory or distortive of one another. Dealing with the symbols that have arisen out of long traditions of worship and thinking, theology has to accept these mutually overlapping and sometimes competitive symbols. Sometimes they can be connected consistently with one another simply by sorting their appropriate contexts. But often the contexts are so intrinsically related to the symbols themselves that this is not possible. Theology then seems like a dense resonant overlay of many different symbolic patterns, more like the textures in a Victorian room than like a clean system with each symbol in a function connected to the other functions.

Therefore, fourth, theology implicitly, and in its systematic forms explicitly, gathers its symbols according to hierarchical distinctions of levels of vagueness, where vagueness is a particular logical trait. A symbol is vague if both its internal meanings and its distinction from other symbols on its own level of vagueness are tolerant of diverse, perhaps unrelated, incommensurable, or inconsistent, instantiations by symbols on a less vague level. Thus, for instance, the symbol of God as head of the divine kingdom is vague with respect to instantiation by Moses' warrior hero or Jesus' loving Abba; the symbol of God as personal is vague with respect to instantiation by symbols involving political images or symbols of the divine companion preferred by process theologians; the symbol of God as creator is vague with respect to instantiation by less vague symbols of a personal God or of a creative principle, or a mystical creative abyss. Only by moving up and down the ladders of vagueness is it possi-

---

31. See the treatment of these themes in chapter 5 below.

ble for theory to acknowledge the diverse integrities of the various symbols systems it needs to acknowledge, and to control for the negations of symbols that need to be made when they are taken out of appropriate context.[32] Of course, theology has many different forms or genres. Not all of these explicitly attempt to systematize a hierarchy of levels of vagueness. Nevertheless, I believe that all employ distinctions, in sorting symbols and their meaning-contexts, that reflect such a hierarchy.[33]

A final point needs to be made about the theological intention with religious symbols, namely, that theology is most of all concerned about truth. There are a great many tests of truth, including the obvious ones of consistency, coherence, adequacy, and applicability. But there are less obvious ones such as the enrichment of experience, the deepening of spiritual life, and the flourishing of the community that come out when we realize that theological symbols are true insofar as they engage us correctly with divine matters. Symbols are inadequate simply at the level of imagination if they do not engage us. Many secular people are not engaged at all by traditional religious symbols. Religious experience is not possible at all without engaging symbols. No aspect of divine matters can be experienced for which we lack symbols with which to engage it. Much of theology's work toward understanding divine matters truly consists of identifying, sorting, and integrating symbols by which the divine can be engaged and experienced. Revelatory religions sometimes argue that much of theology's work is done by God when symbols appear of no theologian's making. The formal discussion of the truth of religious symbols, in theology and in the other intentional contexts within which religious symbols occur, is posponed until chapter 7.

## 4.3. CULTIC LIFE

The last point about engagement brings the discussion directly to the functions of religious symbols having to do with organizing religious life. The phrase "organizing religious life" needs some specification. By *organizing* is meant that the occurrence of the religious symbols, with

---

32. See the discussions of vagueness in my *Reconstruction of Thinking* and *Recovery of the Measure*; for the role of vagueness in systematic theory see the *Highroad around Modernism*, chapter 6, and *Normative Cultures*, chapter 4.

33. The distinction between levels of vagueness is not at all the same as the Aristotelian distinction between genera and species. Aristotle's distinction is incapable of handling symbolic overlays that do not have clear differentia. I have treated the difference between hierarchies of vague symbols and Aristotle's point in *Normative Cultures,* chapter 3.

implicit or explicit interpretation, shapes life or makes a difference to it in ways that might be discerned through a cultural-linguistic analysis. This is to say, the relevant shaping comes from the interpreted meaning of the symbol, or at least some part of that. A statue of a saint in a college courtyard might encourage at least a subliminal awareness of the religious devotion of at least one college donor, and raise questions as to what this might mean. Insofar, the statue functions as a religious symbol to organize the life of the college. But insofar as the placement of the statue merely organizes traffic so that people have to walk around it, this is not organizing in the sense intended, for the statue is not functioning as a symbol in any religious dimension.

By *religious life* is meant something normative, namely, life as lived in ways that partially respond to the holy or divine for better or worse, as discussed in 1.1. There the distinction was made between ritual, spiritual practices, and representations that have the function of shaping life in responses to the holy or divine. But obviously the religious dimension has a broader scope than that. Both private family life and public social life can have elements of orientation to the divine; meals are blessed and officials are sworn into office with one hand raised to God and the other on a holy object. Religious symbols function in contexts like these to organize life in response to the holy. Chapter 1.3 took note of the roles of religion in articulating the human condition of obligatedness and of devising platforms from which societies might be judged relative to their obligations. There are many other roles of religion in society, affecting art and imagination, communications, education, and other institutions of social and personal life. Religious symbols make a religious difference there.

Of course religious symbols function much more densely in organizing the cultic life of religious communities, the topic of this section. Monastic communities in Buddhism, Christianity, and Daoism can approach total institutional control in organizating behavior, thought, and affect according to complicated systems and overlays of religious symbols.[34] Most religious communities, however, are not so totally organized. They involve members coming together for worship, teaching, and the orientation of religiously directed work in the community, and then also going their separate ways, with participation in many symbol systems other than the religious, perhaps that are in direct conflict with the religious symbols principally orienting the community. This is surely

---

34. On total institutions, see Irving Goffman's *Asylums*.

true when religious communities are enclaves in secular societies or in pluralistic societies shaped also by other religious traditions.

Much that happens in a religious community might not be shaped by religious symbols. A church dinner can be cooked according to secular recipies. A Seder, however cooked, needs to have certain foods present, for instance the bitter herbs, as part of the religious symbolism. The issue is complicated when religious symbols are present and effective in shaping the community but not according to their religious meaning. When hot cross buns are purchased in a supermarket by people who do not recognize the cross for its Christian lenten meaning, the crosses of icing fail to function as religious symbols. When rules for dress or diet within a religious community are observed as part of the community definition but without any sense that the rules are related to the holy, the symbols cease to be religious and become only social or ethnic. That the rules were once symbolic of religious functions, however, means that they might recover that meaning. Most of the world's great religions have a literature of complaint about the degeneration of religious symbols into mere forms, social shapers without religious reference, perhaps even used hypocritically; the point of the complaint is to recover the religious reference. What makes the symbolically organized behavior religious, when it is, is that the symbols orient it in part to the holy. The implications of the cultic intentional context for religious symbolism can be discussed in terms of the interpretants of symbols, their material reality in practice, and their reference.

With regard to interpretants, my hypothesis is that the intentional context of the cultic life of a religious community generally requires doubled interpretants. On the one hand, the religious symbol is interpreted in a representational way so that the meaning is thrown back on the religious object. On the other hand, the symbol is interpreted in a practical way so that the implication of the religious object so symbolized is drawn out for the practice or activities of the community. Therefore, when it is asked of a cultically contextualized symbol what it means, say, the architectural symbols of a sanctuary, the symbolic meaning of religious vestments, scriptures read or hymns sung in a liturgy, one answer interprets the symbol as a meaning applied to its object, and another interprets the symbol in terms of how it shapes, might shape, or ought to shape the life of something in the community. So, the representational meaning of the high vaulted ceiling of a gothic cathedral, for instance, is to point to the loftiness and light of God; the practical meaning is to give worshippers a certain feeling of their place, dwarfed by lofty divine majesty and yet illumined by the light. The plain, unadorned, and distinctive robes of Buddhist monks on the representational hand mean that true emptiness treats fashion as evanescent and on the practical hand mean that the monks too should abandon ego for plain simplicity. Scriptures and hymns mean representationally what their authors mean (more or less), and practically they mean whatever moral they bear for the congregation at hand. And so on.

These examples, of course, are exaggerated as exemplars. Architecture, vestments, scriptures, music, all mean a very great many things at once, and the meanings I have drawn out may not be their most important ones. Surely, many of their meanings shade the difference between the representational and practical. Furthermore, the examples have not respected important distinctions discussed earlier between the schemata and schema-images of symbols, the replications of symbols, and the relations among symbols and their fragments. Nevertheless, I suggest that the practical contextualization of religious symbols, in cultic life and in the other practical contexts to be discussed shortly, draws out the two extremes of meaning. In any given context one may be dominant over the other. One may be closer to consciousness, and one may be more powerful without being more conscious.

The integrity of the meaning of a symbol in a practical context consists in large part in the proper relation between the representational and the practical interpretants. That is, does the practical interpretant rightly call for the shaping of behavior, attitudes, practices, and specific activities that indeed would be the practical implication of the representational meaning, taking into account the entire set of practices and the religious symbol systems shaping them? The ideal relation between the representational and practical interpretants is that the latter is an implication of the former. The relation of practical integrity is vastly complicated for two obvious reasons. First, symbols never stand alone and always impact on one another; both representational and practical interpretants of a given symbol may be themselves implicated in other symbol systems, some of which are not shared. Second, it is a logical point that something that can imply one thing can imply many things, perhaps not all of them relevant. The question of practical integrity has to do with drawing the appropriate and relevant practical implication for the practical interpretant from the representational interpretant. Relevance and appropriateness are not decided by matters of the symbol and its interpretations alone.

Nevertheless, when the practical meaning of a symbol is questioned, the response is usually to ask whether it is the practical implication of the representational meaning of the symbol for the concrete situation. The thesis about doubled interpretants and their relation perhaps can be made more persuasive by recurring to our extended example of the eucharist.

The first meaning-level we distinguished concerns the eucharist as food, and we noted two meanings here, the interpretation of the representations of blood and broken body as epitomes of suffering, and their interpretation as nourishment, God sacrificing the Son for the world, and also nourishing believers. But on the practical side, regarding the first, consuming the eucharistic elements means the parishioners take upon themselves suffering and crosses as the lot of life; regarding the second the practical meaning is that Christians are nourished to new life, risen life. The implication relation is that Christians are supposed to be like Jesus in both cases, expecting a life whose emblem is crucifixion and resurrection joined.

The second meaning level has to do with Jesus as the sacrificial lamb, the representational meanings of which have to do with his atoning for the sins of all. The practical interpretants have to do with Christians behaving as redeemed people, no longer in debt to sin or bound by it and obligated rather only to give thanks for the sacrifice of Jesus. The implication relation is not the same as in the first level of meaning, namely that Christians ought to be like Jesus. That would be to say in this instance that Christians ought willingly to allow themselves to be sacrificed and that this has redeeming virtue. On the contrary, the representational meaning of the atonement symbols is that Jesus performed the sacrifice no one else could and that he did it once and for all. Nobody else's suffering after him has any redeeming value in the sense relating to sacrifice, and sacrifice involving suffering ought to be avoided unless it has pragmatic value. On the contrary, redeemed sinners have a life in this respect very unlike Jesus' life, and they should give thanks for him. At this level of meaning the representational interpretant, the atonement theory, does not give rise to the practical implication of imitation, denies it in fact, and gives rise to a different practical implication of thanksgiving.

The third layer of meaning has to do with the eucharist being a common meal. Its representational meaning is the unity, commonality, historical continuity and connection of the Christian congregations and other occasions for celebrating the eucharist across the ages. The practical meaning is that the congregants should feel part of this larger fellowship, not merely caught up in their own situation and practice. The implication relation here is that individuals and congregations should take to heart the symbolically constituted large cultural reality of which they are a part (and which it is very hard to do practically, given people's propensities to think that their own is the only local embodiment of meaning).

The fourth layer is that the eucharist reenacts Jesus' table fellowship. The representational meanings have to do with his use of the meal to teach his disciples, his building of friendship and solidarity among them, and so forth. The practical meaning is that congregations should find ways of doing the same among their members. The means would not be the same: the eucharist is not in fact a meal with long talk, stories, and jokes. But other elements of congregational life should be cultivated to serve the purpose. The differential power of the eucharist at this level of meaning is seen in the fact that so many other powerful symbols might channel energies into activism or worship rather than table-fellowship teaching, into cooperation rather than friendship and solidarity which were the point of the meal. The implication relation here has to do with finding ways to do in a contemporary context what Jesus did in his by other means, where the context was very different.

The fifth layer of meaning distinguished is Jesus as an historical person who is commemorated. The representational meanings have to do with his historical character, the "historical Jesus" as this level of meaning has been called, and with the history of the Christian community from his time to the present. The practical interpretants have to do with defining the contemporary contours of the church and its current members in continuity with Jesus' historical particularity. The implication relation here has to do with deriving contemporary identity from Jesus' identity in historical terms. The representational meaning does not entail that the contemporary church has to have the same form as Jesus' community, or the first- and second-century church that compiled the historical accounts of Jesus, but that it has to identify itself as an historical outgrowth or development of that original situation, adapted to different circumstances. The difficulty of determining just what forms of possible church life are in authentic practical continuity illustrates the difficulties mentioned above about finding the appropriate implication.

The sixth layer of meaning is the symbolism of the Word of God in Jesus' words of institution. The representational meanings of this have to do with creation and the normative ordering of the world. The practical meaning is that the words of institution create the potential of a new ordered community around the eucharistic meal. The congregation as a church is a new kind of reality, transcending ordinary meals and social gatherings, a new community of redeemed people who ought to behave as such. The implication relation here moves from a representational basic theme or motif—the activity of the word in creation—to the concrete instantiation of that theme around the eucharistic meal—building a congregation that behaves like redeemed sinners.

The seventh layer of meaning is the Axial Age point that the Christian community gathered around the eucharist is voluntary and relates first to God and then to people who are not necessarily bound to one another by kinship or other communal ties, save in the church. The representational meaning is to draw all that out. The practical interpretants are to make the congregation at hand focused first on God and then welcoming to all who come, irrespective of kinship and so forth. The implication relation between the representational and practical interpretants have to do with living up in the present to the cultural sensibilities taken to express a proper human-divine relationship in the religion's founding.

The eighth layer of meaning has to do with the eucharistic symbol of Jesus as lord. Its representational meaning involves the imposition of justice and Jesus' rule in the kingdom of God. Its practical meaning is to make Jesus the ordering ruler over the congregation's life, the lives of its members, and perhaps over their larger community. In the long run, the symbol of eucharistic lord implies the practical obligations of justice. The implication relation here has to do with discerning just what justice means in practice and how current circumstances might be imaged as the kingdom of God, and taking all this to heart.

The ninth layer of meaning is the cannibalistic one. Its representational interpretants involve understanding how eating the body or drinking the blood of a person means taking on that person's powers and virtues. The practical interpretants are very direct: by taking the communion elements people are committing themselves to at least the attempt to lead a Christ-like life, governed by the mind and heart of Christ, and taking energy, if not magic, for this from the eucharist itself. The implication relation is that of instantiating a general belief in cannibalism in the particular symbolic relation between Jesus and the communicants.

In each of these interpretations of meaning there are at least two kinds of interpretants, the representational and the practical, and they are related such that the former has implications for the latter. Indeed, the latter are implications of the former. Again it is important to stress how the symbols are systematically interconnected, and systems laid down on systems, with many interactions that complicate the simple correspondences listed here. There is much plausibility, I believe, to the hypothesis that, in practical contexts such as the cultic life of a religious community, symbols are interpreted with two kinds of interpretants, representational and practical. This hypothesis of doubled interpretants is related to, but to be distinguished from, the hypothesis of doubled referents put forward in the next chapter in the case of symbols in a devotional context.

As regards the material functions of symbols themselves in cultic contexts, prescinding for the moment from their interpretants and referents (yet to be discussed), their main practical function is to shape imagination. The practice of a religion has a deep need to imprint the symbols in the habits and imaginations of people, and to make their practical implications baseline traditions and policies for religious institutions. All this is done through rehearsing the symbols in imagination-forming behavior, the primary example of which is ritual, especially homiletical rituals. Rituals and liturgies of course serve many purposes. The most important, perhaps, is that their repetition, either in anticipation, memory, or actual practice, serves to shape people's imagination. Frequently to participate in the Christian eucharist, for instance, is to cultivate the deep psyche around the crucifixion-resurrection figure according to which just about all of human life can be interpreted. Liturgical services that move through the rhythm of praise, self-examination and confession, expressing and receiving the creative word, prayer, acts of dedication to the particularities of the religious life, and dismissal to carry grace to the world, by their very repetition create the habit of moving through life with that rhythm.[35] The placement of religious symbols in liturgies is a model for placing them in appropriate contexts in the rest of the community's life, in daily life, and in religion's contribution to the public. Without ritual formation of individual and community imagination, religious life can hardly be organized according to religious symbols. Thus while the primary purpose of worship might be to praise and acknowledge God, at least in theistic religions, a very close secondary purpose is to shape the imaginations of people to be oriented to the divine through the religion's basic symbols. Praise cannot spring from the heart unless the heart is shaped to praise in the first place.

---

35. This is a general order of Christian ritual typical of many services, for instance the liturgies for morning and evening prayer in the *Book of Common Prayer*. It derives from Isaiah's vision of God in Isaiah 6.

Ritual is not the only place, of course, where religious symbols are rehearsed so as to shape people's imaginations in cultic life. The architecture of religious buildings, and religious art everywhere does this. Invocations of the divine in prayers at meetings and meals shape imagination. Hagiography does the same. So do songs and the chanting of mantras and sutras. Even the language that religious people speak is replete with religious symbols that affect much of how they interpret the world. Lindbeck's point that a tradition's theology ought to articulate how to understand today's life in the basic motifs of the tradition is fundamentally about imagination. With the religious symbols repeated and reinforced in religious living, a person interprets daily events not only in the pragmatic terms of the secular world but also in the terms that derive from the symbolic tradition.

Plato was perhaps the first to point out that repetition and imitation are the main ways of educating the spirited part of the soul, in contrast to the education of desires and of the rational part of the soul. This was in his discussion of the education of the military in the Republic. The division of the soul into these parts is not a universal understanding among religions. But the point about the practical formation of imagination, and thereby of the behavior that follows from it, has a large truth.[36]

The practical function of symbols is not only to shape imagination, although through this the life of the community is primarily formed and competence is gained at living the tradition's religious life. But in addition there are matters of practical deliberation. Religious communities need to make all sorts of decisions about specific issues and activities. Among these are the critical examinations of the implication relations between the representational and practical interpretants of their symbols. These deliberative matters are topics of theology and ethics.

As to reference, my hypothesis is that in cultic contexts religious symbols are primarily referred to their objects *performatively* and only secondarily representationally. By "representational reference" here I mean to combine the senses deriving from the doubled interpretants as representational and practical. That is, in one dimension of reference, the symbol refers representationally to the divine as interpreted in the representational meaning. It also refers representationally to the divine as implying the practical meaning of the divine for the interpreting community. But in

---

36. See the Republic, books 2 and 3; also my *Soldier, Sage, Saint* which identifies the spirited part of the soul with the model of the soldier, the rational part with the sage, and the desiring part with the saint.

addition to both of these meanings, reference in a practical context also performs the reference to the divine as doubly interpreted.

The notion of performative acts was developed by John Searle (following John Austin) and it means that some symbolic acts, "speech acts" he called them, do something other than express propositions, although expressing the propositions is part of the act.[37] So for instance, when in a wedding ceremony the bride and groom say "I do" they not only express their willingness to marry but also, along with the minister's pronouncements, perform the act of marrying. When two parties write their signatures on a contract, that not only expresses their names but performs the act of contracting. When a congregation sings "Holy! Holy! Holy!" it not only describes God (the representational interpretant) and indicates that the congregants appreciate that holiness (the practical interpretant) but it also performs an act of praise of divine holiness. When a religious community hears a sermon about divine condemnation of some of their practices they not only understand the practices as wrong (the representational interpretant) and that they have to change them (the practical interpretant) but the hearing and taking to heart perform an act of contrition in reference to God; to the extent contrition is not performed in the hearing, to that extent the sermon is not referred to the divine judgment but to the preacher's opinion. Chanting mantras or singing *AUM* are speech acts that are not seriously representational.

The last example makes clear that religious symbols can occur within practical cultic and other contexts without being intentionally referred to the divine. The only reference might be to some extensional interpretation in the tradition's symbolic code. For instance, the code (as is true for Christianity's) might allow the extensional interpretation that "God expects loving treatment of all people, including gays and lesbians" and also the alternative extensional interpretation that "God does not expect loving treatment of gays and lesbians." If the preacher preached the first, say, the congregation can take it to heart as referring intentionally to God, whereupon the hearing of the sermon involves something of an act of contrition for any homophobia; or the congregation can interpret the sermon as intending only the preacher's opinion, God's opinion being expressed by the second proposition.

Among the occurrences of religious symbols in practical contexts, therefore, it is important to distinguish those that are interpreted religiously, as referring to the divine, and those that are denied that inten-

---

37. See Searle's *Speech Acts*.

tional reference, although people know that the symbol might be intentionally referred that way because of its extensional references. When religious symbols are intentionally referred to the divine, they are taken religiously and the reference is in part performative.

Liturgical acts are most obviously performatives in their reference. But other kinds of occurrences of symbols in cultic intentional contexts are also performatives. A religious community reads scripture not only for the sake of understanding and conforming to it but also to perform an act of receiving the divine word. Hearing Torah is not reduced to understanding it and acting in conformity. Saying grace before meals or praying toward Mecca five times a day are not merely expressions of thanks and submissions but also the act of thanking and submitting to God. Worshipping in a gothic cathedral is not only to note the majesty of God and the divine light but also to make an act of self-humbling and enlightenment. This is because the way in which the symbolic elements are interpreted is that they are referred to their referents by performing something of their meanings.

One might ask why the performative aspect of interpretation is put on the reference rather than the interpretants. The reason is that an analysis of the extensional interpretations within the code can give rise to both the representational and practical interpretants without any intentional act of engaging the divine. The earlier paragraphs of this section did just that. Few if any readers would employ this text here to engage the divine. In such an analysis, although the interpretants can be understood, developed, assessed, and criticized, no reference need be made beyond the extensional references in the tradition's symbol systems themselves. Performative reference occurs only in intentional reference. My hypothesis is that the practical intentional contexts such as cultic life make many if not all intentional references with religious symbols to be performative as well as representational. Interpretations are no less interpretive for being performative. The meaning of the performative interpretaton is the combination of the representational and practical interpretants.

In sum, the practical contextualization of religious symbols in cultic religious communities involves drawing out doubled interpretants, both representational and practical, the formation of the imaginations of the people involved, and the performance of acts of religious comportment toward the divine as structured by the symbols. These are all senses in which religious symbols shape practice. What is true of cultic communities with regard to these senses of shaping is true as well of the shaping functions of religious symbols in other practical contexts. In the following section I shall not rehearse the practical implications of the interpretation, function, and reference of religious symbols but shall discuss some of the interesting characteristics of and differences among certain of those other contexts.

## 4.4. PUBLIC LIFE, ORDINARY LIFE, AND EXTRAORDINARY LIFE

Religious symbols are to be found in all domains of culture. In 1.3 I discussed briefly the role of religious symbols in defining the sense of obligation in public life. Religious symbols also function importantly in ordinary life and in extraordinary life projects. Each of these is an intentional context for the interpretation of symbols.

Only in recent centuries, and even now not in all religious cultures, has it been sensible to distinguish public life from religious cult. Religious ritual was once the same as court ritual. But the concerns of public life seem to have little to do intrinsically with relations to the divine. Public life deals with such things as the development and enforcement of laws, the administration of a judicial system, promotion and regulation of the economic and perhaps educational systems, diplomatic relations among societies, keeping public order and maintaining military force for defense or other purposes. To anticipate an argument that will be made in more detail in 6.2, life has many dimensions, each subject to certain norms. Thus, to use the above examples, there are norms for good laws for various situations, for effective and fair administration of justice, for the production and distribution of wealth, for social support of good education, for diplomatic probity and effectiveness, and for military development and deployment.[38] Many of life's activities are under obligation to different norms at once.[39] Hence we should call them "dimensions" because they interpenetrate rather than separate *areas* of discrete activities or *layers* of activities such as Aristotle's levels of soul.[40] The dimensions listed might be lumped together as subdimensions of public

---

38. I have discussed the multiplicity of norms for various interdependent but also quasi-independent social processes and institutions in *The Cosmology of Freedom*, part 3, and especially in *Normative Cultures*, chapters 6–8.

39. On the problems of handling conflicting norms in the balancing of life, see my *The Puritan Smile*, chapter 10.

40. See Tillich's very important discussion of the metaphor of *dimensions* versus that of *levels* in his *Systematic Theology III*, pp. 11–30.

religious symbols in ordinary life is even more important than it is in cultic life. Or if ordinary life is not shaped by religious symbols in a serious way, it is bereft of its religious dimension. According to Taylor, Christianity has been particularly important in developing the modern emphasis on ordinary life, and part of contemporary confusions about the Good Life come from the evacuation of its symbols in ordinary life.

By "extraordinary life" I mean a modern phenomenon set beside but contrasted with ordinary life. Many people are not satisfied with ordinary life and undertake life-projects of heroic, if modern proportions. One thinks of artists and poets, of athletes, dancers, actors, musicians, of political leaders, of leading educators, of explorers, even of outstanding religious leaders. Not satisfied with the fulfillments of ordinary life they stretch the envelope of ordinary work to have careers aiming at great accomplishments. Many ordinary people live extraordinary lives vicariously, perhaps most often in reference to athletes and media figures.

The extraordinary lives are not guided principally by religious goals, by endeavoring to relate rightly and deeply to the divine, except perhaps in the case of some religious figures. They are guided rather by the norms of their field of endeavor—cultural, athletic, political, military, scientific excellence, for instance. They might think of themselves as secular and even hostile to cultic religious practice. Yet religious symbols often shape their understanding and projects of extraordinary life. On the one hand religious symbols can shape their sense of their own identity as striving, reaching for perfection or accomplishment. On the other hand they can also shape the content of the projects, as in the religious symbolic character of the arts, the religious importance of public life, the religious character of adventure and questing. It is extraordinary, for instance, how Einstein appealed to religious symbols in his quest for a unified physical theory, as in his reaction to the Copenhagen interpretation of quantum mechanics ("God does not play dice").

The analysis given above of the structure of religious symbols in practical intentional contexts applies as well to the practical context of attempting to live an extraordinary life. That is, the religious symbols form the imagination, they have both representational and practical interpretants, and they refer performatively. What is significant for at least some people defining themselves by the quest for extraordinary life is that their project itself is a performative religious reference. By their pursuit of art, political eminence, or adventure they offer their lives as ways to be rightly related to the ultimate boundaries of things, to the divine as defined by their religious symbols. The content of their project might not be defined by religious symbols, but their embrace of it is. Most religious traditions have symbol systems for the religious significance of heroism, archaic as that might seem in the modern culture of ordinary life. The very conception of life as a quest, as giving oneself over to a work, as a test of limits, is religious, Promethean in fact, modelled by Rama, Gilgamesh, Abraham, and others. Extraordinary life in the modern culture of ordinary life is rarely cultic in its religious content. But its religious dimension derives from deep cultic symbols.

I have tried in this chapter to lay out some of the structures of religious symbols as they are interpreted in intentional contexts, focusing primarily on theological and practical contexts. But perhaps the most important intentional context in which religious symbols are interpreted, which in return reshapes religious symbols, is that of devotional life, of individuals and communities. The next chapter is focused on its analysis.

# CHAPTER 5

# Symbols for Transformation

Religious symbols are supposed to be true to what they symbolize and they are also supposed to be effective in transforming their interpreters to be better in accord with what they symbolize. Insofar as the former supposition is emphasized we engage in theology and philosophy, or their equivalents in traditions that use different terms. Theology's interest is to say in as many ways as possible what the truth of a symbol is, its strengths, ranges of application, and limitations. The conditions for theological truth are enormously complex and have to do not only with the objects of symbolism, divine matters in some sense, but also with the conditions of interpretation, the cultures within which the symbols are interpreted. Religious symbols can be very powerful as transformers of persons and cultures, but if they are not true they are idolatrous and perhaps even demonic: idolatry loses one side of the finite/infinite referent, and demonism embodies the wrong representational and practical interpretants in the interpreters.

When the second supposition is emphasized, namely, that religious symbols are supposed to transform their interpreters to be in better accord with what they symbolize, a different set of considerations becomes important. The high abstractions at the outcome of theological investigation are likely to be so removed from symbolic powers of transformation as to be inefficacious and symbolically barren. For the sake of transformative power, symbols are embellished and enriched, mutually engaged and made to resonate with one another, laid down on top of one another and layered with networks of symbol systems compacted and interwoven. Fanciful as these are, is it legitimate for them not to be true? Surely not, but they cannot be true in exactly the same sense that theology wants symbols to be true, that is, to represent the symbols' objects accurately to the interpreters. For the transformative point of religious symbols is to adjust the interpreters so that they themselves, personally and in community, come into better and deeper accord with the religious objects. The tension between the interests of truth and those of transformation is the subject for this chapter.

The argument here has four parts. In the first section I shall discuss religious transformation itself and make four main points. The first is that the transformative power of religious symbols is specific to the *state* of a person's soul. Second, a distinction will be drawn between a person's psychological state and the process of spiritual growth. Third, it will be argued that there is something of a sequence of *stages* in spiritual matu-ration, different from psychological stages. The last, and perhaps para-doxical, point is that religious symbols are *not* helpfully sorted by appro-priateness for different stages, although their differential function is appropriate by stage and state.

The second section will analyze the reference of devotional symbols, and suggest that they have dual reference, primarily to finite-infinite contrasts and secondarily to the state and stage of the specific devotee. The third section will focus on the meaning of devotional symbols and argue that they function in networks so as to create a transformative *world of meaning* for devotees. Then the fourth section will take up special issues of the contexts of the use of devotional symbols and ask how the concern for their truth relates to the control of the exaggerated and fantastic qual-ity of devotional symbols.

A word should be said about my use of the word *soul* in this chapter. *Soul* has a fairly technical and controversial history in Western theology, signifying for some a contrast with body and for others the unity of the whole person; it has sometimes been identified with the self, and at other times distinguished from it. The word has been used to translate the Sanskrit atman, of which there are different theories in the samkhya, yoga, and other traditions, and the existence of which is denied in Buddhism. There are hardly even rough parallels in Chinese, although meditative Daoists conceive of something like a disembodied soul that can be cultivated to extend life. Yet we need a word that signifies a person considered in relation to finite/infinite contrasts. Let the word *soul* be used generally to mean a person as expressed in the religious dimension of life, leaving aside dis-putes about what that might be, except insofar as they are discussed below.

## 5.1. DEVOTIONAL LIFE AS TRANSFORMATION

Religious symbols, as we have noted, are of many sorts: pictorial, musi-cal, architectural, artifactual, natural, including places, times, processes, and things, and, of course, words; verbal symbols include scriptures, liturgies, creeds, stories, and theologies. Religious symbols also function in many intentional contexts, as discussed in the previous chapter, including theology and other forms of straightforward reflection about the objects of religious symbolism, practical contexts of organizing religious life, the wider public contexts that borrow religious symbolism for domains such as politics or art, and devotional contexts of spiritual formation in which religious symbols are developed, cultivated, and employed to lead the soul.

I have so far been careful not to suggest that there are different religious symbols for different intentional contexts. There is not one set of theological symbols contrasted with another set that have practical bearing on leading the religious life, in turn contrasted with another group of symbols that have devotional currency. Rather, most symbols function in all these contexts, often at the same time. Nevertheless the intentional contexts exert a force on the shaping of the symbols. The theological use of symbols nudges them toward clarity, systematic definability, perhaps abstract applicability to different instances, and a readiness to affirm or deny in ways that can be understood as representational and true or false. The practical use of symbols nudges toward analogical generalizibility, discrimination regarding consequences, and readiness to be exemplified in social relations and actions that can be given non-religious descriptions. The devotional use of symbols, while perhaps a species of practical usage, stretches symbols beyond safe theological representationalism and responsible practical application to have a power of transforming the soul. The transformations at stake are radical, such as dissolving the soul completely, filling it with the infinite, transporting it across the finite/infinite boundary. No wonder the devotional use of symbols shapes them in exaggerated and fantastic ways. Much confusion about religious symbols arises when symbols shaped dramatically for one context are used in another. Imagine a sober theologian trying to understand eschatological matters by having to pick among heavenly images of cities, mansions, and gardens!

The place to begin a discussion of religious symbols in devotional contexts is to note the wide variety of such contexts. There are many social locations for devotional life—the cultus of a religious community, active public life, rustication in nature, with others in worship, alongside others in coenobitic monasteries, in anchoritic isolation, with a guru, and so forth. This discussion, for the sake of relative brevity, will be focused mainly on the devotional life of individuals, especially individuals in congregations. Individuals are specific with regard to the spiritual state in which they are, and with regard to the stage of their spiritual maturity.

By spiritual state I mean the intersection of the person's relation to the divine with all the other things descriptive of that person. These include the person's gender, social class, historical identity, family relations, age, friends and enemies, kinds of participation in society and culture, education, psychological health and maturity, and whether she or he has been to Paris. Perhaps most important for the differential impact of devotional symbols is the religious culture within which the person has been raised or is familiar, and the associations of this with other religious cultures and with secularism; religious cultures provide a kind of baseline self-interpretation in spiritual matters. That the ways symbols would be effective for transforming a person depends on the state of the person in this sense is obvious, although the specific differences between the ways are not obvious. Feminists have called attention to the differences between women's and men's spirituality.[1] Liberationists have called attention to the role of social class.[2] The differential effects of language and membership in historical groups have been understood since Babel and contemporary pluralistic societies provide constant reminders. Sociologists and social psychologists have shown how one's "state of soul" is determined in part by the specifics of one's relationships to others in the family and community, by occupation or calling, by neighborhood. Education makes an enormous difference to which symbols are transformatively significant, and so, of course, does one's psychological state.

---

1. Because of my own gender bias in discussing the devotional use of symbols, it might be helpful to list some feminist perspectives. Phyllis Zagano's *Woman to Woman* presents brief biographies and selections from classical women writers on spirituality, from Hildegaard of Bingen to the twentieth century. Judith Plaskow and Carol P. Christ's *Weaving the Visions* contains essays from most of the important contemporary feminist writers on spirituality. Carol Gilligan's *In a Different Voice* presents a detailed scientific case for differences between women's and men's psychological development; although psychology ought not be confused with spirituality, it often is and is important for understanding the feminist discussion. Susan Cady, Marian Ronan, and Hal Taussig's *Sophia* is the study of a Biblical idea that has inspired quite radical feminist spiritualities, including the return to Wicca. Carter Heyward's *Touching Our Strength* develops a powerful spiritual vision based on stereotypic "feminine" traits such as mutuality and eros. Rita M. Gross' *Buddhism after Patriarchy* is a marvelous study by an American feminist of Buddhist history and structures, including spirituality. Susan Thistlethwaite's *Sex, Race, and God* is a reminder of the diversity of women's spiritualities even within American Christianity.

2. See Margaret R. Miles' *Practicing Christianity*.

One way of studying the history of the development of religious symbols would be to explore how they are modified to address newly encountered states of soul. Buddhism was developed by a coterie of people deeply committed to the religious quest in the form of ascetic life; yet it quickly developed symbols for relating to non-ascetics and for people who had to be taught that they had religious needs.[3] Christianity began as a small-town provincial movement and yet in one generation had developed a symbology addressing sophisticated urban dwellers.[4] Where religions lack symbols to relate to the rich or the poor, they have to develop them. When their symbols seem to distort or marginalize the experience of people in this or that state, the symbols need to be amended or supplemented. A symbol such as the Exodus can be the ground of Zionist nationalism to some Jews, the ground of hope for freedom from the effects of slavery for African-Americans, and the ground for identifying God in salvation history for German theologians, each barely comprehending what the symbol means for the others, and not transformed by those other meanings. A person's identity, made up of a far greater array of interactive factors than those epitomized here, constitutes a complex state of soul that the transformative devotional symbols need to address. A person can learn theology and move abstractly with ease among many symbols that do not have devotional transformative power. A person can participate effectively in a symbolically shaped religious community whose symbols include many that do not have much devotional significance for that person, although they might have for others in the community. In their devotional function, religious symbols are state-specific for persons.

Psychology, the science of soul, has often been confused with spirituality. This is particularly true in its practical application as psychotherapy. Pastoral psychology as a modern theological discipline has been ambivalent as to whether it is an updated version of spiritual formation and direction, making use of what has been learned from scientific psychology, or rather a form of psychotherapy engaged in by religious people who are at home with religious symbols.[5] Psychotherapy aims to treat psychopathologies and character disorders, and to help people to a prop-

---

3. See Eckel's *To See the Buddha* and Gross's *Buddhism after Patriarchy*.

4. See Wayne Meeks's *The First Urban Christians*.

5. My colleague, Merle Jordan, has pointed out this confusion in his *Taking on the Gods: The Task of the Pastoral Counselor*, which attempts to translate some psychological notions into theological ones.

erly mature emotional life. Emotional maturity is closely related to psychopathologies and character disorders because the latter are thought to derive in part from emotional fixations at earlier stages in the person's emotional development. Psychotherapy aims at psychological health, which is variously defined as the capacity to work and love, the manifestation of a mature personality, realism, self-knowledge and acceptance, and a flexibility to relate to the world without having to filter it through one's own, often repressed, pretences. Self-actualization or self-fulfillment is very important for psychological health.[6]

Spirituality, by contrast, is concerned with the relation of people to the divine whatever their state or their stage of psychological growth. It aims to conform people more and more to the divine, and has something like a sequence of stages for doing this. Obviously, persons' psychological states will make a difference to the religious symbols that can be transformative. People who have been abused as children by their parents will relate to parental symbols of the divine differently from those who were not so abused, either rejecting them completely or idealizing them. People who are deeply narcissistic will have as hard a time relating to God as to their human friends. People who are psychologically and socially healthy might have little motivation to quest for something bigger in life, and hence be uninterested in religion. The psychologically healthy can be in deep ignorance of any traditional religious symbols whatsoever. Twentieth-century psychology as a science has itself been fairly hostile to religion and generally has interpreted religious symbols reductively, that is, as not referring to God but to rebellion against parents or the projection of psychological needs.[7]

Some thinkers have attempted to develop a sophisticated psychological understanding of "stages of faith," to use James Fowler's phrase.[8] This takes its form from developmental psychology, and its inspiration to generalize to spiritual matters from Kohlberg's and Gilligan's theories of moral development.[9] "Stages of faith" theories should be understood

---

6. Especially in the thinking of Abraham Maslow, who is influential in pastoral psychology.

7. The most famous text is Freud's *The Future of an Illusion*. For an interpretation of the effects of this on subsequent theology, see Peter Homans' *Theology after Freud*. For a discussion of the hostility transformed to displacement, see Philip Rieff's *The Triumph of the Therapeutic*.

8. From the title of his book, *Stages of Faith*.

9. See Lawrence Kohlberg's "Stage and Sequence" and "From Is to Ought"; see Gilligan's *In a Different Voice*. See Kohlberg and Gilligan, "The Adolescent as Philosopher."

as psychological theories that describe various states of soul that religious symbols might have to address. They are not descriptive of stages of spiritual growth. Often the failure to recognize this leads to deeply conflicted interpretations of the roles of religious symbols. In psychological growth, for instance, it is important for children before adolescence to lay down a sense of basic trust and of competence in their own ability as agents.[10] The spiritual encounter with the holy, on the other hand, sometimes even in maturity scares the bejesus out of people and renders them impotent in the face of the divine. Religious symbols sometimes need to convey awesomeness and evoke terror and a breakdown of "basic trust," a destruction of the sense of competence. This is so the more advanced one is spiritually: Isaiah trembling before the throne of God was not having an infantile regression (Isaiah 6). Psychotherapy seeks to overcome the debilitating effects of neurotic guilt; spirituality often needs to transform even minor guilt into total wretchedness before God, if only for a while.[11] Psychotherapy works for wholeness, fulfill-

---

10. This thesis has been made central by Erik Erikson. See his *Childhood and Society*.

11. John Calvin opens the *Institutes of the Christian Religion* with the argument that, if we contemplate the true wretchedness of the human condition, we are led immediately to the glory of God, and if we contemplate the glory of God, we are led immediately to perceive the wretchedness of the human condition; but most of us are blind and irreligious because we begin with banalities about God or with self-deceived complacency about the human condition: true spirituality requires moving to one limit or the other. His argument is classic and worth quoting:

> Nearly all the wisdom we possess, that is to say, true and sound wisdom, consists of two parts: the knowledge of God and of ourselves. But, while joined by many bonds, which one precedes and brings forth the other is not easy to discern. In the first place, no one can look upon himself without immediately turning his thoughts to the contemplation of God, in whom he "lives and moves." For, quite clearly, the mighty gifts with which we are endowed are hardly from ourselves; indeed, our very being is nothing but subsistence in the one God. Then, by these benefits shed like dew from heaven upon us, we are led as by rivulets to the spring itself. Indeed, our very poverty better discloses the infinitude of benefits reposing in God. . . . For, as a veritable world of miseries is to be found in mankind, and we are thereby despoiled of divine raiment, our shameful nakedness exposes a teeming horde of infamies. Each of us must, then, be so stung by the consciousness of his own unhappiness as to attain at least some knowledge of God. Thus, from the feeling of our own ignorance, vanity, poverty, infirmity, and—what is more—depravity and corruption, we recognize that the true light of wisdom, sound virtue, full abundance of every good, and purity of righteousness rest in the Lord alone. To this extent we are prompted by our own ills to contemplate the good things of God; and we cannot seriously

ment, and competence of personality, with rewarding interpersonal relations; spirituality in many traditions seeks a broken spirit, the abandonment of self, the sacrifice of fulfillment, and the ability to face God alone as well as in community. The failure to recognize the distinction between the aims of psychological health and those of a spiritual career in relation to the divine usually leads to the reduction of religious symbols to psychological analogues, and so often their very force is reversed.

But the devotional use of religious symbols is not independent of the psychological state they must address. If persons have not developed a psychologically adequate sense of basic trust, they find it extremely difficult to relate to the religious symbols of God the destroyer or the God who says not to put your trust in chariots and bowmen, without giving those

---

aspire to him before we begin to become displeased with ourselves. For what man in all the world would not gladly remain as he is—what man does not remain as he is—so long as he does not know himself, that is, while content with his own gifts, and either ignorant or unmindful of his own misery. . . .

Again, it is certain that man never achieves a clear knowledge of himself unless he has first looked upon God's face, and then descends from contemplating him to scrutinize himself. For we always seem to ourselves righteous and upright and wise and holy—this pride is innate in all of us—unless by clear proofs we stand convinced of our own unrighteousness, foulness, folly, and impurity. Moreover, we are not thus convinced if we look merely to ourselves and not also to the Lord, who is the sole standard by which this judgment must be measured. For, because all of us are inclined by nature to hypocrisy, a kind of empty image of righteousness in place of righteousness itself abundantly satisfies us. And because nothing appears within or around us that has not been contaminated by great immorality, what is a little less vile pleases us as a thing most pure—so long as we confine our minds within the limits of human corruption. . . . So it happens in estimating our spiritual goods. As long as we do not look beyond the earth, being quite content with our own righteousness, wisdom, and virtue, we flatter ourselves most sweetly, and fancy ourselves all but demigods. *Institutes*, pp. 35–38.

Calvin's own spirituality is by no means universal. His description here of pride, for instance, illustrates what Valerie Saiving, in "The Human Situation," and others have characterized as men's spirituality from which women's is quite different. She would argue that women start off with the wretchedness and self-debasement Calvin believes comes only from a contrasting vision of God. But Calvin's point about the banality of complacency is well taken, whether of the masculine or feminine form, and it bears upon the difference between psychological and spiritual development. Psychologically, it might be important for people to get to feel a little better about themselves, particularly if they suffer from character disorders; spiritually, that might in the long run be a step toward having the courage to encounter God, but in itself it merely builds greater defenses against spiritual progress.

an infantile interpretation relating to the dependency of infancy. If persons have not overcome neurotic guilt and become able to assess real guilts and failures accurately, then they cannot easily understand the wretchedness of the human condition in relation to divine glory without taking it to be a childish insult. If persons have not developed a psychologically healthy sense of themselves as competent people with strong and resilient egos, they cannot give themselves over to the divine, abandoning their egos, without that being likely a useless, childish gesture. Although there is a great danger that the psychological mind-set will reductively distort and destroy the transformative power of religious symbols in devotional life, there is an even greater danger that real psychological pathologies, character disorders, and immaturities will render religious symbols merely psychological, not capable of referring to the divine.

Having said this, it is also important to notice that sometimes people who are deeply crippled psychologically still are heroes of devotional life. They reverse the psychological reductionism and can use their psychological infirmities as ways to relate to genuine engagements of the divine. Poor, mad William Cowper, the eighteenth-century poet who spent much of his life in insane asylums, wrote some of the most spiritually moving hymns in Christendom. We in the Freudian age cannot take his references to "bathing in fountains of the savior's blood" without smiling; but to get inside his imagery is to see holiness there, not only psychopathology.[12] John Wesley, an obsessive-compulsive, anal-retentive

---

12. Around 1771 Cowper wrote:

There is a fountain filled with blood drawn from Emmanuel's veins;
And sinners plunged beneath that flood lose all their guilty stains.

The dying thief rejoiced to see that fountain in his day;
And there may I, though vile as he, wash all my sins away.

Dear dying Lamb, thy precious blood shall never lose its power
Till all the ransomed church of God be saved, to sin no more

E'er since, by faith, I saw the stream thy flowing wounds supply,
Redeeming love has been my theme, and shall be till I die.

That hymn is number 622 in the current *United Methodist Hymnal.* That hymnal does not have his far more serene "Light Shining Out of Darkness":

God moves in a mysterious way,
 His wonders to perform;
He plants his footsteps in the sea,
 And rides upon the storm.

neurotic who took his "spiritual temperature" many times a day and could never have a serious friend, let alone a mature sexual relation, overrode this infantile character that would have crippled most people to become the highly successful leader of a religious movmement in which most of his contemporary leaders failed.[13] He also developed an exquisite sense of spiritual balance that allowed him to avoid the excesses of the revivalist movement, without benefit of a clear theology that allowed him to state his own way positively. Psychological disabilities, like social alienation, poverty, and physical infirmaties, can be overcome by the heroes of spiritual life. But it seems to require heroism, just as heroism is required for psychological health in the state of deep poverty or for a successful career with psychological disabilities. Attention to devotional formation does not have to wait upon glowing psychological and physical health, nor upon a full stomach and the honoring of one's race and gender in a decent society.

The principle distinguishing spiritual concerns from psychological ones, and from all the other concerns that define a person's "state," is that

Deep in unfathomable mines
Of never failing skill;
He treasures up his bright designs,
And works his sovereign will.

Ye fearful saints fresh courage take,
The clouds ye so much dread
Are big with mercy, and shall break
In blessings on your head.

Judge not the Lord by feeble sense,
But trust him for his grace;
Behind a frowning providence,
He hides a smiling face.

His purposes will ripen fast,
Unfolding ev'ry hour;
The bud may have a bitter taste,
But sweet will be the flow'r.

Blind unbelief is sure to err,
And scan his work in vain;
God is his own interpreter,
And he will make it plain.

Compare that to the passage from Calvin quoted in the note above.

13. Henry Rack's *Reasonable Enthusiast* is a detailed and friendly analysis of Wesley's life and character. Henry Abelove's *The Evangelist of Desire* is less friendly because it usually takes psychological assessments as the bottom line.

in spiritual matters, the religious symbols function to relate the person to the divine in transformative ways. Symbols arising primarily from psychological, social class, gender, occupational, and historical matters can themselves be reshaped to engage one with the divine.

Now we can ask about the developmental structure of spiritual life itself. The yogic traditions of India provide far more complex models of spiritual development than I will employ here, often conceived as stretching through many life-times. My present purpose is to make some rough distinctions for an ordinary life-span. Four levels of spiritual growth can be distinguished, blocked out on life stages typical of modern society: the student, the boundary crosser, the embodier, and the seeker for union. These perhaps overly dramatic titles will be explained shortly. They obviously are not discrete stages such that one stops being a student when one encounters the finite/infinite contrast, nor does one abandon the shattering encounter with God when one comes to shape an ordinary life with its responsibilities in terms of that encounter; nor does one abandon the responsibilities of life when focusing on union with God, or the Vision, or Nirvanic enlightenment. Nor are they necessarily ordered in sequence: one might become a student of divine things only after a dramatic encounter. But by and large, one begins by learning the meanings of religious symbols, then most likely in adolescence comes to see something previously taken for granted to be a boundary condition revealing the divine, and then comes to integrate this into the texture of a family and career, and then shifts the emphasis to union with God as death becomes more real. The key to the logic of the stages is the semiotic structure we have already analyzed: learning the meanings of the religious symbols, learning to refer them to the divine, learning to embody them in the practical contexts of life, and then finally bringing the engagement with the divine to culmination. These will be discussed in turn.

The student stage involves the learning of religious symbols as parts of a religious semiotic code. This can begin very early, with the learning of language, and it is obviously related to what children are ready for in their psycho-social development. For instance, as children learn basic trust and personal competence, they can learn the religious symbols that interpret this. A child in a Christian family, for instance, can learn to sing "Jesus Loves Me" when the emotional experience of love is derived from the family setting; the extensional referent in that song, however, is not mother or father but Jesus as interpreted in Biblical symbols. The child can learn to sing "Jesus wants me for a sunbeam to shine for him each day" and understand the song by means of an emerging sense of competence and approval for being good; the religious extensional referent again is Jesus, however, and the imagery of the light that glorifies is not quite the same as getting to the toilet in time or remembering to say "please" and "thank you."

Religious symbols are not coextensive with the goals of psychosocial development, however. Children encounter sickness, death, and tragedy, wickedness at home in those who are supposed to love them, humiliation and brutalization at school and play. If they do not learn the songs of grief and comfort, the symbols of sin and forgiveness, courage and endurance, they not only miss the realistic scope of things symbolized in religious systems but also are deceived about the religious character of life. Psychological approaches to religious symbolism sometimes over-emphasize the healthy-minded symbols associated with positive stages of emotional growth. They also sometimes depreciate the symbols of death, tragedy, betrayal, and wickedness out of fear that children will internalize the causes of suffering to themselves, blaming themselves for mother's alcoholism or father's incestuous abuse, believing they deserve the bad things that happen to them, or even cause them.[14] But this is to fail to see that the religious symbols refer to the divine, even if only in extensional ways within the religious semiotic systems; it is to treat them instead as if, for children, the symbols refer to the significant people around them. By a perverse logic, some psychologists have taken the analogy between symbols of the divine and symbols of psychological relations with significant others to mean that children have to experience the emotional quality as referring to the relations with those others when they think they are experiencing the divine. Pseudo-research into images of God supposes that these have to derive from images of parents and signficant others, and then on that supposition prove the supposition to be true. This of course begs the question. But there are very many images of God accessible to children, for instance the warmth of sunlight, birth and growth in nature, as well as death and destruction, that have little or nothing to do with personalistic images modelled after parents. Religious symbologies distinctly mark differences between God and parents, and children can experience their parents in a religious world-view of symbols, as fellow creatures, just as they can think of God loving in vastly different ways from the parental love they experience.

---

14. See for instance Marie Fortune's *Sexual Violence.* See also Sheila Redmond's "Christian 'Virtues' and Recovery from Child Sexual Abuse."

What psychologists can do to anthropomorphize religious symbols, societies can do too; perhaps a therapeutic society is prone to this. Then of course the symbols in question are not religious symbols but personalistic ones with a peculiar archaic shape.

The point to notice is that the religious semiotic is not identical to the psychological one, but has a structure of extensional referents and interpretants that allows for a different interpretation of the things that might also be interpreted secularly or in terms of non-religious symbols. As children grow, they can explore the complexities of the systems of religious symbols and perhaps even interpret their lives, or at least their world, in religious terms. This is obviously an unending process, for even the most sophisticated religious person at whatever spiritual stage can gain greater understanding of and competence at the intricacies of the systems of religious meanings.

Childhood vests one with a host of doubled symbols of religious matters, doubled in the sense that they are given a childish expression accompanied with an asterisk signifying that there is an adult version one cannot understand yet. These symbols are picked up from the media, from school, perhaps from participation in a religious community, and from friends who have their own religious communities. Many people, perhaps even most, never go on to receive the adult version of the symbols, however much their spiritual lives might mature in other respects. Likely this is because the adults around them are themselves limited to childish versions of the symbols and are half-conscious of the fact. Another cause of perpetual childishness is that media, religious and otherwise, usually have to address a broad audience and therefore pitch to the lowest, that is, most childish, common denominator. Yet another reason is that the distinction is hard to draw sometimes between a merely childish symbol and one that has been made exaggerated and fantastic so as to relate to the spiritual state of a person at a later stage of development, as I shall discuss below.

It is typical for a child, a student of religious meanings or one bereft of religious symbolism, to become a boundary crosser around the onset of adolescence. Something is experienced that shocks the person suddenly to see the limits, the particularity, the peculiarity, the finiteness of the life-world, sensing the infinite or sublime beyond that. For a great many people this is an experience in nature, of the night sky, of the mountains, the sea, or the vastness of the prairies; nature itself contrasts with the conventionality of the ordinary lineaments of the life-world, including the conventionality of the system of religious symbols in which the person might have been raised. For others the beyond–limits experience is occasioned by encountering an especially wicked or especially saintly person, or by the sudden recognition of obligation beyond convention, or by facing disease or death in an existential way. Something truly beautiful, recognized as such for the first time, can constitute such an experience of the boundary.[15] Prior to this time in a child's experience, none of these things symbolized the limits. When the occasion arises, however, the person sees the ordinary world as circumscribed, perhaps not yet as one world among many, or one construal of life among many, but still as bounded by the non–world.

Some thinkers like to call that which lies beyond the limits "the transcendent," because it transcends the limits of worldliness. But, satisfactory as that is in some contexts, it also suggests that the operative movement is from within the world to the outside. On the contrary, the beyond–limits is experienced as the sustaining context for the world. The world is apprehended as contingent upon that which is not, as the Earth and its human scale is but a speck in the vast cosmic whirl of gasses. The beyond–limits is experienced as the most real, or the reality that cannot be questioned, whereas the world within–limits is suddenly experienced as dependent, fragile, and perhaps evanescent. My language here is highly interpretive of what is actually experienced in terms of far more concrete things taken to be symbolic.

The result of the adolescent beyond–limits experience is that the person now is conscious, through some symbols or others, of having a career relative to what is beyond the limits as well as a career within the limits of the world. Perhaps this is nothing more than feeling small in the face of the night sky. Perhaps it is a resolve to be saintly instead of just good. But it complicates the teenager's sense of self by laying a problematic relation on top of all the other problematic relations of the adolescent's world, namely, how to comport oneself in the face of that which is not determined by the ordinary world at all.

Many young people have ready–made systems of religious symbols into which to translate their limit experiences. The beyond–limit context of contexts is taken to be God, and their religious community has a plan for how properly to relate to God. Or the beyond–limit is limitless Brahman, the experience of which is bliss. Many other young people, however, have few or no symbolic resources at this point and the limit expe-

---

15. See James Alfred Martin's *Beauty and Holiness*.

riences are forgotten, repressed, or translated into quite mundane symbols of psychology, politics, or morality, perhaps even into demonic symbols. The point remains that typically during adolescence, resulting from some kind of limit-experience, people attain some consciousness of the religious dimension of life and begin to organize their lives so as to include that. They imagine their previous religious understanding to be conventional and now ask whether those conventions are adequate to what they have encountered. They envision or imagine their careers not only as budding lovers, athletes, workers, citizens, and family members, but also as related to the world's limits and what lies beyond. This religious dimension begins to be articulated and grasped in informal and formal rituals and in conceptions of various kinds. Young people also feel the need to do something with themselves so as to be worthy or open or attuned to the limit situation.

In some religious traditions these boundary-crossing experiences are regarded as conversions. Sometimes this is entirely appropriate, as when repeated experiences cause shift after shift in the orientation of one's religious engagement. The point to be emphasized, however, is the shift from merely interpreting one's life within the play of religious symbols to using those symbols to engage the divine. This requires actual interpretive engagements of the divine, often sparked by limit-situation encounters, by employing the symbols intentionally. Instead of limiting reference to the extensional referents within the semiotic system, the boundary crosser makes interpretive acts in which the finite/infinite contrasts are intentionally referred to by means of the symbols. This is not to say that the divine was not in fact being interpreted by the child; indeed if the symbol systems is a good one, then the divine effectively engages the child. But the child was not aware, before becoming a boundary crosser, of the difference between interpretive play within the semiotic system and the act of using the symbol system intentionally to refer to the divine. The boundary crosser is aware, at least vaguely, of the fact the symbols are all broken, all problematic. Something is encountered that needs to be symbolized, not something that is automatically carried by the semiotic system. The symbol system at hand might be quite adequate to interpret the boundary crossing, and can be affirmed as such. For many adolescents, this is the occasion for becoming serious about their inherited religion. But with the boundary crossing, the person becomes aware that intentional reference is dealing with a real object to which the symbols need to be adequate, rather than with an object as defined by the code of symbols. Before the boundary crossing, the student interprets life in a network relating himself or herself to God and the world; after, the boundary crosser is existentially aware of having a career in relation to the divine. The divine makes some kind of claim on what the person is to do and be.[16]

At this point, the life of devotion becomes that of the embodier. How can the divine be made relevant to life? Or, more likely, what needs to be done with life to acknowledge the encountered divine? The relation between the boundary crosser and the embodier is peculiarly dialectical. The boundary crossing experience is likely to lead to all sorts of exotic quests for better symbols and for a special way of life. The boundary crosser attempts to understand all his or her previous life from the standpoint of the divine. Everything looks different. Parents and friends are trapped in old ways of looking at things; even one's old religious symbols seem conventional and need to be interpreted from a new perspective if not just exchanged for others. As Mahayana Buddhists put it, there is a lower truth about the wheel of ordinary life, and there is a higher truth encountered in the discovery of the suchness of things and consequent liberation from binding attachments to the world. But then, say the Buddhists, one comes to understand that the enlightened life in accord with the divine truth of emptiness is not something transcendent but is in fact the wheel of ordinary life. The higher truth is that the lower truth is the truth, without the binding attachments that tried to turn the lower truth into some higher truth. So, the way to live the religious life is not necessarily to do something special, although the Buddhists like most other religious traditions had monasteries; the way to live the religious life is to do the ordinary things in the world, but conformed to the liberating higher truth.[17] As Kierkegaard put it in the case of Christian-

---

16. Notice how strikingly different this account of adolescent religious awakening is from Fowler's in *Stages of Faith*. His account makes no reference to relating the ordinary world to the divine but focuses on the psychological aspects of moving out of oneself to conform to the expectations of others and then moving out of that, which he interprets as conventionality, to a stage of taking responsibility for oneself over against the expectations of others. See his discussions of stages 3 and 4, chapters 18 and 19. On the philosophic side his approach reflects' Kohlberg's use of Kant's notions of autonomy and heteronomy (stage 3 is heteronomous, 4 is autonomous) and also Hegel's idea of the self developing out of itself in relation to others, not in relation to a religious object or condition.

17. A concise Chinese Buddhist statement of this is Chi-tsang's "Treatise on the Two Levels of Truth" in Chan, p. 360. A very elaborate philosophical analysis is Malcolm David Eckel's *Jnanagarbha's Commentary on the Distinction between the Two Truths*. A very subtle and straightforward interpretation, placing the doctrine of the Two Truths in

ity, the knight of faith cannot be distinguished from ordinary people in social context.[18]

Nevertheless, it is very difficult to conform ordinary life with all its responsibilities to the divine. Most of practical religious life has to do with embodying the divine in various activities and engaging in those activities that can be symbolically grasped as embodying the divine. Family life, work, participation in society and culture—all these are practical loci for the embodiment of the divine. Devotional life at this stage has to do with understanding and conforming oneself to the divine in the midst of life's responsibilities.

The Vedic tradition of Hinduism distinguished four stages of devotional life similar but not identical to those distinguished here. For the ancient Hindu, one is first a student, then a householder, then a forest dweller who has left home (often with spouse) for spiritual wandering, and then an ascetic. I have elided the last two into one stage of seeking union with the divine, and have inserted the dramatic turning point of the boundary crosser between the student and householder stage. The elision comes from the lack of universality in the social situation supposed in Vedic religion, in which parents with grown children need to vacate the premises to let the next generation become householders, and in the lack of universality in asceticism as the form of the spiritual journey. The insertion of the boundary-crossing stage reflects the post-European Enlightenment fact that the shift from conventional mastery of a symbol system to its use in interpreting the encountered divine is likely to be a big bump, not a slow transition. But the Hindus were profoundly apt in characterizing the stage of *embodying* the divine as that of the householder. People take up responsibilities for themselves and others in late adolescence and become ever more thickly involved in family, friends, work, and community life until very late. The devotional life of the householder is very practical indeed. Of course it can include many experiences of boundary crossing; religious communities often attempt to regularize this in numinous liturgies, retreats, and the like.[19] And of course, study of the symbols, both theological and practical, continues throughout the householding stage. The transformative powers of devotional symbols are specific to the states and stages involved.

---

the context of the system of Buddhist soteriological symbols, is Park Sung-bae's in *Buddhist Faith and Sudden Enlightenment*, chapter 6.

18. See Kierkegaard's *Fear and Trembling*, "Preliminary Expectoration."

19. See Charles Taylor's discussion of *ordinary life* in his *Sources of the Self*.

The householder stage is occupied, in its religious dimension, with making the matters of religious symbolism concrete. The symbols need to be made effective in informing the behaviors of organized life in private and public, and devotionally they need to be explored, understood, and made vital. The network meanings of the religious symbols need to be transformed into content meanings. These general remarks can be made more specific by taking the Christian tradition as a test case; similar points can be made for other religions' symbol systems, although each system itself is particular. Christian symbol systems generally move in spiritual growth from responding to God in wonder and fear alone to responding also in love. This growth involves advancing in symbols about God, grasping God's nature in relation to the world and oneself more deeply. The growth also involves transforming the symbols of oneself in relation to God. One's relation to God is never separate from one's relations to other people, institutions, and nature within the world; but it is not to be reduced to those worldly relations. Indeed, even those worldly relations are qualified by one's relation to God. Sketched roughly, within the Christian symbol systems one symbolizes oneself not only as small and contingent in the face of God but also as participating in a broken and wicked world, with some responsibility for wickedness oneself. Yet this symbolization of personal and social guilt cannot effectively be taken to heart, except in intra-worldly moral senses, because it is the peculiar power of guilt to alienate oneself from oneself. After Kierkegaard, who can miss this point? To break through the alienation one needs to experience what Christians symbolize as God's love for the world and oneself despite the flaws. This is where the peculiarly Christian symbols concerning Jesus the Christ come in, for Jesus is the mediator and actualizer of God's love. Accepting God's love, one can come to terms with the evils in the world and oneself, repent, give thanks for the love and also the power to make amends where possible, and then get on with the path of becoming more holy, most often in conjunction with other Christians.[20]

The Hindus, at least in the stereotypical formulation of life's stages, regarded the stage of seeking union with the divine as coming after the necessary business of householding. Perhaps there is something to this. But the quest for union, for fulfillment, for abandonment in the divine, can be formulated very early, even in childhood. Often the boundary-

---

20. I have developed this logic less abruptly than here in *A Theology Primer*.

crossing experience takes the form of a commitment to the task, like the
bodhisattva's, or the novice monk's or nun's vows.[21] In most religions,
the goal of union is part of the notion of salvation or holiness, along with
behaving in a holy manner in the course of life. Religions, of course,
symbolize union differently. *Union* is itself a symbol with historical specificity, albeit very general specificity. Images of a journey to God, going
home, entering the divine house or heaven, are all images of union. So
are the images of enlightenment, of non-duality, of emptiness or suchness, as are the images of attunement resonant in Chinese religions. Kenneth Kirk shows that the "vision of God" is a primary form of union
within Christianity.[22] We will explore some of these images further to
give meaning to this fourth stage of devotional life. Suffice it for now to
remark that the fourth stage is concerned to complete the engagement
with the divine meant in the symbols, referred to in encounter, and
embodied in practical life.

   This discussion of stages of transformation can end with the remark
that the stages do not necessarily require different symbols. It is not the
case that one can identify some symbols that belong to a more mature
stage, or that are appropriate to one stage rather than another. Sometimes
the "stage" imagery can be taken too seriously in analogy with developmental psychology. When that happens it is sometimes assumed that particularistic imagery is associated with the earlier stages of spiritual development, with the more general and universal images coming later, as
Kohlberg's and Fowler's Kantianism would lead one to expect. But on
the contrary, sometimes young adolescents can understand that enlightenment consists in the experience of non-duality and Brahman without
qualities long before they can understand how to relate to their guru; they
just do not understand non-duality very profoundly. Adolescents, like
smaller children, are often far more effectively grasped and oriented by
large abstractions than by individuated symbols. Similarly, it often takes
an old mature Christian, one who has prayed and sang through many
storms of life, to know what a personal relation to Jesus is. Perhaps it is
indeed true that youthful devotional life seems focused on allegiance to

---

   21. See Park Sung-bae's *Buddhist Faith and Sudden Enlightenment*, chapters 1–3.
Park demonstrates the importance of the work of faith even in Zen Buddhism by pursu-
ing the question of why the bodhisattva needs to take a vow if Enlightenment shows him
already to be a Buddha. Few scholars have brought out the dimension of faith or the
pursuit of holiness in Buddhism as clearly as Park.
   22. See Kirk's *The Vision of God*.

one tradition or set of symbols, and that mature devotees can resonate more easily with saints in other traditions, relativizing their own in some sense; but it is also true that only with the maturity that has coped with practical, theological, and ascetic or mystical matters can one come to see the depths in any one symbol system. The issue is not so much what symbols are appropriate at each stage, but how the symbols are appropriated.

The transformative dynamics of religious symbols vary with different stages of spiritual maturity and with other circumstances having to do with the state of soul of the people involved. Perhaps the vast majority of modern Western people do not have much of an encounter with religious symbols at all apart from public participation in religious communities, and many do not even have that kind of participation. Nevertheless even many of the most secular people have flashes in which something functions symbolically to reorient their soul, at least temporarily. Most people who seem to have only superficial religious lives also have some transformative symbolic experiences shifting their spiritual contours. And seriously religious people devote themselves to meditation, prayer, discipline, and courses of work and devotion, in addition to their public participation in religious communities, in order that their soul might be led toward perfection.

The transformative goals of spiritual formation are variously symbolized, and they are not necessarily specific with regard to stages of spiritual maturity. Some have to do with the will, building discipline, personal strength, abilities to act, and then abandoning ego in giving oneself over to God or to the empty character of the wheel of Samsara. Others have to do with cultivating spiritual knowledge, of oneself, of the spiritual dimensions of the world, and of God and ultimate things, finally abandoning self in mystical transformations. Yet others have to do with cultivating desires into love, building passion, and transforming one's orientation to God from fear, in the Biblical sense, to love.[23] Each of these lines of development has negative elements that must be broken and surmounted. Buddhism's images of gory goddesses girdled in skulls and swinging swords of destruction depict graphically the painful and spiritually violent battles against fear, the bondage of guilt and shame, weakness, clinging, self-deception, willful ignorance, hysteria, obsessions, and all the other obstacles to spiritual growth.

---

23. This list of goals for spiritual development, involving will, mind, and desire, comes from my *Soldier, Sage, Saint*, where they are analyzed in some detail in chapters 2–4.

Further progress is made as people find, enter into, or even invent, symbol systems that allow them to understand the course of their life in connection with their experience of what lies beyond life's ordinary definitions. For all of the conflicts and sometime stupidities of the symbol systems of organized religions, they have the merit of connecting the important passages and events of life, such as schooling, family, work, public responsibility, sickness, and death, to God or that which lies beyond the limits of worldliness.[24] True, many systems of religious symbols these days have been retranslated back to secular categories, especially those of morality and psychology. But where religious symbols are religiously alive and truthful, they maintain the contrastable orientation of life: on the one hand it is lived within the world with the opportunities, values, and obligations defined therein, and on the other hand life is lived in a posture addressing what lies beyond those things constituting the limits of the world.

These general remarks about typical stages in a spiritual career, as has been said, do not imply that different symbols are required for each stage, or for substages within them, although sometimes of course there are radical replacements of one symbol system by another. The more usual and surely more profound growth consists in appropriating more and more of the layers of meaning in symbol systems, their resonances and complications, and taking on those layers as content meaning whose senses are appropriate emphases for one's stage. The more mature one's spiritual life, the more complicated interweavings of symbols can be embraced in content feeling.

## 5.2. DEVOTIONAL SYMBOLS

To understand how religious symbols work in a devotional context, I propose the following hypothesis. Whereas the extensional reference of religious symbols is to something taken to be a finite/infinite contrast, the intentional reference is doubled. That is, the symbol is used in a devotional act to refer on the one hand primarily and directly to the finite/infinite contrast as an intentional referent and on the other hand secondarily and indirectly to the devotee as engaged by the divine so symbolized. A devotional symbol is used as much to address and engage the devotee's soul as it is to engage the divine. From the standpoint of the semiotic code,

---

24. In connection with this list, consult John E. Smith's discussion of the religious dimension of life in *Experience and God*, chapters 2 and 6. Smith relates the idea of experience in religion to these life-events relative to the divine.

the symbol's extensional referents are to the divine. But from the stand-point of the intentional use of the symbol, it is referred also to the devotee as defined in relation to the divine. Thus the interpretants of the symbol take the symbol as standing for some relation between the divine and the devotee in a certain respect. The concrete interpretation is thus some interpretive response to the dually signified relation. In the course of a symbol's development, its actual dual reference, to the devotee as well as to the finite/infinite contrast, affects its shaping; sometimes the exagger-ation and fantastical qualities of devotional symbols come from the need to connect with the devotee in reference.

The dual reference is hidden in symbols' semiotic codes. The codes structure an apparent extensional reference to the divine. Thus, the symbol of blond, blue-eyed Jesus waiting in the garden by the roses extensionally refers to the Biblical Jesus, and does so perhaps mendaciously. But inten-tionally, for at least some Anglo-devotees, that symbol refers to Jesus as he might be understood by and related intimately with a devotee who can imagine only Anglo-typic friends. Fearsome Kali with the girdle of skulls is a symbol of the goddess of destruction and renewal, but also refers to the devotee whose structured worldview needs to be broken and renewed. The Lord of Hosts depicts Yahweh as a warrior leader because that is what the Creator God giving destiny to Israel must be in the cir-cumstances. The Dao is symbolized by the striated grain running through marble because the *taiji* player can visualize moving her *qi* through space, through bodies and empty places, as the lines move through rock.

Symbols can be developed out of many contexts, and symbols can be used for devotional purposes that arose from other contexts. But as symbols are used devotionally, they are shaped more and more by the requirements of double reference, and they become extravagant and fan-tastic.

One of the most powerful kinds of religious symbolization in devo-tional discipline is visualization. *The Spiritual Exercises of St. Ignatius* is probably the most famous Christian text with an organized set of pro-gressive visualizations. Many preachers use verbal instructions for visual-izations to move the souls of their hearers. Mahayana Buddhism, espe-cially its Tibetan forms, makes visualization central to spiritual life. Visualizations are the imaginative creations of fragments of schema-images of important religious symbols, such as the life of Christ during Passion Week in the case of St. Ignatius.

The visualizations may have little or no relation to how historical events would have been perceived by an observer but rather are a function of the individual's own imaginative roots, and are double referenced. They are not mere mental pictures, however, but schema-images of religious symbols that might sustain their own independent theological justification. The purpose of the visualizations is to particularize the place or position of the individual's own soul and life in reference to the religious object. The point of the visualization is precisely its perspectival relation to the devotee, the very fact that its elements come from his or her own imagination.

Here is the major difference in the use of religious symbols in devotional practice from their use in most other contexts of organizing life. In those other contexts the function of the symbols is to organize life by assimilating thought and behavior to the world and divine matters as expressed in the symbols. In the devotional context the symbols themselves need to be transformed so as to be particularized to the person. They need to address the person in the person's psychological and social context, appropriate to the stage of spiritual and psychological development and sensitive to strengths, weaknesses, pathologies, and particularities of circumstance. Then, forming the symbols to grip the soul, the exercise of the symbols is aimed to move the soul to spiritual advancements that might not themselves be prefigured in the symbols. The Buddhist symbols of terror are necessary to awaken narcoleptic souls, but of course there is no terror in the long run, only compassion, according to Mahayana. The Christian images of judgment might have the same provisional status relative to the fullness of loving God.

The fantastical quality of much devotional symbolism comes from the particularization of the symbols to the position of the person. A blue-eyed blond Jesus is unhistorical and perhaps offensive to those whose race is close to the historical Jesus; but that might be the only image of a serious friend that makes sense to simple Wasps who have never known a Jew and have to start somewhere. Just as the medieval windows of Christian cathedrals depict first-century people in fourteenth-century dress, and African-Americans have Christmas creches of all black people, so any spiritually functioning symbol has to be particularized to the meaning world of the devotee, and that particularization gives it a double reference.[25] With advancement in spiritual life, substantive relations with

---

25. This point is forcefully developed in James Evans' *We Have Been Believers*, especially chapter 4 in which he analyzes various metaphorical and literal claims about Jesus as black or African. The crafting of the image of Jesus to be in solidarity with the destiny of African-Americans allows persons whose background is traditional African

circumstances marked by striking differences are quite possible. But that is very advanced indeed, far beyond the limits of tolerance and politeness that people struggle to instill in civilized behavior in pluralistic societies. The fantastical qualities of religious symbols in the devotional context are difficult to assess as to their appropriateness. Childish lingering with symbols past their appropriate usefulness can be limiting to growth just as symbols too mature can be unparticularizable.

The extravagance of religious symbols in devotional contexts is a function not only of how they need to be shaped to the particular circumstances and identity of the devotee but also of the roles they play in spiritual progress. Waking people up through shock and fear is not the only instrumental role for religious symbols. Each tradition articulates stages of discipline such that the symbols appropriate for one stage might be extravagant for the others. The appropriate judgment here is neither theological, looking into the meaning and truth of the symbols at hand, nor practical in the sense of fitting the devotee in more and more closely with a religious way of life, but soteriological. The soteriological judgment of a spiritual director is not the same as that of a theologian or practical organizer of life. The truth of religious symbols in the devotional context has to do with their effectiveness in moving the particularities of the individual's soul toward perfection, however the spiritual tradition conceives that. As spiritual life progresses, visualizations can be improved upon in this respect.

These observations about the extravagance and double reference of devotionally based religious symbols are brilliantly illustrated in a hymn by Charles Albert Tindley, "Stand by Me."[26] Its five verses are as follows:

When the storms of life are raging, stand by me;
When the storms of life are raging, stand by me;
When the world is tossing me, like a ship upon the sea,
    thou who rulest wind and water, stand by me.

In the midst of tribulation, stand by me;
In the midst of tribulation, stand by me;
When the host of hell assail, and my strength begins to fail,
    thou who never lost a battle, stand by me.

---

religions to refer to God by means of the doubled-referenced symbol of Jesus. Evans' own interpretive strategy is to consider the figural quality of the image of Jesus, e.g. pp. 77–83.

26. *The United Methodist Hymnal*, #512.

In the midst of faults and failures, stand by me;
In the midst of faults and failures, stand by me;
When I've done the best I can, and my friends misunderstand,
  thou who knowest all about me, stand by me.

In the midst of persecution, stand by me;
In the midst of persecution, stand by me;
When my foes in war array undertake to stop my way,
  thou who saved Paul and Silas, stand by me.

When I'm growing old and feeble, stand by me;
When I'm growing old and feeble, stand by me;
When my life becomes a burden, and I'm nearing chilly Jordan,
  O thou Lily of the Valley, stand by me.

Notice the repeated time and place indices: when, when, in the midst, in the midst. The singer is addressing God but as related to the particular crisis points of the singer. Notice also the extraordinary progression of the symbolism in each of the first four stanzas. The first line states a universal problem and repeats it: the storms of life, tribulation, personal faults and failures, and persecution. The stanzas in order move step-wise from the general to the more pointed and particular. The second line after the reduplication personalizes the first: the world is tossing *me* like a ship upon the sea, the host of hell assail and *my strength* begins to fail, *I've done the best I can* and *my friends* misunderstand, *my foes* in war array undertake to stop *my way*. Each line again gets closer to the blunt particularity of the singer. The third line characterizes God relative to the trouble: thou who rulest wind and water for the storms of life, thou who never lost a battle for tribulation, thou who knowest all about me for faults and failures, and thou who saved Paul and Silas for persecution. That progression is from the God of nature to the God of nations to the God of persons to the God of redemption.

The fifth stanza is a sea-change. No *general* trouble in the first line but the most intimately personal: when I'm growing old and feeble. Not personalization in the second line but the putting off of person: when my life becomes a burden and I'm nearing chilly Jordan. The reference to Jordan moves the soul back to the symbols of the cosmic voyage through death to God. But in a brilliant reversal the symbol for God is moved from the cosmically vast divine agent of nature and history to the beloved object of the singer's heart: "O thou Lily of the Valley, stand by me." The phrase cited, Lily of the Valley, is from the Song of Solomon 2:1. As the problems move from the universal to the particular, to finitude itself, as the personal references move from nature dislocating my human scale, to the assaults of evil, to my efforts and failures, to the human undoing of my destiny, to the finish of my life itself, the symbols of God move from ruler, to victor, to knower, to redeemer, then amazingly to *my beloved*. The punch line is not God's creating and saving love for me, but my love for God. The hymn is a complex symbol for bringing God into focus.

Tindley's African-American, Biblically literate audience likely would have known the "I am" reference from the Song of Solomon: "I am a lily of the valley." "I am your shield" (Gen. 15:1); "I am the Lord your God, the Holy One of Israel, your savior" (Is. 43:3); "I am the bread of life" (Jn. 6:35); "I am the light of the world" (Jn. 8:12); "I am the good shepherd" (Jn. 10:11); "I am the resurrection and the life" (Jn. 11:25); "I am the way, the truth, and the life" (Jn. 14:6); "I am the vine and you are the branches" (Jn. 15:5); "I am the alpha and the omega" (Rev. 1:8); "I am coming soon" (Rev. 22:7); "I am who I am" (Ex. 3:14). But for you who love me, "I am a lily of the valley." The soul who bears through troubles to the banks of chilly Jordan meets God not as agent, not even just as lover, but as beloved, and hence comes home. To a Biblically literate group, there is not only a progression of metaphorically overlain images—ruler, victor, knower, savior, beloved bringing the point home, there is the indirect reference by means of the association with Christ who is taken to say, "I am the lily of the valley" to all the "I Am" sayings. A deep Christology indeed, but not one that would have much impact if the symbol were the creedal theological statement. Furthermore, the developmental overlayment of the symbols moves through identifying the singer as passive in face of the storms of life to being active at the end: in the striking double reference, God is identified as the one beloved by the devotee.

These symbols of God are not theological descriptions but metaphors whose limitations theologians can easily lift up; yet they serve to transform the soul to face the infinite through the finite at its worst, not just as passive to divine action but as lover for whom the divine beloved is as a lily of the valley. That God is a lily is far more extravagant and fantastic than that God is a rock; Israel thought Yahweh was truly fighting for them in their rock fortress, but the reference to the lily is from erotic poetry with no internal metaphoric reference to God at all. Yet the assimilation of that image through the "I am" statements sends shock waves through the progression of symbols for God who is called upon to stand by me. To call on the cosmic magician is understandable for those whose souls are shaped mainly by storms, tribulations, failures, and persecution. How far an advance it is, then, to call in the hour of death on the beloved, not the steward of the afterlife but the one you have come to love!

The magnificence of Tindley's spiritual imagery should not blind us to the power of religious symbols functioning corruptly, indeed Satanically, in leading the soul. Perfectly good symbols of God's creativity and redemptive love can cultivate a childish, irresponsible passivity of soul. Symbols of discipleship to the God of power can lead to maniacal pride. Spiritual life, like the practical organized life of religious living, needs theological criticism of its symbols. But the test is whether the symbol functions to orient the soul accurately to the divine. The intellectual meaning of the symbol might not be what is true or false in the soul.

On the one hand, religious symbols can be treated one by one, analyzing their meanings and references, doubled references in the case of symbols functioning devotionally, doubled interpretants in the case of symbols used in practical intentional contexts. On the other hand they can be treated as they are sequenced in an act of devotion such as singing a hymn. In this instance the important point is how the soul is moved by the cumulative overlaying of symbols, carried along, as it were, through a change. The important point of Tindley's hymn is not the conclusion, that God comes as the singer's beloved, but the rehearsal of the devotional movement, the turn, the pivot, from apprehending God as the transcendent mover steady in times of the singer's troubles, increasingly personalized, to the apprehending of God as loved through the singer's own love. The spiritual accomplishment is being able to perform that little psychic dance so that every cry to God in time of trouble concludes with a vision of the beloved.

The spiritual life can be viewed as learning certain competencies of soul. Some yoga masters are quite explicit about the overt powers of the soul to change things, not just psychic things but physical things; the psychic-physical distinction is not helpful. More ordinary transformations of soul have to do with learning spiritual habits, which of course have their practical effects in life. Generalizations about this are common—learning to see ordinary life in an enlightened way, learning how to retreat and advance so as to be in tune with the Dao, learning to act in the heart in accordance with Torah, learning to love God and neighbor. The specifics of these general paths of spiritual perfection are the little details of spiritual accomplishment that people work on in spiritual discipline all their lives. The souls of most people in hard times simply feel sorry for themselves, perhaps congratulating themselves on perseverance, or contemplating suicide as a way out. A few people have souls shaped to look to God, to the foundation of the whole world, when things get tough enough to threaten their position in the world. But most of these would complain that God has not worked hard enough for them lately or, if more sophisticated like Job, might ask why God allows them to suffer so. What a rare spiritual accomplishment for a soul to have the habit of responding to deep trouble by turning to God for companionship—"stand by me"—first as awesome protector and then moving ever more personally to be the soul's beloved. For most theistic people, the God who allows trouble is not the beloved. By spiritual exercises like Tindley's, devotees can acquire the competence, the spiritual habit, of being able to turn even trouble into a vision of the divine beloved.

5.3. CREATING A TRANSFORMATIVE WORLD

The array of spiritual competencies that make for a religion's perfection is not merely competencies at relating to individual symbols, or to perform spiritual movements with a complex moving symbol like the hymn, but constitutes a kind of way of being in the world. The world is the same as that to which everyone else has to respond, and any devotee has to make the pragmatic intepretations others make, and also many of the interpretations of things dealing with dimensions of life other than the religious. But over and above this, a spiritual devotee comes to enrich the interpretation of everything by placing it in the divine perspective. This includes the devotee's own identity and activities. Thus the householder comes to the tasks of paying the bills and raising the children as expressions of who the devotee is in relation to the divine; householders who are not religious might do many of the same things, but would not understand their tasks and themselves the same way.

Thus over time a devotee needs to develop the semiotic habits of soul that embody the divine in the things that make up the person's identity. This requires a transformative world of symbols. The spiritually transformative world is not a substitute interpretation that displaces the non-religious interpretation of the world. Rather, it is a new dimension, the related-to-the-divine dimension. Moreover, the symbols of the transformative world are not so much as to be looked at themselves, nor even used instrumentally to interpret the world. Rather, they are the symbols shaping the habits of soul by which the person responds to the world. So the question with the Tindley hymn is not how far to take the symbols of God as ruler of storms or as a flower, but how the symbols nudge the soul to respond to trouble and the threat of death by thinking on God the beloved. The map of transformative religious symbols is not like a map of the world. It is rather like a map of the interconnected habits that lead to spiritual advancement and perfection. The symbols of the "transformative world" have whatever interconnections, networks, and overlayments are appropriate for transforming the specific state and stage of a person's soul. The symbolic transformative world is an icon of the real world with a doubled reference: to the real world in its finite/infinite contrasts and to the devotee in process of transformation.

Sermons are often attempts to configure symbols into a transformative world, addressing the state and stage of the congregation. Nearly every religious tradition has some version of the sermon. Of course congregations are diverse, and so preachers deal a bit more generally that spiritual directors do with those whom they address; and no sermon is equally fit for everyone who hears it. Nevertheless, sermons are excellent symbol-complexes for analyzing the transformative-world function of devotional symbols. The following sermon will serve as an example of a putative transformative world of symbols. It is a Christian sermon set in the context of a Christian worship service, and is used not only because I understand it better than I would someone else's sermon from another tradition, but also because it develops some of the symbols already discussed at length here. Jewish or Buddhist sermons could illustrate the same function of a transformative world of symbols.

The sermon picks up the clues to its transformative world from the liturgical service of which it is a part. The choir had sung the gospel song, "Deep River." The Biblical texts are from the thirty-second chapter of Exodus and Jesus' parable of the wedding feast in the twenty-second chapter of Matthew; the relevant texts are quoted here:

> When the people saw that Moses delayed to come down from the mountain, the people gathered around Aaron, and said to him, "Come, make gods for us, who shall go before us; as for this Moses, the man who brought us up out of the land of Egypt, we do not know what has become of him." Aaron said to them, "Take off the gold rings that are on the ears of your wives, your sons, and your daughters, and bring them to me." So all the people took off the gold rings from their ears, and brought them to Aaron. He took the gold from them, formed it into a mold, and cast an image of a calf; and they said, "These are your gods,

O Israel, who brought you up out of the land of Egypt!" When Aaron saw this, he built an altar before it; and Aaron made proclamations and said, "Tomorrow shall be a festival to the Lord." They rose early the next day, and offered burnt offerings and brought sacrifices of well being; and the people sat down to eat and drink, and rose up to revel.

The Lord said to Moses, "Go down at once! Your people, whom you brought up out of the land of Egypt, have acted perversely; they have been quick to turn aside from the way that I commanded them; they have cast for themselves an image of a calf, and have worshiped it and sacrificed to it, and said, 'These are your gods, O Israel, who brought you up out of the land of Egypt!'" The Lord said to Moses, "I have seen this people, how stiff-necked they are. Now let me alone, so that my wrath may burn hot against them and I may consume them; and of you I will make a great nation."

But Moses implored the Lord his God and said, "O Lord, why does your wrath burn hot against your people, whom you brought out of the land of Egypt with great power and with a mighty hand? Why should the Egyptians say, 'It was with evil intent that he brought them out to kill them in the mountains, and to consume them from the face of the Earth'? Turn from your fierce wrath; change your mind and do not bring disaster on your people. Remember Abraham, Isaac, and Israel, your servants, how you swore to them by your own self, saying to them, 'I will multiply your descendants like the stars of heaven, and all this land that I have promised I will give to your descendants, and they shall inherit it forever.'" And the Lord changed his mind about the disaster that he planned to bring on his people. . . .

As soon as he came near the camp and saw the calf and the dancing, Moses' anger burned hot, and he threw the tablets from his hands and broke them at the foot of the mountain. He took the calf that they had made, burned it with fire, ground it to powder, scattered it on the water, and made the Israelites drink it.

Moses said to Aaron, "What did this people do to you that you have brought so great a sin upon them?" And Aaron said, "Do not let the anger of my lord burn hot; you know the people, that they are bent on evil. They said to me, 'Make us gods, who shall go before us; as for this Moses, the man who brought us up out of the land of Egypt, we do not know what has become of him.' So I said to them, 'Whoever has gold, take it off'; so they gave it to me, and I threw it into the fire, and out came this calf!" . . .

The Lord said to Moses, "Go, leave this place, you and the people whom you have brought up out of the land of Egypt, and go to the land of which I swore to Abraham, Isaac, and Jacob, saying, 'To your descendants I will give it.' I will send an angel before you, and I will drive out the Canaanites, the Amorites, the Hittites, the Perizzites, the Hivites, and the Jebusites. Go up to a land flowing with milk and honey; but I will not go up among you, or I would consume you on the way, for you are a stiff-necked people." Exodus 32:1–14, 19–24; 33:1–3.

The passage from Matthew is equally dramatic.

Once more Jesus spoke to them in parables, saying: "The kingdom of heaven may be compared to a king who gave a wedding banquet for his son. He sent his slaves to call those who had been invited to the wedding banquet, but they would not come. Again he sent other slaves, saying, 'Tell those who have been invited: Look, I have prepared my dinner, my oxen and my fat calves have been slaughtered, and everything is ready; come to the wedding banquet.' But they made light of it and went away, one to his farm, another to his business, while the rest seized his slaves, mistreated them, and killed them. The king was enraged. He sent his troops, destroyed those murderers, and burned their city. Then he said to his slaves. 'The wedding is ready, but those invited were not worthy. Go therefore into the main streets, and invite everyone you find to the wedding banquet.' Those slaves went out in the streets and gathered all whom they found, both good and bad; so the wedding hall was filled with guests.

"But when the king came in to see the guests, he noticed a man there who was not wearing a wedding robe, and he said to him, 'Friend, how did you get in here without a wedding robe? And he was speechless. Then the king said to the attendants, 'Bind him hand and foot, and throw him into the outer darkness where there will be weeping and gnashing of teeth.' For many are called, but few are chosen." Matthew 22:1–14.

Now to the sermon itself. The opening paragraph relates to the specific congregation where I had preached on the analogous date the previous year.[27]

---

27. This sermon was preached on October 10, 1993, at Marsh Chapel, Boston University. The University Chaplain is the Reverend Robert Watts Thornburg to whom reference is made.

❖

Last year the lectionary arranged it so that I could deal with only the lead-in material to the texts on divine wrath and judgment, leaving the hard part for Preacher Thornburg on his return. This year the hard texts come today and I am not disappointed. For, it is impossible to preach the good news of the Christian gospel without acknowledging first the depths of where we are. Know it or not, we are launched over a deep river, beating toward the shores of the campground. This is a religious matter, a matter of the spirit. It is more than moral, more than psychological, more than political, more than family prosperity, more than personal fulfillment, more than getting by, more than survival, more than everlasting life. This is a matter of God's vast holiness, its unmeasured power, and what it does to us. What it does, is measure our folly and call us out over the deep. God's holiness calls us out over the abyss of the deep river where the fragile rafts of our structured lives are as nothing to the wild winds, waves, and undertows. The texts from Exodus and Matthew fairly rattle in their shaky attempts to represent God's terrifying holiness in terms of the human story.

Consider the Exodus story of the golden calf. It is, of course, a story of taking and betraying responsibility in holy matters. What struck me reading it and the surrounding material this time is the lame effort of the author to soften matters with humor. So at the beginning of the text for today, when Moses was delayed on the mountain, the people said, "as for this Moses, the man who brought us up out of the land of Egypt, we do not know what has become of him." Moses was blamed both for leading them into the desert and for being inattentive, as if they had no responsibility themselves. Up on the mountain Moses got it from the other side. "The Lord said to Moses, 'Go down at once! Your people, whom you brought up out of the land of Egypt, have acted perversely.'" As if the burning bush, the plagues, the Red Sea passage, and the pillars of fire and cloud were all Moses' doing. Moses quickly passed the people back to God saying, "O Lord, why does your wrath burn hot against your people, whom you brought out of the land of Egypt with great power and with a mighty hand?" Back in the camp, Aaron assumed that if his brother was gone, so was God; he acceded to the wishes of the people for a home-made god and created the golden calf. The text is clear that he made the calf himself, either with a mold for molten gold or with a shaping instrument—the Hebrew allows both readings. Yet later, in a passage after the text for today (Exodus 32:24), when Moses confronted Aaron, Aaron said "I threw [the gold jewelry] into the fire and out came this calf!"

Poor Aaron should have known more about fire, for it marks the unlimited holiness of God. He missed the encounter with God in the burning bush. But he was at Sinai when Moses first went up, according to Exodus 19, and the people were warned not to touch the mountain, and the Lord descended in fire, and smoke shrouded the mountain like a kiln, and the mountain shook and sounded like a trumpet louder and louder, and the people could not come close or the Lord would "break out against them." God is always on the verge of breaking out of the constrictions of a finite meeting to consume those who get too close.

Now Moses succeeded in rebottling God's wrath about the golden calf by saying the Egyptians would make fun of a liberating God who consumed his own people, and by reminding God of the promises to Abraham, Isaac, and Jacob. That is, Moses argued that if God is indeed going to enter finite history and care for particular people there will have to be a deliberate self-delimitation of the divine. The outcome of the golden calf story, which is told in the next chapter, is that God sends the people of Israel on to the promised land guarded by an angel but without his own presence as up to then. "Go up to a land flowing with milk and honey; but I will not go up among you, or I would consume you on the way, for you are a stiff-necked people."

We have tended to draw only half the inferences from this story. We have noted that God's wrath is negotiable and that with domesticated substitutes we can be led to the promised land. From this many have gone on to infer that God's wrath is a psychologically harmful fiction and that God's goodness without wrath will build up ego strength and lead to self-fulfillment. We hang on the anthropomorphic conversation between Moses and God and approach God as a friendly interlocutor with whom to bargain for prosperity and justice. And in this we define ourselves as dependent children whose God is equal parts parent and therapist. The specifically Christian version of this is all those faint Christologies for which Jesus is a distant and domestic substitute for the holy God. The Arians in the fourth century and the Unitarians in the ninteenth wanted not the Holy God in Jesus but a safe angel, an enlightened, human, non-scary, moral guide.

But a half-truth is a dangerous falsehood. For, the Holy God who talks to us does so out of fire and smoke and we are in constant danger that God will break out against us. The presence of the infinite God to a finite folk is a terrifying miracle. Finite things tend to burst when God indwells. The depth of God's holy fire is infinite. God's saving grace, God's boundless love, God's forgiving mercies mean nothing unless we receive them from the fiery abyss over which we are suspended in our foolishness and evasions as from a spider's thread.

But fiery abyss and deep river are the same, fire and water, both names of God. And we are being carried across by God's holiness, scary as that is. For Christians the raft across Jordan is Jesus, and we need to attend to his parable.

Jesus' metaphor for holiness is the wedding feast, with its eating, drinking, and dancing. Those who have been to Jewish weddings know how important the dancing is as the dancers carry the bride and groom around the symbolic circle of life, fertility, and death. Many things are going on in Jesus' parable. The guests are invited by the king's servants to participate in the wedding, but they have become jaded and go about business as usual, resorting to violence to silence the call from the king. So the king makes his invitation universal. But one of the strangers called still does not get the point of the royal wedding and is cast into the outer darkness.

Notice that Jesus' king does not negotiate, as Yahweh did on Sinai. Jesus's parable is resolutely uncompromising. What is arresting about the story is not merely that God extends salvation universally, but the seriousness of the wedding feast, the seriousness of salvation. Here is the New Testament's most famous symbol for the torments of hell—weeping and gnashing of teeth—applied not to some axe-murderer, drug-dealer, or embezzling banker but to a poor schlep who did not dress right. When confronted he did not lie like Aaron or beg forgiveness but stood speechless; he did not know what he did wrong and probably never understood what happened to him or why. This is not right ritual, nor just desserts, nor empathic suffering. This is the religious substance of the spirit. Jesus is tougher than Moses. His parable is painful to people whose God is the tame angel.

Jesus says come to the feast, it is your very being. Do not go about business as usual, your spirit is at stake. Do not destroy those who call you, for there is no life without the feast. Do not blunder to the wedding without the right garment, for you are about to meet your God. Do not fail to be attentive because all else is outer darkness with weeping and gnashing of teeth. The king of the banquet is the Holy One of Israel before whom foolishness is disaster and whose celebration is the joy of heaven.

How hard this parable is for us, how terrifying, how despairing! For we are nothing if not foolish, unfit, unready, wrongly dressed, distracted, busy, evasive, sinful, wicked, mean-hearted, sucking after golden calves, and on good days cheerfully searching out tame angels. How can we stand before the Holiness that deigns to contract itself in fire and smoke, shaking the foundations of mountains with the sound of ever louder trumpets? One whiff of that smoke, our knees turn to reeds, we cry out for domesticated gods or, which is the same thing, we despair.

Now the gospel's Good News makes sense. God has come to us not only in the temporary transfigurations of fissured mountains but in the person of Jesus, the preacher of parables. Wholly a man, wholly Holy God, Jesus came to us foolish, sinful, idolatrous people with the invitations to the banquet. The invitations say things like I AM the Holy Fire who loves you in your obsessions, your addictions, your dependencies, your weaknesses, your hysterias, your flights, and evasions. I AM the Deep River who loves you in your pain when you fall ill, break bones, lose your house, are oppressed by war, by want, by madness, by failure, and grow old, get left behind, and creep to death. I AM the Abyss who loves you while creating and destroying you, spinning you a short time for living, shutting down projects before completion, making vain your works, partial your justice, and time-bound your vision. I AM the Creator who loves you when you cannot come to me, when you cannot stand before me, when you have no strength, nor courage, nor resolution, nor acceptance of the infinite with the finite, nor capacity to put aside the idolatries by which vainly you seek to diguise your fear from yourself.

These invitations of love are not on paper but in persons. First in the person of Jesus and then in the persons of his disciples. They have to be delivered individually on the street corners, and to make them convincing the bearer often has to suffer greatly to illustrate the love. But these lovers, this Jesus and his band, are not just ordinary lovers with ordinary sufferings. They use ordinary love conveyed to ordinary people to contain the holy presence of God, Creator and Redeemer. What shook Sinai to its foundations with blazes, smoke, and the rumbles of destruction fits neatly into Jesus and those in whom his spirit dwells. The incarnation means God fits in people as God cannot fit in mountains.

The lesson to be drawn from this is not relief at the meek humble humanity of Jesus but holy terror at this man who is God inviting us home. Jesus is the scariest man who ever lived with his awesome invitations to the banquet, and when we finally realize just who he is and how he works in us "every knee should bend . . . and every tongue . . . confess that Jesus Christ is Lord, to the glory of God the Father" (Philippians 2:10–11).

But of course Jesus does not begin scary. He comes first as friend and healer, story teller and teacher, advocate and bringer of cheer. He comes as we are prepared to receive him and works with who we are. Only after living with his love for a while does it dawn on us whom we have. Only after we have begun to respond do we see that we have been given an invitation from the Shaker of Mountains, from the Divine Fire, from the Deep River, from the Abyss of creation. And then we are properly afraid.

"The fear of the Lord is the beginning of wisdom." Anyone who claims to have met God's love and is not terrified is either faking, self-deluded, or in for a big surprise. St. Augustine said that the process of holiness is the transformation of fear of God into love of God. Fear of divine holiness is the stuff out of which love for God is made. Love for God that does not rise out of fear is fake. It is rather love of a golden calf or a tame angel or a domestic Jesus. Jesus is wild, untamed, the bridegroom carried on the cosmic dance.

For, the feast to which we are called, the love for God to which we are summoned, is Holiness itself. We are invited into the Holy Fire where our obsessions, addictions, dependencies, weaknesses, hysterias, flights, and evasions will be purged as dross by God's refining fire and turned to virtue. We are invited by the Deep River to abandon the sufferings of our illnesses, broken bones, loss of home, ravages of war, want, madness, failure, aging, abandonment, and death to the grace of God in whose life we are brought home. We are invited by the Abyss to embrace our creation and destruction, our short-life allotment, the frustration of our projects, the vanity of our works, our partial justice, our time-bound vision, because our finite life arises from the infinite in whom we live and move and have our being. We are invited to come by the Creator who moves us to do so, to stand before divine holiness despite our foolishness, who gives us divine strength, the courage of sanctity, the resolution of Christ's heart, the vision of finite and infinite together, and the heart to live before God.

We are called to love God with the wildness of Jesus, to dance through the Fire, through the River, through the Abyss, into the Creator. We are called to the wild love that steps to the edge of the everyday dark and throws itself into the light with the confidence of the children of God. We are called to follow the Bridegroom Dancer whose dance gives flesh to the Holy. We are called to dance God's steps that touch Terror and Love and consume us.

There is no more serious holy business than this, and all our other business is transfigured in this feast. To ignore the invitation is to be half-dead and to die, and to come without attention is to meet only the Terror, not the Love. When you stand at the edge, and the Light comes up that does not blind but ever brightens, step off into the vastness of the divine Abyss, come through the Fire and Smoke, push out across the Deep River, for your Creator calls you with a Love that receives you wildly and makes you holy. For we have met this love, we have touched its source, and we live to pass it on.

Sermons in Christianity and other religions are complicated iconic symbolic acts and the structural intent of this sermon is to complicate symbols on top of one another even more than usual. Simply as a sermon it attempts to exegete scriptural texts without flinching at the hard parts. The texts prescribed by the *Revised Common Lectionary* for the date of this sermon are very sharp indeed. In the Exodus reading the Chosen People commit grievous idolatry, God decides to murder them, Moses plea-bargains, Aaron lies rather than take responsibility, and God grudgingly sticks to his patriarchal covenant but absents himself from the people. That passage is set in the larger context of the the Sinai account in which God comes to meet the people. Exodus 19:16–19, 24 reads:

> On the morning of the third day there was thunder and lightning, as well as a thick cloud on the mountain, and a blast of a trumpet so loud that all the people who were in the camp trembled. Moses brought the people out of the camp to meet God. They took their stand at the foot of the mountain. Now Mount Sinai was wrapped in smoke, because the Lord had descended upon it in fire; the smoke went up like the smoke of a kiln, while the whole mountain shook violently. As the blast of the trumpet grew louder and louder, Moses would speak and God would answer him in thunder. . . . The Lord said to him, "Go down, and come up bringing Aaron with you; but do not let either the priests or the people break through to come up to the Lord; otherwise he will break out against them."

More than the morally justified come-uppance of Sodom and Gomorrah, the epiphany on Sinai was the paradigmatic fire and brimstone event. Insofar as it shook with divine vengeance, it was holy vengeance rather than moral wrath. The sermon glosses this point with the citation of Jonathan Edwards' famous image of the spider over the fire in the classic fire and brimstone "Sinners in the Hands of an Angry God." Jesus' parable in Matthew is no more congenial to domestic liberal sentiments. Though we are pleased to learn that many are called to the kingdom of heaven, it is a hard saying that few are chosen and that the reason for not being chosen is merely being ignorant of what is going on, like the man who did not know to dress for the wedding. This parable is set among a group of equally stark stories and parables, all having to do with being awake, being ready, being properly responsive, and being rejected for failure in these matters; see Matthew 21:18–22 concerning the fig tree, 28–32 concerning the two sons one of whom promised to work but did not and the other of whom said he would not but did, 33–41 concerning the owner who kills the ungrateful tenants of his vineyard, 24:36–44 concerning those taken up and those left standing, 45–51 concerning the dissolute slave, 25:1–13 concerning the foolish virgins, and 14–30 concerning the investment of talents. Hard as it is to reconcile to liberal morality or to a theology that sees God as no more than a benevolent father, the parable of the wedding feast is at home with Jesus' other parables. A sermon on these texts needs to take them seriously without backpeddling.

Concerning intent, a sermon should be poetic in the ancient sense (if not the artistic sense) of attempting to create or at least foster a new and improved heart in the hearers, a heart closer to the Christian goal of loving God, or to Buddhist enlightenment, or Confucian sageliness. This sermon seeks to create the spiritual competence of seeing God as holy, even when God is seen as loving, and of moving from awe at holiness to its embrace, a giving of ourselves over to holy God. A sermon is self-consciously a Word, and thus resonates with the creative Word of God in Genesis 1, the Words of the law and the prophets, and the Word Incarnate as described in John 1.[28] The creative function of the Word in devotional life is the advancement of spiritual formation.

A sermon should be a publically accessible genre of the deployment of symbols for devotional purposes. Unlike devotional symbols involved in an individual's private life of prayer or in one-to-one spiritual direction, the devotional symbols in a sermon need to address a wide range of conditions of people. They need to be used in ways that can be inter-

---

28. I learned the point about the analogy between the divine creative word and the creative preached word from a sermon by Charles Addams.

preted on many levels by people at different stages of their spiritual careers and in different social positions. Of course, as noted, no one sermon can speak to all people with equal force. Moreover, there are different kinds of sermons, all of which have some intent to create a new soul but most of which are more concerned with the social context of religious living than this sermon. Perhaps most sermons are as much involved with organizing religious life as they are with devotional life as such, although the sermon here stresses the latter. All kinds of sermons have their season. But to the extent the devotional function is stressed, the symbols are developed far beyond their descriptive meanings in the attempt to reorient the soul to a more accurate and deep relation to the divine object of the symbols.

Having noted three traits that apply to sermons as a genre of the devotional use of symbols, namely attention to scripture, intent to move the heart, and publicity, the sermon here can be analyzed in more specific detail.

In this sermon there is a three-level development of symbols. First is the development of the symbols for God, beginning with an uncompromising presentation of the infinite power of the Holy One of Israel who burns things up when they get too close; infinite holiness is not politically correct within Christianity these days except among astrophysicists who think about the Big Bang. Then God is depicted as the saving lover who enters into Jesus for the sake of redemption, and finally as the object of sanctified human love, although both of these symbolic representations, which are now popular and politically correct, are set in the context of infinite and terrifying holiness.

Second, there is the development of symbols for the human condition, beginning with the fearful idolatry of those who made the golden calf. The litany of human sufferings and malefactions—foolishness, sinfulness, idolatry, obsessions, addictions, dependencies, weaknesses, hysterias, flights, evasions, illness, broken bones, homelessness, war's devastations, want, madness, failure, old age, obsolescence, death, short life, incomplete projects, partial justice, time-bound vision—is repeated in part or whole as guilty people face the Holy One of Israel on the plain before Sinai, as unworthy people are invited by the welcoming king to the banquet, and as devoted people are moved toward God in the train of Jesus, Lord of the Dance. The list of sufferings and evils is not derived directly from scripture but from the experience of people in the congregation. The repetition of the litany in overlapping lists is intended to intensify the listeners' own identification with the human condition addressed in the point of the sermon.

Third is the development of symbols for the mediation between God and people, beginning with Yahweh's clumsy attempts to approach a mountain without breaking it and speak to people for whom God has no patience. Then there is the tame angel God sends to lead the people from Sinai to the Holy Land, an image to which many would like to conform Jesus. Finally there is the symbolic characterization of Jesus as the perfect vessel for the Holy One of Israel on the one hand and the friend who meets us on our own terms on the other, a brief symbolic schematization of the theological doctrine of the two natures of Christ. The image of Jesus as dancer arises only indirectly from the lectionary texts on which the sermon is based. By virtue of Jesus' title of Son of God, he can be likened to the bridegroom son of the king in the parable; although the parable does not mention dancing, we know that dancing the circle of life was and is central to Jewish weddings. The scriptural warrant for the metaphor comes from the episode in 2 Samuel 6 where David, the prototype messiah, brought the Ark to Jerusalem dancing naked before the Lord. Following the sermon the congregation sings Sydney Carter's 1963 hymn "Lord of the Dance" which integrates the Christological story of Jesus as Word Incarnate, as preacher, healer, crucified and raised, around the image of the dance:

I danced in the morning when the world was begun,
and I danced in the moon and the stars and the sun,
and I came down from heaven and I danced on the earth.
At Bethlehem I had my birth.
    Dance, then, wherever you may be;
    I am the Lord of the Dance, said he.
    And I'll lead you all wherever you may be,
    And I'll lead you all in the dance, said he.
I danced for the scribe and the Pharisee,
but they would not dance and they would not follow me;
I danced for the fishermen, for James and John;
they came to me and the dance went on.
    I danced on the sabbath when I cured the lame,
    the holy people said it was a shame;
    they whipped and they stripped and they hung me high;
    and they left me there on a cross to die.
I danced on a Friday and the sky turned black;

it's hard to dance with the devil on your back;
they buried my body and they thought I'd gone,
but I am the dance and I still go on.
> They cut me down and I leapt up high,
> I am the life that'll never, never die;
> I'll live in you if you'll live in me;
> I am the Lord of the Dance, said he.
Dance, then, wherever you may be;
I am the Lord of the Dance, said he.
And I'll lead you all wherever you may be,
and I'll lead you all in the dance, said he.

Like the sermon, the hymn uses the I AM phrase, in which Yahweh announced his name to Moses, to connect Jesus' doings to the power beyond the limits of worldliness.

Arching over the three structural developments of symbols for God, for the human condition, and for the mediation of these are four deeply mystical symbols for the boundary between the finite and infinite: the Deep River, the Holy Fire, the Abyss, and the Light. Each of these is a traditional symbol with many meanings and references, and they cumulatively stack up within their interweavings and overlays an intense concentration of images for crossing over, going through fire, launching into emptiness without worldly helps, and entering the light. Although by no means integrated or made compatible in the sermon, they are compacted onto one another by the image of Jesus whose dance leads us across the water to the other shore, through the fire that burns mountains and our dross but not us, into the abyss of the nothingness out of which creation comes, and into the light of creation itself. In all of those images Jesus' dance leads us home, for in this Christian transformative world we belong to the power beyond limits as much as to our place in the world. The night sky stars are ours, as the adolescent thought. Furthermore, dancing after Jesus across, through, with abandon, and into the infinite, giving ourselves to the dance, we abandon self and even appreciation of God's love and simply love God like the home we never knew. All this in a dance whose steps in the world are simple discipleship to Jesus in the Christian manner. The dance image never represents God as a person or personal being except in Jesus.

The spiritual transformations sought in this sermon have to do with leading the soul to approach the infinite across the boundaries of finite worldliness with a devotional attitude of love. Love in this context cannot be mere gratitude or affection but rather the kind of love that consists in transformed fear of the infinite as holy. Otherwise love is an intra-worldly emotion, where what is needed is love across the boundary limiting finitude. Although different individuals are in radically different places of spiritual development, and not many move deliberately toward the mystical elements fostered in the transformations at hand, each of the many symbol systems involved can be engaged at many levels.

This sermon, unlike many others, is directed to a congregation familiar with the traditions of Christian symbolism. In this age of indifferent religious literacy in North Atlantic countries, such a direction would be self-indulgent except for the facts that there are other occasions for other kinds of sermons and that this one was preached to a university audience. This sermon does attempt to introduce the symbols afresh, given their citation in songs and biblical texts, and to develop them internally within the sermon's own form. But it helps if people know the story of the Exodus, if they catch the I AM reference to Yahweh's self-naming, if they know the status of sonship frequently attributed to Jesus, if they know the development of the symbol of light in patristic writings, the symbol of the abyss in Meister Eckhart, and the symbol of crossing Jordan to campground in African-American Christianity. The more one knows, the more intense the inner resonances and counter-themes of the symbols.

Each of the major symbols in this sermon involves a symbol-system of its own. Moreover, each has an historical depth that might mean different things to different people. The layering and repetition with variations attempts to set up resonances that produce tones not struck by any symbol alone. The intended cumulative resonance here, for devotional purposes, is the ability to release oneself so as to love God, a point that is not made either by the scriptures or by the major symbols of Deep River, Holy Fire, the Abyss, or Light. The point of the sermon is not *about* God, the human condition, or their mediation. The point is to stimulate a movement of love for the Holy that can begin anywhere this side of the Divide, appreciate the holy contrast of infinite and finite, and abandon oneself to the blissful loving of the infinite so contrasted. This transformative world of symbols, if taken to heart in the deep resonances of the soul, aims to make that movement to God habitual and ready. There are many overlaid symbol systems in this transformative world, and each one can function as a trigger or an inference-path for the movement turning the soul to loving devotion when they are compacted as a symbolic world.

5.4. REPRESENTATION AND FICTION IN DEVOTIONAL SYMBOLS

How are these symbols true? They surely are not true in a direct descriptive sense. The difference between the finite world and the situation that would obtain if there were no world is not a river nor an abyss. For Big Bang cosmologists the coming into being of fire or light might be metaphors for explosive energy, but that is not the meaning of passing through tempering fire or entering the blinding light of mystical vision. The parable of Jesus was never intended to be history but a story iconically illustrative of the kingdom of God which itself is "not of this world," as Jesus said. Although there surely is some historical truth to the Exodus story, textual and historical issues make any of the Biblical narratives problematic as straight history.[29] The forced character of the image of Jesus as dancer has already been mentioned. Even the representations of the salvific goal are not meant literally. No one has to dance for salvation. Although abandoning oneself to God in love is a satisfactory statement of the Christian purpose from a theological perspective, it is very abstract. It has to be connected with how to live responsibly in this life while practicing that abandon. Even the meaning of loving God, who as infinite is no object to be loved as we love people, is conveyed in the sermon by a complicated criss-crossing of the apophatic movement toward love from fearing the Holy One of Israel and the kataphatic movement of dancing home to God after Jesus.

Another way of making that point, however, is to say that all of these symbols are broken symbols. Not only can they not be taken literally themselves in any descriptive sense, they impact one another so as constantly to correct and shift the symbolic frame. As in sermons, so in

---

29. By this I mean only to call attention to the problems of traditions-criticism in taking the Biblical stories as history. Few if any stories of the period are as richly attested with historical writing as the story of King David, who was contemporary with the founders of the Zhou dynasty in China and two centuries earlier than Homer. The accounts in our current Bible derive from both northern kingdom and southern kingdom sources and are reinforced by somewhat independent writings in the Psalms and prophets. But only very recently has there been any confirmation from outside the Biblical tradition itself that David ever lived; that was an inscription in a neighboring kingdom that mentions an unnamed king of Israel as being "of the House of David." Were it not for that fragmentary reference, a skeptic might conclude that the whole story of the united Israel, of David the messiah, and of the Zionist interpretation of the meaning of Israel's special relation to God is but a Biblical fiction feeding on itself. As a religious symbol, however, what is important about the story is not its historicity or lack thereof but its iconic rendering of what social life before God is like.

prayer and meditation: the images catch one up, move on, and shift from one system of symbolic meaning to another. To be "lifted in prayer," as the saying goes, is to mount from one symbolic stretch to another, embodying each step of the ascent in the goal.

Broken symbols are a dime a dozen, however, if they are dead. A legitimate question is whether these symbols collectively engage the devotional imagination (not the theological imagination, strictly speaking). The answer to that question is ultimately pragmatic; either they do or they don't; or they do for some people and not for others. The pragmatic tests of engagement should not be limited to superficial feelings of being turned on or off. As an episode in the life of the congregants worshipping in the service with this sermon, surrounded by its scriptural texts and songs, this congeries of symbols is engaging if it shapes their imagination so as to effect something of a transformation of soul. They had encountered most if not all of the symbols before, but the sermon, if engaging, gives them a new level of juxtaposition and meaning. Or if not new, it reinforces a transformative world of symbols encountered in other symbolic media. Furthermore, if truly engaging, by transforming imagination the symbols also transform the people's practical attitudes toward religious life; they alter people's possibilities of thought, so that they can wonder about and engage things in ways closed off before. And they should affect people's behavior. The behavior relevant to this sermon may not be as overt as the kind of behavior relevant to sermons about stewardship, social justice, and overt religious practice; the relevant behavior here has to do with the cultivation of the soul. Nevertheless even the inner life of prayer has overt effects. Then, the cycle from imagination to practical attitudes to behavior moves back to imagination so that one's whole structure of symbolic imagination is altered through the effects of experiential transactions. Whether the symbols in the sermon, as conjoined there, are truly living so as to engage people with divine matters is something to be discerned only through delicate analyses of imagination and life.

As noted here and in the previous chapter, the intentional contexts in which religious symbols are interpreted are interrelated, and the rough distinctions between the theological, practical, and devotional contexts are rough indeed. Moreover, symbols move rather freely from one context to another. Nevertheless, particular symbols are often more importantly shaped by one context or another. The eucharistic symbols analyzed in some detail in chapter 3 are most importantly shaped by the practical context of Christian communities organizing their lives around a center of worship. The eucharistic symbols are not so fantastic and exaggerated as those in the sermon or in Tindley's hymn, and they relate to realistic consciousness of the world and to practices within it. Yet they also function in devotional contexts. Worship itself is often taken to be devotional practice, even though it does not always involve the concentration of meditative imagination typical of the spiritual disciplines of devotional life. Christians often meditate in private on the eucharistic symbols, and sometimes are deeply moved spiritually, that is, transformed, during a liturgy.

The symbols I analyzed in detail for the devotional context are themselves taken from public liturgies, that is, a congregational hymn and a sermon. In this respect, both reinforce the devotional aspects of public worship. That point would not be made if I had analyzed the procedures of St. Ignatius *Spiritual Exercises* or the text of Kempis' *Imitation of Christ* or breathing and centering-prayer exercises, devotional examples from the Christian tradition. Yet clearly the imagery of the hymn and sermon are to be understood primarily in terms of the dual reference to God and the devotee, practicing and rehearsing movements of soul, constellated in a world of symbols aiming to transform the soul so as better to address God in a Christian way. Set in the context of the practical life of the congregation, those devotionally oriented symbols are not only too extravagant and fantastic but also barely applicable, perhaps silly, even dangerous. The symbol of the parable of the wedding feast would need a radically different interpretation in the practical context, as it will be given in 7.1 in the context of guiding the religious community's guest list for festival meals. In that practical context, the important element of the parable is the inclusiveness of the invitation, not the damnation to outer darkness of those who do not appreciate the holiness of God, much less the punishment of those who do not dress right. Viewed in the practical context, the parable's attack on the man who came without wedding clothes is a grave danger to charity if taken to heart literally by those planning the festival celebration; from the practical context, the most helpful response to the improperly dressed person is to think the king unjustifiably harsh. Insistence on correct dress in practice is in extreme dissonance with the vast majority of Christian symbols about accepting people into fellowship. So symbols transform their meanings and functions as they are moved from one intentional context to another.

But then there is the question of truth. Do the symbols here in the devotional context engage people accurately with the divine, or are they idolatrous or even demonic? Not being descriptively true, the truth of the symbols lies in whether they cause the souls that engage them to be truthfully oriented to the divine, as will be argued in detail in chapter 7. More specific than that, the causation is not mechanical but semiotical. When people do indeed take these to be symbols of the divine, of the boundaries of finitude and their crossing, when people see and touch the divine through these symbols, does the divine come to be resident in people truthfully? That is, does the human registering of the divine through these symbols contain what is of value to be registered concerning the relevant divine matters? Does the divine dwell in the spiritual habits shaped by the cultivation of inner life by these symbols?

These questions need to be answered in particular cases by two routes; both are necessary and either without the other is flawed, perhaps even dangerous. One is the critical route of theology that examines the nature of the divine and the human to determine when they are in accord and how the human can interpret the divine. Theology too works with symbols, and perhaps never leaves symbolic levels of discourse. But it has a control on symbolic extensions by virtue of its ability to move through many layers of abstraction and sensuosity.

The other route is internal conviction or certainty. Like any signs, the symbols of the divine are supposed to enable real engagement so that through them the divine is concretely experienced. That is, with true and living symbols we do not experience the symbols but the divine through them. We cannot express this save symbolically. Yet the experience of the divine is concrete and real if the symbols make it possible. The conviction and certainty of direct engagement is the same here as it is when you are sure that you are driving a car, that you are hearing music, and that you are enjoying a friend's company. Of course we can talk ourselves into false convictions in religious matters, as we can dream that we are driving, hearing music or are in the presence of a true friend. That is why we need cool critical judgment of the sort good theology brings. But even the best of theology is only about the symbolic experience of the divine, not the thing itself. Theology's symbols have to be engaged with the divine in order to make the genuine transformative experience possible.

There is no finite set of algorithms by which to test engagement. Theology can only go so far in straightening out contradictions and anomalies in symbol systems and their apparent bearing on the conduct of life. The pragmatic insistence on thinking in the middle of things is important to recall here. We are always already engaged with life, well or badly, focused here or there. The function of thinking is to correct and improve that engagement, discovering more discerning symbols so that our engagement bears more truthful enjoyment and responsiveness. In religion, we are always already engaging whatever it is that religious symbols refer to. Reductionisms claim that the symbols are very mistaken about the realities to which they refer, that the real referents are better symbolized by anthropological, political, moral, or psychological symbols. Religious thinking claims, rather, that the symbols are only partial, dark, and broken. The argument that religious engagement is only a dream needs to be answered by criticism of the symbolic interpretations in people's lives; perhaps it is a dream, perhaps not. Each case needs to be argued against a background of correcting engagement. That a particular engagement seems right, that it carries conviction and a certainty that centers the heart, is a good if not infallible mark of genuine engagement.

The tentative conclusion is that religious symbols can be alive and true, even when they are not descriptive, if in fact they transform the imaginative and behavioral structure of experience so that people engage divine matters truly. This chapter has been focused on the experiential structure of devotional life, although the point holds for more overt practical behavior. The truth consists in the shaping of the soul and its effects so as to register and be oriented to the divine as it is juxtaposed to the limits of finitude. For Christians this is loving God as creator, with "loving," "God," "Creator" and "the Christian way" interpreted according to the symbols of the tradition. So understood, religious symbols may be taken at face value. It is good and true for Christians to image Jesus dancing across the abyss into the light with disciples weaving in his train. Or, as C. S. Lewis observed, Yes, there are cigars in heaven.

But how conscious need people be that their symbols are broken? Surely everyone recognizes that deep water, fire, the abyss, and light are symbols and not meant literally. This is so even when we can find no better language than crossing over, purification through fire, self-abandonment, and affirmation. Moreover, Jesus' parable is clearly labeled by him as a parable. But how non-literally should we think about the God who rages against idolatrous Israel and argues with Moses? Throughout at least Christian history many if not most believers have thought of God as a personal being with emotions and capacities for linguistic communication, and have taken this to be literal and non-symbolic.

Beyond Christianity the point holds for the other theistic traditions, and even for non-theistic traditions such as Buddhism in which practical devotional life more often centers on the deity Guanyin or the Lord of the Pure Land than on Emptiness or the Unconditioned. When theological symbols are adapted to devotional use and made appropriate to the spiritual state of the devotee, it seems almost universal that there be a reification and personification of a divine object. Is it "fair" that these symbols not be broken for many people? Is it idolatrous for them not to be broken? Can they be believed innocently? Or is the harder problem whether they can be believed at all if they are recognized as broken?

Are these questions about the nature of religious symbols? Or are they direct theological questions, such that a legitimate answer might be that God is indeed as Yahweh appeared on Sinai, literally and truly? The theory of symbols presented here has argued that the primary referent of religious symbols is at and beyond the boundary of world-making. Thus personhood is a finite boundary condition such that a world with persons in it must reflect fundamental person-making. But as a boundary condition, personhood is finite and what lies beyond the boundary cannot be personal, any more than it can be a tree or an explosion.

In many respects, the devotional use of religious symbols is a practical intentional context like those discussed in 4.3–4. In those respects, the devotional symbols have a doubled interpretant as well as a doubled reference. So, for instance, a representational interpretant for Guanyin as an object of devotion might be that there is divine aid for your sickness which would imply the practical interpretant that you should not give up hope; a representational interpretant of an image of Jesus in the garden waiting for you might be that you have a friend which would imply the practical interpretant that you should pull yourself together to present yourself to someone who loves you. But these practical considerations are often not all that important in devotional life. The important interpretant of devotional symbols is that the devotee take on the elaborate transformative world as the iconic frame within which everything is experienced. Therefore, the doubled referent, which is where the iconic "taking" of the world lies, is more important than the interpretant. Approaching ultimate things is like crossing a deep river, entering the consuming fire, launching out over the abyss, or entering the light. Without ever believing in metaphysical deep water, fire, abyss, or light, a devotee can interpret reality as such that his or her relation to ultimate things is like going through those things. The practical interpretants of those things are the implications of the large symbol systems overlaid and intermixed that serve as the devotee's icon for life. The overall icon allows life to be engaged in a centered way. In devotional symbols, the important thing is to bring the doubled referent into the experience of the devotee; the subsequent interpretation can follow with practical effects. But a concern for practical implications of devotional symbols is almost ludicrous; devotion is not about doing something but about finding something and being transformed by that.

The argument of this chapter has been that religious symbols are properly made fantastic and exaggerated when they function in devotional contexts. To a lesser degree they are similarly fictionalized when they are used not theologically but to organize religious life. Though not descriptively true, religious symbols in the devotional and practical contexts can be existentially true when they conform the soul and practice so as to embody what the religious referent means for the persons and community in their situation. But how does theology tell about this? And how dangerous is it that theology not speak well?

Before addressing these questions directly with a theory of truth, one more complication needs to be introduced, the negative case where accurately interpreted and (for the sake of argument) true symbols nevertheless have bad consequences.

# Judging Religious Symbols by Consequences

Most of my discussion of religious symbols so far has been biased toward taking them seriously as symbols. Indeed, I have insisted upon this in the face of various other approaches that are reductive in one way or another. I have dwelt on how religious symbols refer, on what they mean, and on what is involved in their interpretation. With regard to their interpretation I have discussed their straightforward assertive elements, as in theology, their practical roles in shaping religious life, and, in the previous chapter, some of the ways in which religious symbols themselves are shaped by the religious needs of those to whom they are addressed so as to set up tensions with theological understandings of their truth. But recall that the discussion opened in chapter 1.2 with a consideration of the view that the interpretation of religious symbols is not important at all compared with what might be the consequences of the use of the symbols in religious life or in society. That view was dismissed after some consideration because it blocked the road to inquiry about the interpretation of religious symbols. But now, with an elaborate theory of interpretation in hand, and without an apriori attempt to balance the relative importance of interpretation and extra-interpretive consequences, it is time to return to the issue of consequences.

In one sense, of course, all the issues of interpretation are consequences of religious symbols. Theological truths, falsehoods, distortions, and adumbrations are consequences of religious symbols. The roles symbols play within the intentional contexts of organizing religious life have consequences precisely for shaping that life; our discussion has focused on the shaping consequences that come from the interpretation of the symbols in those practical contexts. Similarly for the devotional context of religious symbols: the relevant consequences of the symbols developed in ways made applicable to the devotee, perhaps feeding back to develop the symbols to exaggerated and fantastic forms that in turn are involved with the ongoing shaping of the person's spiritual life. All these are consequences of interpreting the symbols, and the relevant evaluative questions are about reference, meaning, interpretation and the engagement of the religious object in the interpreters.

On the other hand, there are consequences of religious symbols that are not tied to the meaning or truth of the symbols but that come from the ways the social context can react to the symbols. The reaction involves an interpretation of the symbols, it is true, but an interpretation whose main lines are formed by social structures, not the symbols. The line between interpretive consequences and social consequences is difficult to draw. But it is important for the criticism of religious symbols and is connected with more general concerns about the criticism of religion as a social and cultural phenomenon.

Perhaps the most obvious cases of extra-religious consequences of behavior shaped by religious symbols are those apparent to people from another culture who apply moral categories but do not understand or identify with the religious symbols. The English, for instance, took great exception to the Hindu practice of suttee, in which a widow would throw herself onto her husband's funeral pire. The Western conception of the holiness of matrimony is little help in understanding the Hindu. Similarly the English thought that the Indians' protection of the sacred cow was a waste of good beef among often starving people, not appreciating the senses in which cows could be holy. Northern Europeans have difficulty appreciating how people from the South could live in poverty while devoting most of their little wealth to adorning cathedrals and mosques, insisting that human material welfare is of first-order in holiness. Westerners have difficulty applying any but moral and political categories to stratification of social classes that other cultures take to be of religious significance concerning the transmigration of souls and resonance of the cosmic order. The caste system in India and the practices in China of incapacitating upper class men with long fingernails and upper class women with bound feet are cases in point. In our own time, for modern people, inequities in social class and oppressive treatment of women, racial and national minorities, gays and lesbians, and the disabled, are described in moral and political categories (as in this sentence), and the religious rationales that have been used to justify them are dismissed as rationalizations. But there is a subtler issue here than the mere dominance of moral and political categories. There may in fact be serious conflicts of norms of judgment. A case study can display some of the subtleties and difficulties of the issue, one that picks up some of the Christian symbols developed earlier.

In a challenging article, "For God So Loved the World?," Joanne Carlson Brown and Rebecca Parker argue that the Christian doctrine of the atonement—that God gave his only son to suffer for the redemption of the world—legitimates child abuse and also the belief that women's place is to suffer and accept abuse.[1] Their argument will be viewed as extreme by many and for that reason I summarize it mostly in their own words:

Women are acculturated to accept abuse . . .[2]

Our acculturation to abuse leads us to keep silent for years about experiences of sexual abuse, to not report rape, to stay in marriages in which we are battered, to give up creative efforts, to expend all our energy in the support of other lives and never in support of our own, to accept it when a man interrupts us, to punish ourselves if we are successful, to deny so habitually our right to self-determination that we do not feel we have an identity unless it is given to us by someone else.

Christianity has been a primary . . . force in shaping our acceptance of abuse. The central image of Christ on the cross as the savior of the world communicates the message that suffering is redemptive. If the best person who ever lived gave his life for others, then, to be of value we should likewise sacrifice ourselves. Any sense that we have a right to care for our own needs is in conflict with being a faithful follower of Jesus. Our suffering for others will save the world. The message is complicated further by the theology that says Christ suffered in obedience to his Father's will. Divine child abuse is paraded as salvific and the child who suffers "without even raising a voice" is lauded as the hope of the world. Those whose lives have been deeply shaped by the Christian tradition feel that self-sacrifice and obedience are not only virtues but the definition of a faithful identity. The promise of res-

---

1. Joanne Carlson Brown and Rebecca Parker, "For God So Loved the World?", in *Christianity, Patriarchy, and Abuse: A Feminist Critique*, edited by Joanne Carlson Brown and Carole R. Bohn, pp. 1–30. Brown is a professor of church history and ecumenics at St. Andrews College in Canada and Parker is President of the Starr King School for the Ministry in Berkeley, California.

2. Ibid., p. 1

urrection persuades us to endure pain, humiliation, and violation of
our sacred rights to self-determination, wholeness, and freedom.
Throughout the Scriptures is the idea that Jesus died for our sins.[3]

Critical traditions have formulated the issue of redemption in different terms but still have not challenged the central problem of the
atonement—Jesus' suffering and death, and God's responsibility for
that suffering and death. Why we suffer is not a fundamentally different
question from why Jesus suffered. It may be that this fundamental tenet
of Christianity—Christ's suffering and dying *for us*—upholds actions
and attitudes that accept, glorify, and even encourage suffering.[4]

The authors then discuss three classical theories of the atonement. The
*Christus Victor* theory asserts that the resurrected Christ triumphs over
evil and suffering and that Christians can enter into this triumph. On this
theory, sufferings are like illusions, they say, or at least are to be borne
but temporarily in confidence of glory. Moreover, they say that this theory entails God's intention of suffering:

> In this tradition, God is the all-powerful determiner of every event in
> life, and every event is part of a bigger picture—a plan that will end
> with triumph. When people say things such as, God had a purpose in
> the death of the six million Jews, the travesty of this theology is
> revealed.
>
> Such a theology has devastating effects on human life. The reality
> is that victimization never leads to triumph. It can lead to extended
> pain if it is not refused or fought. It can lead to destruction of the
> human spirit through the death of a person's sense of power, worth,
> dignity, or creativity. It can lead to actual death. By denying the reality
> of suffering and death, the Christus Victor theory of the atonement
> defames all those who suffer and trivializes tragedy.[5]

Next Brown and Parker consider the *satisfaction tradition* of the
atonement as articulated by St. Anselm. On their reading of this tradition

---

3. Ibid., p. 2.
4. Ibid., p. 4.
5. Ibid., p. 7. It is interesting that the sources cited for the Christus Victor theory
are a rhetorical passage from Gregory of Nyssa and the contemporary, Matthew Fox. A
subtler version might have been found in Gustav Aulen's *Christus Victor* or John Macquarrie's *Principles of Christian Theology*, pp. 318–321, which should be consulted.

justice demands that evil must be balanced by punishment. Only the punishment of God's own son is sufficient to balance out the evil of the world. God, on their interpretation,

> is portrayed as the one who cannot reconcile "himself" to the world because "he" has been royally offended by sin, so offended that no human being can do anything to overcome "his" sense of offense. Like Lear, God remains estranged from the children God loves because God's honor must be preserved. God's position is tragic, and it is to free God that the Son submits to death, sacrificing himself, it is imagined, out of overwhelming love for the two alienated parties: God and the human family.[6]

They conclude from this that "the image of God the father demanding and carrying out the suffering and death of his own son has sustained a culture of abuse and led to the abandonment of victims of abuse and oppression".[7] Furthermore, Brown and Parker indict a list of symbolic developments in scripture of the idea of blood in sacrifice, namely, that blood protects, that blood intercedes, that blood establishes covenant, and that blood makes sacrificial atonement. They note that none of this honors the natural flow of women's blood in menstruation or childbirth but instead treats women's blood as unclean. Rather than appreciating the nurturing blood of women, they point out that Jesus, a male, has been depicted as a maternal nurturer, which "suggests that the religious imagery of the atonement is founded upon the robbery and subsequent defamation/degradation of women's experience".[8]

They finally analyze the *moral influence* tradition of atonement thinking as developed by Abelard. "The moral influence theory," they say, "is founded on the belief that an innocent, suffering victim and only an innocent, suffering victim for whose suffering we are in some way responsible has the power to confront us with our guilt and move us to a new decision"[9] Brown and Parker extend the point to say that:

---

6. Ibid., p. 8.

7. Ibid., p. 9.

8. Ibid., p. 10. Brown and Parker do not point out that this retributive theory of justice aims to respect human freedom and responsibility by taking it seriously, in contrast to the drift of the Christus Victor tradition which saw the situation of sin as a contest between larger-than-human powers. Hegel developed the satisfaction theory of atonement in modern ways.

9. Ibid., p. 12.

Theoretically, the victimization of Jesus should suffice for our moral edification, but, in fact, in human history, races, classes, and women have been victimized while at the same time their victimization has been heralded as a persuasive reason for inherently sinful men to become more righteous.[10]

They then ask:

How can we explain the condition of women, and others who are the chosen victims in a society, who live in constant fear of rape, murder, attack, verbal assault, insult, and the denial of rights and opportunities except as a condition of terrorization? To glorify victims of terrorization by attributing to them a vulnerability that warrants protection by the stronger is to cloak the violation. Those who seek to protect are guilty. Justice occurs when terrorization stops, not when the condition of the terrorized is lauded as a preventive influence.[11]

Brown and Parker point out that much twentieth-century theology has rebelled against these classical atonement theories, and they consider three instances of theological rebellion.

The first is the now popular claim that God suffers with the world and suffers in solidarity with people who suffer. Crediting an article by Ronald Goetz, the authors cite Barth, Berdyaev, Bonhoeffer, Brunner, Cobb, Cone, "liberation theologians generally," Kung, Moltmann, Reinhold Niebuhr, Pannenberg, Ruether "and feminist theologians generally," Temple, Teilhard and Unamuno.[12] They add and discuss the theology of Edgar Sheffield Brightman. While the suffering and solidarity of God might be a comfort to some of those who suffer, it only glorifies suffering all the more, they argue.

The second is the revival within some liberation theologies of the view that suffering is positive because it builds up character and helps people take possession of their own achieved freedom. So, for instance, Martin Luther King, Jr., was able to make the sufferings of his people into a virtue that undergirded their strength. Brown and Parker object

---

10. Loc. cit.

11. Ibid., p. 13.

12. Ibid., p. 14. See Ronald Goetz, "The Suffering God: The Rise of a New Orthodoxy."

that, even though there might be something to the positive discipline of suffering in some cases, that theology lets the oppressors off the hook and fails to challenge the source of suffering, which they identify mainly with oppression, although they do not explain how this applies to King.[13]

The third theological rebellion takes place within liberation theologies and argues that, although all suffering as such is wrong, suffering is not the whole of the Christian doctrine of the atonement. William R. Jones, a black liberation theologian, argues that the crucifixion symbolizes the suffering of black people but that resurrection is the source of their political hope.[14] Carter Heyward, a feminist theologian, agrees that suffering is always bad, that Jesus was fully and only human whose suffering was "an evil act done by humans," and that Jesus challenged both "the unjust systems under which he lived" and "the theological idea of a sadistic God."[15] Heyward attempts to redeem the doctrine of the atonement by saying that Jesus shows us that salvation "consists in being in an intimate, immediate love relationship with God."[16] Jones and Heyward fail, according to Brown and Parker, only in that they do not simply reject the doctrine of the atonement.

Brown and Parker conclude:

Christianity is an abusive theology that glorifies suffering. Is it any wonder that there is so much abuse in modern society when the predominant image or theology of the culture is of "divine child abuse"—God the Father demanding and carrying out the suffering and death of its own Son?[17]

We do not need to be saved by Jesus' death from some original sin. We need to be liberated from the oppression of racism, classism, and sexism, that is, from patriarchy. . . .

Our adventure into freedom is empowered by rejecting and denying the abuse that is the foundation of the throne of sacrifice. We choose to call the new land we enter Christianity if

Christianity is at heart and essence justice, radical love, and liberation.

---

13. Ibid., pp. 20–21.
14. Ibid., p. 22.
15. Ibid., pp. 25–26.
16. Loc. cit.
17. Loc. cit.

Jesus is one manifestation of Immanuel but not uniquely so, whose life exemplified justice, radical love, and liberation.

Jesus chose to live a life in opposition to unjust, oppressive cultures.

Jesus did not choose the cross but chose integrity and faithfulness, refusing to change course because of threat.

Jesus' death was an unjust act, done by humans who chose to reject his way of life and sought to silence him through death. The travesty of the suffering and death of Jesus is not redeemed by the resurrection.

Jesus was not an acceptable sacrifice for the sins of the whole world because God does not need to be appeased and demands not sacrifice but justice. To know God is to do justice. . . . Peace was not made by the cross. . . . No one was saved by the death of Jesus.

Suffering is never redemptive, and suffering cannot be redeemed.

The cross is a sign of tragedy. God's grief is revealed there and everywhere and every time life is thwarted by violence. God's grief is as ultimate as God's love. Every tragedy eternally remains and is eternally mourned. Eternally the murdered scream, Betrayal. Eternally God sings kaddish for the world.

To be a Christian means keeping faith with those who have heard and lived God's call for justice, radical love, and liberation; who have challenged unjust systems both political and ecclesiastical; and who in that struggle have refused to be victims and have refused to cower under the threat of violence, suffering, and death.

Fullness of life is attained in moments of decision for such faithfulness and integrity. When the threat of death is refused and the choice is made for justice, radical love, and liberation, the power of death is overthrown. Resurrection is radical courage.

Resurrection means that death is overcome in those precise instances when human beings choose life, refusing the threat of death. Jesus climbed out of the grave in the Garden of Gethsemane when he refused to abandon his commitment to the truth even though his enemies threatened him with death. On Good Friday, the Resurrected one was Crucified.[18]

18.  Ibid., pp. 27–28.

Brown and Parker's challenging article raises a truly important question about the truth or falsity of religious symbols. But it is likely to be overlooked because of several outrageous elements of the article, outrageous except for those who agree with the position and its rhetoric antecedently.[19] In order to focus the real issue, I would like to mention and set aside certain controversial points that are not the issue at hand.

First, the article is not really about divine child abuse, that is, about God the Father abusing Jesus the Son by making him suffer for the Father's purposes. The article is about how Christian symbols of suffering lead to the abuse of women. Had the article been about the first two persons of the Trinity it would have had to note that Jesus had a remarkably happy childhood, by all accounts, and did not suffer until he was an adult; he could have escaped the suffering of crucifixion up until the trial itself. It would have had to note that God sent Jesus to save the world, according to the title quote, and Jesus suffered out of love for the world, not because suffering is good. Families, parents and children alike, suffer nobly for causes in which they believe, and kings send their sons to fight righteous battles for them, often with approbation. These and like justifications for suffering are ignored in the article because the real topic is the suffering of abused women.

Second, the article is written in a rhetoric that is likely not to be shared by those Christians who do believe in the doctrine of the atonement and who would need to be persuaded to abandon it. Rather, the article's rhetoric is aimed to bolster enthusiasm among those already committed to its general orientation. In so doing it declines the context of inquiring with the reader about the truth of the matter and assumes the context of building power for its own side. Let us abstract from this rhetorical orientation and shortly re-ask the questions of truth.

Third, the article also employs the rhetoric of large generalization from small samples. What is undoubtedly true of some women and some men and some parts of Christianity is generalized to be asserted of women in general, men in general, and Christianity as such, where exceptions in vast numbers and kinds occur to any thinking reader.

---

19. Its style might tend to put off the serious theologians who are the very audience that needs to attend to the argument. Lest people dismiss it too quickly, I note that the book in which it occurs (Bohn and Brown's *Christianity, Patriarchy, and Abuse*) is the first item in the bibliography for the article on "Atonement" by Eugene Teselle in Musser and Price's *A New Handbook of Christian Theology*, p. 43, and the Brown and Parker article is the only one in that book directly on the doctrine of atonement.

Among the unintended consequences are that patriarchy is blamed for all
evil and suffering, as just quoted; that men in general are blamed for
patriarchy; that Christianity as such glorifies suffering and encourages
abuse; and, most ironically, that all women are encouraged by the article
to think of themselves as abused, even if they are not, and thereby to suffer certain of the major ill-effects of abuse. This is genuinely outrageous
scapegoating of men and victimizing of women of the very sort other
feminists warn about.

Fourth, Brown and Parker's understanding of evil and suffering, that
from which salvation is needed, is unusually simple. As quoted above, it
consists in "the oppression of racism, classism, and sexism, that is, from
patriarchy."[20] Salvation for them consists, negatively, in liberation from
oppression and, positively, in living justly and with intimate and immediate
love. Reflective persons who have read Paul Ricoeur's *The Symbolism of
Evil*, or Kierkegaard's *Either/Or*, or any of Paul Tillich's or David Tracy's
discussions of ambiguity know how superficial this understanding of evil
and suffering is, even if true so far as it goes.[21] Brown and Parker's understanding of salvation makes no reference to God except as a witness, reducing the matter to morals.[22] That is better called *justice* than *salvation*.

Fifth, Brown and Parker deeply err about Christianity by making it
hang, or even seem to hang, on the doctrine of the atonement. Although
atonement symbols are found in the New Testament, so are many other
elements that have not been made central to Christian faith. The doctrine of the atonement is not one of the central elements. The early
creeds all testify to God as creator, to Jesus as the crucified and risen
Christ, and to the Holy Spirit, but not to atonement through Jesus' suffering.[23] Where are the classical loci of the doctrine of atonement

---

20. Ibid., p. 27.

21. For Tillich, see *Systematic Theology I*, pp. 81–93; *Systematic Theology II*, pp. 19–
78; *Systematic Theology III*, pp. 30–110. For Tracy, see *Plurality and Ambiguity*.

22. As quoted above, God calls for justice, radical love, and liberation, grieves in a
musical form, and has love for the world no more ultimate than grief. None of these is
salvific unless there is more to divine love than Brown and Parker mention.

23. The Apostles' Creed has been basic in the Western Christian Churches; it
reads:

> I believe in God the Father almighty, creator of heaven and earth; And in Jesus
> Christ, His only Son, our Lord, Who was conceived by the Holy Spirit, born
> of the Virgin Mary, suffered under Pontius Pilate, was crucified, dead and bur-
> ied. He descended to hell, on the third day rose again from the dead, ascended
> to heaven, sits at the right hand of God the Father almighty, thence He will

through Jesus' suffering? Not the Apostles' Creed, not the Creed of Nicaea in 325, not the Creed of Constantinople of 381, not the Definition of Chalcedon of 451, not the Council of Orange of 529, not the Anathemas of the Second Council of Constantinople of 553, not the Statement of Faith of the Third Council of Constantinople of 681, not the Synod of Constantinople of 753, nor the Seventh Ecumenical Council at Nicaea of 787.[24] Most of these creeds say that the logos became incarnate in Jesus for the sake of our salvation, and also that Jesus suffered crucifixion. But the concerns about Jesus' suffering are not as to its redemptive powers but as to its marking Jesus' true humanity; the concerns in the creedal discussions usually are about the relation of the suffering human nature to the divine nature that might or might not suffer.

To be sure, there are crucial theological problems that the doctrine of atonement was developed to solve. These include the nature of that from which people need to be saved, just how God in Christ goes about effecting that salvation, the difference that salvation makes to human beings, and human beings' own roles in the salvific process. The New

---

come to judge the living and the dead; I believe in the Holy Spirit, the holy catholic Church, the communion of saints, the forgiveness of sins, the resurrection of the body, and the life everlasting. Amen. [Quoted from Leith, *Creeds of the Churches*, pp. 24–25.]

The Nicaean Creed has been basic in the Eastern Christian Churches:

We believe in one God, the Father All Governing, creator of all things visible and invisible; And in one Lord Jesus Christ, the Son of God, begotten of the Father as only begotten, that is, from the essence of the Father, God from God, Light from Light, true God from true God, begotten not created, of the same essence as the Father, through whom all things came into being, both in heaven and in earth; Who for us men and for our salvation came down and was incarnate, becoming human. He suffered and the third day he rose, and ascended into the heavens. And he will come to judge both the living and the dead. And in the Holy Spirit.

But, those who say, Once he was not, or he was not before his generation, or he came to be out of nothing, or who assert that he, the Son of God, is of a different hypostasis or ousia, or that he is a creature, or changeable, or mutable, the Catholic and Apostolic Church anathematizes them. [Leith, pp. 30–31]

24. These may be checked in Leith's *Creeds of the Churches*. The Constantinopolitan Creed of 381 does have the phrase, "was crucified for us," but as part of the history with Pontius Pilate, suggesting only that God wills human salvation, not Christ's suffering. The phrase was dropped from the Definition of Chalcedon which was preoccupied with the two-natures doctrine and does not even mention suffering.

Testament presents many different images of atonement, with no consistent or dominant image; but generally suffering and Jesus' crucifixion are subordinated to the role of resurrection in salvation.[25] (I myself have a theological interpretation of salvation as understood by Christians that does not make use of the notion of atonement as the sacrificial benefit of Jesus' suffering.)[26]

Sixth, Brown and Parker move without warning or control between careful theologies of the atonement, as in their discussions of *Christus Victor*, Anselm, and Abelard, and popular images of atonement having to do with blood and beneficial suffering. In all the theologies of atonement, whatever their differences or internal difficulties, the point of the doctrine is that Jesus' sufferings were once and for all sufficient and that no subsequent suffering has salvific power. People might imitate Jesus' faithfulness in bearing up under suffering, and they might remain faithful through suffering and death as witnesses or martyrs. There might also be a place for suffering in penance for specific sins; but penance is to increase holiness, not to accomplish salvation. To say that anyone's suffering after Jesus imitates Jesus' own cosmic atoning suffering is precisely to deny the heart of the doctrine of the atonement. If popularized images of Jesus' suffering were commonly construed to mean that Christians ought to imitate Jesus' redemptive activity so as to bring it home in their own context, that is a rejection of the theological content of the once-for-all atonement of the Christ. What could be a more extreme form of Pelagianism?

This is not to deny that the popular response to Christian symbolism has in many instances been what Brown and Parker claim. But the problem is with the popular use of images, not with the doctrine of the atonement. Indeed, the doctrine of the atonement is intended as a theological bulwark, however ineffective, against that very popular response. The failure to point this out, or even to note it, is the greatest theological failure of the Brown and Parker article. Nevertheless, because our concern here is with religious symbols, including images of suffering, the exculpation of theology does not get around their complaint. They misnamed their audience, which is popular or folk religion, not theologians and theological doctrines; and they misnamed their topic, which is the abuse

---

25. See the review article on Atonement in the New Testament by C. M. Tuckett in *The Anchor Bible Dictionary*.

26. In *A Theology Primer*, chapters 6–8, especially pp. 93–97.

and oppression of women, not divine intent to abuse the messiah. But they have a real criticism of the consequences of religious symbols.

Having made these points, we can now address the extremely important issues in their writing, namely, how to understand and respond critically to religious symbols, those associated with a doctrine in this case, that have bad effects as measured by other dimensions of life. For surely Brown and Parker are right that many women are abused, that at least some of them participate in that abuse and affirm the culture legitimating that abuse, and that some come meekly to the abuse, refusing to fight against it, because they think that attitude is entailed by Christianity. Brown and Parker might exaggerate in their claim that Christianity causes patriarchy which causes abuse and the oppression of racism, classism, and sexism. Many cultures have managed to be abusive and oppressive in those ways without benefit of Christianity. Indeed abuse and oppression appear to have become exacerbated within Christendom *as secularism has gained power over Christianity* and all religion. Men as well as women have suffered from abuse and the oppression of racism, classism, and sexism. Nevertheless, insofar as religious symbols have some responsibility somewhere, the matter requires theology's critical examination. The following sections will attempt to lay out some of the structure of that critical examination, although the criticism of the doctrine of the atonement is not the specific topic of this book.

## 6.2. RELIGION AMONG THE DIMENSIONS OF LIFE

The exceedingly complex interplay of religious symbols with the various conditions of the intentional contexts in which they are interpreted has been discussed at some length in chapters 1, 4, and 5. We have seen religious symbols to have two intrinsic normative functions, first authentically to engage people with the divine matters, such as Enlightenment, God, the Dao, redemption, that are their topic, and second truthfully to relate people to these divine matters. The first intrinsic normative function comes from the fact that symbols are elements of imagination the function of which is to engage. The second comes from the fact that symbols are interpreted and it is the function of interpretation to aim for truth, that is, to carry over the nature and worth of what is interpreted into the experience of the interpreters. Religious symbols can relate people to divine matters in practical ways by having doubled interpretants, and in devotional ways by having doubled referents.

The case about divine child abuse, however, demonstrates what Proconsuls and social scientists have long known, namely, that religious symbols have many extrinsic functions with normative consequences. In the above instance, a good argument can be made that, while the doctrine of the atonement seems in its intrinsic normative function to intend only good things for people, overcoming sin of all kinds and setting them right with God, in fact it has had bad consequences. It has served, for instance, to legitimate the plain immorality of people in power causing direct physical, mental, and life-career harm to those over whom they have power, if in fact it was ever used as a justification for dominance. Under the same condition it has served in a related way to legitimate unjust political structures that institutionalize the immorality; it has the same unjust legitimating effect on other kinds of institutionalized structures such as those in family relations, the work place, and church organizations. The popularization of the doctrine of the atonement has had the effect, at least in some people, of causing psychological harm, of turning women and abused children against themselves, of infantilizing them as victims so that they will and perpetuate their suffering. Verdi, or at least his librettists, Joseph Mery and Camille du Locle, realized that the point applies to the suffering of men too when, in *Don Carlo,* Act 3, Scene 1, the Grand Inquisitor tells King Phillip that he must put his son to death for supporting a rebellion; the King asks how he, a Christian father, could acquiesce in the death of his son, and the Grand Inquisitor replies that God sacrificed his own to redeem us. When the King asks how the Inquisitor can sustain such a severe law, the latter replies that Calvary does not need his sanction! Although Brown and Parker did not develop the point this way, they illustrate how the doctrine has perverse aesthetic consequences, not in the superficial sense of making things ugly but in the profound sense of clouding our abilities to see things straight, to focus on them in context, to see what matters and what does not.

To understand this it is insufficient to note that the interpretations of religious symbols have consequences beyond their direct implications, or to say only that social structures can carry the implications of symbols into consequences that contradict the symbols' intent. This is to say far too little, and to ignore the fact that there are norms going well beyond religion according to which affairs are to be judged good or bad. The norms for religious symbols have to do with engaging people with divine realities, the finite/infinite contrasts at the foundations of worldliness, and to do so in truthful ways so that people are well-related to those divine realities. But what about personal righteousness, political justice, psychological health and well being, aesthetic acuity and satisfaction (to name just those areas mentioned above in connection with the doctrine of the atonement)? An understanding of the extrinsic consequences of religious symbols must deal with these other dimensions as well. Religious norms are not the only ones pertinent to the judgment of religious symbols.

The word *dimension* is chosen carefully, reflecting Tillich's reasons for liking the word.[27] Distinguishing a variety of dimensions allows us to talk about affairs from several different normative angles, where the distinction of angles comes from the employment of different normative values, for instance holiness, morality, political justice, psychological health, aesthetic acuity and satisfaction. An affair might be going well in some dimensions but not in others. Indeed, it might be going well in some because it is corrupt in others; Brown and Parker tend to blame religion for immorality, injustice, psychological abuse, and so forth, assuming that where the religious dimension is successfully served, the other dimensions are ruined.

The word *dimension* is preferable to *levels*, Tillich argued, because it does not presuppose any neutral hierarchy of importance. Each dimension relates to the others in ways reflecting its own norms, and thus puts itself at the center. *Dimension* is also preferable to *areas* or *fields* because it recognizes that the competition among norms covers the same affairs. The very same activities are at once religious, moral, political, psychological, and aesthetic.

Any aspect of life for which there are norms distinguishing good from bad, better from worse, fulfilling from frustrating, can be considered a dimension overlapping and pervading the affairs to which its norms are relevant. The scope of a dimension is determined by what things are relevant to be judged by the norms defining the dimensions. This is a somewhat informal notion because it can be applied to large-scale norms such as those of relating rightly to the divine, producing and distributing goods, making and enjoying beauty, and so forth, as well as to small things such as a person doing well in school, cultivating a garden, or finishing a book. The large-scale dimensions are by no means the only ones, nor has a case been made that, except for religion, those names cut reality at natural joints. Obviously there is an economic dimension to life, and a domestic, nurturing and caring dimension. Personality types

---

27. Tillich and his texts on *dimensions* were discussed in 4.4 above. His main text is *Systematic Theology III*, pp. 12–29.

and kinds of career-excellences too can be understood in terms of dimensions, as some people excel in sociability while others in internal reflectiveness, some excel as leaders while others excel as artistic creators.[28] The differences among the dimensions are constituted in large measure by the various norms governing them.

Many thinkers would like to believe that all norms are consistent with one another in their demands on specific situations and that norms can be ranged in a hierarchy of importance. Much foolishness has been passed as wisdom in the name of the general and embracing value of goodness. Anyone with both a family and a job knows that being faithful to the norms of one often compromises the other. Maximal economic productivity often requires political tyranny, and justice often leads to inefficiency. Creative geniuses such as Beethoven can treat their neighbors immorally. Empathic souls such as St. Francis can spread the plague. Sometimes saints are crazy and prophets call the she-bears to eat the children.[29] The diverse dimensional norms for affairs are not always in contradictory tensions, but they are often enough so that it is foolish to believe, with Kant, that "ought implies can." Too often it is impossible to pursue holiness, personal righteousness, political justice, one's psychological well-being, and aesthetic acuity and satisfaction together, let alone fit these into earning a living.[30] Brown and Parker in effect argue against attending to the religious dimension because of the price paid by the consequences of the doctrine of the atonement, or at least of some of its images, in other dimensions of life: in defense of justice they abandon all religious considerations.

Because many people will believe that religion is the ultimate or most important dimension, it is good to dwell a bit longer on its relations to certain other dimensions. Religion, it was argued in chapter 1.1, is

---

28. Paul Weiss has developed an extensive philosophical position distinguishing areas of endeavor governed by different norms as reflecting different modes of being. See his *The World of Art*, chapter 2. The metaphysical background for his distinctions is in *Modes of Being*. He does not give norms the prominence I do in distinguishing dimensions or realms of activity, although he recognizes them in each case. In contrast to my Platonism, his position is an Aristotelianism that argues that tasks are defined by the need to complete something otherwise incomplete.

29. 2 Kings 2:23–25.

30. I have attempted to show how the religious dimension has its own way of reconciling the other dimensions, as each of the others also reconciles them all, with generally incompatible forms of reconciliation, in *The Puritan Smile*, chapter 10.

how people relate to the sacred, now understood in terms of the finite/ infinite contrast, by means of representations, rituals, and spiritual practices aiming at perfection or holiness. The representations, rituals, and spiritual practices might in some respects be specific religious institutions. But in most respects they are symbolically shaped things that affect a great many of the institutions of life. Religious representations are integrated into overall cultural thought patterns and affect how people think about most things, not merely religious things. Religious rituals also affect many areas of life outside of specifically religious institutions such as churches. If they did not, they would be ineffective at forming life as a whole regarding how to relate to the world and its ground. Spiritual practices too might be specific among and different from other practices, but they should affect all of a person's practices if they are effective. Furthermore, just as religious representations are parts of cultural systems of representations, so rituals are integrated into social habits and spiritual practices with systems such as singing, speaking, imaging, cultivating attention, will, and the like. Religion is a dimension of life that interpenetrates nearly everything in life with the influence of its representations, rituals, and practices.

Put another way, the purpose of religious living is to modify everything we do, in household life, providing for economic needs, organizing communal life, maturing through life's stages, creating things of excellence—everything—so that those activities and their projects are rightly related to the sacred. Religious effort struggles to conform the whole of a society and the whole of individuals' lives to whatever would be an appropriate stance toward the sacred in that situation. In this way religion seeks to leaven all the other dimensions of life.

So, to mention only the dimensions featured above, religion seeks to conform personal morality or righteousness to the sacred. Sometimes religions contribute explicit moral codes, as in the Torah and Qur'an. But these codes are rarely purely secular in content; they mix laws for moral righteousness with laws of ritual purity, laws for making proper deference to the sacred. Furthermore, often what is morally important, as opposed to ritually important relative to the sacred, is the religious grounding of morality. Obligation itself is what it is, religions say, because it is divinely made, or because it forms the human Dao, or because it expresses sacred Dharma. Religion articulates how living under obligation is itself one of the boundary conditions defining worldliness, and the moral is one important kind of obligation. A person can be moral without being religious. One can deliberate about how to help people and not harm them with clarity and thoroughness, one can develop a character that acts readily and consistently with what one knows to be the morally right, one can encourage others in righteousness, all without attending to the religious dimension. One can even attempt to purge moral practice of the representations of religion, and of the influences of ritual and religious practice, the secularist's dream, and still carry on a moral life. But such a moral life will be strangely shallow where the moral dimension usually feeds on the religious, as in the motivations for moral behavior. The norms of the moral dimension can provide the content of obligatory actions and practices, and they can say what the content of moral character is. But the moral dimension says little to the question, Why be moral?, except that this is the moral thing to be. Religion is what says that the project of being moral is a fundamental boundary marker of human reality as such. The religious dimension impinges on the moral dimension to give it holiness. Duty, for religion, is sacred duty, and failure to do it is not merely immoral or a non-achievement of an obliged good, but an affront to the sacred in the finite/infinite contrast defining obligatedness.[31]

The political dimension roughly can be distinguished from the moral by its focus on the regulation of social institutions instead of personal and interpersonal life. In matters of justice what counts for people is not so much their personal traits that are so important for morality but rather how the social structures affect them impersonally. In politics, people function according to public roles, not personal traits; questions of justice have to do with equality of rights, due process before the law, openness of opportunity, access to institutions of the economy, of education, of communication, and so forth. Social structures distribute power to classes of people, not to individuals per se.[32] The norms of justice have to do with what is good and bad in social institutions insofar as they affect people according to the roles they play or the types into which they fall. Justice of course is far more complex than this. There is a political dimension to households and workplaces as well as to societies at large. Ecological concerns are causing political thinkers to ask whether non-human animals and species of plants, maybe even mountains and lakes, should be given parity with people in the just structuring of social

---

31. On religion as lying at the limiting conditions of ethics, see Stephen Toulmin's *An Examination of the Place of Reason in Ethics*, chapter 14, "Reason and Faith."

32. On the political dimension, see Paul Weiss's *Toward a Perfected State*.

institutions that affect them all. But enough has been said to distinguish the political dimension from the religious.

Regarding the relation of the religious to the political dimension, much that was said about morality is analogous. Religion needs to articulate the ontological truth that it is human nature to be under obligation, obligation to the good in matters of social institutions as well as in interpersonal relationships. Religion attempts to articulate *obligatedness* in the ways societies think about the obligatedness of their obligations, and sometimes religious people take on the social role of the prophet, complaining about the ignoring of obligations. When societies attempt to suppress or ignore religion, and still be just, they tread the soft ground of relativism and are open to the parochial claim that there is no obligation on questions of power.

The psychological dimension of life has to do with the health of one's emotional and mental organization, its capacities to withstand and respond appropriately to life's traumas, its cultivation of various important areas of emotional and cognitive life, its achievements and habits regarding relating to specific persons, to persons in particular roles, and to roles one has to play oneself in familial, educational, economic and other social systems. These matters are all related to personal development and are defined variously in terms of stages of growth and maturation. The criteria for psychological strengths and weaknesses, achievements and failures, wholeness and partiality, integration and dissociation, are all susceptible to being worked out without reference to the religious dimension, with two exceptions. There needs to be a reference, analogous to those in morals and politics, to why it is ontologically good or obligatory to be psychologically healthy and mature. The answer to the question, Why do I have to grow up? is not a psychological answer, although psychology might say in what growing up consists. Also, religious participation is one of the areas of life in which one needs to develop psychological health, if one participates in religion.

In North Atlantic cultures now the religious dimension is very often confused with the psychological. The development of psychology as a science of the soul in the modern Enlightenment seemed to replace much of religion's unscientific reflections on the soul. Often the psychological pains people feel had been treated as problems of spiritual formation. But there is a significant difference between psychological growth and health, on the one hand, and spiritual growth and health on the other, however much they interact, as I argued in 5.1. Spiritual matters have to do with how the individual relates to the sacred, to the infinite at the defining finite/infinite contrasts of the world. Spiritual matters are worked out in the context of all the rest of life, and are particularly shaped by specifically religious practices such as participation in religions and thinking about theological topics. Spiritual development is a matter of maturation in some respects, but also has to do with transforming character traits. Most of all it has to do with defining oneself in the most intimate parts of life with those symbols that carry over the divine realities into one's concrete living. Psychological health might treat these concerns as incidental. Many psychological theories suppose, in fact, that there are no divine realities and that the concern for them is an illusion with pathological sources. Moreover, spiritual matters are often psychologically destabilizing. Powerful religious symbols in devotional use tend to be abrupt and absolutistic, making demands difficult to harmonize with other demands. Religions' stark spiritual contrasts between ignorance and enlightenment, competition and attunement, damnation and salvation are usually anathema to psychology's proper concern that we assess realistically and with balance just how good and how bad we are. Psychology's concern is to find wholeness and balance within the world. Spirituality's concern is to conform all postures within the world to the ultimate which founds the world but is not merely a part of it.

The aesthetic dimension is intended here in a special sense. It is not merely the activities of creating art or appreciating it, though inclusive of those. The aesthetic dimension has to do with the norms for seeing things clearly, with understanding what matters, and what matters for what. The word *aesthetic* goes back to the Greek problematic of transforming the effects of all the things with which we interact into perceptions. Perception is an attainment, not a merely automatic natural condition, and good perception is difficult to attain. The obstacles to good perception are not merely, and not importantly, impaired hearing, seeing, smelling, and so forth. The obstacles are enduring pain, poverty that dulls the soul, oppression that obliterates or fixates attention, a crude culture that does not allow subtle distinctions, reductive habits that force perceptions into rude classes determined by our needs rather than by things' own contours. Obstacles to good perception include a social style where the sensibility is overstimulated or sated and a style of thought occupied with jargon, buzz words, and politically motivated judgments about non-political matters. Art causes us to perceive better, to make discriminations, to develop taste regarding what matters. Producing art is a struggle to come to better perception. But art alone is insufficient to provide the imagination for good perception. It is a matter for all the roles of imagination in culture.

Concerning the religious dimension, the aesthetic dimension is important for developing good perception in religious matters, as we have seen in the discussions of imagination and engagement. But religion is merely a topic area for the aesthetic dimension. Most proper aesthetic concerns deal with other topics for perception. As in the other dimensions, the religious supplies the motive for perceiving well in the first place: the debasement of perceptive thought by jargon not only trivializes but blasphemes. Religious representations, rituals, and practices can debase perception as well as enhance it. Whether perception is good depends on the norms for good perception, not on the norms for properly relating to the divine.

I have dwelt, however informally and anecdotally, on other dimensions of life than the religious in order to indicate that human life and its activities stand under many norms at once. What religious symbols do perhaps well in the religious dimension might be indifferent or even wicked in other dimensions. The opposite can also hold. What is the situation with regard to Brown and Parker's case?

## 6.3. RELIGION JUDGED BY OTHER DIMENSIONS

We now are in a position to inquire more deeply into the sources of the complaints made by Brown and Parker about the Christian symbol of the atonement. A religious symbol is authentic, that is, a real religious symbol, if it engages people with what it symbolizes. Whether symbols are natural or conventional, or a combination of both, they are authentic when they shape imagination so that people engage their subject matter. Authentic symbols are living because they effect a kind of interaction between divine matters and the people that interpret them. This is as true for abstract theological symbols such as the doctrine of the atonement as it is for representations such as baptismal water, crosses, or psalms to be sung.

Nothing is more apparent in this secular age, however, than that many ideas and objects that had effectively engaged people in previous ages now are dead. Perhaps the symbols were once authentic and true, or even would be true again if the means could be found to engage them today. But they simply have died and cannot live in our culture as it stands. Therefore, if a religion wants to assert and make symbolically efficacious some truth once carried by a now dead symbol, it needs a new symbol, or it needs to change the present situation.

The chief reason I do not hold to much of a doctrine of atonement to understand Christian salvation is that I believe that the atonement imagery depends on the symbol of sacrifice rectifying wrongs and that that symbol is dead for us in the North Atlantic world in the late twentieth century. We can understand intellectually what sacrifice meant in the Torah, how people believed, once they had broken the covenant, that only God could restore it, and that the rituals for performing sacrifice were instituted by God to be the vehicles for restoring the covenant. The sacrifices were thought to be effective, not because God likes the smell of cooking meat—Yahweh much preferred justice—but because God instituted them as the way back into the covenant. Far from Yahweh being a sadist, as Brown and Parker claim, the sacrifices were means of divine grace by which people could be brought to reconciliation. The Pauline and Johannine interpretations of Jesus as a sacrifice for the sins of the whole world work off of this sense of God sending both the rites and the sacrificial lamb to renew the covenant.

But that sense of sacrifice plays no role in our modern sensibility. If anything, it only arouses our feelings of solidarity with sacrificial animals. Almost inevitably, then, the sacrifice imagery in the atonement either gives rise to anger at the abuse of victims or the radical misconstrual of the image to mean that we should act like sheep. In the Torah, people were not supposed to act like sacrificial victims, and the victims themselves were prized and loved for the roles they played in renewing the covenant.

What do we do? Perhaps with a strong educational campaign we could expand our current sense of symbolic sensitivities so as to recapture something of the ancient meanings of sacrifice. But that would be very hard. In Judaism that sensitivity began to slip when the Second Temple was destroyed and rabbinic Judaism replaced the cult of actual temple sacrifice. I doubt we could practice real animal sacrifice in the ancient sense enough to valorize its symbolic power. The alternative would seem to be to find other symbols to replace that of sacrifice. What needs particularly to be addressed is that primitive sense of stain or impurity, described so accurately by Ricoeur, that results not from responsible wicked action but from being in disconformity to the covenant.[33] Alter-

---

33. See Ricoeur's *Symbolism of Evil*, chapter 1.

native symbols for salvation would need to recognize that the problem is the shame of corruption and disattunement, not merely moral guilt.

As the Christian community struggles with this, the community must be extraordinarily sensitive to what happens when dead symbols are employed: if they are interpreted at all, they are misinterpreted, and perhaps with disastrous results. Brown and Parker have shown that, for at least some women, the symbols of the atonement have nothing authentic to do with salvation but are misinterpreted as legitimating the very things salvation is supposed to replace.

Not only are symbols living or dead for interpretation, the important symbols for religion need to be broken. Religious symbols fasten on something that marks the boundary of fundamental lineaments of the world, I have argued, on the other side of which is the infinite or divine. The boundary condition points both to the finite it expresses and to the infinite that must be acknowledged for the boundary to be recognized as boundary. Perhaps the most common symbols in theistic religions are those marking the sheer existence of the world, its contingency, pointing thereby to the creator. The creator, of course, is not the world created, nor is the creation of the world much like creation in the world such as law-giving or ceramic pottery. So the images of the creator as law-giver or potter and gardener in Genesis 1 and 2 need to be qualified; God is not like that, we noted above, because the creation includes making law-givers, potters, and gardeners. Sophisticated theologians such as Augustine and Thomas can provide subtle and abstract renditions of what makes the world contingent and of what the creation of that might mean; yet nevertheless all we know of the creator is the creating of this world and the creator is not merely that. These points made within the traditions of Christianity hold for Judaism, Islam, Hinduism, and other religions with some sense of creation.

There are other borderline conditions around which religious symbols have focused. For instance, the world is filled with obligations for human beings, and God is the source of obligatedness as such, not exactly a super-obligated being as Job learned, but the source of obligatedness. A central religious boundary condition is how human beings posture themselves with respect to God, not so much with respect to one another in morality or to nature in harmony but with respect to God as the author of themselves, their moral contexts and their places in nature. Various images express this human existential boundary condition—the relation of subjects to a king, children to a parent, sheep to a shepherd, partners in covenant, creatures to creativity, and so forth. Of course none of these can be taken literally because the God-term in the relation is infinite rather than finite as the relation depicts, although God can enter into the finite roles required by the relation. Because the human side of the existential relation to God is disturbed, salvation is required and, in the theistic religions, salvation comes from God. The doctrine of the atonement is a set of symbols attempting to articulate the relation of people to God, what has gone wrong with this relation, and what God does to remedy that.

But all of those symbols in the atonement theory, whatever their merit, have also to be broken. God is not a touchy monarch offended by disobedient subjects. God is not a doting father conflicted about sending his only son into danger. God is not a monster-Moloch salivating for sacrificial victims. God is not a senior partner sending an heir to tend to junior partners who are ruining the business. God is not a person in any plain sense but the creator of persons, personality, and personhood. The deepest travesty Brown and Parker make of the doctrine of the atonement is that they use the symbols for God without breaking them. They treat God as if the personal symbols could be taken literally, and of course then the infinite looks silly masquerading as a big tyrant.

Even school children know that the image of God as an old man in the sky with a white beard is only an image and that God has no gender, age, shape, or place. But it requires a developed ear for symbolism, a refined taste, to be able to use finite symbols as legitimate in their place but broken, to use them without drawing silly or malicious implications, as Brown and Parker do with the atonement symbols. One learns through religious practice to hear symbols resonating in one another without the conflicts that literally would obtain. One learns to hear limits and inapplicabilities and to move with discernment through the connections among symbols, drawing faithful implications for communal and personal religious life. Religious life requires a developed art of symbolic discernment. At a minimum, the cultivation of this art is a major function of public worship that lifts up and contextualizes a religion's symbols. Healthy religious communities also cultivate the art of symbolic discernment in explicit educational programs and in all the other activities that have educational consequences.

The wretchedly false interpretations of the atonement imagery cited by Brown and Parker among the women and men who think the life of Christ justifies abuse come thus from two sources. For these people, the atonement symbols are dead in their original meanings, and stupid other meanings have been assigned them, such as, that like Jesus we must suffer to save the world. Furthermore, for these people the religious symbols are not broken but are used idolatrously. These people lack the art of discerning religious symbols in their powers and limitations and thus are more childish than children. They are snared and brutalized not by the doctrine of the atonement but by their inability to break its symbols and see through their popularization. At the very least, there is a failure of religious education here, not just in the churches in which these people grew up but in the society at large.

Turning from the conditions for interpretation to the conditions for larger consequences following from religious symbols, it is important to be reminded that consequences can be good as well as bad. Indeed, both Jesus, in saying "thus you know them by their fruits" (Matthew 7:20), and Paul, in citing "love, joy, peace, patience, kindness, generosity, faithfulness, gentleness, and self-control" (Galatians 5:22–23) as pragmatic tests for the authenticity of a gospel, advocated looking to positive and good consequences for evaluating the truth of certain religious symbols. Generally, religious communities would like the entire sphere of their activities, in fact the whole culture in which they live, to be shaped in accord with the practical application of basic religious symbols. This is why the problem is so serious when negative and wicked consequences follow from symbols that are supposed to cultivate the kingdom of God. Two remarks need to be made about this.

The first is that the conditions connecting religious symbols with structural social consequences involve many things besides the symbols themselves. The symbols are only one kind of contributing cause of the consequences, one that should not be overestimated. Elisabeth Schussler Fiorenza and other feminist scholars have argued, for instance, that the earliest symbols within the Christian movement expressed a radical sense of equality among persons and respect for leadership roles of women as well as men; but as the Christian movement spread through Hellenistic culture it took on more and more of the symbolic definitions of authority in family and state characteristic of patriarchal Rome.[34] In this instance the cultural conditions of Roman patriarchy simply overwhelmed the original Christian symbols and practices that should have had consequences in the opposite direction. Similarly, the symbols of the atonement, which mean that no suffering after Jesus has salvific significance, have been overwhelmed in the cases cited by Brown and Parker by social habits of violence and abuse; among the consequences is the serious misinterpretation of the symbols of the atonement.

---

34. See her *Bread Not Stone* and *In Memory of Her.*

The second remark opens a whole new topic. Are the consequences to be judged by religious or moral criteria? The answer, of course, is both, and by many other criteria stemming from other normative dimensions of life such as the aesthetic, psychological, political, historical and so forth. Large-scale social structures and habits are consequences of religious symbolizations but also of many other things, and are to be judged by whatever normative perspectives might be applicable.

Yet it is peculiar that Brown and Parker use exclusively non-religious criteria to judge the consequences of the religious symbols of the atonement. Their reconstruction of an acceptable Christianity appeals only to moral criteria of liberation from oppressive conditions of abuse and to psychological criteria of interpersonal intimacy. References to God trivially appropriate God to psychological and moral categories. The non-religious approach in Brown and Parker is most apparent in their criticism of the *Christus Victor* theory of atonement for saying that suffering can be justified or endured for the sake of resurrection. Without even bothering explicitly to deny the resurrection, they merely assume there is no such thing in any religiously important sense and condemn the position for suggesting that suffering itself is not the last word. Suffering may well be the last word morally; but there is no major religious tradition—Christian, Jewish, Buddhist, Daoist, whatever—that says suffering is the last word religiously. Buddhism is the religion to focus most intensely on suffering. It claims that all of life is suffering, even if unrecognized: all success leads to the grave and the best party leads to hangovers. Ecclesiastes in the Hebrew Bible comes close to this in the lament that all is vanity; but vanity is not suffering in the profound Buddhist sense. Andrew Sung Park has argued that the Christian notion of sin, which addresses the sinner, ought to be complemented by the Korean notion of han, a version of the Korean Buddhist notion of suffering.[35] But even here, in Buddhism and in Park's *minjung* theology, suffering is only the first word. The conditions of suffering ought to be removed, of course. But the message of religion is that suffering itself, in its surface appearance, is not the true Unconditioned, not the true God. Religion has to do with a radical displacement of the worldly character of suffering victim.[36] The religious dimension simply did not occur to Brown and Parker as relevant.

---

35. See Park's *The Wounded Heart of God.*
36. Park would not agree with this point wholly. He astutely notes, ibid., pp. 132 ff., that suffering or *han* is "shared by all major religions." The closest he comes to a divine decentering, however, is in a concluding discussion of transcendence, which means transcending human difficulties, not reorienting to the divine. Interestingly, his

By the religious dimension, as must be clear by now, I mean, among other things, that the major living religious symbols engage us with divinity whatever else they do. Therefore in matters of atonement and its alternative symbols, regardless of consequences for social justice and psychological intimacy, the affirmation and use of the symbols ought to turn Christians to God in certain ways. Brown and Parker neglect entirely to inquire into whether or how the symbols of the atonement orient people relative to God, and what consequences for public and personal life follow from this. Perhaps this is because the symbols of the atonement are indeed dead and thus are not religious in any authentic sense, which is my own reluctant conclusion concerning most of the atonement imagery. Then Brown and Parker should have said this. For, their discussion leaves open the possibility that *authentic* religious consequences—how we *should* stand toward God—might conflict with at least certain moral and psychological imperatives. Regarding suffering, it is perplexing to ask how the religious approach of Theresa of Calcutta can be reconciled with the heroic models Brown and Parker embrace of social liberation, personal intimacy, and justice.[37]

The conclusion is that the consequences of religious symbols can be judged by whatever normative standpoints might be relevant. Insofar as there is a concern for the religious or theological dimension of the symbols, at least one of those standpoints should be the religious. To make such a judgment one must determine the meaning of the symbol, analyze the intentional use of the symbol, discern whether the meaning is properly carried over into the interpretations arising with that use, and answer causal questions about what those interpretations contributed, along with other causes, to the consequences being judged. Religious symbols can be harmful by being demonically false, dead, or idolatrously misinterpreted. But even if true, live, and properly interpreted, other condi-

---

first approach to the resolution of suffering is Gnostic: "Pain that is shared is pain no more. The han that is understood is han no more," p. 138. He goes on to advocate a transformation of social conditions that cause pain, led by the Christian church in connection with other religions. But he seems not to conclude that the pursuit of justice and the alleviation of suffering is a political matter regardless of any religious commitment, and that the redefinition of religion as a political project threatens religion's concerns for the unconditioned, the dao, the divine.

37. Doubtless they would object to their ideals being called heroic. *Heroism* is antipathetic to their rhetoric. Nevertheless, freedom, love, and justice, if they are not to be qualified by the compromises of community and the otherness of one's companions, are truly heroic ideals.

tions might make them accessory to consequences that contradict their own intent. All these questions need to be answered before blame is levied or an intervention attempted on the symbol, its use, its interpretation, or its consequences.

To understand how they are used, recall four related aspects of religious symbols: their meaning, their intentional use, their interpretation, and their consequences.

The meaning of religious symbols is what they assert or assume about what they are supposed to symbolize. A major purpose of theology and other kinds of religious reflection is to develop, analyze, articulate, and criticize the meanings of religious symbols. As is obvious in the case of the complex of symbols involved in the doctrine of the atonement, there are many competing meanings to some symbols, and there is a history of the development and interaction of those meanings.

The phrase "intentional use of religious symbols" refers to the roles those symbols play in various contexts. It would be too much to say that religious symbols are always used for some explicit purpose or other. Too often they form the background and context for activities that are purposive irrespective of the symbols or that are not even particularly purposive. These contexts can be called "intentional" because they are shaped by human intentions and those shapes determine many of the roles of symbols. Religious symbols have three main families of intentional contexts that have been examined above:

Closest to pure communication is the theological context of attempting to understand divine matters through the development, criticism, and use of religious symbols, especially verbal and intellectual ones. In theology, religious meanings themselves are examined, and the conditions under which they can be used to assert things about their topics determined. There has been a history of attempts within Christianity to formulate an understanding of salvation—its problems and mechanisms—and the symbols of atonement have been candidates for providing good formulations. There are similar theological histories in other traditions. Religious symbolic meanings are not interpreted at all unless they are at least in the intentional context of reflection.

In addition is the intentional context of the use of religious symbols to organize religious life, including the activities of religious communities such as worship, teaching, and mutual care, the activities of daily life insofar as religion bears upon them, and the activities of the larger community in their religious dimension. Brown and Parker refer to the use of the various symbols of the atonement as they are verbalized, sung, depicted, and sometimes explicitly taught in church activities, and also to how those symbols are fastened on by women in other parts of their lives when they are faced with the potentiality of abuse and oppression.

Finally, there is the intentional context of personal spiritual formation in which religious symbols are intended to lead the soul to God or enlightenment or perfect attunement. Religious symbols might be radically transformed through visualization and other means in personal spiritual devotions beyond what theologians would assert as legitimated by their strict meanings, and also beyond what ecclesiastics might say would be healthy in a religious community. The practical intentional context here is not so much religious life in public but the private life of the soul.

In the practical uses of religious symbols there may be little or no conscious interpretation of the symbols, as there would be in explicit theology or religious reflection. Rather, they simply shape the hermeneutic world of the practical activities according to some interpretation that might be unnoticed. Here is precisely the place where symbols, regardless of their theological meaning, might do great damage. Two further elements need to be distinguished.

Symbols do not symbolize anything unless they are interpreted, or potentially interpreted. Sometimes the interpretations are hedged about with critical intellect, as they are supposed to be in theology. But in most practical intentional contexts in which religious symbols occur their interpretation is vastly enriched with other elements. Indeed, is that not precisely the point for most symbols? The interpretive response to them is not only an intellectual Aha! but an incorporation of the meaning of the symbol into the life of the community and its members. To understand the atonement and related or alternative doctrines, according to Christians, is to see that Jesus' crucifixion and resurrection save us! It is to organize our community's life around gratitude and praise for this so as to live in accordance with salvation. The devotions of the Saivite and other bhakti traditions of India have a similar function.

Or put the other way around, when we organize our religious communities we want the proper placement of appropriate religious symbols so that they shape the various activities and habits of the community. Aristotle distinguished practical syllogisms—his version of interpretations—from theoretical ones by saying that the conclusion of the latter is a proposition whereas the conclusion of the former is an action— major premise: "white meat is good for a fever"; minor premise: "Socrates has a fever"; conclusion: the practical reasoner feeds Socrates some chicken. Of course the interpretive impact of religious symbols is rarely syllogistic, but it does consist in actions that are shaped the way they are because of how the symbols represent divine matters in the behavior. Nothing could be clearer from the argument by Brown and Parker than that the interpretations that a theologian would see legitimated by the meaning of the symbols of the atonement are a far cry from the interpretations that sometimes are made in popular religion.

The consequences of religious symbols in their various intentional contexts are not limited to the interpretations of them made there. Indeed, the interpretations may have consequences that go far beyond any interpretive reference to the symbols or what they symbolize. The development of a culture in which the abuse of women is legitimated need make no reference to the sacrifice of Jesus for the sins of the world. Nevertheless, if the practical interpretation of Jesus' suffering is that what was good for Jesus is good for me, and therefore I should embrace suffering as if it helped others and myself, then that interpretation could reinforce the culture of abuse, especially if other people want me to suffer. There are, of course, many causes, indeed necessary conditions, for a culture of abuse having nothing to do with religious symbolism. But certain interpretations of religious symbols can reinforce such a culture, and therefore lead to that culture, perhaps indirectly, as their consequence. Patriarchy itself is a set of consequences of many factors, among which can be found certain religious symbols.

In analyzing the problem exposed by Brown and Parker, we need now to bear in mind the distinctions between the meanings legitimated by the structure of religious symbols, their various roles in intentional contexts of life, their interpretations in those contexts, and the consequences of those interpretations.

## 6.4. THE TRUTH AND RELATIVITY OF RELIGIOUS HERMENEUTICS

All of the above has demonstrated that religion and religious symbols exist in cultures and societies that contain many things besides religion, and that understanding religious symbols means understanding more than their religious significance. There are five practical observations I would like to make about these matters.

First, the case presented by Brown and Parker once again illustrates the importance of the question of truth regarding religious symbols.[38]

---

38. The question seems to have escaped them, however.

Put most bluntly, the questions that should have been asked by Christian theologians through the centuries are whether the symbols of the atonement mean that Christian disciples should imitate Jesus' suffering on the cross for the sake of salvation, whether, if so, this falls as a special burden on women, and whether the Father's dedication of Jesus to a dangerous task by analogy legitimates the abuse of children. I believe in each instance the answer should be a resounding No, but the question should have been asked and answered relative to each of the instances in which a society might have drawn those practical inferences. To answer those theological questions requires theological interpretations both of the atonement symbols and the other symbol systems with which they resonate and also of the various social and cultural circumstances in which suffering is found and abuse is possible.

In light of these considerations we can appreciate the importance of traditional concerns about orthodoxy and heresy. Especially with regard to practical implications it is important to set the boundaries of symbols and their meanings, to define symbolic assertions by contrast with their near neighbors, and to know what ought not be symbolized that might look like the symbolic reference at hand. Modern liberal culture tends to look askance at the concern to define heresies and affirm orthodoxies. That concern is nearly universal among the major religions. Sankara, Bavaviveka, Maimonides, al'Farabi, and Zhuxi thought polemically as much as Athanasius and Thomas Aquinas. A heresy is a symbolically twisted doctrine that leads to bad theological, practical, or devotional interpretations. Gnosticism, for instance, was decided to be heretical in part because of its theological affirmation of the material world as bad, the creation of an evil rather than good God. But it was also heretical for its practical implication that salvation is oriented only to elite knowers, not to common people, and for its devotional consequence of creating a mystical orientation without a corresponding orientation to reform the concrete neighborhood. The symbols of the atonement are theologically heretical when and where they assert that salvation comes not from God but from the human imitation of Jesus' suffering; they are practically heretical where they imply the legitimation of suffering for salvific purposes, among women, men, or children, and devotionally heretical when and where they inculcate a victimized mind-set. A true or orthodox doctrine of the atonement would have to have symbols that do not lead to these heretical consequences. Theology's business is to determine the truth of such symbols and to spell out how the symbols refer and are to be interpreted so that heresies do not result.

Second, theology as the watchdog for the truth of religious symbols, and critic of heresies, is not a mere intellectual enterprise but quickly becomes, or should become, an agency for legitimating and delegitimating religious symbols in a religion and in the larger society. Christian theologians should have been warning women against heretical versions of the atonement doctrine, telling them not to think suffering would save them or their loved ones, encouraging them rather to behave like those whom God loves dearly unto death. The orthodox implication of the atonement doctrine is that Christians should assert their dignity, refuse to take seriously those who accord them less respect than God who died for them, and get on with perfecting themselves and their community. Theologians should have been saying these things, and doing so with authority in the appropriate places where common people encounter the symbols. As Brown and Parker demonstrate, there is a great need in religious communities and in the larger society to regulate critically the legitimate and illegitimate religious symbols.

But what a shock this conclusion is! Does not theological intervention with power conjure up all the images of the inquisition, of Muslim leaders calling for the assassination of critics, of fundamentalists in all religions attempting to regulate belief? Is not the exercise of power in direct contradiction to the freedom theology itself needs in order to be critical and not dominated by a powerful but false symbol? These are indeed the practical problems and they were what led modern European skepticism to make religion a private matter. If only religious symbols could be construed to have no public consequences, so that no public exercise of critical theological power is required, then societies could be spared the pains, sometimes wars, associated with the effective deployment of theological power, and theology itself as an intellectual discipline could be free to play. Brown and Parker demonstrate, however, that religious symbols, even in societies that have attempted to privatize religion, have enormous public consequences. Somebody ought to do something about the abuse of women and children, and in part, they show, theologians that keep the symbols straight ought to be part of the effort. Having said this, we can affirm all the democratic safeguards on the wielding of theological power, limiting the scope of churches, pitting sides against one another in public debate, sharply regulating means for expressing power—no stakes and flames for heretics. We can note also, in anticipation of the discussion in the next chapter of the nature of the community of theological discourse, how difficult it is to identify authoritative theological judgment. We can take comfort in the emerging consensus that the best way to enforce good ideas and drive out bad ones is by having everyone understand both. But societies will never be able to say that the truth of religious symbols does not matter.

Third, the theological task is complicated by the fact that the practical intentional context for religious symbols gives them doubled interpretants, and that the devotional context gives them doubled referents as well. Thus in possibly two ways religious symbols are relativized to people's contexts. This relativity does not compromise the truth of the symbols, only their universality, because they refer, mean, or imply different things in different contexts. Suppose, for instance, that Valerie Saiving is more or less right in her claim that whereas "sin" for men takes the form of pride and egoistic over-assertiveness, "sin" for women is much the opposite, a self-debasement, a diffuseness of identity overly dependent on others.[39] The symbols of the atonement or any alternative theory of how salvation works that convey the practical message to women are thus likely to be different from those that convey them to men, different at least in the derivation of practical interpretants from representational ones. In the devotional context, symbols that present the saving God to a selfishly assertive sinner are likely to be different from those that present the saving God to a sinner too diffuse to be confronted on her own terms. In this example, it is to be expected that the differences between the symbols easily can be reconciled theologically so that we can see that the same thing is being symbolized in different forms; the differences. But consider the example suggested by Paul Tillich in his claim that the "problem" of religion in the Christian first century was finding life in a world of death, that the "problem" in the sixteenth century was finding moral forgiveness in a world of immorality and personal sin, and that the "problem" in the twentieth century is finding meaning in a scientific world where all meaning is human projection.[40] Is there a common problem underlying all these expressions? Tillich thought that anxiety is the common element, with three forms. Is there a common salvific answer? Tillich thought that faith, divinely given, as the courage to carry on in the face of anxiety is the common element of salvation, with three forms. But what about the symbols that convey the problem and the answer? Surely they must be highly diverse and difficult to connect and criticize so as to be clear about the truth and nearby heresies.

---

39. See her "The Human Situation: A Feminine View." She is clear that she is speaking only about tendencies, not about absolute differences in classifications.

40. See his *The Courage to Be*, chapter 2.

Now consider that the contextually relativized truth of religious symbols needs to be understood in conjunction with all the other dimensions of life in which those symbols play a role. For instance, the normative relations of relative dominance of men and women is just as contextual as the religious dimension. According to Tikva Frymer-Kensky, the earliest Sumerian pantheon honored gods and goddesses about equally, but distinguished them according to different functions within civilization associated with males and females. Men and gods slowly came to dominate women and goddesses by taking over the female roles. Encouraged by modern conceptions of equality, many feminists today want to reverse the dominance of women by men through dissociating gender from social roles, making all opportunities open to all with equal rewards. The political symbols of balance in a culture that associates gender with roles are very different from the political symbols that denies the association. To decide which symbols truthfully represent what end in what context is a difficult and confusing matter for political philosophy, but something obviously related to judging the function of religious symbols in the political dimension. Theology is not the same as political philosophy, or morals, or psychology, but it relates to them directly regarding the understanding of the truth of religious symbols.

Fourth, the task of assessing the truth of religious symbols is complicated even further by popular religion. Two senses of popular religion need to be distinguished. One is the religious life open to a wide variety of people—religions differ regarding how wide their legitimate membership should be—in which religious symbols shape practical activities and devotional life, as discussed earlier. Regarding this sense of popular religion, I have argued that religious symbols aim to be true and should be judged regarding their truth, with truth defined in theological, practical, and devotional senses (to be specified further in the next chapter). The other sense of popular religion is where religious symbols are coopted by the needs of other dimensions of life and the religious dimension itself is disguised, distorted, and sometimes plain neglected. Some kinds of fundamentalism consist in the use of religious forms for political ends, with the political ends in turn distorted by the ultimacy appropriate for religious objects. Crusades and jihads idolatrously identify political goals, which may or may not have legitimate political justification, with the divinity of finite/infinite contrasts. Other kinds of fundamentalism use religious forms for psychological ends, to provide a sense of identity and security in a changing world people do not understand and with which they are not prepared to cope. Given the frightening character of ultimacy, and the deeply eschatological locus of the bliss of divine love, security and psychological stability is the last thing one should expect from truthful symbols of the religious dimension. But many fundamentalists co-opt religious symbols for their psychological needs. Similarly fundamentalisms can be driven to co-opt religious symbols for economic needs, and so on. The divisions are not neat.[41] Popular religion in the second sense is the appropriation of religious symbols and symbolic activities and attitudes for matters not of the religious dimension of life.

Actual social situations, of the sort about which Brown and Parker complain, are complicated mixtures of popular religion in both senses. It is possible to look at the popular use of symbols such as those of the atonement from the standpoint of the religious dimension and ask whether they properly bear religious truth. In this example there are nice issues to be decided as to whether the symbols of the atonement are orthodox in attributing salvation to God, or heterodox in attributing salvific powers to human suffering, as to whether the symbols involving sacrifice are genuinely alive, or can only be taken in idolatrous senses, as to whether the practical implications are rightly drawn in their interpretation and whether the saving God is rightly presented to devotees of this and that stage and state of soul. Brown and Parker asked none of these

---

41. These examples of fundamentalism reflect the enormous research and original conceptual work of the Fundamentalism Project at the University of Chicago whose published volumes are edited by Martin E. Marty and R. Scott Appleby. The first volume, *Fundamentalisms Observed*, reviews the breadth and diversity, as well as commonalities of contemporary fundamentalisms. It has major articles on North American Protestant fundamentalism, Roman Catholic traditionalism and activist conservatism in the United States, South American Protestant fundamentalism, fundamentalism among religious Jews, Zionist fundamentalism, Sunni fundamentalism in the Arab world, Shi'ite fundamentalism in Iran, Iraq, and Lebanon, Islamic fundamentalism in South Asia, Islamic resurgence in Malaysia and Indonesia, Hindu fundamentalism, Sikh fundamentalism, fundamentalist movements in Theravada Buddhism, Confucian fundamentalism in industrial East Asia, and the mix of religious and political fundamentalism in Japan. The project volume, *Fundamentalisms and the State*, contains essays looking at the political connections with fundamentalisms around the world; its subtitle is *Remaking Polities, Economies, and Militance*. The volume, *Fundamentalisms and Society*, discusses fundamentalisms as they have impact on science, family structures in various societies, and education. All of these volumes show fundamentalisms to be far more complicated than my simple scheme of the co-opting of religious symbols for non-religious purposes. My scheme, however, is complicated enough to make the point that popular religion in this second sense deeply confuses the situation with regard to the assessment of religious symbols.

questions, for which reason I have said that their analysis is not religious but moral or political.

They have in fact demonstrated that it is possible to look at the situation of popular religion from the standpoint of its second sense, namely, as the use of religious symbols for the purposes of other dimensions of life. From the standpoints of the political, moral, and psychological projects of North American feminists such as Brown and Parker, the use of the symbols of the atonement in forming political, interpersonal, and personal developmental life has been odious. Of course the religious symbols are not the only factors, and indeed might be relatively minor factors; but they might well have the effects Brown and Parker cite. From the hermeneutical standpoint of interpreting and assessing religious symbols in terms of their functions in dimensions of life other than the religious, their truth as religious symbols is irrelevant. Christian symbols of the atonement are no more interesting than Jewish symbols of obedience to Torah or Confucian symbols of the great relations, except insofar as they happen to be involved in the situation under analysis. The hermeneutical interest is not in their religious truth but in how they have impact on the political, moral, and psychological structure of the society in question, how they help or hinder the norms of those respective dimensions.

Part of the theological difficulty of the Brown and Parker article is the disingenuous quality of its conditions for Christianity quoted at the end. That seems to be a theological statement about what true Christian religion ought to be. But in fact it is a political call for justice, a moral call for radical love and intimacy, and a psychological call for personal liberation, especially for women. It considers Christian doctrines not at all with regard to their truth about what they symbolize but only in terms of their potential roles in the political, moral, and psychological projects. They could just as well have considered Jewish, Muslim, Buddhist, Confucian, Daoist, or Hindu symbols, with the same normative, non-religious conditions. Their attempts to redefine doctrinal symbols such as divine compassion, resurrection, and crucifixion do not deal with what those symbols were attempting to represent theologically, practically, or devotionally, but with what they ought to mean if they are to be adopted for Brown and Parker's political, moral, and psychological projects.

My conclusion is that it is one thing to trace out the social and personal consequences of religious symbols according to causal lines, a difficult empirical task, and quite another to know what norms to bring to bear in assessing those consequences. From the standpoint of the other dimensions of life, religious symbols have various non-religious roles which they play for good or ill. One cannot understand the political impact of religious symbols by considering the religious dimension alone. At least some of those non-religious roles are indifferent to whether the religious symbols are religiously true. On the other hand, at least some of those non-religious roles might very well be affected by the religious truth or falsity of the symbols as they are assumed or asserted. I discussed earlier the role of religion in representing the political, moral, psychological, and aesthetic contexts to be under obligation. If a religious symbol undermines the obligatedness of the human condition, it undermines normativeness in the other dimensions of life. If a religious symbol is idolatrous, organizing religious energies in ways that neglect either the infinite or the finite in finite/infinite contrasts, that can lead to political, moral, psychological, and other projects that are represented as ultimate when they are not. If a religious symbol is demonic, engaging the divine but misrepresenting it, that can lead to depravity with unbounded energy.

The purposes of this book do not include examining the norms of dimensions of life other than the religious. But they do include examining the conditions of religious truth, to which we now turn.

CHAPTER 7

# Truth in Religious Symbols

The argument of this book has promised to study religious symbols by concentrating on four general topics, each of which contains many issues and all of which bear upon one another. The topics are the reference, meaning, contextual functions, and the truth of religious symbols. The separation of the topics is somewhat artificial and they all have been discussed together since the beginning. But each of the topics save that of the truth of religious symbols has had at least one chapter in which it is the chief focus; the focus on truth in this concluding chapter serves also to collect and summarize some of the conclusions that have been put forward so far.

The general theory of truth within which my discussions of the truth of religious symbols have taken place was stated in the Preface in summary form as the carryover of value from the object interpreted into the interpreter, subject to certain qualifications.[1] The summary statement is surprising to some because it departs from more customary theories of truth in Western philosophy. But in the long run, this theory of truth is not so different and can be understood in terms of the traditional categories of correspondence, coherence, and pragmatic theories. It is a straightforward correspondence theory in the sense that it claims that the nature of the object is carried across to the interpreter in some respect. The theory reflects something of the insights of the coherence theories in its insistence that the signs mediating the correspondence need to be in consistent semiotic systems, and also that the body of assertions of truth needs to function holistically in some contexts, with no vicious

---

1. The theory of truth was elaborated in great detail in *Recovery of the Measure*, with a direct statement in Chapters 3 and 4 that is summarized here in the text.

inconsistencies. Nevertheless, there might be no possible summary statement of the wholeness or completeness of the body of truths. Many expressions have only metaphorical logical connection, and the body of assertions might articulate diverse pockets of order only vaguely related to one another, so that there is no necessary organic ordering of assertions. The theory also derives much from pragmatic theories, but with respect to identifying the meanings of signs and with respect to criteria and tests for truth, not with respect to identifying truth itself, which is correspondence, not "usefulness."[2]

What makes the present theory surprising is that it takes the *nature* of things which is to be carried across to the interpreter to be primarily the *value* of the things rather than the *form* of the things. Aristotle, who, like this theory, presented a causal account of truth for carrying across the nature of the thing to the knower, said that what is carried across is the *form* of the thing, from the matter of the object into the matter of the knower's mind. Aristotle's form-matter distinction is no longer a viable metaphysics or cosmology. It can be shown that what he and much of the Western tradition has meant by *form* can be derived from *value* interpreted a certain way.[3] The question for truth is not whether a form is repeated but whether what is of worth in the thing is grasped by the interpreter. The form of that grasp in the interpreter's experience might be quite different from its form in the object interpreted. Surely the interpreter's form will be influenced by the purposes and contexts of interpretation, as well as by the forms of the interpreter's body, culture, and semiotic systems.

The formula for the general theory of truth used for religious symbols here is: *Truth is the carryover of value from the object into the interpreters' experience by means of signs, as qualified by the biological, cultural, semiotic, and purposive contexts of the interpreters.* The formula can be unpacked briefly and then illustrated in the treatment of religious symbols.

The first point to notice is the role of intentionality. Whereas this is a statement of the nature of truth in causal metaphors, the reference to

---

2. Peirce himself, the founder of pragmatism, strongly held to a correspondence theory and disavowed the name *pragmatism* when he thought that William James had confused truth with meaning and testing; CP 5.414–416.

3. See my *Reconstruction of Thinking*, Part 2, which argued this point in detail. This eases up the pressure on correspondence theories such as Aristotle's or Descartes' to explain how the form of a spatial thing, for instance, could be in a non-spatial thing such as a mind.

signs means that the interpreting experience *intends* objects, or attends to objects, as having the value carried over. The interpretation takes the object to be as the sign says in the respect required and, in that taking, the value of the object becomes ingredient in the interpretation or the interpreters' experience in an intentional way.[4]

Second, although *carryover* is a causal term, the formula is vague with respect to the various kinds of causation involved in carryover. They always include the kinds of synthesis involved in imagination, and sometimes, as in vision or hearing, elaborate physical processes that might not have the forms of synthesis characteristic of human experience.

Third, the formula mentions four kinds of qualification to the carryover: biological, cultural, semiotic, and purposive. These are shorthand terms for much more complicated qualifications, but they make the necessary point. The carryover must respect the difference between the kind of reality the object has and the kind of reality interpreters have in which the object is represented. Although mental representations might not be spatial, as some of their objects are, still they are functions of the human body and nervous system, responsive to stimuli that register on human sense organs and organized in ways reflecting the structure of the human brain. Aspects of objects that cannot be registered within the human apparatus are not experienced or known. Human experience is also organized by cultures which provide terms, habits, tastes and appreciations that lift up certain things as important to notice and others as not so important. To be more exact, cultures define the various contexts in which things have some degree of importance relative to one another. Semiotic systems perhaps should be viewed as subsets of cultures, yet they are directly involved in providing the signs for interpretation. Things can be registered in some sign systems and not others, registered one way and not others. Finally, the qualifications include the purposive activity of the interpreters, for the purposes, overt or habitual, determine in part what is picked up for carryover and what not, and the form in which the value carried over will be expressed. Body, culture, semiotics, and purpose are all involved in determining the respects in which signs interpret objects, and hence the respects in which the value of the objects will be carried over. Intentionality means, among other things, taking objects to be as the signs say, in certain respects.

---

4. *Recovery of the Measure,* chapter 15, analyzes intentionality.

Truth itself is a dyadic relation within the triadic relations of interpretation. Either the value in the object is what is carried over, given all the qualifications, or it is not. Or part of the value is what is carried over and the rest not. Or what is carried over is the object's value in a certain respect but not others. All of these formulations maintain the either–or structure of truth. This goes back to Aristotle's thesis (Metaphysics, 4/7 1011b26) that truth is saying of what is that it is, and of what is not that it is not. The reality of the object measures our interpetations, which either get the object right or do not. Both explicating the meaning of interpretations, however, and testing whether they are true is a matter of more interpretive work. Whereas an interpretation is either true or false in a dyadic sense, determining what it means and whether it is true is a matter for more interpretation, and perhaps a re-engagement of the object.

There are peculiar difficulties to understanding the truth of religious symbols because of the peculiar character of their objects or referents. But these difficulties should not be compounded by a common confusion of logical objects with physical objects or cosmologically determinate objects. Logical objects, as mentioned earlier, are referents in interpretation; they take on the status of logical objects by being intended or by being among the extensional referents of a sign determined within the network of a sign system. The intrinsic determinateness of logical objects comes from their roles in interpretations or in sign systems. The signs attribute various other kinds of determinateness to the logical objects, such as space-time location, shape, weight, movements, and so forth, or the determinations of emotional qualities, or of ownership, or any among an indefinitely large array of orders of meaning. Although signs always attribute some kind of determinate character to their logical objects, they might also attribute kinds of indeterminacy, as in the openness of the future, the diffuseness of an emotional atmosphere at a meeting, or the transcendence of determinateness by Nirguna Brahman or Eckhart's Godhead. We can even think of Absolute Nothingness as a logical object, although not as a real object. The bare requirements of determinateness in the case of Absolute Nothingness come from the subjunctiveness in the signs referring to it: *if there were* no determinate things, . . . Because there are some determinate things, at least signs, there is Somethingness rather than Nothingness. But it is a determinate thing to say that Nothingness is not because something is, and "Nothingness" in that statement is a logical object. Religious objects that transcend determinateness, or that involve a peculiar kind of determinateness, can be involved in interpretation as logical objects or logical referents with a puzzling form. The puzzle comes in understanding what their nature is, that is, how they ought to be interpreted, including the question of whether they are real. Logical objects do not have to be real, as when we truly say of something that is not, that it is not.

From the beginning I have argued that only religious symbols that are broken are true. In an intellectual world that debunks religion and references to the transcendent, this might be construed as a mere defensive strategy; but it is not. On the contrary, the insistence on the brokenness of religious symbols is to protect and highlight their apophatic reference to the transcendent or infinite. The criticism of religious symbols by the scientistic spirit is the smaller part of the argument. The mystics' criticism is far more powerful. Against the debunkers I have offered an hypothesis, concerning the reference of religious symbols to finite/infinite contrasts, that justifies the possiblility that religious symbols legitimately refer to the infinite or transcendent. Against the mystic rejection of all symbols, I have argued that finite symbols do have determinate meaning, that they function with discrimination in various contexts, and that the finite elements in their reference are legitimate because of the finite side of finite/infinite contrasts. Of course, mystics reject all symbols only at the end of a long highly symbolic journey, often recounted afterward in long highly symbolic books. There is no reason to deny that in the context of such a structured symbolic path it is possible to go beyond symbolic experience.

Making this general hypothesis concrete with respect of religious symbols, or any kind of symbols for that matter, requires showing how the symbols in question structure and effect the carryover. The value in the interpreters corresponds to the value in the interpreted objects in the respects in which the symbols interpret the objects.

With regard to religious symbols, the emphasis on value and carryover seems a happy approach because of religion's soteriological concerns. Religious symbols are true if they transform people's practices so as to embody the religious object, properly qualified; they are true if they effect transformations in devotional life so that the soul becomes more and more conformed to the religious object, properly qualified. They are true if they carry over the values in the religious object so that the intentional understanding of the mind is conformed to them, properly qualified. Even in the last, the theological, context within which religious symbols function, their truth can be given a pragmatic interpretation. Yet the first chapter here opened with a contrast between the truth of religious symbols and pure soteriological instrumentalism. If religious symbols are mere mechanical instruments of salvation or enlightenment, they do not symbolize anything and hence can be neither true nor false. Throughout I have argued that, whatever religious items there might be that are purely instrumental to soteriological goals, and whatever merely instrumental and non-symbolic uses religious symbols might be put to sometimes, religious symbols as symbols do represent their objects to interpreters and therefore are true or false, true in some respects, false in others, more or less adequate as representations of what they symbolize. The heart of the argument, therefore, has been that religious symbols are first and foremost to be understood in terms of the structure of signs, with referents, meanings, and interpretations.

The plot of this concluding chapter shall be to consider each of the contexts in which religious symbols function that have been discussed earlier and elaborate the senses in which religious symbols are true or false in those contexts, and perhaps indicate something about how we can judge the truth. The first section will consider practical contexts, the second devotional contexts, and the third theological contexts. The final section will discuss how the contexts can intermingle in religious life so that religious symbols might be here referential, there not, here meaningful, there not, here interpreted, there not, here true, there not. I shall argue that religion itself is an ironic enterprise that keeps the contexts together without making them commensurate with a formula, so that religious symbols are both referential and not, meaningful and not, interpreted and not, true and not. That is, they are true but broken.

## 7.1. TRUTH IN RELIGIOUS PRACTICE

Chapter 4 discussed how religious symbols have reference, meaning, and interpretation in four kinds of practical religious contexts, namely, in the life of a cultic community, in public life, in ordinary life, and in extraordinary life. I want now to discuss each of those contexts with respect to truth.

The phrase, "life of a cultic community," covers a broad range of communal phenomena, from sects and churches, temple-communities and monasteries, to traditions of practice such as reading texts and commentaries as in Advaita Vedanta, the songs and poetry of the cults of Krishna, and cultivating meditative or special aesthetic experiences as in philosophical Daoism. What they have in common is that participation is aimed to cultivate capacities and habits responsive to the divine that express themselves not only within the cultic community but in the rest of life.

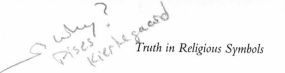 

The reference to "cult," it will be remembered, is not to a particular kind of sect but to the purpose of cultivating a religious character in individuals and groups by means of activities developed through tradition, participation in which is important for the individuals' religious identity.[5]

The truth of a religious symbol in the practical intentional context of a cultic community consists in its shaping a relevant aspect of cultic life so as to be a faithful response to the symbol's referent. *Faithful response* can be analyzed according to three dimensions of truth, the interpretive, symbolic, and referential.

The interpretive dimension of truth in the sense of practical faithfulness has to do with relating the religious object by means of the symbol to an event or practice within the community in a way that is differential and relevant. Consider the question of whom to invite as guests to a community's festive meal. Advaitins would reflect on their symbols of inclusiveness, exclusiveness, and on the permeability of the distinction of who is a member or potential member of the community from those irrevocably outside, and would invite only twice-born males who have received the sacred thread, and never untouchables.[6] Modern practicing Advaitins might reject caste system taboos and associate with untouchables in other contexts, at other meals, but likely not at a meal celebrating the faith as such. Christians asking the same question would find that their dominant symbols are explicit about crossing over caste and class boundaries, particularly to be inclusive in a downward direction, as discussed in the eucharistic example in chapter 3.1. In both traditions, the interpretive dimension of truth involves finding relevant symbols for establishing the guest list, and drawing the differential faithful conclusion. The difference in this illustration is a difference in the classes eligible for invitation.

The symbolic dimension of faithfulness has to do with whether there is an assemblage of symbolic networks and overlays that connects the

---

5. Perhaps I should use the Latinized word *cultus* to indicate that I mean a religious group considered as a cultivator of habits and character. *Cult* recently has come to mean rather what H. Richard Niebuhr, following Weber and Troeltsch, called a *sect* in contrast to a *church*. Both sects and churches, in Niebuhr's usage, are symbolic shapers of people, institutions, and behavior. See his *The Social Sources of Denominationalism*, chapter 1.

6. See Clooney's subtle discussion of the tension between ritual and institutional readiness to know Brahman in Advaita and intellectual readiness, in *Theology after Vedanta*, pp. 135–141. Classical Advaita down to very recent times maintained its close relation to the Mimamsa traditions.

religious object to the practical matter at hand, the guest list in the above example. In Christianity, for instance, there are complex relevant symbolic systems and overlays. The question of potential fellowship in the cultic community with regard to social class and status was explicitly addressed by Jesus and recorded in the Bible. Jesus and the core of leading disciples came from small-town entrepeneurial families, Jesus the son of a carpenter and Peter and Andrew sons of a fisherman who owned several boats and employed both his own sons and other workers. Jesus' movement reached out to much poorer people and to much richer people, to women as well as men, to outcasts like Mary Magdalene and lepers as well as leading citizens of the community such as Joseph of Arimathea, to Romans, Canaanites, and Samaritans, as well as to cultic Jews, to legal thieves like tax collectors and to revolutionary zealots. Jesus' table fellowship was explicitly criticized, according to the Biblical tradition, and he rejected the criteria of status and class in favor of criteria of need (Luke 5:27–32). That symbol system concerning table fellowship has been reinforced throughout the Christian tradition. There are also overlapping symbol systems that are relevant. In the parables, for instance, Jesus distinguished between those who have a prior claim on table fellowship and those who do not, and explicitly advocated inviting both, as in the parable of the wedding banquet discussed above in chapter 5.3; in the prodigal son parable the father welcomes back the son who had rejected the duties of the fellowship as well as the son who thought faithfulness to duties gave him a prior claim (Luke 15:11–32); in the good Samaritan parable a member of a hated religious group regarded as apostate was the example of the good neighbor (Luke 10:25–37). In addition to the tradition of parables Jesus reconceived human relations in universalized family metaphors: all human beings are brothers and sister, and God is father of all, whereas he downplayed the importance of his own blood kin family (Mark 3:31–35); even on the cross he reconstructed the responsible relations in his own family by assigning his mother maternal responsibilities for the disciple John and vice versa (John 19:25–27). In terms of later church discipline, St. Paul gave directions for celebrating the eucharist in which the common meal should embrace rich and poor so as not to embarrass the poor (1 Corinthians 11:17–22). All these overlayed symbol systems reinforce the practical conclusion of an inclusive guest list, which is thus faithful to the tradition's symbolic networks. These systems are compatible, although perhaps in some tension, with the systems that are specific about more circumscribed meals such as the eucharist for which some groups of people might be ineligible because that meal requires allegiance to the community, others might be unready because not yet baptized, and others excommunicated for moral or doctrinal errors. Practical controversies within the Christian tradition often have had to do with balancing, adjusting, reconciling, and analogically extending these symbol systems to apply to specific or new circumstances.

All these Christian symbol systems lie within a more basic cultural symbolic system in which the conditions of people in this life are very important; hence the explicit traditions of inclusiveness that recognize differences of class, status, gender, and the rest, and deliberately cross them. The Advaitin tradition, by contrast, operates within an alternative cultural orientation expressed through reincarnation and karma. Although the conditions of people today are important for how they are to be treated today, it is assumed that the condition of any individual today expresses but one of many lives for that sentient being. If not this lifetime, perhaps in some other the individual will be a high caste male and ready to be welcomed to a festive Advaitin meal. A guest list viewed as exclusivistic from a Christian standpoint is reinforced within the Advaitin community not only by the traditions of the caste system but also by the symbol systems articulating the careers of animals whose own karma might in some lifetime ready them for fellowship with the Advaitin community. Furthermore, within the Advaitin tradition, the elite readiness to respect and practice a life of careful literate study, while important for a festive meal with Advaitins, is not something to be expected even of all brahmin males. So the Advaitins' symbol systems would lead them to view the Christian symbolic principles for the guest list as inattentive to concrete conditions on the one hand and disrespectful of other sentient beings on the other. Faithfulness regarding the symbol systems of both traditions requires figuring out the practical implications of those systems and drawing the differential conclusions. This was analyzed above in terms of the doubled interpretants, one representational, the other practical and following by some kind of contextualized implication.

Regarding the referential dimension of truth, the practical situation of festive meals must interpret the ways to make the founding finite/infinite contrasts matter. Although the issues of reference cannot be expressed purely and without symbols, the issues include something like the following. For the Advaitin tradition the ultimate religious reference is to Brahman who is the true meaning of sentient life (and all matter), Brahman on the one hand with qualities in respect to the search for life's

meaning, and on the other hand without qualities as the non-dual resolution of life's meaning. The mode in which Brahman in the finite (with
qualities) and infinite (without qualities) contrast is relevant to life is
through the process of enlightened liberation through many lifetimes, a
near culminating one of which is the Advaitin's concrete cultic practice
of literate study. Brahman as finite/infinite referent is to be symbolically
carried over into the cultic festive meal and faithfully engaged there by
the guest list that includes only those whose lives this time around are in
exclusive affinity with Advaitin practice.

The Christian divine referent is also to a creator God but one whose
fundamental founding implication for life's meaning has to do with the
realization of divine-human and human-divine love that is immediately
accessible to all human beings regardless of conditions and that has a different immediate connection with the non-human parts of creation. The
practical way of carrying this over into the guest list for a festive cultic
meal is to be inclusive of all conditions of human beings and never to
consider non-humans. St. Francis would invite the birds and animals but
according to a principle of sharing love, not according to the principle
that they might in some future lifetime be persons.

This extended illustration of the truth of religious symbols in the
practical context of the lives of two cultic communities perhaps cannot
be generalized too far. But it does illustrate the dimensions of interpretation, symbolic systems, and their reference as they bear upon practical
truth. That is, we can see how each of the traditions, in their guest lists,
carries over the value or importance of the religious object into a concrete cultic behavior. Assuming the poetic license taken in setting up the
illustrations, each tradition truly or faithfully, by means of its systems of
religious symbols, conforms that bit of behavior to its founding religious
object.

We can, of course, ask the further theological question of whether
their ultimate religious objects are the same. Both Brahman and the
Christian Trinitarian God are creators of all determinate, discriminable
reality. Perhaps the self-realization of life through liberating enlightenment is not so different from divine-human and human-divine love, or
perhaps they are complementary; each tradition has symbol systems that
pick up on analogous themes in the other. But the vast differences
between the traditions' symbol systems do not allow of an easy comparison, and much theological work of the sort Clooney characterized as
reading one tradition's symbols within the other tradition needs to be
done before theology can make much progress on that larger question.

Concerning the truth of the symbols within each tradition, truth as faithfulness in the practices of the cultic communities is to be understood in something of the way illustrated here.

The practical context for religious symbols is not limited to cultic communities but extends to public life as well, as noted in chapter 4.4. The same three dimensional structure of truth as faithfulness, illustrated above in reference to interpretation, the symbol systems, and their religious referents would extend into public life, although vastly complicated by the fact that many people in the public would not be participants in the cultic tradition, and that the practices to which the religious symbols are to be made relevant are ones primarily to be understood in terms of other dimensions of life such as politics, morals, psychological growth, and the aesthetics of discerning perception, as discussed in chapter 6.2–4.

It is not difficult to see, however, that the religious symbols of the Christian tradition lifted up in the example of the guest list for the festive cultic meal would direct the public force of Christianity to an emphasis on universal human rights, and perhaps even on democracy broadly understood. The recognition of concrete human differences and the deliberate crossing of them to make all people immediately and equally ready for the two-way love relation with God pushes in this inclusive and universalist direction. By the same token, it is possible to see that the public import of the Advaitin symbols would push to an appreciation of the continuities of human life with all other forms of life and of a hierarchical ordering of forms of life, even within human classes, toward those ready for liberative discipline. Interpretive faithfulness to the symbolized religious objects would lead to these different public emphases in each case.

Again, public theology can ask how these different emphases are related. Are they contradictory or complementary? Enough other symbol systems within Christianity having to do with divine and human covenantal responsibilities to all creation now are being seen as critical of the sharp break the public import of Christianity has fostered between the human and non-human realms.[7] Ecological problems have revealed this to be a weakness or partiality in the public expressions of Christianity and the public emphasis on natural continuities in the various Hindu symbol systems have become better appreciated within Western societies.

Similarly, the public emphasis on hierarchy and the downplaying of imperatives to change social conditions for people living the lives they

---

7. See, for instance, John Cobb and Herman Daly's *For the Common Good.*

inhabit now within the Hindu traditions, of which Advaita is one, are now appreciated as reinforcing oppressive injustice. The bhakti symbol systems within Hinduism, such as those of Saivism, which in this respect parallel Christianity, are coming to have greater public relevance. As a matter of comparative religious symbol systems in their public expressions, our theological understanding has far to go to discern the true elements of comparison. Comparative assessments of the religions from the standpoint of the political dimension seem easier at this point, although the diverse symbol systems for articulating political justice might be just as confused and incommensurate as the religious. Because of the Western dominance of the United Nations and other international organizations that set the context for comparative politics, contemporary comparative political theory is likely to be little advanced beyond the stage at which Western comparative religious theory was at the end of the nineteenth century. At bottom, religious symbols in both traditions have been extremely influential in shaping political symbol systems.

In addition to interpretation in practices of cultic communities and in public life, religious symbols are interpreted in ordinary life and ought to be true there too. The same three dimensional structure of truth holds in ordinary life as in cultic life. The conditions of ordinary life differ so radically among the world's various societies that neat generalizations and comparisons are even more difficult here than in the cases of the other intentional contexts. Many of these complexities with regard to the modern North Atlantic societies have been traced by Charles Taylor who has singled out "ordinary life" as an important context of practice.[8] Other societies and cultural traditions are just as complex. In the view of anthropologists, the practical bearing of religious symbols on ordinary life is often their main bearing. A "thick description" of a society would call upon religious symbols to interpret the shape of many ordinary practices.

The question of the truth of religious symbols in ordinary life in the view of religious leaders and theologians, however, is extremely problematic. In some senses, though varying, cultic practitioners would like to see ordinary life as an extension of cultic life, an adaptation of cultic life to domestic circumstances. For Islam no legitimate distinction is admitted between the two, except in the case of the ordinary lives of non-believers. For modern western cultures, religion in the cultic sense

---

8. See his *Sources of the Self,* Part 3.

is taken to be only one among many dimensions and in many respects separate from the impingements of those other dimensions on ordinary life. The Muslim distinction between believers and non-believers is important with regard to the truth of religious symbols in ordinary life. The ordinary lives shared by people of different religious traditions within the same society will be shaped in different ways.

The important point to observe regarding the truth of religious symbols in the present context, however, is that they impact the conditions of ordinary life within a society irrespective of whether the people are believers. They shape ambitions and opportunities, attitudes toward work, family responsibilities, and interpersonal relations. Their truth is relative to the ways their symbol systems connect the religious object to the ordinary conditions, and in this respect the symbols interpreted into ordinary life are not only differential regarding how to live but differential between one tradition's symbol systems and another's. But the point about truth and falsehood has to do with the faithful mediation of the religious object into ordinary life. It is either differentially present in the respects interpreted or it is not, or partially present and partially obscured. Put in the terms used in contrasting the Advaitin and Christian traditions, ordinary life's practices are either expressive of and conducive to the quest for liberation at some stage, or they are not. Ordinary life either expresses and conduces to appreciation of God's love and the practices of loving God (and because of this loving neighbors), or they are not. Nearly all religious traditions employ religious symbols in ordinary life to push against selfishness while at the same time religious symbols push to make the religious project or quest an important part of ordinary practices. Even in wholly secular cultures within which religious symbols have barely residual affects, the "life is worth living" issues are religiously shaped, either truly or not.

The extraordinary contexts of life, engaged perhaps by only a few, are more explicitly shaped by religious symbols and illustrate the questions of truth graphically. The attempts to be a great artist, a person of great honor, a great leader, a great sage, a great saint, all have their content determined by the nature of those extraordinary projects. But in addition, part of the motivation for greatness comes from the attempt to find excellence in human fulfillment, and that is largely a religious matter. For, excellent fulfillment is impossible without relating to the finite/infinite contrasts that give meaning to life and its fulfillments. If the shaping religious symbols are false, a great artist will produce great art but still not find heroic fulfillment, the person of honor will do great deeds and be honored, but not fulfilled, and so forth. Only in religious heroism might there be a pure convergence of greatness with the fulfillment of greatness. In most religious traditions, the impact of the symbols claimed to be true on extraordinary life projects is extremely dialectical. On the one hand, the extraordinary accomplishments approach the role of being "world-founding," although within a finite and limited sphere. On the other hand, the hero or heroine needs to get out of the way of the infinite in the project for it to be truly world-founding, however limited. This means a kind of self-effacement or humility coupled with the extraordinary ambition to transcend ordinary accomplishments. The religious symbols shaping extraordinary quests are truly received in practice when they accomplish that humble losing of the self in the project. Religious fulfillment is to leave the dancer and become the dance. Of course different religions' symbols interpret this differently. They are true in practice when they accomplish the peculiar mirroring of the hero or heroine with the divine founder, particularly when the emptiness of self mirrors the infinity in the finite/infinite contrast.

This section has explored some of the aspects of the difference between true and false interpretation of religious objects into the practical shaping of life. To be talking about the dimensions of faithfulness as mediated by religious symbols is to be doing theology, not the practice itself. A religious practice can be true to the religious objects because of the symbols shaping it without anyone thinking much about it. What counts in this context is the practical doing. But then practice is concerned to be true, which means that questions arise as to how practice should be shaped by symbols, as to which symbols are relevant and what their practical implications are, and which symbols refer to the religious objects to be engaged in the relevant respects. So, theology, or intellectual inquiry into these questions, becomes part of practice. Section 7.3 will deal with the special issues of truth in theology. Section 7.2, however, turns to the truth of religious symbols in devotion.

## 7.2. TRUTH IN RELIGIOUS DEVOTION

In some respects the functions of religious symbols in devotion are practical in the senses discussed above, and in these respects the observations about truth made in the previous section pertain to the devotional functions as well. The pragmatic meaning of truth is whether, in the three elements of interpretation, symbolic structure, and reference, the reality of the religious object is carried over into the devotee. Because the nature of devotion is to be radically transformative, the carryover is something like the realization of the divine in the person. But of course different symbol systems express this differently, both regarding the nature of the divine and the kind of human state thought to realize this. The cumulative interpretation of religious symbols in their devotional functions then ought to be realization of Brahman and liberation, enlightenment and the release of Nirvana, a vision of God, perfect attunement, perfect sageliness in the Neo-Confucian sense, or whatever. And the truth of the symbols in their devotional functions along the way would consist in their interpretation exercising an appropriate state of soul for this stage or accomplishing the "transformative next step" on the way to fulfillment.

But as noted in chapter 5, there are certain traits of the devotional function of religious symbols that need special treatment. First, unlike some other, purely pragmatic, elements in devotional life, such as breathing and concentration exercises, religious symbols are representational. They are ways the devotee thinks about, visualizes, hears, or otherwise represents the religious object. Therefore we need to ask about the senses in which those representations might be true.

Second, unlike the other practical contexts in which religious symbols function, the devotional context requires that they be intentionally interpreted as such. It is not only that they shape the soul while the person engages in other religious work or in public or ordinary life, or in an extraordinary project, affecting what the person does. This would be enough in the practical contexts, although symbols in those contexts are also often reflected upon theologically. It is that they are self-consciously employed by the individual to transform or shape the person's self-identity by what they reveal of the divine. When a morally upright, minimally sinning, Calvinist devotee meditates on his or her utter wretchedness, complete wickedness, absolute undeservingness, and total lack of spiritual health, it is neither to contemplate a descriptive assessment of self-worth nor to have the practical effect of feeling guilty and otherwise bad. Rather it is to apprehend the infinite glory of God in the only way that relates personally and integrally to the individual.[9] Religious sym-

---

9. This, at least, was the point with which Calvin opened the *Institutes of the Christian Religion*, as I noted above. He said in the passage previously quoted that the thought of one's wretchedness leads immediately to God's glory, and if one began by contemplating the glory of God one would be immediately led to see one's wretchedness.

bols in the devotional context are themselves structured to relate the
divine to the individual's personal spiritual state and journey. Therefore
the question of truth in the devotional context needs to ask not only
about whether the finite/infinite referent is carried over into the soul of
the devotee but also whether the signs alleged to effect the carryover
rightly refer to both the divine and the state of the devotee. There is a
double reference in devotional symbols, to both the divine and the devotee (often with one explicit and the other implicit, as personal wretchedness is explicit about the devotee and implicit about the divine). That
double reference, not a reference to the divine alone, is what the symbol
and its network carry over into the devotee's interpretation. Devotional
symbols in their complicated double reference need to be true of both
the divine and the devotee if they are to carry over the divine into the
devotee when interpreted.

Third, the appropriateness to stage and and personal state cannot be
emphasized too much with regard to the devotional function of symbols.
In the other practical contexts it is often the case that current practical
behavior should be conformed as much as possible to the traditional
symbols and their way of seeing what the situation is; at least this is what
Lindbeck has in mind when he says that Christians should understand
their situation through the types, stories, and ideas of the Christian Bible.
The technical way of expressing this is that the practical interpretations
should stick mainly to the extensional interpretants of the symbols and
not take poetic license with novel interpretants, so far as possible. Where
the traditional symbol system's view of the world cannot be taken at face
value, the symbols ought to be extended in practical contexts with care
and caution. By contrast, symbols in the devotional function need to be
shaped immediately by whatever forms address the state and stage of
development of the devotee. These forms might not be those the person
would recognize apart from the devotion; they might not involve conscious self-descriptions; and they might all be part of the traditional symbolic repertoir. Whatever their source, they must accomplish the
addressing of the person through a recognizable connection of the divine
with that person. For Romans of antiquity, Jesus was dressed as a philosopher; for seventeenth-century Dutchmen, the disciples were burghers;
for many unsophisticated twentieth-century Americans of English background Jesus is blond and dressed in a long white choir robe. None got
the first-century appearances historically right, but none could have
related personally and deeply to a wandering Galilean teacher, at least not

until their devotional experience was stretched to accomodate Jesus in his historically alien form.

Noting these three points, that religous symbols in the devotional contexts need to bring the divine to mind as relevant to the soul, in connection with the soul, we can ask what is special about their truth.

To determine whether a devotionally contextualized religious symbol is true, ask whether its imaginable denials, in that context, would be true. Could Jesus be made devotionally present to a person when represented with historical accuracy? For sophisticated people who can relate to very different others and speak Aramaic, the answer is yes, and a blond, Anglophantic Jesus would be a false symbol. For others, the historical Jesus would be devotionally unintelligible and an accurate historical representation would be false for them; their truth requires a representation translated in language, physiognomy, and dress to something they can imagine as a friend and teacher. Is the symbol of personal wretchedness as the personal mirror in which one reflects and thus holds God's glory true? Not for a victim of sexual abuse who sees guilt in only psychological terms, for the divinity mirrored in that kind of guilt is an abuser. Not for someone who sees guilt only in moral terms, for if there is divinity mirrored in moral guilt it is the accuser, not the Infinitely Glorious; more likely, moral guilt in twentieth-century people reflects no divinity at all but only self. For the symbol of personal wretchedness to be true, it must in context be distinguishable from psychological and merely moral determinations and be existentially connected with self-definition over against felt divine glory.

These examples have been explicated in terms of their state dependency. Their truth is also dependent upon stage. Part of the symbolic network of the symbols concerrning Jesus is that, if he becomes the devotee's friend and master, eventually the devotee will be able to relate to people far different from himself or herself. On the one hand, Jesus will turn out to be God, according to the Christian symbols, and there is hardly anything more alien than that; on the other hand, Jesus' friends are supposed to leave home to carry the consequences of his friendship to people who can be as alien from the devotee as the devotee is from first-century Galileans. Furthermore, part of the direction of a devotional life fixed on Jesus is to advance in historical knowledge about Jesus so that one's images tend to converge on the historically accurate; in the devotional context that advance cannot be so abrupt as to make Jesus alien, but must take the form of expanding the devotee's sense of self to become a wanderer in a strange land loving with an inclusive fellowship.[10] A Christian somewhat advanced in devotional life would look on the Anglophantic Jesus as false, or at least as useful only at an earlier stage.

Similarly, a symbol such as a meditation on one's own wretchedness has truth only at certain stages. Persons limited to psychological and merely ethical interpretations of it are not ready for such a meditation; it could only be distortive for them. On the other hand, personal wretchedness ought not be the last step for a Christian devotee, for God loves the sinner, according to the Christian gospel. To experience God as forgiving and transforming is to circumscribe personal wretchedness radically. To be a forgiven sinner is still to be a sinner, but an extremely happy one. On beyond the forgiven sinner stage is the sense of a deeply beloved identity, in which one loves oneself because God does. Beyond that is regarding oneself as only important as God's lover. The stages have an integrity to them that makes leapfrogging difficult. Without deeply forming the soul around the contrast between God's glory and human wretchedness, the subsequent experience of oneself as a forgiven sinner is likely to be shallow and merely psychological. Without the deep formation of God's glory and *one's own* wretchedness, later experiences of divine love are likely to be generalized and not existential. The Christian conception of spiritual stages is somewhat simple compared with the yogic traditions in several Indian religions.

Asking the contextual questions of the significance of the denials of a symbol is complicated by the fact the symbols are in systems and hedged in by overlying symbol systems. The devotional functions of Jesus, however represented, presuppose the overlying symbols that relate him to God as the founding finite/infinite contrast for Christians. Apart from those other related systems that connect Jesus with the Holy One of Israel, the Judge, devotion to Jesus can become little more than a form of psychological self-congratulation, the enjoyment of an imaginary friend who tells you you're OK. That is a common enough corruption of Christian spirituality.

But spiritual maturity is necessary to take into the soul the vast complications of symbol systems required for the proper contextualiza-

---

10. The Christian's symbol systems in this regard are quite different from the Confucian's within which the deeply alien could be only barbarians and of no spiritual interest; the Confucian's spiritual progress requires staying at home. The Daoist's systems place great emphasis on wandering from home to learn from the deeply alien who are often divine teachers.

tion of Jesus in a devotee's stage and state. Aren't there important symbols for the spiritually immature, symbols that lack contextualization with correcting symbols? Surely there are, and popular presentations of Jesus are common in the Christian tradition. Jesus himself shocked his disciples with his holiness and authority, and made them his students, long before they understood him in connection with Jewish messianic expectations. The simple story of Jesus can turn around a life lost to licentiousness, drugs, despair, or deliberate evil and start that person on a devotional path. Sometimes those primitive, unsophisticated, unsystematic, unhedged responses to certain religious symbols—a Buddhist reliquery, a Daoist wild man, a Muslim almsgiver, a recitation of the Torah, the bow of a Confucian sage—have profoundly transformative power to introduce the holy into the soul in the right form for the devotee's state and stage. Are not these symbols true, without the nuancing and enrichment of mature symbolic networks? The answer is that they might be as regards the existential state of the devotee, but that neither the devotee nor a spiritual director can tell except in potential relation to those other symbols. Mere power in a symbol might be demonic. The importance of spiritual direction consists in the fact that the truth of religious symbols contextualized to an individual often depends on the potential qualification of those symbols by others to which the person still lacks existential access.

Most religious symbols derive their form, their networking and systematic interconnections, from the devotional context. In many religious communities the devotional symbols are most often expressed in communal liturgies rather than in private meditation and prayer. Therefore there is some tension between the public rehearsing of the devotional symbols, where in a sense they are all present regardless of the differing states and stages of the liturgical participants, and the private taking of them to heart. The tension is expressed when individuals ask about the truth of a particular symbol, especially a symbol that is very central to the liturgy. For the individual it might be true or false, depending on the person's state and stage, whereas for the community it is supposed to be true because everyone is to pass through the state and stage for which it is true.

Perhaps the most controversial instance of this tension has to do with whether the divine is personal. There is no doubt that the representation of God as personal has some nearly universal places in the devotional structures of most religions. If Advaita Vedantins say that Brahman without qualities transcends the personal, they also recognize the legitimacy of worshipping the person Isvara, and Brahman with qualities is personal in some sense. Vishistadvaita Vedantins such as Ramanuja say that Brahman is personal all the way through.[11] Mahayana Buddhists say that form, including personal form, is emptiness, but worship through personal devotions to Maitreya, Guanyin, and the cosmic Buddha-mind. Daoists have many revealing Gods, known by their dress and accouterments.[12] Confucians have shorn the personal traits of the Shang-ti from abstract principle, but worship principle through its expression in the sages of the past. Judaism, Christianity, and Islam all represent God as personal, worshipping through scriptures that show God as male, jealous, talkative, and of great personal affection. By the same token, there are other devotional strands in those religions that deny or drastically qualify personal attributions. The East Asian religions emphasize the immanence of the transcendent in the finite world which is not all personal, to use Tu Weiming's phrase.[13] The South Asian religions emphasize that there is no place apart from a created order for a personal God to stand over against creation. The West Asian religions emphasize the creator's simplicity. In all these religions, there are places to devote oneself to the personal divine, and other places to set that aside as a qualified representation and devote oneself to what transcends the personal. But the diverse religious traditions vary widely among themselves, and almost equally widely within themselves, regarding the structures of those places for the personal and impersonal. We are not in a scholarly position to make accurate comparison.[14]

The temptation with regard to confusions about the truth of religious symbols in their devotional function is to rephrase the question in terms of the theological function of those symbols. To be sure, theology is required in order to lay out the structures of the symbols even within their devotional function; the assessment of devotional truth requires theology. But theology also has its own intentional context, wanting to

---

11. On Ramanuja, see John B. Carman's *The Theology of Ramanuja* and also *Majesty and Meekness*, chapter 5. In the latter book, Carman advances the persuasive thesis that religions employ polar symbols to harmonize or hedge their main representations; so God can be represented as personal only if also represented as transpersonal, as transcendent only if also immanent, as majestic only if also as meek.

12. See Michael Saso's *The Teachings of Taoist Master Chuang*, part 2, and Livia Kohn's *Taoist Mystical Philosophy*.

13. See his *Confucian Thought*, chapter 8.

14. John Carman's theory of polarities in *Majesty and Meekness* is an important step toward the construction of such a scholarly position.

assess symbols on all sides, not only as related to the personal states and stages of devotional life. Theology is concerned with the nature of the divine, and only secondarily with devotional or practical matters. For theology in its primary occupation, symbols developed in practical and devotional contexts are tools.

## 7.3. TRUTH IN THEOLOGY

Theology is an intentional context that differs in important ways from the practical and devotional contexts. Like them, its truth consists in a carryover of the religious object into the interpreters, the theologians in this case, in the respects in which the symbols interpret that object. But whereas in the devotional context the form of the carryover, and therefore of the symbols used, needs to be appropriate to the stage and state of the devotional purpose, in theology the devotional purpose is not important except insofar as it bears on understanding. Whereas in the practical contexts the forms of the carryover, and thus of the symbols, need to address the practical purposes, in theology the practical purposes are not important in the first instance except as aids to understanding, and are important in the second instance only to help theology shape its understanding so as to provide practical orientation and advice. The first purpose of theology is to understand the divine.

The purposive structure of understanding itself needs to be understood in terms of two roots. Perhaps the most important in the modern day is the need for a theological position, or assertion, or claim, to be able to communicate itself to those who are interested and to respond to questions and criticisms from other perspectives. In our time the other perspectives include not only different theological positions but also the range of other disciplines that study religion, collectively called religious studies. These include textual studies of both philological and historical sorts, anthropological, sociological, and psychological studies, literary studies, and studies of specific institutions and practices of religion such as music, dance, liturgies, festivals, ceremonies of passage; there also are philosophical disciplines focused on religion, morals, and metaphysics. These are some of the relevant disciplines found in the academy in the West. There are other configurations in other cultures. Also, questions for theology might come from individuals who cannot be identified by discipline; questions can be raised for theology by important events. The first root of theology's definition of understanding then is the community of discourses with which it must be in touch and from which it might learn and be corrected.[15]

The other root for understanding theology's kind of truth is the collection of diverse particular kinds of theological reflection that have developed over history, with their own internal aspects and diversities. To put the matter roughly, theology in Judaism is deeply formed by rabbinic commentary, in Christianity by doctrinal controversies classically shaped during the period of creedal formation and influenced by Greek and Roman philosophy, in Islam by the elaboration of law as it applies in cultures far beyond its founding culture, in some kinds of Hinduism around various competing kinds of commentary on the Upanisads, in other kinds of Hinduism around and through devotional poetry, in Buddhism by commentaries on reported conversations and teachings of the Buddha, often highly metaphysical and speculative, in philosophical Daoism by poetry, stories, and philosophic literature that resonates with classic Daoist texts, in religious Daoism by revelations plus commentaries descriptive of gods and prescriptive for spiritualizing behavior, and in Confucianism by recorded sayings and brief essays of the masters and a long commentarial tradition often oriented to public affairs. Each of these is its own genre of theology, containing competing genres of theology within it, competing themselves with neighboring genres within their own tradition, sometimes with a history of interaction with other traditions, as between Hinduism and Buddhism in India and among Buddhism, Confucianism, and Daoism in China. Each genre has its own way of asking questions. Each is easily responsive to certain kinds of questions and responds to others with difficulty.

Furthermore, theology in each tradition has had to be responsive to the interpretation of symbols in devotional life, in the practical life of religious communities, in the public life of their various social settings, in the ordinary lives of their participants, and in the extraordinary human projects of their cultures. Thus whatever the dominant theological genre in a tradition, the other genres are present too where they help give theology critical access to the locus of religious symbols. The

---

15. I have stressed this responsiveness to the contingencies of public discourse in my "Religious and Theological Studies." A much more qualified appreciation of the norms of public discourse would be given by someone who believes that theology is exclusively located within a religious confessional community; see, for instance, Avery Dulles' careful argument in *The Craft of Theology*.

prayers of St. Chrysostom, the songs and sermons of Bernard of Clairvaux, the poetry of Rumi, the Tamil erotic songs about Krishna, the Daoist, Buddhist, and Confucian poetry of Chinese literati, have much in common with one another, more perhaps than each has with the dominant modes of theology in its own tradition. Yet each of these "rhetorical" expressions is theological and crucial for lifting devotional symbols to reflective consciousness. In addition, in Western Europe there is a skeptical theological tradition that began loyally enough with Deism but allied itself with, indeed often led, a philosophical movement of epistemological thought that has given rise to sharply formulated atheisms as in Marx and Sartre, that shaped philosophy of religion as a respecter of the skeptical standpoint, and that has influenced not only the growth of secular humanism but even the form of late modern Jewish and Christian theology. Christian theology in the nineteenth and twentieth centuries has been more deeply formed by theological debate with the skeptical tradition than with debate with Buddhists or Hindus. Other religious traditions too have spawned and then been informed by debate with skeptical traditions.

These two roots, the need to be responsive to all questions about theological claims, and the particular historical formation of those claims and the genres within which they are expressed and defended, combine to produce the contemporary situation in theology. Any theological work is historically particular with respect to its sources. Usually these sources are participation by the theologian in some tradition's religious practice; but not always, especially in the case of theologians influenced by skeptical traditions. At the same time, in order to make a claim for the truth of theological claims, a position needs to be able to answer questions and objections from any direction. And therefore there is a much larger theological public than has characterized theology in the past, formed in part by dialogue among religious traditions, continuing controversies within religious traditions, the mediation of religions by other disciplines studying them, and the need on the part of all theologians to articulate religious claims in reference to the conditions of the modern world which in themselves are upsetting to traditional religious practices.

Furthermore, many of the new dimensions of the theological public are in very early stages of development. The dialogue among world religions has just begun to develop comparative categories that might allow for a commensurate consideration of the symbol systems of different religions. The studies of religion by secular social sciences are only slowly overcoming positivist reductionisms that define away the religious qualities of religions by making them merely psychological phenomenon, or social forces, and so forth. Therefore the making of public theological claims has a tentativeness entirely appropriate for the stage of maturity of the conversation. Whereas within a religious tradition there might be an ancient and fully matured way of doing theology, that way suddenly seems privatized, reduced to the mere exercising of intellectual habits from its intended purpose of understanding the divine, if it cannot present its claims and defend them within the larger public of theologies also interest in the truth about the same topics.[16]

Within Christianity alone there appear to be at least four different theological strategies developed in response to this situation. One, associated with John Hick, is to attempt immediately the development of a common language for world theological discussions, with all the learning that has been amassed in the historical studies of religions and in philosophical reflection.[17] Not that all theologians would agree with one another, but they would speak in an increasingly common language. The heart of this approach is the conviction that at bottom there is indeed a common topic to theology, an ultimate reality that all religions express, each with its own symbols. In the language of our study here, this is to suppose that all the finite/infinite contrasts come down to one, or can be coordinated in summary fashion.

A second, associated with Ninian Smart, is the attempt to elaborate a theology arising out of and giving orientation to a particular religious tradition with its own symbol systems, Christianity in his case, but explicitly learning from and responding to the counter-suggestions and criticisms, as well as the different nuances associated with different symbol systems, of the other world religions.[18] Although a Christian theologian might never be able to know enough of Buddhism, Advaita, or Islam to be wholly at home in those traditions of theology, the Christian

---

16. It is such cosmopolitanism that makes the theologies of Raimundo Panikkar, say in *The Silence of God: The Answer of the Buddha*, and of Ninian Smart, say in *Christian Systematic Theology in World Context*, so attractive; that they are cosmopolitan and learned does not keep them from also being Christian theologies.

17. See Hick's *Problems of Religious Pluralism* and *The Metaphor of God Incarnate*. The latter is an interpretation of Christology based on the universalism defended in the former. See also *The Myth of Christian Uniqueness* that Hick edited with Paul Knitter, and the essays edited by Gavin D'Costa entitled *Christian Uniqueness Reconsidered* that rebut.

18. See his *A Christian Systematic Theology in a World Context*, with Steven Konstantine.

nevertheless might learn enough from them to make important corrections to what is still obviously a Christian theology. This position does not assume that religions at bottom address the same ultimate reality, but leaves that question for the outcome of the mutual theological reflection.

A third position, associated with Francis X. Clooney, takes the public character of theology in this expanded situation to focus at heart on the close reading of other traditions by theologians steeped in their "own" tradition.[19] The purpose of the close reading is not to repeat the way the theologians of the "other" tradition would read themselves, but to subject the theologian's own tradition to the slow, subtle moulding of the theological artifacts of the other tradition. This position aspires to no world theology, nor to a Christian theology in world perspective, nor even to pushing inter-religious theological readings to the expression of explicit comparisons, although that is not bad. It rather aims to enrich the practice of theologizing in any tradition by the influence of practices of theologizing in other traditions.

The fourth position, associated with George Lindbeck, extends the emphasis on practice but insists that it is enough for theology to define itself as within a given tradition, to be that tradition's theology, and to exert its efforts to shape its contemporary theological expressions by its ancient symbols.[20] That is a deep enough task given all the other forces that shape contemporary understanding. This position assumes that the truth of a theological position is embodied in its primary symbols and determined by the subtle criteria of faithfulness. The position is not hostile to interreligious dialogue; indeed it arose, at least in Lindbeck's case, out of ecumenical and interreligious dialogue that pressed the issue concerning just what his own tradition has to contribute. But interreligious dialogue is not essential for any tradition's theology, nor is much attention to the other disciplines that study religion, however much they are useful (Lindbeck's use of Geertz' anthropology has already been noted).

I have drawn out these complications of contemporary theology before directly addressing the question of theological truth to emphasize the complexity of the problem, and also to emphasize that any particular expression of the problem is itself within the public and not above it.

---

19. See his *Theology after Vedanta*.

20. See his *The Nature of Doctrine*. Avery Dulles' *The Craft of Theology* is close to Lindbeck although within a Roman Catholic context. Lindbeck aims his theory of theology or doctrine to be appropriate for any religion's work.

The time has come, however, to say how religious symbols are true when functioning in the theological context.

Like the other intentional contexts, truth in the theological one means that the nature and worth of the religious object is carried over into the interpretation by means of the symbols that are interpreted to represent the object in a certain respect, as qualified by the human condition, the theologians' culture, symbol systems, and purposes. Generally, the truth consists in the correspondence of the representations in the interpretation with the religious object from which they are carried over subject to the qualifications, and so forth. The representations thus are right or wrong in the respects in which they are alleged to interpret the objects.

The purposes of theology, however, in contrast to the practical and devotional purposes, are to understand the divine. Therefore the interpreting symbols in the theological context need to be set within the disciplines of understanding. I have characterized these generally as being responsive to questions that might be asked. Particular theological genres have their own ways of asking questions. But generally theological understanding needs to ask, for instance, what the symbols mean in terms of their own symbol systems, how their symbol systems network with others, how the systems overlay and are overlain by other systems, how the relations among the symbols shift in meaning according to the different practical, devotional, and other theological contexts, how the symbols relate in meaning to potentially alternative symbol systems that might say contrary things about the divine, both within the same religious tradition and in other religions, how the symbols function within the various structures analyzed by the various social sciences, how the symbols can be expressed in other symbol systems, how they can be rephrased in more general symbols, how they can be exemplified in more particular symbols, how far they can be expressed in more nearly literal symbols, how far they can be extended in more poetic symbols, and so forth and so on. All these questions are about the meanings of religious symbols. Each has a way of being re-expressed as an interpretation of the religious object in terms of the symbols. Thus theology asks whether the religious object truthfully can be represented by a symbol in its symbol system, by the symbol when overlaying this or that other symbol system, by the symbol as an affirmation or denial of an alternative symbol or symbol system, and so on. These are the kinds of considerations that go into *understanding* the religious object by means of religious symbols.

Therefore when the question of theological truth is raised concerning a claim with a particular religious symbol, it is assumed that the claim is amenable to parsing in regard to this wide array of questions required for understanding. Of course no claim is framed by an antecedent consideration of all these elements of understanding. But the drive toward systematic theology reflects just this condition. The system serves as the antecedent context for understanding the theological claim and the various kinds of truth it alleges. The system aims to provide a ready answer, or a map for finding answers, to the kinds of questions listed above. The very mapping function of systems often relates symbols to broad philosophical considerations. But philosophy is not the only kind of system; there are broad symbol systems such as grand narratives or stages of devotional growth that can also serve to provide systematic orientation. Regardless of whether a theological claim is couched within a system, its presentation as true requires a readiness to explain and justify it to those who ask the kinds of questions listed above.

The peculiar truth of a theological claim or position, then, is that of an hypothesis subject to further correction, as I argued in chapter 4.2. The claim is put forward as representing its object in the way it says and as capable of being explained and justified in any of the terms required for understanding. *Understanding* means "understanding the religious object," not merely "understanding the meaning of the theological claim." Theological truth is thus defined partly in terms of the various processes of corroboration, verification, and falsification associated with the extensions of its meaning in the various kinds of directions listed above. The definition of theological truth requires reference to criteria for truth. The criteria are specific to the various aspects of understanding involved. A theological assertion can make a stronger claim on truth the more it can be shown to have survived and been reframed through the relevant intellectual processes of correction, including comparison with serious alternatives. Always fallible and subject to further correction, a theological position is protected by its vulnerability. A theological claim made invulnerable in form cannot say it has stood the test of criticism. A theological claim that is vulnerable to correction can claim that, so far as the resources for correction go, if it were false that would have been found out and corrected before. If claims are vulnerable, the false are likely not to survive.

The truth of religious symbols in the theological context thus requires a theological public, not only of competent theologians within a given tradition's symbol systems but of theologians of other traditions' symbols systems and of disciplines interested in other things about religious symbols than their truth. Such a public is only an ideal at the present time. The relevant conversations take place locally and in fits and starts. Miscommunication is as common as helpful communication that might actually make a correction. But this is only to emphasize the fallible character of theology's use of religious symbols to understand the divine. Not only are claims true subject to further correction but we should expect serious further correction.

One last point should be made in this section to emphasize a theme that has run throughout, namely that the purpose of theology is to understand its religious object, the divine, the appropriate finite/infinite contrasts. Theology is an actual interpretation that engages the divine to understand it. Theology is not merely the understanding of religious symbols of the divine; art history, literary critics, and semioticians are concerned to understand the *meaning* of religious symbols in that sense, and this is a necessary component of theology. But theology also and primarily proposes to understand the religious objects themselves. If it did not do that, it would be useless as a guide to practice and devotion, for practice and devotion indeed purpose to engage the divine.

## 7.4. TRUTH IN RELIGION: BROKEN SYMBOLS

The transition to a summary of our study of religious symbols can be made by remarking a point assumed from the beginning but often forgotten in considering theology, namely, that we are always operating in the middle of a context taking for granted religious realities to be as symbolized by at least some symbols. The question is not how to get some symbols to represent some reality to which we have non-symbolic access, but rather how to correct the symbols we have, or how to correct our symbols through an encounter with other symbols.[21]

This understanding of intellectual work as learning and correction was formulated by Charles Peirce but underlay the approach even of such a systematician as Hegel. It contrasts, however, with an understanding more characteristic of the European Enlightenment, namely, that reality lies awaiting our invention of symbols which can be justified by the method

---

21. This is an alternative version of "liberal theology" to the one Lindbeck describes as *experiential-expressive*, as attempting to express an inner thought or feeling that is not itself symbolic. My kind of liberalism does not have to refer to inner thoughts and feelings, although I certainly have and respect them, but only to the process of correcting symbolic forms that are already shaping our behavior and thought.

of their invention; invention through science is the preferred method. The Enlightenment understanding thus advocates skepticism of any symbol because its systematic networks are biased functions of historical factors that are authoritarian rather than methodic. The Enlightenment understanding also puts a heavy requirement of justification by literal means, because only a literally intended process can be checked for methodical faithfulness. Of course this Enlightenment approach has been severely criticized.[22] It arose itself not as a wholly new unbiased principle but as a correction of various forms of medieval thought too enthralled by authorities. It itself embodies representations of founding elements of the world, finite/infinite contrasts, often without expressing and criticizing them. The methods legitimated by Enlightenment thought have been shown to rule out apriori the possibility of certain kinds of phenomena, not only religious but ethical phenomena in the larger sense, and thus Enlightenment methods are anti-empirical in these cases. Yet for all the criticism of Enlightenment thought regarding religion, its influence remains powerful regarding a skeptical approach to religious symbols.

The importance of the fact that we are always in the middle of symbolic usage seeking correction, rarely in the invention of symbolization itself, applies to the other intentional context of religious symbols, not just to theology. Although in the practical contexts there is a point to the emphasis on truth as faithfulness, the countervailing point is that practice requires steady correction of forms of faithfulness. Likewise in the devotional context the point that religious symbols need to be tailored to the stage and state of the devotee as well as to the religious object needs to be balanced by the point that the symbols need to be under steady corrective watch. This is to say, there is a theological dimension to both practical and devotional contexts.

The discussion above has been oversharp in its distinctions of the various practical contexts of the religious cultic community, the public, ordinary life, and extraordinary projects, and of the practical contexts from the devotional and theological. Yet it should be obvious that they interpenetrate, if not always in happy perichoresis then in muddled confusion.

No practices are wholly unreflective, especially in times such as ours when symbolically formed religious habits are frustrated again and again. Practical affairs in such circumstances depend on theology for orientation

---

22. Dulles neatly summarizes the criticisms in the first chapter of his *The Craft of Theology*.

and advice, counting on theology to understand not only how better to get along practically but also how the divine bears on what to do, the divine as understood in the truest possible ways. Devotional life, because of the very power of its effective symbols, is always in jeopardy to the demonic; it too needs reflective correction from theology which understands not only how the symbols powerfully relate the divine to the devotees' spiritual stage and state but whether they make the relation correctly.

Regarding the other intentional contexts, hardly any practice shaped by religious symbols can fail to be affected by the devotional lives of important practical symbolizers. Practical religious symbols often take their rise from devotional symbols expressed in liturgies and communal practices. Similarly the practical contexts of life as shaped by religious symbols affect individuals' and communities' devotional use of symbols. Furthermore, the symbols with which theology has to work, and their contexts of confirmation, exist in their exercise, not only in their contemplation. Although the corrective procedures in theology are complicated, in the end they come down to the issue of whether life in all its contexts better engages the divine with these symbols rather than with some other symbols denying them.

It would be helpful at this point to recall the outlines of the analysis of religious symbols. The principal thesis, to which reference has just been made, is that religious symbols are among the means by which people engage the divine. Thus, although religious symbols can and should be studied on their own in terms of their networks and semiotic systems, they also should be studied in the dynamic context of their use, that is, in relation to the interpreters using them and the objects with which they are to engage the interpreters. Therefore chapter 3 focused on the semiotic meaning structure of religious symbols, on systems of meanings, and overlaying of systems. Within its semiotic code, a symbol's meaning has a range of extensional referents to which it might refer, and a range of extensional interpretations which it legitimates of its extensional referents. These matters are all within the semiotic systems.

There also, however, are the real referents to which symbols are referred by actual intention in interpretation, rightly or wrongly. In the common interpretation, these intentional referents are among those indicated by the symbol's semiotic extensional referents, as selected in the act of interpretation. In metaphoric reach, however, the intentional referent might be different from the coded extensional referents; such a

*[handwritten margin notes:]* extensional → denotative / intentional → w/ intent / semiotics → interpretation of signs

novel reference can be encoded within the semiotic system as a new metaphor. Chapter 2 focused on reference.

Similarly, an intentional interpretation is an actual act of interpretation, different from the semiotic system's range of extensional interpretants. The act of interpretation is set within an intentional context, such as theological reflection, the organization of practical life, or devotional formation. Those contexts give interpretation purpose and set conditions for determining what is of importance to interpret about the religious object. The roles of interpretation in the context determine how the object is to be made an intentional referent and what signs are to interpret it in what respects. Ordinarily, the intentional interpretants in the actual context are indicated by some among the extensional interpretants within the semiotic system; where they are not, the semiotic system is stretched, enriched, and adapted for a new use in context. Extensional interpretants that no longer have a context for use decay within the semiotic code. Chapter 4 discussed these matters.

The peculiarity of the religious object, analyzed in chapter 2 as a finite/infinite contrast, and the highly idiosyncratic states of individuals and differences in stages of spiritual development, called for a special analysis of religious symbols in the devotional context. It was argued there that in devotional contexts, religious symbols have a doubled referent, to the religious object and to the devotee's state and stage. The meanings of devotionally charged symbols are fantastic and extravagant for this reason. Their interpretation is an actual exercise or advancement of the spiritual life of the devotee so as to embody the religious object in respects carried by the symbols. This was the point of chapter 5.

Religious symbols and their interpretation do not lie only within the domains of religion, of course. They intersect with political and moral life, with economic and domestic life, with social and psychological structures, with art and culture, and with many other dimensions. They are consequential in these other dimensions far beyond their legitimate meanings and their truth and falsity. Chapter 6 analyzed a particular case where symbols have psychological and political consequences that run in apparent contradiction to the symbols' customary intent.

The relation of religion and its symbols to other aspects of human life, each with symbols that engage their objects, is an issue far more complicated than this fairly simple study of religious symbols. I may seem to have strained the reader's credulity by requiring as much trust as has been demanded in the orienting definitions of religion, the religious object as a finite/infinite contrast, and the Peircean approach to semiotics. Think how much worse it would have been to have floated hypotheses about the political dimension of life, the moral, the aesthetic, the economic, and all the rest. In fact, that much strain would call into question what is here only a heuristic device, the analysis of life into dimensions. That the divine is to be understood in terms of finite/infinite contrasts is no more controversial than that political justice is to be understood in terms of universal human rights rather than differentiated social fulfillment.

This study has taken a few steps toward a more comprehensive interpretation of human life, however. In contrast to approaches that would have concentrated on the logic of religious symbols, this approach has concentrated on their functions in interpretation. The contexts of these interpretations are the same as the contexts informed by the other dimensions of life, and it should be possible to see how religious symbols bear upon them as they and their symbols are analyzed. The symbolic networking and overlaying of systems of religious symbols are not limited to religious symbols but influence all the rest, and are influenced by them.

Furthermore, this study has not approached religious symbols as open for inspection only by insiders. Their meanings can be analyzed by anyone willing to undertake the nuanced study of religious semiotic systems. Their intentional referents are open to anyone willing to engage them the way a biologist would engage an organism or a pianist a score. That students of religious referents are required to use some symbols or other to engage their objects, and thus must engage in religious interpretation in some way, is like a biologist having to look somehow or other and perform some kind of experiment, or like the pianist having to be willing to read and at least imagine the sounds.

Not only have I represented the study of religious symbols as a public one, I have tried to show that the religious use of religious symbols is publically open to anyone willing to engage the contexts in which they function. This would involve participation in religious communities and undertaking devotional practice, but this participation in most instances is open to anyone willing to gain the competence. Only restrictions such as the Advaitins' requirement of twice-born maleness would stand in the way. In particular, I have argued that theology in any tradition, and theology transcending traditions, is public in its need to be vulnerable to correction.

Now as to the cigars, we know that heaven is a broken symbol. Heaven is no place at all, let alone a No Smoking place. Yet in the devotional contemplation of the relation of a person to the divine, a relation that has not yet been consummated as immediate, being with the divine in a place is a wholly understandable and appropriate metaphor. It conveys togetherness with distance and intentional relation. Nearly every religious tradition has elaborate symbolism for "being with the divine in a place": Hindu heavens, Buddha-lands, the Muslim's Paradise, the Confucian heaven of ancestors and the Daoist heavens of souls maturing to supernatural infancy. The special symbol systems of the different religions shape the place and mode of being with the divine with interesting variants. I'm told that Roman Catholic saints in heaven stare at God in a beatific vision, whereas Protestants sing; furthermore, Protestants sing Bach when God is paying attention, Mozart when Her attention is elsewhere. That the divine is such a personal audience is an entirely appropriate symbol when the devotee is intending the divine as an object founding the devotee's own personality and consciousness. But not all practical and devotional contexts relate persons intentionally to the divine as object. Sometimes the divine is discovered as the principle within, sometimes as the original abyss into which the mystic falls when imagining beyond the boundaries of the world, sometimes as the truth of ordinariness itself. All these and other categorially different kinds of representations might be legitimate and true in some context or other, and if they are, theology needs to coordinate them all.

Devotees who take pleasure in a good cigar and who long for perfection in something like this life but with the divine, know that having a cigar is more perfect than no cigar when all one's efforts are past and God's grace alone abounds.[23] They may rest assured that it is symbolically significant and possibly true that our loved ones await us, God is the mansion's perfect host, and, Yes, there are cigars in heaven.

---

23. On this see Kirk's comment in *The Vision of God*, p. 62, on "the prevalently world-accepting outlook of the Jews" of antiquity: "The body, as created by God, is not a thing to be condemned. God shall redeem it, and the righteous shall enjoy bodily well-being in Paradise. But—if so—Paradise must be furnished with all that makes for bodily well-being. So far from being the utter antithesis of this present life, it represented the full realization of all that in this life men count good."

# BIBLIOGRAPHY

Abelove, Henry

    1990    *The Evangelist of Desire: John Wesley and the Methodists*. Stanford: Stanford University Press.

Altizer, Thomas J. J.

    1980    *Total Presence*. New York: The Seabury Press.

    1982    *Deconstruction and Theology*. With Max A. Myers, Carl A. Raschke, Robert P. Scharlemann, Mark C. Taylor, and Charles E. Winquist. New York: Crossroad.

    1985    *History as Apocalypse*. Albany: State University of New York Press.

    1990    *Genesis and Apocalypse: A Theological Voyage toward Authentic Christianity*. Louisville, Ky.: Westminster/John Knox Press.

    1993    *The Genesis of God: A Theological Genealogy*. Louisville, Ky.: Westminster/John Knox Press.

Appleby, R. Scott

    1991    *Fundamentalisms Observed*. The Fundamentalism Project, Volume 1. Edited with Martin E. Marty. Chicago: University of Chicago Press.

    1993    *Fundamentalisms and Society: Reclaiming the Sciences, the Family, and Education*. The Fundamentalism Project, Volume 2. Edited with Martin E. Marty. Chicago: University of Chicago Press.

    1993    *Fundamentalisms and the State: Remaking Polities, Economies, and Militance*. The Fundamentalism Project, Volume 3. Edited with Martin E. Marty. Chicago: University of Chicago Press.

Aulen, Gustaf

    1953    *Christus Victor*. London: SPCK.

Bantly, Francisca Cho

    1992    "Buddhist Philosophy in the Art of Fiction," in Reynolds (and Tracy), 1992, 83–107.

Berger, Brigitte

  1973    *The Homeless Mind: Modernization and Consciousness.* With Peter
          Berger and Hansfried Kellner. New York: Random House.

Berger, Peter

  1961    *The Noise of Solemn Assemblies: Christian Commitment and the
          Religious Establishment in America.* Garden City, N.Y.: Dou-
          bleday.
  1966    *The Social Construction of Reality: A Treatise in the Sociology of
          Knowledge.* With Thomas Luckmann. Garden City, N.Y.:
          Doubleday.
  1967    *The Sacred Canopy: Elements of a Sociological Theory of Religion.*
          Garden City, N.Y.: Doubleday.
  1973    *The Homeless Mind: Modernization and Consciousness.* With
          Brigitte Berger and Hansfried Kellner. New York: Random
          House.
  1981    *The Other Side of God: A Polarity in World Religions.* Editor.
          Garden City, N.Y.: Doubleday.

Bellah, Robert N.

  1975    *The Broken Covenant: American Civil Religion in Time of Trial.*
          New York: Seabury.
  1985    *Habits of the Heart: Individualism and Commitment in American
          Life.* With Richard Madsen, William M. Sullivan, Ann
          Swidler, and Steven M. Tipton. Berkeley: University of Cal-
          ifornia Press.
  1991    *The Good Society.* With Richard Madsen, William M. Sulli-
          van, Ann Swidler, and Steven M. Tipton. New York: Alfred
          A. Knopf.

Berling, Judith

  1992    "Embodying Philosophy: Some Preliminary Reflections
          from a Chinese Perspective," in Reynolds (and Tracy), 1992,
          233–260.

Bernstein, Richard J.

  1971    *Praxis and Action.* Philadelphia: University of Pennsylvania
          Press.
  1992    "Reconciliation and Rupture: The Challenge and Threat of
          Otherness," in Reynolds, 1992, 295–314.

Berthrong, John H.

  1993    "Master Chu's Self-Realization: The Role of *Ch'eng*," in
          *Philosophy East and West*, 43/1 (January, 1993).

1994     *All under Heaven.* Albany: State University of New York Press.

Bielefeldt, Carl

1986     "Ch'ang-lu Tsung-tse's *Tso-Ch'an I* and the 'Secret' of Zen Meditation," in Gregory, 1986, pp. 129–161.

Birdwhistell, Anne D.

1989     *Transition to Neo-Confucianism: Shao Yung on Knowledge and Symbols of Reality.* Stanford: Stanford University Press.

Bohn, Carole R.

1989     *Christianity, Patriarchy, and Abuse: A Feminist Critique.* Edited, with Joanne Carlson Brown. New York: Pilgrim.

Bol, Peter K.

1992     *"This Culture of Ours": Intellectual Transitions in T'ang and Sung China.* Stanford: Stanford University Press.

Bouker, John

1978     *The Religious Imagination and the Sense of God.* Oxford: Clarendon Press.

Bracken, Joseph A., S.J.

1995     *The Divine Matrix: Creativity as Link between East and West.* Maryknoll: Orbis.

Brockelman, Paul

1992     *The Inside Story: A Narrative Approach to Religious Understanding and Truth.* Albany: State University of New York Press.

Brown, Joanne Carlson

1989     *Christianity, Patriarchy, and Abuse: A Feminist Critique.* Edited, with Carole R. Bohn. New York: Pilgrim.

Buchler, Justus

1951     *Toward a General Theory of Human Judgment.* New York: Columbia University Press. Second revised edition; New York: Dover, 1979.

1955     *Nature and Judgment.* New York: Columbia University Press.
1966     *Metaphysics of Natural Complexes.* New York: Columbia University Press. Second edition with new material edited by Kathleen Wallace, Armen Marsoobian, and Robert S. Corrington: Albany: State University of New York Press, 1990.

1983 "A Strain of Arbitrariness in Whitehead's System," in *Explorations in Whitehead's Philosophy*, edited by Lewis S. Ford and George L. Kline. New York: Fordham University Press.

Buri, Fritz

1985 "American Philosophy of Religion from a European Perspective: The Problem of Meaning and Being in the Theologies of Imagination and Process," in *Journal of the American Academy of Religion*, 53/4 (December 1985), pp. 651–673. Translated by Harold H. Oliver.

Buswell, Robert E., Jr.

1986 "Chinul's Systemization of Chinese Meditative Techniques in Korean Son Buddhism," in Gregory, 1986, pp. 199–242.

Cady, Susan

1986 *Sophia: The Future of Feminist Spirituality*. With Marian Ronan and Hal Taussig. San Francisco: Harper & Row.

Calvin, John

1559 *Institutes of the Christian Religion*. Edited from the 1559 edition by John T. McNeill and translated by Ford Lewis Battles. Philadelphia: The Westminster Press.

Campany, Robert F.

1992 "Xunzi and Durkheim as Theorists of Ritual Practice," in Reynolds, 1992, 197–231.

Cannon, Katie G.

1988 *Black Womanist Ethics*. Atlanta: Scholars Press.

Caputo, John D.

1987 *Radical Hermeneutics: Repetition, Deconstruction, and the Hermeneutic Project*. Bloomington, Ind.: Indiana University Press.

Carman, John Braisted

1974 *The Theology of Ramanuja: An Essay in Interreligious Understanding*. New Haven: Yale University Press.

1994 *Majesty and Meekness: A Comparative Study of Contrast and Harmony in the Concept of God*. Grand Rapids, Mich.: William B. Eerdmans.

Carr, Anne E.

1988 *Transforming Grace: Christian Tradition and Women's Experience*. San Francisco: Harper & Row.

Casey, Edward S.

  1976   *Imagining: A Phenomenological Study.* Bloomington: Indiana University Press.

  1987   *Remembering: A Phenomenological Study.* Bloomington: Indiana University Press.

  1993   *Getting Back into Place: Toward a Renewed Understanding of the Place-World.* Bloomington: Indiana University Press.

Cassirer, Ernst

  1923–1929   *Die Philosophie der symbolischen Formen.* In three volumes. Berlin: Bruno Cassirer.

Chan, Wing-tsit

  1963   *A Source Book in Chinese Philosophy.* Princeton, N.J.: Princeton University Press.

Chappell, David W.

  1977   *Buddhist and Taoist Studies I.* Edited with Michael Saso. Honolulu: University Press of Hawaii.

  1986   "From Dispute to Dual Cultivation: Pure Land Responses to Ch'an Critics," in Gregory, 1986, pp. 163–197.

  1987   *Buddhist and Taoist Practice in Medieval Chinese Society: Buddhist and Taoist Studies II.* Editor. Honolulu: University of Hawaii Press.

Ching, Julia

  1977   *Confucianism and Christianity: A Comparative Study.* Tokyo: Kodansha International.

Chittick, William C.

  1983   *The Sufi Path of Love: The Spiritual Teachings of Rumi.* Albany: State University of New York Press.

  1992   *Faith and Practice of Islam: Three Thirteenth Century Sufi Texts.* Albany: State University of New York Press.

Chopp, Rebecca

  1989   *The Power to Speak: Feminism, Language, God.* New York: Crossroad.

Christ, Carol P.

  1989   *Weaving the Visions: New Patterns in Feminist Spirituality.* Edited with Judith Plaskow. San Francisco: Harper & Row.

Clooney, Francis X., S.J.

  1990   *Thinking Ritually: Rediscovering the Purva Mimamsa of Jaimini.* Vienna: Indological Institute of the University of Vienna.

1993    *Theology after Vedanta: An Experiment in Comparative Theology.* Albany: State University of New York Press.

Cobb, John B., Jr.

1989    *For the Common Good: Redirecting the Economy toward Community, the Environment, and a Sustainable Future.* With Herman E. Daly. Boston: Beacon.

Cupitt, Don

1986    *Life Lines.* London: SCM Press.
1987    *The Long-Legged Fly.* London: SCM Press.

Daly, Herman E.

1989    *For the Common Good: Redirecting the Economy toward Community, the Environment, and a Sustainable Future.* With John B. Cobb, Jr. Boston: Beacon.

Daly, Mary

1973    *Beyond God the Father: Toward a Philosophy of Women's Liberation.* Boston: Beacon.

D'Costa, Gavin

1990    *Christian Uniqueness Reconsidered: The Myth of a Pluralistic Theology of Religions.* Edited. Maryknoll, New York: Orbis.

DeBary, William Theodore

1975    *The Unfolding of Neo-Confucianism.* Edited. New York: Columbia University Press.
1981    *Neo-Confucianism Orthodoxy and the Learning of the Mind-and-Heart.* New York: Columbia University Press.

Derrida, Jacques

1976    *Of Grammatology.* Translated by Gayatri Chakravorty Spivak. Baltimore: The Johns Hopkins Press.

Dewey, John

1916    *Essays in Experimental Logic.* Chicago: University of Chicago Press.

Driver, Tom F.

1991    *The Magic of Ritual.* San Francisco: Harper.

Dulles, Avery, S.J.

1983    *Models of Revelation.* Garden City, N.Y.: Doubleday.
1992    *The Craft of Theology: From Symbol to System.* New York: Crossroad.

Durkheim, Emile

1915    *The Elementary Forms of the Religious Life.* Translated by Joseph Ward Swain. London: George Allen & Unwin; New York: Free Press, 1965.

Dye, James, W., and Forthman, William, editors.

1967    *Religions of the World: Selected Readings.* New York: Appleton-Century-Crofts.

Eagleton, Terry

1983    *Literary Theory: An Introduction.* Minneapolis: University of Minnesota Press.

Eck, Diana L.

1993    *Encountering God: A Spiritual Journey from Bozeman to Banaras.* Boston: Beacon.

Eckel, Malcolm David

1987    *Jnanagarbha's Commentary on the Distinction between the Two Truths: An Eighth Century Handbook of Madhyamaka Philosophy.* Albany: State University of New York Press.

1992    *To See the Buddha: A Philosopher's Quest for the Meaning of Emptiness.* San Francisco: Harper and Row.

Eliade, Mircea

1957    *The Sacred and the Profane: The Nature of Religion.* Translated by Willard R. Trask. New York: Harcourt Brace, 1959; New York: Harper Torchbook, 1961.

1978–1985    *A History of Religious Ideas.* In three volumes. Volume 1, 1978, translated by Willard R. Trask, *From the Stone Age to the Eleusinian Mysteries*; Volume 2, 1982, translated by Willard R. Trask, *From Gautama Buddha to the Triumph of Christianity*; Volume 3, 1985, translated by Alf Hiltebeitel and Diane Apostolos-Cappadona, *From Muhammad to the Age of Reforms.* Chicago: University of Chicago Press.

Eno, Robert

1990    *The Confucian Creation of Heaven: Philosophy and the Defense of Ritual Mastery.* Albany: State University of New York Press.

Erikson, Erik H.

1963    *Childhood and Society.* Second edition; New York: Norton.

Farrer, Austin

1959    *Finite and Infinite.* Second edition; London: Dacre Press.

Faure, Bernard

    1986    "The Concept of One-Practice Samadhi in Early Ch'an," in Gregory, 1986, pp. 99–128.

Felder, Cain Hope

    1991    *Stony the Road We Trod*. Edited. Minneapolis: Fortress.

Fiorenza, Elisabeth Schussler

    1984    *Bread Not Stone: The Challenge of Feminist Biblical Interpretation.* Boston: Beacon.

    1985    *In Memory of Her: A Feminist Theological Reconstruction of Christian Origins.* New York: Crossroad.

Fingarette, Herbert

    1972    *Confucius: The Secular as Sacred.* New York: Harper and Row.

Fortune, Marie M.

    1983    *Sexual Violence: The Unmentionable Sin: An Ethical and Pastoral Perspective.* New York: Pilgrim.

Fowler, James W.

    1981    *Stages of Faith: The Psychology of Human Development and the Quest for Meaning.* San Francisco: Harper.

Frazer, James George

    1890    *The Golden Bough.* Theodore H. Gaster, editor, *The New Golden Bough*; New York: Criterion Books.

Frei, Hans

    1974    *The Eclipse of Biblical Narrative: A Study in Eighteenth and Nineteenth Century Hermeneutics.* New Haven: Yale University Press.

    1992    *Types of Christian Theology.* Edited by George Hunsinger and William C. Placher. New Haven: Yale University Press.

Freud, Sigmund

    1927    *The Future of an Illusion.* Translated by W. D. Robson-Scott, revised and newly edited by James Strachey. Revised edition; Garden City, N.Y.: Doubleday Anchor, 1964.

Frymer-Kensky, Tikva

    1992    *In the Wake of the Goddesses: Women, Culture, and the Biblical Transformation of Pagan Myth.* New York: Free Press. New York: Ballantine/Fawcett Columbine.

Geertz, Clifford

    1968   *Islam Observed: Religious Development in Morocco and Indonesia.* New Haven: Yale University Press.

    1973   *The Interpretation of Cultures.* New York: Basic Books, 1993 reissue by Fontana Press, London.

    1979   "Deep Play: Notes on the Balinese Cockfight," in Sullivan and Rabinow, 1979.

    1983   *Local Knowledge.* New York: Basic Books, 1993 reissue by Fontana Press, London.

Gilligan, Carol

    1971   "The Adolescent as Philosopher," with Lawrence Kohlberg, in *Daedalus*, 100 (Fall 1971).

    1982   *In a Different Voice: Psychological Theory and Women's Development.* Cambridge: Harvard University Press.

Girardot, Norman

    1983   *Myth and Meaning in Early Taoism.* Berkeley: University of California Press.

Goetz, Ronald

    1986   "The Suffering God: The Rise of a New Orthodoxy," in *The Christian Century* (April 16, 1986), p. 385.

Goffman, Erving

    1961   *Asylums: Essays on the Social Situation of Mental Patients and Other Inmates.* Garden City, New York: Doubleday Anchor.

    1971   *Relations in Public.* New York: Harper.

Goodman, Nelson

    1978   *Ways of Worldmaking.* Indianapolis, Ind.: Hackett.

Green, Garrett

    1989   *Imagining God: Theology and the Religious Imagination.* San Francisco: Harper & Row.

Gregory, Peter N.

    1986   *Traditions of Meditation in Chinese Buddhism.* Editor. Honolulu: University of Hawaii Press.

Gross, Rita M.

    1993   *Buddhism after Patriarchy: A Feminist History, Analysis, and Reconstruction of Buddhism.* Albany: State University of New York Press.

Hall, David L.

    1994   *Richard Rorty: Prophet and Poet of the New Pragmatism*. Albany: State University of New York Press.

Hansen, Chad

    1983   *Language and Logic in Ancient China*. Ann Arbor: University of Michigan Press.

    1992   *A Daoist Theory of Chinese Thought*. New York: Oxford University Press.

    1993   "Term-Belief in Action: Sentences and Terms in Early Chinese Philosophy," in Lenk and Paul, 1993.

Hart, Ray L.

    1968   *Unfinished Man and the Imagination: Toward an Ontology and a Rhetoric of Revelation*. New York: Herder and Herder.

Hartshorne, Charles

    1962   *The Logic of Perfection and Other Essays*. LaSalle, Illinois: Open Court.

Heidegger, Martin

    1954   *The Question Concerning Technology and Other Essays*. Translated by William Lovitt. New York: Harper, 1977; 1954 is the original publication date of the title essay.

Herrin, Judith

    1987   *The Formation of Christendom*. Princeton, N.J.: Princeton University Press.

Heyward, Carter

    1989   *Touching Our Strength: The Erotic as Power and the Love of God*. San Francisco: Harper & Row.

Hick, John

    1973   *God and the Universe of Faiths*. London: Macmillan.

    1985   *Problems of Religious Pluralism*. New York: St. Martin's Press.

    1987   *The Myth of Christian Uniqueness: Toward a Pluralistic Theology of Religions*. Edited with Paul F. Knitter. Maryknoll, New York: Orbis.

    1989   *An Interpretation of Religion*. New Haven: Yale University Press.

    1993   *The Metaphor of God Incarnate*. London: SCM Press.

Homans, Peter

    1970   *Theology after Freud: An Interpretive Inquiry*. Indianapolis, Ind.: Bobbs-Merrill.

hooks, bell

    1984    *Feminist Theory: From Margin to Center*. Boston: South End Press.

Hoyt, Thomas, Jr.

    1991    "Interpreting Biblical Scholarship for the Black Church Tradition," in Felder, 1991, pp. 17–39

Husserl, Edmund

    1913    *Ideas*. Translated by W. R. Boyce Gibson. New York: Macmillan, 1931.

James, William

    1902    *The Varieties of Religious Experience: A Study in Human Nature*. New York: Longmans, Green.

Jaspers, Karl

    1954    *Way to Wisdom: An Introduction to Philosophy*. Translated by Ralph Manheim. New Haven: Yale University Press.

Johnson, Elizabeth A.

    1993    *She Who Is: The Mystery of God in Feminist Discourse*. New York: Crossroad.

Jordan, Merle R.

    1986    *Taking on the gods: The Task of the Pastoral Counselor*. Nashville, Tenn.: Abingdon.

Kant, Immanuel

    1787    *Critique of Pure Reason*. Translation including both the first (1781) and second (1787) editions by Norman Kemp Smith. London: Macmillan, 1956.

    1788    *Critique of Practical Reason*. Translated by Lewis White Beck. New York: Liberal Arts Press, 1956.

Kapstein, Matthew

    1992    "Samantabhadra and Rudra: Innate Enlightenment and Radical Evil in Tibetan Rnying-ma-pa Buddhism," in Reynolds and Tracy, 1992, 51–82.

Kasulis, Thomas P.

    1992    "Philosophy as Metapraxis," in Reynolds and Tracy, 1992, 169–195.

Kaufman, Gordon

    1981    *The Theological Imagination: Constructing the Concept of God*. Philadelphia: Westminster.

Keller, Catherine

    1986    *From a Broken Web: Separation, Sexism, and Self.* Boston: Beacon.

Kellner, Hansfried

    1973    *The Homeless Mind: Modernization and Consciousness.* With Peter Berger and Brigitte Berger. New York: Random House.

Kelly, J. N. D.

    1960    *Early Christian Doctrine.* Second edition; New York: Harper & Row.

Kierkegaard, Soren

    1843    *Fear and Trembling* and *The Sickness unto Death.* Translated by Walter Lowrie. Garden City, New York: Doubleday Anchor, 1955. 1843 is the original date of publication of *Fear and Trembling.*

    1846    *Concluding Unscientific Postscript.* Translated by David F. Swenson and Walter Lowrie. Princeton, N.J.: Princeton University Press, 1941.

    1844    *Philosophical Fragments.* Translated by David F. Swenson. Princeton, N.J.: Princeton University Press.

Kirk, Kenneth E.

    1932    *The Vision of God: The Christian Doctrine of the Summum Bonum.* London: Longmans, Green and Co.

Knitter, Paul F.

    1987    *The Myth of Christian Uniqueness: Toward a Pluralistic Theology of Religions.* Edited with John Hick. Maryknoll, N.Y.: Orbis.

Kohlberg, Lawrence

    1969    "Stage and Sequence: The Cognitive Developmental Approach to Socialization," in David A. Goslin, editor, *Handbook of Socialization Theory and Research.* Chicago: Rand McNally.

    1971    "The Adolescent as Philosopher," with Carol Gilligan, in *Daedalus* 100 (Fall 1971).

    1971    "From Is to Ought: How to Commit the Naturalistic Fallacy and Get Away with It in the Study of Moral Development," in T. Mischel, editor, *Cognitive Development and Epistemology.* New York: Academic Press.

Kohn, Livia

    1991    *Taoist Mystical Philosophy: The Scripture of Western Ascension.* Albany: State University of New York Press.

1992    *Early Chinese Mysticism: Philosophy and Soteriology in the Taoist Tradition.* Princeton, N.J.: Princeton University Press.

Konstantine, Steven

1991    *Christian Systematic Theology in a World Context.* With Ninian Smart. Minneapolis: Fortress Press.

Lamberton, Robert

1986    *Homer the Theologian: Neoplatonist Allegorical Reading and the Growth of the Epic Tradition.* Berkeley: University of California Press.

Langer, Susanne K.

1942    *Philosophy in a New Key: A Study in the Symbolism of Reason, Rite, and Art.* Cambridge: Harvard University Press.

Leith, John H.

1963    *Creeds of the Churches.* Garden City, N.Y.: Doubleday Anchor.

Lenk, Hans, and Gregor Paul, editors.

1993    *Epistemological Issues in Classical Chinese Philosophy.* Albany: State University of New York Press.

Lewis, C. S.

1961    *A Grief Observed.* London: Faber & Faber. New York: Bantam, 1976.

Lindbeck, George A.

1984    *The Nature of Doctrine: Religion and Theology in a Postliberal Age.* Philadelphia: The Westminster Press.

Lentricchia, Frank

1980    *After the New Criticism.* Chicago: University of Chicago Press.

Loyola, St. Ignatius

1541    *Spiritual Exercises.* Translated by Anthony Mottola. New York: Image, 1964.

Lovin, Robin W.

1992    "The Myth of Original Equality," in Reynolds (and Tracy), 1992, 141–166.

McFague, Sallie

1982    *Metaphorical Theology: Models of God in Religious Language.* Philadelphia: Fortress.

Machle, Edward F.

> 1993   *Nature and Heaven in the Xunzi: A Study of the* Tian Lun.
> Albany: State University of New York Press.

Macquarrie, John

> 1977   *Principles of Christian Theology.* Second edition; New York:
> Macmillan.

Major, John S.

> 1993   *Heaven and Earth in Early Han Thought: Chapters Three, Four,
> and Five of the <u>Huainanzi</u>.* Albany: State University of New
> York Press.

Martin, James Alfred, Jr.

> 1990   *Beauty and Holiness: The Dialogue between Aesthetics and Reli-
> gion.* Princeton, N.J.: Princeton University Press.

Martin, Michael

> 1990   *Atheism: A Philosophical Justification.* Philadelphia: Temple
> University Press.
> 1991   *The Case against Christianity.* Philadelphia: Temple University
> Press.

Marty, Martin E.

> 1991   *Fundamentalisms Observed.* The Fundamentalism Project, Vol-
> ume 1. Edited with R. Scott Appleby. Chicago: University
> of Chicago Press.
> 1993   *Fundamentalisms and Society: Reclaiming the Sciences, the Family,
> and Education.* The Fundamentalism Project, Volume 2.
> Edited with R. Scott Appleby. Chicago: University of Chi-
> cago Press.
> 1993   *Fundamentalisms and the State: Remaking Polities, Economies,
> and Militance.* The Fundamentalism Project, Volume 3.
> Edited with R. Scott Appleby. Chicago: University of Chi-
> cago Press.

Mason, John R.

> 1993   *Reading and Responding to Mircea Eliade's <u>History of Religious
> Ideas</u>.* Lewiston, N.Y.: The Edwin Mellen Press.

Mathews, Thomas F.

> 1993   *The Clash of Gods: A Reinterpretation of Early Christian Art.*
> Princeton, N.J.: Princeton University Press.

Meeks, Wayne A.

    1983   *The First Urban Christians: The Social World of the Apostle Paul.* New Haven: Yale University Press.

Miles, Margaret

    1985   *Image as Insight: Visual Understanding in Western Christianity and Secular Culture.* Boston: Beacon.

    1990   *Practicing Christianity: Critical Perspectives fo an Embodied Spirituality.* New York: Crossroad.

Moffett, Samuel Hugh

    1992   *A History of Christianity in Asia.* Volume I. *Beginnings to 1500.* San Francisco: Harper.

Murata, Sachiko

    1992   *The Tao of Islam: A Sourcebook on Gender Relationships in Islamic Thought.* Albany: State University of New York Press.

Murray, Robert

    1992   *The Cosmic Covenant: Biblical Themes of Justice, Peace, and the Integrity of Creation.* London: Sheed & Ward.

Myers, William H.

    1991   "The Hermeneutical Dilemma of the African American Biblical Student," in Felder, 1991, pp. 40–56.

Neville, Robert Cummings

    1967   "Intuition," in *International Philosophical Quarterly,* 7 (December 1967), pp. 556–590.

    1968   *God the Creator: On the Transcendence and Presence of God.* Chicago: University of Chicago Press. Corrected edition with a new Preface; Albany: State University of New York Press, 1992.

    1978   *Soldier, Sage, Saint.* New York: Fordham University Press.

    1981   *Reconstruction of Thinking.* Albany: State University of New York Press.

    1982   *The Tao and the Daimon: Segments of a Religious Inquiry.* Albany: State University of New York Press.

    1987   *The Puritan Smile.* Albany: State University of New York Press.

    1989   *Recovery of the Measure: Interpretation and Nature.* Albany: State University of New York Press.

    1991   *Behind the Masks of God: An Essay toward Comparative Theology.* Albany: State University of New York Press.

1991    *A Theology Primer.* Albany: State University of New York Press.

1991    "On Buddha's Answer to the Silence of God," in *Philosophy East and West*, 41/4 (October 1991), pp. 557–570.

1992    *The Highroad around Modernism.* Albany: State University of New York Press.

1993    *Eternity and Time's Flow.* Albany: State University of New York Press.

1993    "Religious Studies and Theological Studies," in *Journal of the American Academy of Religion*, 61/2 (Summer 1993), 185–200.

1995    *Normative Cultures.* Albany: State University of New York Press.

Niebuhr, H. Richard

1929    *The Social Sources of Denominationalism.* New York: Henry Holt. New York: Meridian Books, 1957.

Noss, John B.

1969    *Man's Religions.* Fourth edition; New York: Macmillan.

Ogden, Schubert

1966    *The Reality of God and Other Essays.* New York: Harper & Row.

Otto, Rudolph

1917    *The Idea of the Holy.* Translated by John Harvey. New York: Oxford University Press, 1926.

Panikkar, Raimundo

1989    *The Silence of God: The Answer of the Buddha.* Translated from the Italian by Robert R. Barr. Maryknoll, N.Y.: Orbis Books.

Pannenberg, Wolfhart

1988    *Systematic Theology, Volume I.* Translated by Geoffrey W. Bromiley. Grand Rapids, Mich.: Eerdmans, 1991. Citations are to the translated edition, although by the date of the German original.

Park, Andrew Sung

1993    *The Wounded Heart of God: The Asian Concept of Han and the Christian Doctrine of Sin.* Nashville, Tenn.: Abingdon.

Park, Sung-bae

1983    *Buddhist Faith and Sudden Enlightenment.* Albany: State University of New York Press.

Parrinder, Geoffrey

    1983    *World Religions from Ancient History to the Present.* Editor. New York: Facts on File.

Peirce, Charles Sanders

    1931–35    *The Collected Papers of Charles Sanders Peirce.* Edited by Charles Hartshorne and Paul Weiss. Volume 1, 1931; Volume 2, 1932; Volume 5, 1934; Volume 6, 1935. Cambridge: Harvard University Press. Standard citation as, for instance, CP 6.452–493 (*Collected Papers*/volume 6/paragraphs 452–493 inclusive).

Plaskow, Judith

    1989    *Weaving the Visions: New Patterns in Feminist Spirituality.* Edited with Carol P. Christ. San Francisco: Harper & Row.

Poole, Fitz John Porter

    1992    "Wisdom and Practice: The Mythic Making of Sacred History among the Bimin-Kuskusmin of Papua New Guinea," in Reynolds (and Tracy), 1992, 13–50.

Quinn, Philip L.

    1992    "On Demythologizing Evil," in Reynolds (and Tracy), 1992, 111–140.

Rabinow, Paul

    1979    *Interpretive Social Science: A Reader.* Edited with William M. Sullivan. Berkeley: University of California Press.

Rack, Henry D.

    1992    *Reasonable Enthusiast: John Wesley and the Rise of Methodism.* Second edition; London: Epworth Press. American edition; Nashville, Tenn.: Abingdon, 1993.

Redmond, Sheila A.

    1989    "Christian 'Virtues' and Recovery from Child Sexual Abuse," in Bohn and Brown, editors, *Christianity, Patriarchy, and Abuse.*

Reynolds, Frank

    1992    *Discourse and Practice.* Edited with David Tracy. Albany: State University of New York Press.

Ricoeur, Paul

    1967    *The Symbolism of Evil.* Translated by Emerson Buchanan. Boston: Beacon Paperback, 1969.

Rieff, Philip

    1966    *The Triumph of the Therapeutic: Uses of Faith after Freud.* New York: Harper & Row.

Riffaterre, Michael

    1990    *Fictional Truth.* Baltimore: Johns Hopkins University Press.

Robinet, Isabelle

    1979    *Meditation taoiste.* Paris: Dervy Livres. Translated by Norman J. Girardot and Julian F. Pas as *Taoist Meditation: The Mao-shan Tradition of Great Purity.* Albany: State University of New York Press, 1993.

Roetz, Heiner

    1993    *Confucian Ethics of the Axial Age: A Reconstruction under the Aspect of the Breakthrough toward Postconventional Thinking.* Albany: State University of New York Press.

    1993    "Validity in Chou Thought: On Chad Hansen and the Pragmatic Turn in Sinology," in Lenk and Paul, 1993.

Ronan, Marian

    1986    *Sophia: The Future of Feminist Spirituality.* With Susan Cady and Hal Taussig. San Francisco: Harper & Row.

Rorty, Richard

    1979    *Philosophy and the Mirror of Nature.* Princeton, N.J.: Princeton University Press.

Ross, James F.

    1969    *Philosophical Theology.* New York: Bobbs-Merrill.

Ruether, Rosemary Radford

    1983    *Sexism and God-Talk: Toward a Feminist Theology.* Boston: Beacon.

Saiving, Valerie

    1979    "The Human Situation: A Feminine View," in Carol P. Christ and Judith Plaskow, editors, *Womanspirit Rising: A Feminist Reader in Religion.* San Francisco: Harper & Row.

Saso, Michael

    1977    *Buddhist and Taoist Studies I.* Edited with David W. Chappell. Honolulu: University Press of Hawaii.

    1978    *The Teachings of Taoist Master Chuang.* New Haven: Yale University Press.

Schweiker, William

    1992    "The Drama of Interpretation and the Philosophy of Religions: An Essay on Understanding in Comparative Religious Ethics," in Reynolds (and Tracy), 1992, 263–294.

Searle, John

    1969    *Speech Acts*. Cambridge: Cambridge University Press.

Sharma, Arvind

    1993    *Our Religions*. Editor. San Francisco: Harper Collins.

Silk, Joseph

    1989    *The Big Bang*. Revised and updated edition. New York: W. H. Freeman.

Smart, Ninian

    1989    *The World's Religions: Old Traditions and Modern Transformations*. Cambridge: Cambridge University Press.

    1991    *Christian Systematic Theology in a World Context*. With Steven Konstantine. Minneapolis: Fortress Press.

Smith, John E.

    1968    *Experience and God*. New York: Oxford University Press.

    1978    *Purpose and Thought: The Meaning of Pragmatism*. New Haven: Yale University Press.

Smith, Jonathan Z.

    1987    *To Take Place: Toward Theory in Ritual*. Chicago: University of Chicago Press.

Sorabji, Richard

    1983    *Time, Creation, and the Continuum: Theories in Antiquity and the Early Middle Ages*. Ithaca, N.Y.: Cornell University Press.

Soskice, Janet Martin

    1985    *Metaphor and Religious Language*. Oxford: Oxford University Press.

Sponberg, Alan

    1986    "Meditation in Fa-hsiang Buddhism," in Gregory, 1986, pp. 15–43.

Stevenson, Daniel B.

    1986    "The Four Kinds of Samadhi in Early T'ien-t'ai Buddhism," in Gregory, pp. 45–97.

Stookey, Laurence Hull

    1993    *Eucharist: Christ's Feast with the Church.* Nashville, Tenn.: Abingdon.

Suchocki, Marjorie Hewitt

    1986    *God, Christ, Church: A Practical Guide to Process Theology.* New York: Crossroad.

Sullivan, William M.

    1979    *Interpretive Social Science: A Reader.* Edited with Paul Rabinow. Berkeley: University of California Press.

Suzuki, Shunryu

    1970    *Zen Mind, Beginner's Mind.* Edited by Trudy Dixon with a preface by Huston Smith and an introduction by Richard Baker. New York: Weatherhill.

Taussig, Hal

    1986    *Sophia: The Future of Feminist Spirituality.* With Susan Cady and Marian Ronan. San Francisco: Harper & Row.

Taylor, Mark C.

    1984    *Erring: A Postmodern A/Theology.* Chicago: University of Chicago Press.

    1986    *Deconstruction in Context: Literature and Philosophy.* Edited. Chicago: University of Chicago Press.

Thistlethwaite, Susan

    1991    *Sex, Race, and God: Christian Feminism in Black and White.* New York: Crossroad.

Tillich, Paul

    1948    *The Protestant Era.* Translated by James Luther Adams. Chicago: University of Chicago Press. Abridged edition; Chicago: University of Chicago Press, 1957.

1951–63    *Systematic Theology,* in Three Volumes: Volume I, 1951, Volume II, 1957, Volume III, 1963. Chicago: University of Chicago Press.

    1952    *The Courage to Be.* New Haven: Yale University Press.

    1957    *Dynamics of Faith.* New York: Harper and Brothers.

    1959    *Theology of Culture.* Edited by Robert C. Kimball. New York: Oxford University Press.

    1963    *Christianity and the Encounter of the World Religions.* New York: Columbia University Press.

Tillman, Hoyt Cleveland

    1992   *Confucian Discourse and Chu Hsi's Ascendancy.* Honolulu: The University of Hawaii Press.

Toulmin, Stephen

    1950   *An Examination of the Place of Reason in Ethics.* Cambridge: Cambridge University Press.

Tracy, David

    1987   *Plurality and Ambiguity: Hermeneutics, Religion, Hope.* San Francisco: Harper & Row.

    1981   *The Analogical Imagination: Christian Theology and the Culture of Pluralism.* New York: Crossroad.

    1992   *Discourse and Practice.* Edited with Frank Reynolds. Albany: State University of New York Press.

Trungpa, Chogyam

    1973   *Cutting through Spiritual Materialism.* Edited by John Baker and Marvin Casper. Berkeley: Shambhala.

Tu Wei-ming

    1985   *Confucian Thought: Selfhood as Creative Transformation.* Albany: State University of New York Press.

Turner, Victor

    1969   *The Ritual Process: Structure and Anti-Structure.* New York: Aldine. Ithaca: Cornell Paperback, 1977.

Tylor, Edward Burnett

    1872   *Primitive Culture.* Reprinted in two volumes: Volume I, *The Origins of Culture*; Volume II, *Religion in Primitive Culture.* New York: Harper Torchbooks, 1958.

Van der Leeuw, G.

    1933.   *Religion in Essence and Manifestation.* Translated by J. E. Turner with appendices to the Torchbook edition, incorporating the additions of the second German edition, edited by Hans H. Penner. New York: Harper and Row, 1963.

Weber, Max

    1948   *From Max Weber: Essays in Sociology.* Edited and translated by H. H. Gerth and C. Wright Mills. New York: Oxford University Press

Weiss, Paul

    1958    *Modes of Being.* Carbondale, Illinois: Southern Illinois University Press.

    1961    *The World of Art.* Carbondale: Southern Illinois University Press.

    1986    *Toward a Perfected State.* Albany: State University of New York Press.

Weissman, David

    1993    *Truth's Debt to Value.* New Haven: Yale University Press.

Whitehead, Alfred North

    1926    *Religion in the Making.* New York: Macmillan.

Wildman, Wesley J.

    1995    *The Quest for a Classical Christology: Jesus Christ in the Twentieth Century.* Forthcoming.

Wimbush, Vincent L.

    1991    "The Bible and African Americans: An Outline of an Interpretative History," in Felder, 1991, pp. 81–97.

Wiles, Maurice

    1992    *Christian Theology and Inter-Religious Dialogue.* London: SCM Press.

Wittgenstein, Ludwig

    1922    *Tractatus Logico-Philosophicus.* London: Routledge & Kegan Paul.

    1953    *Philosophical Investigations.* Edited and translated by G. E. M. Anscombe. New York: Macmillan.

Xunzi

    3rd c. B.C.E.    *Xunzi: A Translation and Study of the Complete Works.* Edited by John Knoblock. Stanford: Stanford University Press. In three volumes; Volume I, containing books 1–6, 1988; Volume II, containing books 7–16, 1990; Volume III, containing books 17–32, 1994.

Zagano, Phyllis

    1993    *Woman to Woman: An Anthology of Women's Spiritualities.* Collegeville, Minn.: Liturgical Press.

# INDEX

Aaron, 179–181, 187

Abandonment, in the divine, 168–169; of self

Abelard, 205–206, 212

Abelove, Henry, 160n. 13

Abraham, 107

Absolute, the, 7, 47, 69, 242

Abstraction, xiii–xiv, 68–69, 78, 151; in theology, 13–14

Absurdity, 2–3

Abuse, 213, 225, 229; child, 156, 203, 209, 214; of children, justified by atonement, 231; sexual, 255; of women, 203–213, 230

Abyss, the, 46, 65, 93–95, 132, 182–193, 197–198, 271

Accomplishment, extraordinary, 149–150

Accord, of interpreters with objects, 151

Activism, social, 138

Actors, 149–150

Acts, intentional, 113–121

Actuality, 57; and transcendence, 58

Actualization, 145

Adam and Eve, 107

Addams, Charles, 188

Adequacy, 130, 133

Adolescence, and boundary-crossing, 163–166

Adolescents, deficient religious symbol systems for, 164–165; and the night sky, 191

Advaita Vedanta, xv, 39n, 45, 244–251, 257–258, 262–263, 270

Aesthetics, 104, 226, 236–237; aesthetic sensibility, 220–221; as norm, 214–221

Affirmation, and negation, 66, 70–75, 197

African-Americans, 155, 173; Biblically literate, 176

Agni fire, 94

al'Farabi, 231

Alienation, 18, 94

Allen, Horace T., Jr., xxv

Almsgiver, Muslim, 257

Altizer, Thomas J. J., xiv n, 63

Amalananda, 64n. 39

Ambiguity, 28

Anal-retentive character, 159–160

Analogy of being, xvi

Analysis, of meanings of signs, 36–47

Ananda, 45

Anathemas of the Second Council of Constantinople, 211

Anchorites, 153–154

Angel, tame, 190

Anger, at sacrificing animals, 222

Animals, 222, 247

Anselm, 204–205, 212

Anthropology, 3, 7, 12, 197, 250, 263

Anxiety, in Tillich's theology, 233–234

Apophatic theology, xvi, 41, 73–74, 129, 193, 243

Apostles' Creed, 210n. 23, 211

Appearance, 51–58, 66; in experience, of emotions, institutions, ideas, traditions, cultural projects, obligations, descriptions, theories, 52–58; paradigmatic for world-construction, 54–58

Appleby, R. Scott, 235n

Applicability, 130, 133

Appreciation, 2, 241

Aquinas, St. Thomas, xii, xvi n. 10, 64, 223, 231

Arbitrariness, of the theory of signs, 35–36

Architecture, xxii–xxiii, 13, 23, 26, 121, 135–136, 141, 152–153